Counseling

D1357206

Counseling

A Developmental Approach

Fourth Edition

Donald H. Blocher

John Wiley & Sons, Inc.

New York • Chichester • Weinheim • Brisbane • Singapore • Toronto

Library of Congress Cataloging-in-Publication Data:

Blocher, Donald H.
   Counseling : a developmental approach / Donald H. Blocher.— 4th
ed.
       p.   cm.
   Rev. ed. of: The professional counselor. 1987.
   Includes bibliographical references and index.
   ISBN 0-471-25462-2 (cloth : alk. paper)
   1. Counseling. 2. Counselors.   I. Blocher, Donald H.
Professional counselor.   II. Title.
BF637.C6B48   2000
158′ .3—dc21
                                                99-43402

Printed in the United States of America.

10 9 8 7 6 5 4 3 2 1

This book is dedicated to Betty,
my best friend, partner, lover, and wife.

Preface

IT HAS been more than 30 years since the publication of the first edition of *Developmental Counseling*. During these three decades, many changes have taken place in the practice of counseling and psychotherapy. Many fads and fascinations have come and gone with the years. The basic premises, concepts, and values that defined developmental counseling in 1966 are alive and well today in the professional practice of an untold number of counselors and counseling psychologists.

In 1988, at a national conference devoted to planning the future of counseling psychology, the group charged with studying the future of professional practice (Kagan et al., 1988) listed the primary psychological emphases and value commitments that defined and would continue to define practice in the field. The first four such emphases listed were:

1. A commitment to the empowerment of people
2. An understanding and appreciation of career development
3. A focus on development across the life-span
4. The importance of viewing people in the full context of their life situations

Hurst (1989), in a presidential address to the Division of Counseling Psychology, stated his conclusions in surveying the field. As he put it, "The focus on preventive and developmental interventions with persons in environments is alive and well. . . . We rally around the common cause of facilitating growth processes in persons and environments" (p. 158).

Borders and Drury (1992), reviewing research on the effectiveness of school counseling programs, noted, "Effective counseling programs are proactive in helping students acquire the knowledge, skills, self-awareness, and attitudes necessary for successful mastery of developmental tasks" (p. 448).

Davis (1996), describing the role of counseling psychologists, wrote, "our predominant purpose is to help others get more control over their lives . . . counseling psychologists emphasize preventive, developmental and educational skills and believe in empowering others to use their talents to prevent future difficulties" (p. 153).

These same values, emphases, and commitments have constituted the basic tenets of developmental counseling for more than 30 years. Practitioners know a great deal more about human development and how it can be nurtured today than was known 30 years ago. The whole field of adult development has emerged to provide substance to the counseling of people across their life-span. A cognitive revolution has enriched our knowledge of how people construe themselves and their world.

In this edition, I have endeavored to clothe the basic framework that defines the developmental approach with the knowledge and experience accumulated through current research and contemporary practice. I hope that this edition will contribute to the personal and professional development of another generation of developmental counselors and therapists.

DONALD H. BLOCHER

Acknowledgments

I gratefully acknowledge the help given by Betty Blocher at all phases of the project. I also appreciate the suggestions and advice given by Norman Sprinthall in reviewing the manuscript.

Contents

Introduction to the Reader

This book conceptualizes the process of counselor education and subsequent professional development as the product of a commitment to life-long learning. A major aspect of such learning involves continuing sequences of *action* and *reflection* that allow new experiences to be internalized and integrated with previous learning and personal experience. This process of experiential learning is elaborated in Chapter 15.

At the end of this book is a section called "Action and Reflection Issues." It includes a brief synopsis and outline of each chapter. More importantly it contains a set of questions to consider—that is, to *reflect* on. These are intended to help *organize, integrate,* and *personalize* the principal research findings, values, and concepts contained in each chapter. The serious reader will be able to supplement that list with additional questions and issues drawn from his or her own experience.

The process of reading about and then reflecting on these ideas and issues in a deeply personal way constitutes the beginning of an action-reflection approach to professional development. Following the questions are lists of recommended readings and relevant journals that enable the reader to take the next *action step* of enriching a knowledge base and expanding the scope of professional reading. Action-reflection sequences of course culminate in the application and evaluation of new ways of working with clients and so increasing levels of professional development.

The reader may consult this material before, during, or after reading each chapter, or may choose to do so after completing a set of closely related chapters (Chapters 6, 7, and 8 on counseling theory and process, for example). The reader may choose to refer to these materials after completing the entire book, using them to pull together and internalize the most personally relevant and practically useful ideas.

Using these materials thoughtfully can help the reader to embark on a journey of personal growth and professional development.

CHAPTER 1

The Nature of Developmental Counseling: An Overview

For me the basic principle out of which . . . a synthesis grows is that of *development*. At each moment of life, any person is in the process of changing into something a little different from what he is now. . . . A person to some extent shapes the pattern of his life by the choices and decisions he makes. . . . Once a choice has been made . . . it can never be eradicated. Development is a one-way street.

—Leona Tyler (1958)

OR MORE than 40 years, a growing number of counselors and therapists have quietly agreed with Leona Tyler's identification of the core concept that gives substance and coherence to the theory and practice of psychological counseling. Today, many helping professionals identify themselves as psychotherapists. Psychological counseling is a form of psychotherapy that includes, but is not limited to, assisting with personal problem solving, decision making, and life planning.

Assistance is focused on the goal of facilitating the development of clients by helping them become aware of the factors and forces at work in their own lives and, in the process, to learn to exert some degree of control over those forces. The practice of this kind of professional helping is called *developmental counseling*.

1

A BRIEF HISTORY OF
DEVELOPMENTAL COUNSELING

Professional counseling began almost a century ago in what was called the *Guidance Movement,* a small part of a larger, nationwide call for sweeping social, political, economic, and educational reform that historians call the *Progressive Movement.* The Progressive Movement came into being in response to the great concentration of wealth and power that occurred in America during the latter half of the nineteenth century. That concentration of wealth was accompanied by an abysmal set of conditions that afflicted working people, women, new immigrants, and the poor. The Progressive Era—the period from about 1890 to 1920—saw the institution of many reforms and changes that we take for granted today. Rights for women, regulation of big business, legitimization of labor unions, and greater democracy in government all made significant gains during the Progressive Era.

An important aspect of the Progressive Movement was concern for the welfare and development of children. Compulsory education laws, the elimination of child labor, and the humanization of urban environments through construction of parks and playgrounds were all parts of the progressive agenda.

One of the most important aspects of this reform movement was focused on radical changes in public education. At the turn of the twentieth century, public high schools were essentially academies devoted to preparing a few elite students to enter college or university.

For the great majority of children, formal education ended after six or eight years with entry into the workforce following almost immediately. The Guidance Movement developed from the need to help these early school leavers develop a rational plan with which to begin their careers.

Guidance programs developed first in settlement houses and social agencies. Soon, however, guidance pioneers joined vocational educators in the educational reform movement called *Progressive Education* to demand comprehensive high schools that were devoted to the needs of all young people. These high schools offered vocational preparation as well as college preparatory programs.

As comprehensive high schools came into existence, guidance programs and counselors were needed for the task of helping students choose courses and make plans that would prepare them for vocational life (Kelley, 1916). As more diverse populations entered colleges, counseling and other personnel programs began to be provided on college campuses.

From the very beginning, guidance and student personnel work was concerned with the development of students (Miller, 1961). In its early years, guidance was seen as both a program of services and as a philosophy of education. In this sense, guidance was very closely aligned with Progressive Education. This is not surprising since both came out of the same ideological mix, having both been part of the larger Progressive Movement. Indeed, guidance and Progressive Education were so closely related that John Brewer (1932), in *Education as Guidance*, virtually equated the two.

The great spokesman and architect of Progressive Education was John Dewey. He is credited by social historians with revolutionizing American education (Link & Catton, 1967). Dewey clearly saw facilitation and nurture of development as the purpose of education.

In his classic book *Democracy and Education*, Dewey (1916) defined education as the enterprise of supplying the conditions that ensure growth. As he saw it the criterion for the value of schooling was the extent to which it creates a desire for continued growth and supplies the means for making that desire effective.

After World War I, the dominant influence on counseling and guidance was the *Mental Testing Movement.* With the widespread use of tests in schools and colleges, many counselors became little more than custodians of cumulative records and compilers of test results. The emphasis on development was not dead even though guidance was no longer seen as an instrument of social reform. For example, Hamrin and Erickson (1939) writing about the roles and functions of secondary school counselors stated their conviction about the role of the counselor emphatically: There must be someone in the school with the responsibility, the interest, the time, and the capacity to "know" each child as an individual and to integrate the many influences affecting that child into a positive program of growth and development.

With continued emphasis on development as the overriding goal of both counseling and education came a steadily growing awareness of the importance of person-environment interaction or "fit" on development. Williamson (1939), in his book *How to Counsel Students*, pointed out that the counselor must have an understanding and appreciation of the possible effects on the student of social, educational, and occupational situations. Will they help him or her grow intellectually, socially, and emotionally, or will they lead to maladjustments, wasted effort, and emotional conflicts?

As we can see, the rudiments of developmental social ecology (that is, a perspective based on person-environment interaction) were present in the counseling literature more than a half century ago. The notion that the wellsprings of both development and stagnation are to be found in the interaction between the individual and the environment was well established many years ago.

The point of view that has contrasted with the developmental emphasis has been called the "cult of adjustment." Much of the literature on guidance and counseling before the 1960s interpreted the role of counselors and of guidance programs as centered around the task of adjusting students. Adjustment was accomplished in a variety of ways including homogeneous grouping and assignment of underachievers to nonacademic classes and counseling students in or out of various occupations or programs. Adjustment and conformity were considered primary goals. Traxler (1945) defined this view clearly and succinctly. For him the central idea in guidance was to gather as much relevant information as possible about each pupil, organize it, and use the information for the classification and adjustment of individual pupils.

Personal adjustment referred to a person's ability to conform to given situations and organizations. The personal adjustment orientation unobtrusively reinforced psychological passivity by encouraging individuals to fit in and get along in terms of existing social norms and prevailing practices (D'Andrea, 1988). The adjustment emphasis was as strong in the practice of psychotherapy as in counseling and guidance. One practitioner (Halleck, 1963) referred to psychotherapy as the "handmaiden of the status quo." Counselors and therapists who direct their efforts primarily toward promoting personal adjustment essentially help people become more suitable for given kinds of situations and environments. Adjustment resulted in a kind of rigid and static person-environment fit rather than a mutually adaptive and dynamic engagement or interaction that nurtures development in the individual and responsiveness in the environment.

A simple reading of a major newspaper will demonstrate the hardiness of the adjustment approach to psychotherapy. Today's criminal justice system has made psychotherapy the number one alternative to incarceration. Upon conviction, culprits are routinely sentenced to terms of psychotherapy for a wide range of offenses including drunken driving, domestic violence, child abuse, indecent exposure, window peeping, possession of illegal drugs, and a host of other crimes and misdemeanors. Therapy or jail is a common choice facing violators in our criminal justice system.

In the years following World War II, professional counseling grew very rapidly. The G.I. Bill and other programs related to veterans caused rapid expansion of counseling programs on college campuses and in communities. The profession itself in those years was torn by the directive-nondirective controversy. For nearly 30 years, the question of whether to be directive or client-centered produced a heated and generally unproductive debate and dialogue. These largely pseudo-issues sank into well-deserved oblivion as the realization dawned that all counseling influences clients, and that all counseling that deserves the name is client-centered.

It was remarkable that one of the few things that both of these camps and their respective leaders agreed on was the importance of development as a primary goal of counseling and therapy. E.G. Williamson (1958) a leader of the so-called directive school, defined the counseling relationship as possessing a developmental thrust, and as an affective relationship that is individualized and personalized. He saw it as a thinking relationship in which human reason is applied to problems of human development, and as an endeavor to achieve full human development in a particular individual.

Carl Rogers (1962) gave his endorsement to the developmental approach as he pronounced that the purpose of most of the helping professions, including guidance and counseling, is to enhance the personal development and the psychological growth of its clients. He stated further that the effectiveness of any member of the profession is most adequately measured in terms of the degree to which, in work with clients, this goal is achieved.

Leona Tyler (1958) saw the study of development as the central theoretical and research focus to give direction and substance to the counseling

Leona Tyler, (Archives of the History of American Psychology— The University of Akron).

profession and the new field of counseling psychology. A focus on development was an important part of the definition of "Counseling Psychology as a Specialty" as Division 17 of the American Psychological Association took on its present name.

In describing this newly named professional called a *counseling psychologist,* the Committee on Definition (1956) said:

> He has now emerged as a psychologist. He is, however a psychologist who uses varying combinations of exploratory experiences, psychometric techniques, and psychotherapeutic interviewing to assist people to grow and develop. *This is the counseling psychologist.* [italics added] (Counseling Psychology as a Specialty, 1956)

By the 1950s, developmental approaches were a central part of the emerging identity of counselors and counseling psychologists.

In the late 1950s, counseling in schools received a powerful, if perhaps misdirected, impetus from the competition engendered by the Cold War between the United States and the Soviet Union. Early in 1957, German rocket scientists employed by the Russians put *Sputnik I,* a basketball-sized piece of hardware, into orbit around the earth. A month later, *Sputnik II* was launched with an unfortunate dog named Laika on board. The Russian achievement surpassed the efforts of the group of Germans who were employed in the American space program.

The reaction in this country was one of national humiliation, soul-searching, and backbiting. After a few months of agonized recriminations and a convoluted exercise in illogic by politicians, it was decided that the blame for this catastrophe lay with the public schools and the failure of American school children to take enough science and mathematics courses.

Predictably, the Congress immediately passed the National Defense Education Act that, among other things, provided for the recruitment and training of more school counselors, presumably to remind junior high school students of their patriotic duty to immerse themselves in science and mathematics. Special NDEA Institutes were held in many major universities and teachers and counselors were paid to enter or take additional training in counseling. Within five years after the passage of the NDEA legislation, nearly 14,000 counselors had participated in the institutes (Borow, 1964).

Whether its rather dubious purposes were ever achieved, the NDEA legislation undoubtedly resulted in an influx of new and capable people into the counseling profession. It also increased public awareness of the role of counseling in the schools. In 1960, a large-scale national study of counseling in the schools was undertaken under the direction of Gilbert Wrenn. The final report was published in 1962 under the apt title of *The Counselor in a Changing World.*

Wrenn reaffirmed the commitment of counseling to the nurture of student development and proposed counselors be actively engaged in helping to shape and reshape schools to become more developmentally responsive and potent learning environments. Shoben (1962) urged a social reconstructive role for guidance in helping the school to transform itself into a developmentally productive, growth-enhancing community.

In a strange and ironic way, counseling and guidance had come full circle back to its roots as a social reform movement. Much of the impetus that brought counseling full circle was the influence of social reform movements that were ushered in by the turbulent 1960s.

The 1960s was a time of social revolution. The Civil Rights movement, the Women's movement, the anti-Vietnam War movement together with a general discontent about many features of American life made the 1960s the most turbulent decade in twentieth-century American history. Part of this change in values and perspectives was what has been called a "quiet revolution" in mental health (Suinn, 1979). This revolution began with the 1961 report of the Joint Commission on Mental Health established by President Kennedy that was the take off point for the community mental health movement.

The community mental health movement undertook to move the primary responsibility for the identification, treatment, and prevention of mental health problems out of psychiatric clinics and mental hospitals and into the mainstream community. Community mental health centers were funded on a large scale.

The community mental health movement generated a set of perspectives on the nature of mental health problems that had much in common with the points of view that had emerged in counseling and counseling psychology.

The community mental health approach tended to minimize the usefulness of the concept of mental disease, and instead to view psychological dysfunctions not so much as a result of personality defects, but rather simply as a set of maladaptive responses to situational problems demanding practical solutions (Lehman, 1971). This approach focused on the task of helping people living in the community to solve practical problems of everyday living, a view that is similar to the traditions of counseling psychology.

A second aspect of the community mental health approach that resonates with the value system of counselors was the view that the *prevention* of severe breakdowns in human functioning is more important to human and social welfare than is the intensive, long-term treatment of acute emotional disturbances (Suinn, 1979).

As a consequence of these new values and perspectives, community treatment programs were naturally concerned with a variety of factors that affect the immediate and practical functioning of an individual within the community setting. These concerns may include the client's attitudes and competencies, family interaction patterns, and educational and vocational skills.

These concerns were not limited solely to processes occurring within the client (Hersch, 1968). They also included problems and resources inherent in the client's environment, such as housing, employment or educational opportunities, health care, and physical safety and security. Also included in these concerns and variables around which treatment may be centered were the attitudes of the community or society itself toward the identified client (Iscoe, 1974).

The quiet revolution in mental health that was under way in the 1960s and 1970s brought the fields of counseling psychology and community health much closer together and moved both toward what J.G. Kelly (1966) termed an *ecological approach*. Such an approach views human behavior as the product of transactions with the environment and focuses both the understanding and treatment of human problems and dysfunctions squarely on such interactions.

The establishment of the Division of Mental Health Counseling of the American Counseling Association is testimony to this close connection. Today, many counselors practice in community service agencies.

As the connection between professional counseling and mental health was strengthened in the 1980s and 1990s, the image that began to shape the emerging identity of many counselors was that of the psychotherapist. As a profession, psychotherapy was even newer than counseling. For many years, due to the dominance of psychoanalytic theories and psychoanalysts over the field, relatively few professionals other than psychiatrists engaged in psychotherapy (Humphries, 1996).

Beginning in the 1950s, psychologists and other professionals began to practice psychotherapy on an independent basis. The image of the psychotherapist free of institutional commitments, connected to clients within a deeply personal and private relationship has seemed an exciting

Table 1.1

Growth Line for Developmental Counseling: 1900 to Present by 20-Year Intervals

20-Year Intervals	Settings	Clientele	Goals
1900s	High schools, settlement houses	Youth leaving school	Vocational
1920s	High schools, colleges, employment services	School leavers, college graduates, job seekers	Vocational, educational
1940s	High schools, Junior high schools, rehabilitation agencies, veterans administration, colleges, employment services	Children, adolescents, young adults, veterans	Vocational, educational, rehabilitative
1960s	Elementary schools, middle schools, high schools, colleges, rehabilitation settings, family services, corrections, alcohol and drug agencies	Full age range including women and minorities	Developmental and remedial
1980s	Elementary schools, middle schools, high schools, colleges, rehabilitation settings, family services, corrections, alcohol and drug agencies, employee assistance programs	Full age range including women and minorities	Developmental, remedial, and preventive
2000s	Elementary schools, middle schools, high schools, colleges, rehabilitation settings, family services, corrections, alcohol and drug agencies, employee assistance programs, private practice, organizational consulting, health maintenance organizations, health care	Full age range including women and minorities	Developmental, remedial, and preventive

and liberating model around which to organize an extended professional identity.

Out of this influence has come a tremendous expansion in the range of concerns and the types of clients to whom counselors offer help. The early focus on vocational development and transitions from school to work or from military to civilian life has been expanded to encompass a wide variety of problem situations across the entire lifespan (see Table 1.1).

The emphasis on enhanced development as a primary goal of therapy, however, has remained. A basic creed for developmental counseling and therapy can be found in the words of Fassinger and Schlossberg (1992).

Inherent in our philosophy is a nonpathological focus on normalcy, and day-to-day problems of living with an emphasis on strengths and adaptive strategies in our clients . . . We see ourselves as educators, we emphasize the empowerment of individuals, we value preventive as well as ameliorative intervention efforts, and we work for enhanced functioning in all people. . . .

Our scope includes environmental as well as individual intervention . . . the effective use of community resources and social and political advocacy where appropriate . . . We emphasize developmental approaches to working with people including attention to their sociocultural context and the influence of gender, race, age, ethnicity, sexual orientation, (dis)ability and socio-history. These characteristics give us the unique opportunity to be in the forefront . . . of effective service delivery. . . . (p. 244)

This statement eloquently describes the culmination of a century of the history of psychological counseling and therapy, generally, and of developmental counseling in particular.

Developmental counseling is an approach to psychotherapy that combines the developmental and ecological approaches. It provides a framework and rationale for counseling and psychotherapy that builds on the positive potentials of people to grow, achieve, and build competence in dealing with the inevitable challenges confronting them across their life cycle.

BASIC PRINCIPLES OF DEVELOPMENTAL COUNSELING AND THERAPY

Developmental counseling is an approach to psychological helping that is organized around a set of unifying and clarifying ideas, principles, and commitments regarding human beings and the physical and social world in which they live. Counseling and psychotherapy are very closely related processes. Although they have evolved historically out of somewhat different social and cultural antecedents, it is almost impossible to make neat, clear-cut, and mutually exclusive distinctions between what counselors and psychotherapists actually do. In any individual case, a considerable degree of overlap in techniques and functions is very likely to occur.

COUNSELING AND PSYCHOTHERAPY: INTERTWINED PROCESSES

Generally attempts to distinguish between counseling and psychotherapy have centered around several types of comparisons. Counseling has been viewed as more appropriate for less severely disturbed people and has been described as more oriented toward immediate, specific, and practical outcomes than psychotherapy. Psychotherapy, on the other hand, has been perceived as more often directed toward effecting global and pervasive personality change, or toward "curing" presumed mental illnesses or psychopathology.

Counseling has been seen as stressing rational problem solving, decision making, life planning, and stress management. Counseling has also been construed as focused toward helping "normal" people deal with problems arising out of the vicissitudes of everyday life. Counseling is often viewed as preventive, rather than remedial in the sense that it can offer help before problems and difficulties reach proportions that might trigger profound or catastrophic breakdowns in psychological functioning. Counselors have been traditionally positioned in schools, colleges, or community agencies where they are readily accessible to large segments of given communities and populations.

These differences have been based upon practical, common sense distinctions that have had some practical utility and validity in distinguishing between the practice of counseling and psychotherapy. Increasingly, however, the validity of these common sense distinctions has been steadily eroded by changes occurring in the practice of both counseling and psychotherapy. The rapid increase in the practice of brief psychotherapies reflects the influence of both empirical research findings and the economic realities of the marketplace (Koss & Schiang, 1994). These developments have made duration of treatment a less useful criterion in distinguishing between counseling and psychotherapy.

The advent and evolution of a variety of "behavior therapies" have also tended to blur distinctions between counseling and psychotherapy. These therapies focus very directly on specific, immediate symptoms and purposely avoid dealing with inner or unconscious personality mechanisms or defenses. Similarly, more recent cognitive and cognitive-behavioral therapies have stressed rational, logical approaches to the analysis of troublesome problems and situations facing clients (Dobson, 1988). Certainly, the old onionskin analogy that portrayed therapists as probing into the pungent and conflict-laden "core of personality," while counselors busied themselves with the less volatile surface layers is no longer an apt distinction.

The changes that have occurred have resulted in confusion and even the denigration of counseling. For example, Corsini (1995) defines counseling as "the giving of information, advice, and orders by someone considered to be an expert. . . . (p. 3). Such a definition certainly shows little respect for counseling as a psychologically based, professional activity and is completely out of touch with modern approaches.

Given that approaches to providing psychological help through the medium of personal interaction have a great deal in common, it is more useful simply to consider psychotherapy as the broader and more inclusive term. It is then possible to view developmental counseling as a specialty within the broad and diverse constellation of professional activities termed psychotherapy.

COMPONENTS OF DEVELOPMENTAL COUNSELING

Professional counseling has historically been closely linked to education. Developmental counseling often includes a component involving the dissemination of specialized information and/or the acquisition of specific skills. Educational-vocational counseling may, for example, provide clients with information about occupations or educational opportunities as well as information about self in relation to psychologically relevant aspects of the environment. Similarly, academic improvement counseling may provide skill training in areas such as reading comprehension, test-taking, or time management.

Family counseling may include didactic material on parenting skills as well as basic information about child development. Counseling may also include coaching in social skills or other practical training relevant to the presenting problems of individual clients. Developmental counseling may include any or all of these activities.

Since developmental counseling perceives people as thinking, feeling, and acting beings, it is seen as natural and desirable to couple the exploration of deeply personal hopes, fears, and aspirations with practical, useful information and adaptive skills that can move the client toward the removal of obstacles to goal attainment and thus toward higher levels of development and satisfaction. Issues that deal with successfully handling basic social roles such as those of spouse, parent, worker, student, or friend are crucial in terms of optimal development, while failure or fear of failure in these roles is fraught with profound emotional distress.

DEVELOPMENTAL COUNSELING: AN ECLECTIC APPROACH

Developmental counseling approaches have evolved in much the same way as other psychotherapeutic systems. All such systems represent efforts to deal with a wide range of human needs and characteristics in a comprehensive yet consistent way. Developmental counseling is a framework for understanding clients and helping to set goals on their behalf. *It is not a theory about counseling processes.*

In choosing formulas or techniques to be used, developmental counseling builds on eclectic integrative approaches, that is, an approach drawn from many sources. Eclectic counseling or psychotherapy uses concepts, constructs, and behavior change principles from a variety of psychological or therapeutic models or bodies of research and theory (Poznanski & McLennan, 1995).

For many years, many psychotherapists viewed themselves as eclectic. Generally, however, eclectic has meant little more than a refusal to be classified as an adherent of a single theory (Garfield & Bergin, 1994). In this narrow and negative sense, it could not be expected that any two eclectic counselors or therapists would necessarily reflect any degree of similarity in techniques or approaches. Eclectic approaches have often been criticized as shallow, poorly organized, and conceptually weak because of their failure to articulate clearly how they draw on and organize principles and concepts adapted from different bodies of theory and research (Mahalik, 1990).

For eclectic counseling or therapy to be evaluated in terms of effectiveness, the approach must be *systematic*, that is, it must attempt to articulate the particular sources of gain that it draws on, and must specify how these are *integrated* into an organized and internally consistent approach to clients. A specific example of the way in which developmental counseling can draw on a variety of theoretical concepts and research findings is elaborated in Chapter 8.

PHILOSOPHICAL CONCERNS AND COMMITMENTS

Basically, developmental counseling views people as complex and complete thinking, feeling, and acting beings. The goals of clients, and therefore the goals of developmental counseling generally, involve facilitating lasting changes in the ways those clients think, feel, and act in regard to themselves and in relation to the world in which they live.

Developmental counseling is distinguished by several major philosophical concerns and commitments. The ideas, principles, and values associated with these philosophical commitments help to distinguish developmental counseling from other models of psychological help-giving. These basic assumptions and commitments can be partially expressed in terms of the following positions:

1. The primary goal of developmental counseling is to facilitate the optimal psychological development of clients, both by enhancing higher levels of functioning and by helping to remove obstacles to further growth.
2. Developing human beings can only be fully understood and helped within the context of their interactions with the physical, social, and psychological environment.
3. The ultimate goal of developmental counseling is to facilitate a *dynamic* and *growth-producing* engagement or "fit" between the developing person and a humane and responsive environment. Change in person-environment interaction is inevitable.

The inevitability of change, however, by no means guarantees the progress of further development for any individual. Development is seen as systematic, continuous change in a *valued direction*. Change in human affairs and individual lives is an inescapable reality. Further growth and development is an ever-present possibility.

Developmental counseling is very heavily concerned with choice and consequently with issues of human freedom. Human beings have the freedom to participate purposefully and consciously in change. The failure to engage actively and planfully with change factors at work in one's own life is to abdicate the opportunity to exert any degree of direction and impetus to your life.

People can only participate actively and purposely in the realities of change when they become aware of those realities. Developmental counseling deals very directly with the task of helping clients to become aware of themselves and equally aware of crucial events and opportunities in their environments.

As self-awareness and awareness of the environment grow, new possibilities, new aspirations, new hopes, and consequently new choices and new challenges emerge. Developmental counseling helps not only to increase awareness, but also to mobilize clients' personal and practical resources to convert hopes and aspirations into accomplishments and successes.

Developmental counseling has a strong focus on human potential. It also has an equally strong concern with interactions between people and their environment—human ecology. Human development proceeds from a long-term, optimal set of interactions between the developing individual and the environment. The ecological focus represents a second set of unifying and clarifying ideas that helps to distinguish developmental counseling from other psychotherapeutic systems.

The ecological approach stems from an interactionist view of the sources and determinants of human experience and behavior. It contrasts with those views that see behavior stemming almost solely from intrapsychic events such as unconscious conflicts, defenses, and motivations.

According to the interactionist view, most human experience and behavior arises out of transactions between the individual and the physical and social psychological environment. Attempts to understand or to assess the behavior of an individual in isolation from his or her interactions with the environment are incomplete and usually misleading. Seen in this way, most human problems do not exist inside an individual in terms of a disturbed psyche or a set of deviant traits. Rather, human problems and difficulties tend to arise around specific interactions *between* the individual and the environment (Rubenstein & Zager, 1995).

When developmental counselors attempt to understand a troubled or inadequately functioning client, they do not search primarily for deepseated intrapsychic conflicts that are presumed to reside within the troubled individual. Rather, they focus on the pattern of responses that the client makes to immediate and concrete situational challenges. The approach is to help the client deal constructively with practical problems of living, and in that process learn coping and mastery skills that will transfer and persist in future situations and so lead to further growth and development.

CONSTRUCTS AND CONCEPTS IN DEVELOPMENTAL COUNSELING

The constructs or conceptual tools used by developmental counselors differ considerably from those that have been developed out of abnormal psychology and that are heavily utilized in other systems of psychotherapy. People know from simple observation that the behavior of human beings changes markedly through time and across situations (Mischel, 1984). The discipline of social psychology deals with the many ways in which human behavior is influenced by the presence of and interactions with other human beings.

Social roles, expectations, and relationships are seen as important shapers of human behavior and human experience. Human beings are social animals. They need and depend on others to meet myriad needs throughout the life-span (Ainsworth & Bowley, 1991). Most social interactions through which people meet their needs is organized in terms of social roles. A social role is a more or less clearly structured way of participating in social interaction. Put very simply, a social role is defined primarily by what others expect of an individual occupying a particular position within a group.

The life space of any individual is organized around social role memberships that can be mapped. Competence, conflict, and competition within and among social roles govern the rewards and punishment, successes, and failures that orchestrate the emotional life of every individual. Developmental counseling focuses on the cognitive, emotional, and behavioral resources needed to meet clients' legitimate needs within their principal social roles.

CONCEPTS OF DEVELOPMENT

As people move through the life cycle, passing through a sequence of chronological stages, the number and complexity of social roles in which they engage increase rapidly. Often, these roles conflict or compete, sometimes taking on contradictory and incompatible expectations and conceptions. As this occurs, the life space of the individual is characterized by *role strain*. When role strain among very central and significant roles occurs, the individual may be subject to intense anxiety or stress.

Similarly as individuals move through the life cycle, new roles, relationships, and responsibilities are often thrust on them. They may be poorly prepared to handle these new roles. The anthropological concepts of *continuity and discontinuity* link human ecology and counseling and are important in conceptualizing the functions of developmental counselors.

In very simple societies, cultural and social forces act upon developing individuals at rates and in ways that closely approximate the maturational processes that determine readiness for the demands and expectations inherent in new or expanded roles. Expectations for productive work, for example, may proceed at about the same pace as growth in size and strength, giving a developing child the ability to assume a greater share of family tasks. The growing youngster, thus, experiences a basic *continuity* between physical maturation and social and vocational development.

In relatively simple societies, biological and cultural clocks tend to keep the same time. In modern, complex, post-industrial societies, however, there are many cultural clocks that tick away to give notice of new demands and expectations for the developing individual. These cultural clocks are not necessarily synchronized with the biological clocks that govern maturation. Indeed, these cultural clocks do not even keep time with each other.

In complex societies, most individuals sooner or later experience a marked *discontinuity* in their transactions with the environment. Entry into various levels and types of schooling, beginning work, marriage, parenthood, the termination of active parenting, and retirement from work are all examples of events that are frequently accompanied by severe discontinuities with consequent stress and emotional upset. These kinds of challenges are called *life transitions* (Fassinger & Schlossberg, 1992).

Developmental counseling addresses human needs in helping clients deal with major transition points in the life cycle. Because the nature of an organized society imposes demands and expectations on all of its members, some transition points can be readily identified for most members of the society. Failure to succeed reasonably in meeting these expectations means that further development is disrupted or even permanently stalled. Table 1.2 lists some of the ways in which transitions are smoothed by social institutions including developmental counseling.

The cognitive, emotional, and behavioral changes needed to continue along the path of further growth are called *developmental tasks*. Each life

Table 1.2
Social Institutions for Bridging Life Transitions

Critical Period	Social Institution
Preparation for school entry (3–5 years)	Nursery school, Head Start, family counseling
Entry into school (5–6 years)	Kindergarten, parent consultation
Early adolescence (11–14 years)	Junior high school, middle schools, school counseling
School-leaving Entry into adulthood (16–21 years)	Community colleges, technical and trade schools, juvenile courts, educational-vocational counseling, premarital counseling, personal counseling
Young adult (21–35 years)	Adult education, marriage and family counseling, vocational counseling, personal counseling
Mid-life adult (35–50)	Personal counseling, vocational counseling, family counseling, health care counseling, adult education
Later adult (50–65 years)	Preretirement counseling, health care counseling, personal counseling
Retirement (65+ years)	Personal counseling, health care counseling, adult education, geriatric counseling, family counseling, nursing homes, retirement communities

stage imposes these developmental tasks on individuals before successful entry into an ensuing stage can be achieved. Developmental tasks may include the acquisition of basic educational skills, interpersonal skills, attitudes toward work or authority, functioning within marital or family relationships and myriad others arising out of complex social role structures (Masten & Coatsworth, 1998). Developmental counselors are often expert in assisting clients with specific developmental tasks that are prevalent in particular life stages such as adolescence, young adulthood, midlife, or postretirement.

A final major concept crucial to developmental counseling is that of *coping behaviors*. Coping behaviors permit people to deal with stressful and problematic situations triggered by discontinuities in life transitions. They may also be triggered by a host of other events such as serious illnesses, losses, bereavements, job loss, divorces, victimization, and so forth (Gibson & Brown, 1992).

Coping behaviors have two major components: (1) the acquisition of strategies and skills that directly interface with a problematic and stressful situation such as problem solving, decision making, or planning skills; and (2) ways in which an individual handles emotional distress such as fear, anger, and frustration in the face of threat and uncertainty. Often this emotional control is established by helping the client to develop personal meaning about the stressful situation, assess the situation realistically, and interpret it within a framework of personal beliefs and values.

DISTINGUISHING CHARACTERISTICS OF DEVELOPMENTAL COUNSELING

Developmental counseling differs from other psychotherapeutic systems in the ways in which it conceptualizes human needs and characteristics and how it construes the human condition. The basic concepts are developmental and psychosocial rather than pathogenic and intrapsychic.

People potentially transact with their physical and social environments in patterns that can move them toward higher levels of development with attendant gains in personal satisfaction and capacities for social contributions. They are also vulnerable to cultural discontinuities and personal crises that may interrupt or limit development and lead to chronic frustration and failure.

For the developmental counselor, these concepts mean that clients are counseled and understood in the context of the social systems in which they live and with which they interact. They are ever-changing humans who live in an unstable world.

Clients are not seen primarily as pathological victims of some presumed set of intrapsychic deficits, but rather are viewed as developmentally *stuck*, that is, confronted with obstacles to growth that prevent them from moving onward and upward within a developmental pattern. In a sense, the concept of developmental arrest or being *stuck* replaces the traditional psychotherapist's notion of being sick. Similarly, the notion of *freeing* clients replaces the goal of *curing* them (Okun, 1984).

The counselor's concerns are not limited, however, solely to processes occurring within the client. The developmental counselor is also legitimately concerned with problems and resources that both reside and are inherent in the client's environment, itself. Problems of decent housing, employment opportunities, discrimination, access to health care, financial or physical security, and opportunities for social mobility all represent concerns that affect person-environment interaction (McCloyd, 1998). They are, therefore, of as much concern to the counselor as the client's responses to them (Conyne, 1988).

The developmental counselor is committed philosophically to avoid the stance that sometimes results in people being blamed for situations in which they are the real victims (Jessor, 1993). Communities and the social institutions that they represent such as schools, agencies, and organizations are human inventions that are ostensibly designed to meet human needs and serve human purposes. When it is clear that the obstacles to growth confronting clients arise from inadequate, aversive or exploitive features of the community or society, itself, the counselor moves to improve the quality of those environments.

For many students entering the field of counseling and psychotherapy, one of the most negative and frustrating aspects of the profession is the sense of helplessness that comes from the knowledge that while we can talk with clients and help them to cathart about their pain and problems, the fundamental situation often does not change.

The ecological or interactive model for understanding and assisting people is a fresh perspective that defines a new kind of role for counselors and therapists (Kaczmarek & Riva, 1996). One of the most important realizations of this view is that people live, work, suffer, triumph, or fail within the real world with all of its imperfections and injustices.

Intrapsychic approaches to understanding human behavior, on the other hand, have tended to focus almost solely on behavior potentials that exist *within* the person and have tended, largely, to ignore situational or environmental influences. Such approaches to studying human personality typically come up with long lists of inferred traits, needs, drives, defense mechanisms, mental diseases, and so forth, with which to explain behavior.

When the psychological functioning of an individual in almost any kind of situation seems inadequate, or inappropriate, we explain the problem in terms of inferences about what must be going on *inside* the individual. From this perspective, we begin to think of people as "unmotivated," "stupid," "defensive," "paranoid," "psychopathic," and so on. The intrapsychic view is able to generate an almost endless list of labels with which to categorize and eventually to stigmatize troubled people. Unfortunately, these labels do little to enable us to help people and may, actually result in the refusal or withdrawal of help.

One of the problems with this view is that we often begin to confuse the explanatory constructs that we invented to explain and label behavior with reality. These labels and constructs begin to take on a life of their own, and we begin to treat them as though they were real entities lurking somewhere beneath the skin of the individual. In a sense, we create a kind of mythology to explain things that we do not fully comprehend. This modern version of classical mythology may comfort us in denying our own ignorance, or inability to help, but, like the mythologies of old, it results in very little actual control over the natural world or assistance to those with whom we work.

The ecological or interactive view offers us an alternative to the intrapsychic model that enables us to retain much that is useful from earlier approaches while coming to terms with the realities of environmental and situational influences on human behavior. In the interactive model, we do not have to think of people as interchangeable parts or empty organisms.

Rather than studying or working with the individual in isolation, we can take as our unit for analysis the ecosystem, that is, the person in his or her full social context. An ecosystem is the immediate physical, social, and psychological setting within which the transactions between the individual and the environment are occurring. When we use the system as our unit of analysis, we begin to focus on rather than to ignore or obscure the context within which behavior occurs (Cicchetti & Toth, 1998; Wapner, 1987).

We may see, for example, the rebellious behavior of a child in a classroom in which he experiences constant failure or ridicule. We also may

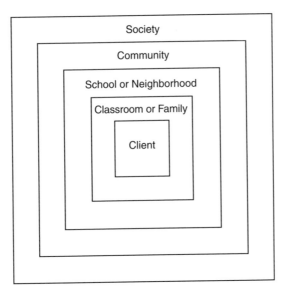

Figure 1.1 The Ecosystemic Model showing boundaries and linkages.

see the violent and tumultuous behavior of a child in a family in which the father has been displaced by the mother's live-in boyfriend.

From this perspective, problems or dysfunctions that are barriers to development are best understood and most effectively prevented or removed in contexts and environments within which they occur. Counseling in systems may involve working with whole families, consulting with parents and teachers, collaborating on neighborhood development programs or participating in curriculum development projects in schools. Figure 1.1 illustrates the ecosystemic model showing boundaries and linkages.

The ecological or interactive perspective, generates larger and more wide-ranging sets of options and alternatives than those available out of traditional personality theories. The approach generates what Tyler (1983) called "multiple possibilities" not available with intrapsychic theories.

CHAPTER 2

Theoretical Approaches to Human Development

Our great advantage over all other social animals is that we possess the kind of brain that allows us to change our minds. We are not obliged as ants are, to follow genetic blueprints for every last detail of our behavior. Our genes are more cryptic and ambiguous in their instructions; Get along, says our DNA, talk to each other, figure out the world. . . .

—L. Thomas (1984)

ALEXANDER, THE 12-year-old hero of Ben Piazza's novel, *The Exact and Very Strange Truth* comes to grips with one of life's ultimate realities when he reflects:

Peculiar how things can change so sudden. Things can be one way today and tomorrow be the very opposite. That is the exact and very strange truth.

A freckle-faced 14-year-old boy suddenly discovers that girls are not just soft boys. A sensitive 16-year-old has her ideals bruised by the realities of a cynical adult world. A blonde cheerleader gazes at an engagement ring with a mixture of exultation and apprehension. A middle-aged executive watches his career disappear in a flurry of corporate downsizing. A distinguished professor approaches retirement with a growing sense of desperation and depression.

All of these people face change—changes occurring within themselves and within the world around them. How do human beings deal with change? How do they cope with stress and turbulence in their environments? Are some kinds of change orderly and predictable? How is it that some people appear to achieve high levels of control and mastery over the course of their lives, while for others life seems to represent a series of unmet challenges and unmitigated disasters?

These and a host of other related questions confront those who seek to understand human development and who dare to try to smooth its course. Psychologists have been engaged in the scientific study of human development for about a century. Long before "scientific psychology," however, thinkers have been struck by the turbulence and transformations that are a natural part of human growth. The concept of adolescence goes back to the fifteenth century (Muuss, 1968). Jean Jacques Rousseau, the eighteenth-century Swiss-born philosopher and student of human nature was one of the first to point out that children were far more than simply miniature adults. Rousseau, in a treatise directed to teachers, begged his reader to begin "by studying your pupils thoroughly." He pointed out that:

> We do not know childhood. Acting on the false ideas we have of it the farther we go the farther we wander from the right path. Those who are wisest are attached to what it is important for men to know without considering what children are able to apprehend. *They are always looking for the man in the child, without thinking of what he was before he became a man.* [italics added] (J.J. Rousseau, from the preface to *Emile,* 1762)

The study of development has flowed from two powerful streams of theory and research. The first of these streams of influence grew out of the thinking of Sigmund Freud and became an integral and indispensable part of psychoanalytic theory. This approach as it has been modified today is often called the *psychosocial* approach to life-span development (Rodgers, 1984). The second body of theory and research focuses on the development of thinking capacities in human beings, and is termed the *cognitive developmental* approach. It has largely grown out of the seminal work of Swiss psychologist Jean Piaget.

In America, pioneering psychologists such as John Mark Baldwin and G. Stanley Hall focused upon the study of development. Baldwin's work anticipated much of Piaget's approach to cognitive development (Cahan, 1984). G. Stanley Hall was one of the first to focus on the study of adolescence, and was instrumental in arranging Sigmund Freud's visit to the United States and in helping to popularize his ideas here.

THE PSYCHOSOCIAL APPROACH

The notion of qualitatively different stages in personality development is a central concept in psychoanalytic theory. Freud posited the existence of a series of *psychosexual* stages of development. The basic energy that drives development was seen as sexual derived from *libido*. Freud believed that the whole body was a source of sexual pleasure, but that this pleasure was concentrated in different parts of the body or *erogenous zones* at different stages of development. These erogenous zones gave each of the stages of development their respective names—*oral, anal, phallic, latency,* and finally the *genital* stage. The first three stages are all experienced in the first five years of life, while the latency stage lasts from about age six to puberty, and the genital stage for the remainder of the life-span.

Freud believed that either under- or overgratification of impulses at any of these stages led to *fixation,* or an interruption of personality development at that stage, which determined formation of a given personality type many years later in adulthood. According to Freud, adults could be classified as oral, anal, or phallic types, and so on, the basis of personality traits that originated in early development.

Various aspects of psychopathology were seen also to develop out of early childhood *fixations* or *traumas.* If an individual experienced problems later in life, the psychoanalyst searched for the origin and the cure of these problems in the psychosexual stages of development going back into early childhood. So was born the "uncover-and-cure" approach to psychotherapy.

As psychoanalytic theory and the many variations spun off by Sigmund Freud's disciples and former disciples evolved, several marked changes in emphasis set the stage for the advent of psychosocial theories of development. First, a group of psychoanalytically oriented theorists sometimes called *ego psychologists* began to put much greater emphasis on the rational, reality-oriented, problem-solving functions of human personality. These ego functions were seen as much more significant than in Freud's earlier formulations. Freud's pessimistic picture of a humankind at the mercy of thwarted infantile libidinal impulses was replaced by an increased appreciation of the positive, resilient and adaptive capacities of the human personality (Fromm, 1941; Hartmann, 1939).

At the same time, these neo-analytic theorists began to envision the seeds of psychopathology sewn much more broadly and pervasively than simply in the curbing or indulging of childish sexual impulses. They saw the whole developmental history of the individual as involved in the formation of patterns of interpersonal and social relationships that virtu-ally defined the personality (Sullivan, 1953).

Finally, analytic theorists like Freud's former disciple, Carl Jung, began to see developmental issues arising not simply as latent reactions to child-hood traumas, but as full-blown crises born out of the realities of life expe-riences reaching across the life-span. Jung labeled the tumultuous upheaval frequently encountered in middle age the *mid-life crisis* (Jung, 1933).

The psychoanalytic theorist who put the complex pieces of the life-span development puzzle together most effectively was Erik Erikson. His classic formulation of the "Eight Stages of Man" (1950) combined the neoanalytic theoretical concepts to produce an integrated developmental model that specified eight chronological stages across the life-span. Each stage was characterized by a central, overriding psychological *task* that must be ac-complished for future development to proceed optimally. This model pointed not only to sources of possible psychopathology inherent in each stage and task, but also to a path of healthy and effective personality devel-opment. An adaptation of the Erikson model as elaborated by subsequent research is presented in Chapter 3.

Erikson's model is psychosocial rather than psychosexual. As we saw in Chapter 1, such a model assumes a continuing life-long interaction between the maturational and aging processes unfolding within a developing indi-vidual and the social institutions and influences constantly at work in the environment.

Robert White (1960) went on to characterize the seeds of personality de-velopment not as growing out of psychosexual stages and libidinal im-pulses, but as rooted in an innate striving or drive virtually "wired" into the growing individual. White described his concept of competence in terms of capacities to survive and develop. To him, the competence of an organism meant its fitness or ability to carry on those transactions with the environment which result in its maintaining itself, growing, and flourish-ing (White, 1960).

White saw the drive for competence both as a key ingredient in the suc-cess of human beings as a species and also as crucial in the development of talents, skills, and potentials in individuals. From this view, develop-ment was seen to proceed out of the life-long strivings of human beings to master and control their environment, and in the process actualizing their own best talents, potentials, and abilities (Masten & Coatsworth, 1998).

The views of development put forth in the theories of Erikson and White were very different from the prevailing picture in psychoanalytic theory, and indeed in much of developmental psychology.

Personality traits or tendencies were not seen as etched in stone in infancy or early childhood. Human beings were not seen to carry within themselves a set of ticking time bombs fashioned out of traumas and fixations buried deep in their developmental histories. People were also not viewed as passive and helpless victims of a tug of war between irresistible sexual impulses and the stern and unforgiving mandates of society or super-ego.

Most importantly, personality development was seen as a continuing, life-long process of challenges and accomplishments. Havighurst (1953) coined the term *developmental tasks* to describe the host of challenges confronting individuals along the thorny path to optimal development. He defined a developmental task as a task that arises at or about a certain period in the life of an individual, successful achievement of which leads to happiness and to success with later tasks, while failure leads to unhappiness in the individual, disapproval by the society, and difficulty with later tasks (Havighurst, 1953).

These new approaches to personality theory triggered a burst of interest in adult development. A whole series of long-term longitudinal studies of the adult years was undertaken in the decades that followed these changes in theoretical formulations. Vaillant (1977), Levinson (1978), Gould (1978), Neugarten (1979), and Lowenthal, Thurnher, and Chiriboga (1975) were among the best known of these researchers on the psychology of adulthood and the transitions and discontinuities that inevitably accompany it.

The results of these pioneering studies were surprisingly similar in terms of results and interpretations. Some differences existed in regard to the extent to which similar patterns of age-related change were apparent across individuals. Several rather clear generalizations emerged, however, across these studies, including:

1. It is not the isolated traumas of childhood that shape the course of human lives, but rather the quality of *sustained* relationships with other people.
2. Developmental change is continuous across the life-span.
3. Developmental change is pervasive, touching psychological, social, and physiological domains.
4. Life-span development is influenced by many factors. No single characteristic such as intelligence, education, or family origin is all-important.
5. The full context of past development and present situation must be considered if we are to understand an individual life.

The insights gained from these longitudinal studies of lives portrayed a view of human nature from this work that sees a capacity for change across the entire life-span and questions the traditional idea that the experience of the early years constrain the characteristics of adolescence and adulthood. The consequences of early childhood are continually being transformed by later experiences making the course of human development more open than had been realized (Brim & Kagan, 1980).

As we noted in Chapter 1, as the realities of life-span development began to be fully understood and appreciated by psychologists, attention was focused on the identification of key markers or *transitions* that punctuate the course of development. Some of these, such as school entrance or leaving, puberty, marriage, child-rearing, or retirement, are rather obvious and predictable milestones accompanied by readily apparent changes in challenges, expectations, and demands. Others are less predictable such as divorce, death of a spouse, or serious illnesses. Promotions, graduations, inheritances, job opportunities, or transfers may also represent major transitions.

Schlossberg (1981) defined *transitions* as occurring if an event results in a change in assumptions about oneself and the world and thus requires a corresponding change in one's behavior and relationships.

This is obviously a very broad definition and one that potentially encompasses a vast array of situations and circumstances. A concept related to transitions that serves to narrow the notion to more manageable proportions is the concept of *developmental crisis*. Most people, most of the time operate in fairly consistent patterns, in apparent harmony with their environments. They tend to deal with problems in familiar ways with minimal delay and reasonable success. When the usual coping or problem-solving responses do not work, people experience stress or tension. A crisis is precisely such a situation.

A crisis is thus an interruption of a stable or steady sort of equilibrium. The individual may experience anxiety, fear, guilt, or shame as well as a sense of helplessness. Self-confidence may be impaired and effective cognitive functioning reduced. A crisis then is a relatively brief period of disequilibrium during which the person in crisis seeks to find new and more effective ways to solve problems, make decisions, and cope with stress.

When transitions precipitate such situations, we call them *developmental crises*. As we noted in Chapter 1, the state of disequilibrium that affects the individual generally arises out of a *discontinuity* between the demands of the situation or transition and the psychological, material, and social resources available to the individual.

The psychosocial approach to life-span development provides a structure that allows us to understand both the challenges confronting developing human beings at various points in the life-span and the resources they bring with them to meet those challenges. The approach identifies a basic drive or motivation toward competence that energizes human beings in their quest to obtain a degree of control and direction to the course of their lives. Out of this quest grows the seeds of further development.

What the psychosocial approach does not do, however, is to specify with any degree of clarity or detail the nature of *psychological* changes that occur in the course of development. Is it possible for people, under some circumstances, at least, to obtain some control or perceived control over their environment without changing psychologically? Is there a basic pattern or template that shapes the ways in which people construe or think about themselves and the world in which they live? Is development a natural part of maturation, or are there sets of environmental conditions that nurture development and others that slow or still its progress?

THE COGNITIVE DEVELOPMENTAL APPROACH

A line of research and theory that endeavors to address some of the questions posed above has grown out of the work of the Swiss psychologist Jean Piaget. Piaget was trained as a biologist, but became interested in studying the thinking processes of young children. He developed a method of studying children by presenting them with various problem situations and then carefully observing and recording their response to a systematic interrogation process.

Out of his research, Piaget became convinced that children pass through a series of *qualitatively* different stages of development in their basic thought processes. Piaget was further convinced that these changes were not simply a function of age or maturation, but rather grew out of the active *interaction* that occurred between the child and his or her environment (Piaget, 1929).

In this respect, Piaget's basic approach was not unlike the psychosocial approach described earlier. Piaget believed that a basic human motivation exists to *understand* and *cope* with the world.

Piaget emphasized that intellectual development, that is thoughts, ideas, or strategies grow out of *actions*. His was an *interactionist* view of behavior and development rather than an hereditarian or purely environmentalist perspective. Piaget saw life as a continuous creation of increasingly complex ways of thinking and a progressive balancing or testing of these cognitive processes with the challenges and realities posed by the environment. Cognitive development, or changes in the way

Jean Piaget (Archives of the History of
American Psychology—The University of Akron).

we construe the world, literally evolves out of our unending struggle with
efforts to make sense of the environment (Piaget, 1929).

The basic need to understand or "make sense" out of our encounters
with the environment means that a kind of dissonance or *disequilibrium* is
established when we confront situations or phenomena that our present

ways of thinking cannot explain or comprehend. This kind of dynamic *mismatch* between our habitual ways of construing events and new and perplexing problems or situations furnishes the basic elements conducive to cognitive development.

Piaget postulated the existence of two kinds of cognitive processes that may occur when an individual is confronted with a dissonance producing mismatch. *Assimilation* occurs when the individual tries to construe the environmental situation in ways that will make it compatible with or understandable in terms of his or her existing cognitive structures or ways of thinking.

The alternative to assimilation that can reduce dissonance is called *accommodation*. Accommodation is a process by which the individual modifies existing cognitive structures to understand or deal with the environmental situation.

The interaction between accommodation and assimilation creates a *dynamic balance*. Cognitive development is seen to occur when and if there is some degree of cognitive *disequilibrium* due to an imbalance in these two processes.

Developmental stages, characterized by relatively stable and pervasive cognitive structures and ways of thinking, are periods of relative balance between assimilation and accommodation processes.

Stages changes or *transitions* on the other hand are periods of disequilibrium and may be accompanied by both emotional turmoil and intense activity interacting with problematic and perplexing situations. Just as developmental transitions in the psychosocial model were seen to represent distressing but promising opportunities for growth, cognitive developmental transitions are also focal points for future development.

Cognitive developmental changes are seen as different from other kinds of human learning in that they are seen to be *irreversible* and to follow an *invariant sequence*. Individuals cannot slide back down the developmental stage ladder to lower levels. While there is no guarantee that any given individual will move to a higher stage, the sequence of stage changes is considered to be similar across individuals and even cultures. In other words, no one can skip a stage on the way to the top of the developmental pyramid. As Tyler put it in the quotation that opened Chapter 1, development is a one-way street.

From their careful observations of children of varying age groups, Piaget and his colleagues postulated the existence of four basic cognitive stages. These are:

1. *Sensorimotor* (Birth to about 2 years)
   In this stage learning is based primarily on direct-sensory experience.
2. *Pre-operational or intuitive mode* (2–7 years)
   The ability to store mental images and symbols using language increases dramatically. Learning is characterized by free experimenting, trial-and-error, or an intuitive approach.
3. *Concrete operations* (7–11years)
   There is a shift from intuition to concrete thought and the child must test solutions to problems in order to understand them. The child may be overly logical and concrete and have difficulty changing his or her mind in the face of new information.
4. *Formal operations* (11–16 years and up)
   The individual is capable of utilizing logical, rational, or abstract strategies. Symbolic meanings, metaphors, and similes can be understood. Implications and generalizations of principles can be made and understood.

The attainment of *Formal Operational* thinking is seen as the great watershed of cognitive development. It is seen to make possible full adult intellectual and social functioning. In the years since Piaget and his associates articulated their ideas of qualitatively different cognitive stages, a number of other theorists have proposed somewhat similar frameworks to describe specific areas of development. Kohlberg (1969), Perry (1970), and Hunt (1961), have all articulated cognitive developmental frameworks. The most comprehensive of these systems was devised by Loevinger (1976). It is discussed in detail in Chapter 4.

The theories and methods developed by Piaget and his followers have inspired a tremendous amount of research. His method of observing subjects as they deal with problems and situations, sometimes called the *genetic* method, has contributed greatly to modern developmental psychology (Siegler & Crowley, 1991).

Piaget's original formulation of cognitive developmental processes was "content free." His notion of changing cognitive *structures* continuously shaped and reshaped out of interaction between the individual and the environment was seen to proceed across content domains, although not always at precisely the same rates. A given individual might be at somewhat different levels of development from one content area to another.

Development was seen, however, always to proceed in the direction of greater complexity. The developing individual always moved to higher levels of *differentiation* being able to distinguish more and more significant factors in a problematic situation, and to higher levels of *integration*, fitting more of the significant pieces of information together in a useful and coherent way.

Developmental change occurs by its very nature and causation in a *valued direction*. Higher stages are always better than lower ones. Value is implicit in the very nature of the developmental process.

SOCIAL DEVELOPMENT

The developmental approach is useful in understanding the nature of interpersonal behavior and its role in personality formation. One of the first cognitive accomplishments of an infant is the ability to differentiate between self and others. The processes involved in this kind of development, and the ways in which it proceeds across the life-span are of crucial interest both to personality theorists and counselors and therapists.

OBJECTS-RELATIONS THEORY

One of the revisions of psychoanalytic theory that reshaped Freudian thinking was the *object-relations* approach originated by Melanie Klein and her associates (1932). This approach focuses on the ways in which children learn to relate to others. According to object-relations theory, the mother-child relationship is the major developmental force in personality development. In this view, the internalized memory of the infant's experiences with the mother serves as the foundation for later interpersonal relationships.

This approach focuses on the disparities between actual relationships between an individual and real people, and the relationship as internalized in the individual's mental representation of these people. The latter is seen to be inevitably colored by the person's early childhood experiences. These experiences then shape and sometimes distort all of the individual's future significant relationships.

ATTACHMENT THEORY

A more recent outgrowth of the object-relations approach is called *attachment theory*. This approach grows out of a long program of ethnological research focused on the bonding processes between mothers and infants across cultures (Ainsworth & Bowlby, 1991).

According to attachment theory, human beings are innately programmed to seek and form attachments with others. This tendency begins in infancy and continues through the life-span. The ways in which human beings manage and regulate their interpersonal needs and relationships constitute major influences and determinants of personality development and personal effectiveness.

Attachment theory is considered by some psychologists to be a key to understanding healthy, positive human development (Lopez, 1995), and in relating concepts of development to personality functioning (Masten & Coatsworth, 1998).

SOCIAL ROLE-TAKING

Cognitive development theory and research has examined the nature of the specific psychological processes that are involved in the formation of significant human relationships. One of the key factors involved in that process is the development of *empathy*. In the cognitive developmental sense, empathy arises out of, and is made possible by, the ability of individuals to assume the perspective, position, and point of view of others. Social role-taking involves both cognitive and affective components. The empathic individual is able to comprehend both the thinking and the feelings of another person.

There are several stage models of cognitive role-taking that have considerable similarity and overlap. These models agree on several basic commonalties (Enright & Lapsely, 1980).

At the lowest level, in early childhood, for example, the individual neither understands another person's viewpoint nor even realizes that differing viewpoints exist. The assumption is that others must have the same perspective or point of view that he or she experiences.

At a higher stage, the developing person begins to realize that others may think and feel differently about a given situation. At this point, although the person understands that others have different feelings and thoughts, he or she may attribute such differences to the fact that one possesses information about which the other is ignorant rather than to more basic differences in values, cultures, or life experiences.

As role-taking ability continues to develop, the individual *may* enter a third stage in which one is able to reverse roles, and to view the world, including oneself, from another person's perspective and feelings. Such role reversal is really the essence of empathy.

Finally, at the highest stage of perspective-taking the individual is able in a sense to "step back" from the immediate situation and to comprehend how two or more people's perspectives interact and influence the way each thinks, feels, and acts in relation to others. Working effectively as a counselor or therapist probably requires this level of development. The importance of empathy to the development of counselors is elaborated in Chapter 15.

In cognitive developmental theory, there is no assumption that growth or stage change will occur inevitably or automatically. Some individuals may climb the developmental ladder unerringly, while others remain locked to the bottom rungs for a lifetime.

What is very clear is that positive human relationships are crucial elements in healthy development at all points in the life-span, and that they are based on acquisitions of cognitive and affective competencies. Research and theory both suggest that social competence, the ability to relate to and get along with others, emerges mainly from prior experience in close relationships. These may include both *vertical* relationships, that is those with people in authority or with responsibility for caregiving or supervision, and *horizontal*, or peer relationships. The quality of these relationships affects the individual not only in childhood but in other enduring ways (Hartup, 1989). Many interpersonal conflicts that beset individuals and social problems that affect society are related to inadequate social development.

IMPLICATIONS OF DEVELOPMENTAL PROCESSES

Theoretical concepts of human development postulate several basic and innate tendencies in human beings that serve to motivate and energize developmental processes. These include:

1. A drive toward competence, in the sense of achieving a degree of control and mastery over the environment;
2. A drive to understand and comprehend the world in a rational and consistent way; and
3. A basic need to attach to and bond with other human beings in enduring and emotionally significant relationships.

For the counselor or therapist committed to the developmental approach, what is inside clients is *not* simply a Pandora's Box of repressed intrapsychic conflicts, frustrated infantile urges, or even a collection of psychological bumps and bruises from a less than joyous childhood. Rather, what is inside clients is a set of deep-seated and innate needs and aspirations to exert some degree of control over their lives, to find and indeed *make* meaning out of the events and situations that confront them, and to reach out to establish and maintain enduring and rewarding relationships.

These are the forces that are engaged in developmental counseling. The process of facilitating human development is very much a process of *mobilizing* the energy provided by these needs on behalf of goals that will empower and enable the client to satisfy them.

DEVELOPMENTAL VERSUS DEFICIT MODELS IN COUNSELING AND PSYCHOTHERAPY

To a considerable extent, traditional psychotherapies have been based on a deficit model that focuses on disease, dysfunctions, and inadequacies. The process of therapy has, in the past, often been built on the uncover-and-cure approach. It has compiled an impressive catalog of human frailties, and failures symptoms and syndromes, but a meager menu of certified "cures."

An alternative to the deficit model is based on the development of both competence and personal meaning. The development of competence seems to function almost as a kind of inoculation against some kinds of psychopathology (Garmezy, 1974). If we wish to remove obstacles to optimal development, our best strategy is to help clients to set and attain goals that increase their control over the course of their own lives. *Empowerment is the best prevention against psychological dysfunction.*

Empowerment grows out of both competence and growth in awareness and the ability to find and to make meaning out of the often bewildering collage of events, situations, and circumstances that beset every life. Human beings are in the business of "making" meaning. As Piaget realized early on in his research, people need and strive to *comprehend, organize,* and finally *understand* life with all of its complexities, anomalies, and absurdities. Experience is not so much what happens to us as what we make of what happens to us.

Kegan (1980) described the change that occurs when people are able to become fully aware of themselves and to understand themselves and their world in a truly personal and deeply consistent way in these words:

> With the capacity to take command of one's impulses (to have them rather than be them) can come a new sense of freedom, power, independence and agency. . . . Things no longer "just happen" in the world; with the capacity to see behind the shadows, to "come in" with the data of experience, the individual now has something to do with what happens. (p. 376)

COUNSELING WITHIN A
DEVELOPMENTAL FRAMEWORK

PERSON-ENVIRONMENT INTERACTION

The overriding task confronting developmental counseling is that of helping clients attain a long-term, growth-producing pattern of interaction
with their environments. Bronfenbrenner (1979) called the study of these
kinds of problems *developmental human ecology*. To understand and so facilitate the kinds of developmental processes that we described earlier, we
must begin to understand the ways in which those processes occur in the
natural environment rather than in the laboratory. We know a good deal
about how people behave in psychological laboratories, but much less
about how they experience the real world.

We need to know how people develop competence or control and understanding *within a given environment* (Masterpasqua, 1989). Certain environments nurture some kinds of competence and cognitive growth and hinder
others. Similarly, certain individuals may grow in one environment and
stagnate in another. Ultimately, many of the issues raised by developmental
human ecology are reducible to questions of person-environment fit
(Takanishi, 1993). As we noted in Chapter 1, interest in this problem has
been part of the history of counseling for most of its existence. Part of developmental counseling is helping clients to understand their own interests, aptitudes, and personal resources and to seek out and engage
environments that will help to nurture their growth.

FACILITATING DEVELOPMENTAL PROCESSES

It is clear from the theoretical concepts and research findings sketched
out above that human development proceeds out of an active and continuing engagement with the challenges and demands that issue forth from
the individual's environment. *Engagement* leads to *development* while *withdrawal* leads to *stagnation*. Development proceeds out of disequilibrium.
Such disequilibrium is almost always accompanied by emotional distress
or a set of crisis conditions such as those described earlier.

Developmental counselors very often face the task of helping clients convert crisis situations triggered by life or cognitive stage transitions into
springboards for further development. Four basic psychological factors are
involved in such a process. The first is *challenge*. Challenges are represented
by problems and demands issuing from the environment. They may be in
the form of developmental tasks as people move from one stage to another,

or they may be the result of unpredictable events. As we saw in the quote from Schlossberg, challenges require changes in assumptions about self and the world, as well as corresponding changes in relationships and coping behaviors. Challenges are potent triggers for further development when they constitute an *optimal mismatch* between the changes required and the personal and social resources available to the individual. If the mismatch is too great, the individual may be overwhelmed and withdraw physically and psychologically from the situation. States of *panic* and *apathy* are often induced by challenges experienced as hopeless and overwhelming.

The second factor involved in a growth producing transition situation is *involvement*. When people recognize that personal psychological and material values such as self-esteem and security are at stake in the problematic or challenging situation, they are likely to remain engaged. Again, however, over involvement can lead to excessive levels of stress and anxiety that can be paralyzing in terms of problem solving and decision making. Challenge and involvement raise levels of stress and anxiety.

Fortunately, two other key psychological variables are available that can be supplied at least in part by the counselor. *Structure* is a cognitive variable that allows clients to analyze and construe challenging and involving situations in ways that make them manageable and make successes and goals attainable. Structure may be supplied in counseling by providing problem-solving or decision-making frameworks. It may be represented in planning activities that break down global goals into a series of practically attainable steps or objectives. Structure may also be supplied by techniques such as role-playing, or behavioral rehearsal, or by providing "homework" and try-out assignments. When people have cognitive structures in the form of *plans, strategies,* and *coping behaviors,* they are able to bring anxiety and stress to levels that *motivate,* but do not *incapacitate.*

The second tension-reducing factor that the counselor can supply is *support*. Social or psychological support is a function of the relationship conditions that people experience within their principal networks. Counselors can supply emotional support for clients within the counseling relationship itself. They can also help clients enter and enhance relationship networks outside the counseling situation in family, work and community settings.

When people are able to experience social support and to develop cognitive structures such as planning, problem solving, and other enabling strategies, they are able to remain actively engaged in challenging and ego-involving interactions that lead to higher and higher levels of development over the entire life-span. Gardner Murphy (1973) called these kinds of developmentally enriching sequences as characterized by "progressive mastery" and saw them as essential part of the "productive personality." When progressive mastery sequences are started early on they can lead to extremely high levels of accomplishment (Ericsson & Charness, 1994). Progressive mastery sequences are evident in high level performances in music, the arts, and sports. They are also possible in other less highly publicized areas of both work and leisure.

Progressive mastery can be part of the lives of many people in all walks of life. In their studies of adult development, Levinson and his colleagues (1978) termed a life-long developmental engagement with a cherished activity the "pursuit of the Dream." For many people developmental counseling can provide an ingredient in this pursuit.

Counseling itself can provide a developmentally responsive environment for clients, but in many situations for development to be nurtured and enhanced over longer periods of time and with more intensive exposure, developmentally potent "learning environments" must be a part of everyday life. Counselors can often help clients find such environments, or help other individuals or organizations to create or enhance them. Counselors need to understand how both developmentally potent and developmentally paralyzing environments operate.

THE NATURE OF LEARNING ENVIRONMENTS

A learning environment, or developmentally potent environment, is essentially a physical, social, and psychological context within which people grow and learn. In a very broad sense, we are all interacting with learning environments all of the time. In that general sense, every environment is a learning environment.

In a more restrictive and developmentally relevant sense, however, learning environments share several special and unique characteristics that distinguish them. Learning environments are those that are especially potent and instrumental in shaping important patterns of behavior that, in turn, set directions for long-term development. Learning environments structure and shape important opportunities, expectations, and perceptions for their participants.

Learning environments gain their potency from several factors. First, their influences tend to be powerful and pervasive in that factors in the environment engage or disengage with very basic needs and motives. The family is a very potent learning environment. It is so, precisely because members strive to meet so many of their physical and psychological needs within it.

Secondly, learning environments are potent because they tend to be intensive and continuing. By this we mean that individuals tend to spend large blocks of time in the learning environment and engage in a wide variety of roles within it. A neighborhood and neighborhood school in which an individual grows up over a period of 10 or 12 years, and in which he or she establishes friendships, undertakes hobbies, has play and work experiences is a potent learning environment. A college campus and community in which students spend four or more years passing from adolescence into young adulthood can be equally potent developmentally.

A third factor determining the potency of a learning environment involves the timing of the interaction. The concept of *critical periods* is an important one in the study of human development. Certain periods in the life of an individual are especially crucial for the development of particular behavior patterns (Ramey & Ramey, 1998). The nature of the learning environment to which an individual is exposed during such critical periods is a powerful influence on subsequent development. Such patterns of interaction, in a sense, determine the presence of continuities or discontinuities.

Nursery schools, Head Start programs, elementary schools, or colleges often are extremely significant influences because of this factor. The elementary school, for example, is a particularly powerful learning environment because children spend about one thousand hours per year in the environment at precisely the most formative and critical periods in their development. Many crucial developmental tasks are mastered or failed within this environment, and the total impact on the developing child is likely to be both crucial and irreversible. Learning environments are not limited to families or schools. Work settings, community organizations, social groups, and neighborhoods all constitute possible important learning environments. Developmental counseling relationships themselves are also important learning environments.

COMPONENTS OF A LEARNING ENVIRONMENT

In studying any learning environment, we can identify at least three crucial elements or components. The first of these we may call the *opportunity structure*. The opportunity structure is defined by the number and range of situations in which the participant is able to attempt or try out new behaviors that may lead to success, mastery, or control in the environmental situation.

In a classroom environment, for example, every mathematics lesson, or spelling list, or class office may offer a new opportunity for achieving success or mastery through acquiring new knowledge or skill. The nature of the opportunity structure is determined in part by the levels of stimulation within the environment. Obviously, when the environment is very rigid and static, or sterile, or when competition for recognition, leadership, or accomplishment is intense or unfair, relatively few real opportunities may be available. When individuals in such environments do not perceive the existence of real opportunities, they tend to disengage from the environment or put little effort into their engagement.

Opportunities within a given environment may involve *exposure* to new ideas, values, or people. They may represent chances to *explore* new activities, relationships, or roles. The richer the environment is in terms of intellectual stimulation, possibilities for accomplishment and recognition, and cultural diversity, the greater the range of opportunities. Finally, the opportunity structure determines the ways in which people are able to make significant commitments to values or causes, and to make investments of time, energy, and material resources on behalf of their convictions and aspirations. Educational and employment opportunities as well as opportunities for long-term, involving relationships and responsibilities are essential to optimal development.

A second aspect of a developmentally potent environment is the *resource structure*. The resource structure includes both physical and material resources, and supporting relationships and practical assistance. Earlier we discussed the role of emotional support and cognitive structure. The availability of teachers, mentors, support groups, and counselors are all important. The availability of practical as well as psychological supports and resources is just as important. Availability of health care, child care, subsistence income, and transportation often make the difference between success and failure in taking advantage of developmentally crucial opportunities (McCloyd, 1998).

The final component in any learning environment can be called the *reward structure*. The reward structure determines two essential elements in the environment. The first is the nature of the rewards that are available to participants when they successfully meet challenges and accomplish tasks. When these rewards are directed to the basic needs and motives of the participating individuals, they have great potency. Rewards may be intrinsic or extrinsic, material or psychological. The most enduring and developmentally potent rewards are intrinsic and psychological in that they help build self-esteem and self-confidence. Environments that allow

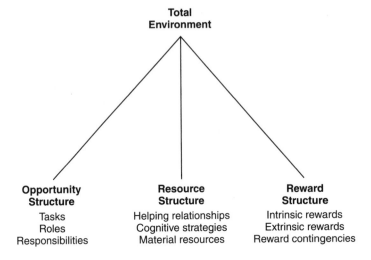

Figure 2.1   Components of a developmentally potent environment.

people the autonomy to assess their own achievements, accomplishments, and successes provide strong, intrinsic psychological rewards. Structures that do not provide for *intrinsic psychological* rewards such as positive feelings of self-esteem, social recognition, and social contribution, may not succeed in tapping and holding high levels of commitment and enthusiasm from participants.

The second aspect of the reward structure involves the kinds of *contingencies* that exist within the learning environment to regulate the dispensing of rewarding consequences. When these contingencies are clear, reasonable, and dependable, participants are willing to invest and risk time, energy, and self-esteem to seek them. When the contingency structure is arbitrary, biased, unreasonable, or capricious, participants soon learn *not* to invest themselves in such a system. Sustained motivation on behalf of important rewards is obtained when participants experience what is called *effort-optimism*, that is, a reasonable belief that the expenditure of effort and hard work will, in fact, yield significant satisfactions or rewards. Figure 2.1 illustrates the nature of potent learning environments.

BASIC PRINCIPLES OF
LEARNING ENVIRONMENTS

We have given a very cursory or "thumbnail" sketch of a way of conceptualizing a learning environment. This sketch allows us to extract a simple set of principles that can be used to illustrate basic patterns in transactions between people and environments.

Developmental counselors are concerned with understanding those balances that sustain growth and development. From our thumbnail sketch of the components of a potent learning environment, we can establish three simple but basic principles:

1. For a learning environment to sustain continued growth and development in its participants, that environment must offer a broad opportunity structure characterized by a variety and range of new challenges and tasks within which participants can acquire new ways of achieving success and mastery.

2. For a learning environment to sustain continued growth in its members, that environment must offer a network of helping relationships, and a source of effective cognitive strategies or frameworks within which participants can manage stress, meet challenges, and accomplish tasks. It must also make available practical and material resources required for effective participation.

3. If a learning environment is to sustain continued growth in participants, it must allow participants to earn significant intrinsic and psychological, as well as extrinsic and material rewards. The contingencies upon which such rewards are made available must be clear, consistent, and reasonable in terms of effort expended and must put such significant rewards within the reach of all participants.

Developmental counselors attempt to create potent learning environments within the counseling relationship itself. They also endeavor to help clients to access and enhance learning environments in other parts of their life in family, school, neighborhood, and community.

CHAPTER 3

The Cycle of
Life-Span Development

One cannot stop or turn back, although one can drift, stall, or
stagnate. One can grow in one area, falter in another, and reach a
plateau in still another. In other words, the life cycle goes on no
matter how or when the various stages are passed.

—Barbara Okun (1984)

IN A very real sense, developmental counseling involves what Robert
White called "the study of lives." Every human life has a kind of
unique integrity and consistency that differentiates it from every
other. Inside each life is all of the drama, humor, tragedy, and pathos of a
work of art.

Understanding the life of another human being involves the willingness and ability to look beyond the immediate and superficial to perceive
both where an individual is coming from on the developmental journey
and where that journey may yet go.

A tool that can help in building such an understanding and appreciation of the mystery and complexity of each human life is what we can call
a life-span, developmental framework. Such a framework helps us to trace
the progress of life-span development in terms of developmental tasks, social roles, and coping behaviors.

Life-span frameworks are normative and the age markers that signal
the beginning or ending of various stages are approximate. When interpreted cautiously and flexibly, such frameworks can help us to appreciate
both the resources that people bring to each new transition and the challenges with which they are confronted.

The following developmental framework draws on the work of Erik Erikson as elaborated by other students of life-span development.

THE ORGANIZATION STAGE

The organization stage is seen as the initial period during which the foundation is laid down for future growth and development. The organization stage comprises roughly the first 15 years of life. The process that tends to dominate this stage involves the physiological growth or unfolding of the organism. The developmental crises of this stage are centered primarily around the individual's socialization, that is the struggle of the maturing person to meet his or her emerging physical and emotional needs within a society that defines and sets limits around the ways in which those needs can be met. Because the organization stage is so complex and eventful, it is useful to break it down into several substages within which we can specify crucial events.

INFANCY (BIRTH TO 3 YEARS)

The human infant at birth is a bundle of potentialities. A baby is essentially a *psychological thing* rather than a personality. During the first three years of life, this psychological thing emerges into separateness and uniqueness in an almost magical transformation that lays down the foundations for the child's entire subsequent development.

It may appear absurd, at first, to think of social roles in infancy. In our child-centered culture, however, an infant is at once an important and closely managed social being. Infants differ widely in terms of activity levels, sleeping routines, and feeding patterns and these differences quickly interact with expectations of parents and other caregivers. Mothers typically talk about even week-old infants in terms such as "He is a good baby," or a "difficult baby."

As the infant grows, this cluster of adult expectations is rapidly expanded. The baby is expected to be responsive to affection, compliant to adult wishes, and alternately cute and quiescent. As the infant grows into early childhood during those first three years, he or she experiences a steadily rising tide of expectations for conformity in habits of elimination, eating, sleeping, and interpersonal behavior. Similarly, there is a steady increase in expectations for accomplishments in language, locomotion, and attention-span.

The ways in which the infant is able to handle these increasingly difficult and complex role expectations determine, in large part the nature of the social interaction through which concepts of self and relationships with significant others will be crystallized. If expectations are unreasonable, arbitrary, or capricious, the child may have difficulty achieving any sense of security and mastery in the environment. If expectations are never communicated clearly in infancy, the child may have difficulty in moving into the more complex social realities of subsequent stages of development.

The developmental tasks of infancy relate largely to the development of trust and affiliation with the mother and other primary caregivers. Erikson (1963) viewed the development of *trust* as the central task of infancy and as the most crucial cornerstone for future development.

As the sense of trust is developed, the infant is able to be separated from the mother for longer and longer periods of time without undue rage or anxiety. The inner security provided by this certainty of being loved and cared for permits the infant to attend to and interact with other sources of stimulation in the environment.

The development of trust is viewed to grow out of the primary bonding between mother and child and then is generalized to other significant figures. Much of the infant's sense of trust is developed out of the confidence and consistency of those who provide care. The ability to trust is not totally dependent simply on the level of need satisfaction. Infants are able to handle increasing levels of minor frustration and gratification deferral when such situations are managed in consistent ways. Parental attitudes that communicate the view that gratification deferral is meaningful and growth-producing, rather than capricious or punitive can help build trust. The basic process of social attachment or relating to others that is crucial to social development begins here (Lopez, 1995).

In addition to basic trust, other important developmental tasks in infancy involve learning to:

1. Feed oneself and eat a variety of nourishing foods;
2. Manipulate simple objects;
3. Walk;
4. Communicate verbally; and
5. Control elimination.

Behaviors or competencies that are important in infancy are primarily those that allow close, loving relationships with an increasing number of significant other people to develop. Self-care, control of elimination, control of anger and frustration all permit the infant to experience an increasing range of positive and caring relationships and to form a variety of emotional attachments.

Another important area of development in infancy involves manipulative and exploratory experiences within the environment. Research on sensory deprivation and environmental constriction suggests that infants should engage actively and frequently with a variety of sensory stimuli. If an infant is over-protected, overly fearful, neglected, or physically unable to explore and interact with various kinds of stimulating environmental factors, full cognitive growth may be inhibited.

Early Childhood (Ages 3 to 6)

As an infant emerges into early childhood, the social environment rapidly becomes more complex. By comparison, the role expectations that defined his or her position in infancy were relatively simple. New roles of *sibling* and *playmate* are thrust on the individual in early childhood. Both of these new roles involve expectations for sharing, cooperation, and communication that are new.

Also in this period, expectations begin to be differentiated in terms of what is considered to be sex-appropriate behavior within family and neighborhood. The child may learn, for example, that little boys are no longer expected to cry or that little girls are not supposed to be brash or adventurous. Such learning may have very serious long-term implications for the child.

Developmental tasks in early childhood revolve around the issue of attaining a sense of *autonomy*. Autonomy is the basis for the child's sense of separateness and responsibility. Only when a full sense of autonomy is attained is the child able to accept responsible independence. This marks the beginning of the process of taking responsibility for the consequences of one's own actions and decisions. This process can be thought of as the beginning of self-regulation. The end of the early childhood period is the beginning of the child's career in formal schooling and marks the beginning of an increasing degree of detachment and emotional weaning from the support and supervision of mother and family. This is a point at which serious discontinuities may appear.

In addition to autonomy, other important developmental tasks include:

1. Developing a sense of self, including a self-image.
2. Developing a sense of extension of self, that is belonging with and relating to a variety others.
3. Learning a set of flexible, reasonable, and appropriate sex roles and identifications.

4. Learning to manage frustration and aggressive impulses in constructive ways.
5. Learning to follow verbal instructions.
6. Learning to focus attention and concentration.
7. Learning to become reasonably independent in self-care (washing, dressing, toilet function, etc.).
8. Developing realistic concepts of the physical and social world (time, space, distance, authority, etc.).

The competencies of early childhood heavily involve interpersonal skills and attitudes that permit sharing, cooperation, handling of aggression, responding to authority, verbalizing feelings, and dealing with fear and anxiety.

In this period, it is especially important that the child gains experience in making choices and decisions and accepting responsibility for their consequences. Those consequences, however, must not be so disintegrating or disastrous that the child will shrink from them, or be forced to repress or deny them.

LATER CHILDHOOD (AGES 6 TO 12)

In later childhood, the social world rapidly becomes more complicated and more demanding. Entry into school brings with it the new role of *student.* As the child becomes more capable, new expectations for roles as *helper* or *big brother* or *big sister* are often encountered. These new social roles require the mastery of a whole new set of developmental tasks. At this point in the child's life, failure to master key developmental tasks may involve drastic consequences in terms of future well-being.

The key developmental tasks at this stage involve the concepts of *initiative* and *industry.* The developing youngster is caught up in undertaking projects for the sake of being active and involved. Soapbox racers, lemonade stands, hobbies, crafts, and sports become the testing grounds for the development of initiative and industry, with their planning and organizing tasks. Initiative requires confidence and energy to bounce back from setbacks and to forget failures. These qualities are essentially the ability to respond to challenges with resilience, resourcefulness, and enthusiasm.

The great danger to further development at this stage is in acquiring feelings and self-images of inferiority. At this stage, the child is acutely aware of rivalry and competition. In this period, children constantly compare themselves and their products and accomplishments with those of others.

Perceived inadequacy can lead to low self-esteem and disengagement with challenges and opportunities.

When the child is able to achieve a track record with a reasonable number of successes, he or she is able to feel a sense of self-esteem and of value in the eyes of others. Such feelings in turn permit the child to invest more of self in each new venture and so reap still greater feelings of worth from each new success or accomplishment.

In addition to developing a sense of initiative and industry, other important developmental tasks that must be accomplished during this period involve learning:

1. Basic educational skills;
2. To value oneself and feel valued by others;
3. To defer gratifications;
4. To control emotional reactions and impulses;
5. To formulate values and make value judgments.

Competencies important in this stage may be grouped into several categories.

1. *Mastery behaviors.* Mastery behaviors are those that give the child, *through his or her own efforts,* a feeling of control and influence over the environment. They involve reaching formerly unattainable goals and the achievement of performances that compare favorably with others. This is the beginning of a life-long pattern of competence-building.

2. *Value-relevant behaviors.* These are behaviors that are based upon internal judgments of good and bad, right and wrong. These are personal and internalized judgments not merely based upon external authority or fear of punishment. These value judgments go beyond "moral realism" to take into account intentions and circumstances as factors in moral judgment.

3. *Work-relevant behaviors.* These are behaviors that involve planning, setting priorities, organizing, and scheduling time for activities such as school work, chores, or practicing skills. They involve deferring immediate gratification for the sake of larger goals. They also involve setting realistic standards for performance and taking pride in personal achievements and productions.

Early Adolescence (Ages 12 to 15)

Early adolescence is well known as one of the most critical and painful periods of human development. The surge of physiological changes of many types, together with the set of escalating expectations for near-adult levels of performance in many areas combine to make early adolescence a time of great disequilibrium. Often, however, mental health professionals "pathologize" adolescence and interpret developmental discontinuities and crises as abnormal or deviant (Newcomb, 1996). More than 80% of adolescents move through this stage successfully (Wagner, 1996).

Two very important changes in role expectations occur in early adolescence. These are the emergence of peer roles and heterosexual roles. These new sets of roles create what has sometimes been called an *adolescent society*. Early adolescence is a period in which family and school relationships and influences begin to wane in terms of their impact in comparison to social influences that arise out of the peer culture, itself. When family-school values and expectations conflict directly with peer influences, the early adolescent may be caught in a "bind situation" that triggers acute anxiety.

Such competing and conflicting expectations for behavior may make it difficult or impossible for the early adolescent to conform fully to either peer or parental expectations. The situation is further complicated by the emergence of new heterosexual relationships with which the early adolescent has had little experience. These new relationships and the social expectations associated with them create very challenging and involving situations in which failure, or perceived failure, can result in catastrophic losses in self-esteem. Discontinuity is virtually a norm at this stage.

Within this confusing and risk-laden psychosocial matrix, the early adolescent is faced with the crucial developmental task of forming the nucleus around which to develop a new identity. The primary developmental task of early adolescence involves what Erikson (1963) called the conflict between identity and role diffusion. Much of Erikson's theorizing and subsequent research by Marcia (1980) and others has focused around the identity development process and its impact on future personality growth. The integration of new roles, the casting off of old emotional ties, and the establishment of new values and aspirations are all part of what is called the period of *identity crises.*

The adolescent must answer the question of "Who am I?" within the context of the masculinity-femininity dichotomy; that is, in terms of the roles and relationships that are shaped out of sexual identification within the contemporary culture.

To a great extent, a stable and comfortable sense of personal identity is derived from a sense of compatibility between *past* experiences of self and others, and one's *immediate* experiencing. When such compatibility between past and present does not exist, and when the prospects for future experiences seem even more ambiguous and uncertain, an inevitable *discontinuity* is introduced. In adolescence, the emerging physiological changes of puberty, together with conflicting and rapidly shifting social expectations, create discontinuities, that can lead to *identity diffusion.*

Many adolescents seek desperately to clarify their own identities through affiliation with peer groups and through establishing close relationships with special friends of either the same or opposite sex. Within the relative closeness and intimacy of such relationships, the adolescent is sometimes able to feel some increased definition of self-identity and escape to some degree from the panic of identity diffusion. One of the dangers or this period is that affiliation will be with groups or gangs that are fundamentally asocial and destructive. Peer relationships are often patterned on family relationships. It is important that close family relationships be maintained in adolescence (Masten & Coatsworth, 1998).

The sense of *belonging to* and *belonging with,* which is often part of these adolescent relationships, can serve as temporary but comforting clarifiers of personal identity. Going steady, being part of the gang, club, or clique, having a "soul mate" or inseparable friend all may help to reduce the "lost feeling" of identity diffusion. The relative impermanence of these relationships, together with the general instability of the world as perceived and experienced by the adolescent, however, often makes such relationships only temporary identity anchors.

While the development of a stable and positive sense of identity is the central task of early adolescence, a number of other important developmental tasks also confront youngsters during this period. These include:

1. Achieving a set of positive and realistic attitudes in regard to work;
2. Achieving control of impulses, particularly in the areas of sex and aggression;
3. Learning to defer gratification over relatively long periods of time;
4. Learning to schedule, organize, and manage time and energy in behalf of long-term goals;
5. Developing personal values and commitments based upon relatively abstract principles (good, truth, beauty, etc.).

The most important competencies of early adolescence can be classified under the following headings:

1. *Social behaviors.* These include general social skills necessary for getting along in group situations. Meeting people, engaging in polite conversation, giving help, and being able to accept help from others are examples of such behaviors.

2. *Sex-appropriate behaviors.* These are behaviors that implement sex role concepts. They involve behaviors that are seen to communicate masculinity and femininity to others.

For many boys, these often center around physical or athletic prowess, driving a car, being physically aggressive, and other essentially narrowly adaptive measures of masculinity. Obsessive concern with implementing masculinity by projecting a "macho" image often interferes with the acquisition of more valuable coping behaviors in intellectual, aesthetic, and social areas.

Similarly, for girls, the same kinds of obsessive attention to sexually attracting elements of femininity or to passive, compliant, or success-avoidant patterns of behavior may detract from overall intellectual and social development.

The acquisition of a balanced, flexible, and wide-ranging set of behaviors around which to express sexual identity is a very important aspect of development in this period.

3. *Achievement-oriented behavior.* These behaviors are those necessary for effective vocational development. They include concentration, organization, planning, time management, appropriate self-criticism, intellectual curiosity, problem-solving, and critical thinking behaviors.

THE EXPLORATION STAGE (AGES 16 TO 30)

The exploration stage begins in mid-adolescence and moves the individual through later adolescence and into early adulthood. This stage of development is dominated by the individual's quest for new values, relationships, motivations, and aspirations. Just as the organization stage involved preoccupation with emerging physiological changes, in this stage the individual is intent upon reaching out into the physical and social environment to identify ways in which to relate to a new-found sense of physical and psychological maturity. This involves a renegotiation of old relationships and an ever-expanding process of entry into new ones (Lopez, 1992).

The key social behaviors in this stage involve movement from essentially *dependent* styles of relating to *reciprocal* modes of dealing with others. In this stage, the individual reaches out to experiment with new relationships in friendship, courtship, education, and career.

Most of these new areas require the individual to learn to give and receive in a variety of situations based upon *mutuality* and *cooperation*. Failure to learn to function within reciprocal relationships may cause very serious problems in family and career development. Entry into marriage and childbearing prior to the development of reciprocal behaviors carries a very heavy risk of failure and the creation of serious obstacles to further growth and development.

We can divide the exploration stage into two periods, later adolescence and early adulthood. The age boundaries that separate these two substages are very difficult to establish. Theorists in the area of adult development (Gould, 1978; Levinson, 1986) maintain that full adulthood is typically not reached in our society until about the age of 30. The exploration stage thus occupies nearly 15 years and is marked by wide individual differences in the rates at which people move toward full adulthood.

For the sake of convenience, we will define the later adolescent period as beginning at age 16 or 17 and running to about age 23. Young adulthood then proceeds to about age 30.

LATER ADOLESCENCE (AGES 16 TO 23)

In the later adolescent period, new social roles are encountered with almost bewildering profusion. The social world of the adolescent mushrooms in complexity in the last years of high school and upon entry into college or full-time employment. The new dimension of emerging sexuality complicates all kinds of relationships. The powerful and newly awakened sexual drives pervade much of the adolescent's activities and consume much energy and attention.

New roles of worker, leader, follower, supervisor, subordinate, and colleague begin to appear as the adolescent starts to participate in a wide range of activities organized around adult rather than childhood models. Failure in these new roles is met with much greater frustration and is marked by much more drastic and lasting costs than ever before. For the first time, some of these new roles begin to compete and conflict with each other. The individual is faced with more complex and far-reaching problems and decisions than ever before.

Individuals are confronted with complex sets of alternatives involving marriage, childbearing, further education, career decisions, and geographic mobility, as well as disturbing issues of morality, religion, and relationships with parents.

Later adolescence is a period of almost inevitable discontinuity. For many youngsters, a kind of *psychosocial moratorium* in which they experience some release from the pressures dictated by these new role expectations is often taken. We often see this kind of moratorium institutionalized within a sort of "youth culture" in which long-term commitments to either career or relationships tend to be minimized and long-term planning is approached gingerly or not at all. Such a moratorium does not guarantee the reduction of stresses however, and may sometimes be purchased at considerable cost in terms of later development.

Key developmental tasks in later adolescence are centered around educational and vocational development. In a sense, the identity crisis of early adolescence shifts from the area of sexual identity to identity as a worker. Decisions about education and career tend to be both inescapable and sometimes irreversible. The vocational development process involves questions of implementing one's identity within the world of work (Super, 1990).

Other developmental tasks of later adolescence include:

1. Developing lasting personal friendships on the basis of individual compatibility rather than mere group membership.
2. Achieving emotional autonomy in learning to make decisions and accept responsibility.
3. Learning to produce in work or study situations under adult performance standards.

As we noted earlier, central competencies involve interpersonal skills and attitudes that allow the individual to function effectively within a variety of cooperative and increasingly demanding relationships. In later adolescence, two new social situations and attendant role expectations put great stress on these reciprocal relationships. Moving out of one's family of origin and into the more egalitarian and loosely structured framework of either dormitory or apartment-sharing often requires the rapid development of these behaviors.

Similarly, experiences in dating and courtship associated with the sharing of sexual and psychological intimacy require both reciprocal behaviors and the ability to begin to make emotional commitments.

Crucial behaviors in this area include trusting enough to disclose oneself honestly, sharing in a material and an emotional sense, fulfilling promises, keeping confidences, becoming sensitive to others' physical and emotional needs, and accepting personal responsibility in joint projects and ventures.

YOUNG ADULTHOOD (AGES 24 TO 30)

The separation of the exploration stage into two substages is somewhat arbitrary. Developmental theorists usually perceive the mid- and late-twenties as extremely important periods developmentally in that much of the foundation for full adulthood is laid down during these years. In a sense, young adulthood is a crucial period in which the adequacy of earlier developmental patterns is put to test.

In terms of social roles, the two major testing grounds are career and marriage and family. For perhaps the first time the young adult finds that he or she is "playing for keeps." Relatively few of the developmental crises encountered earlier were as final or irreversible as those confronted in this period. For the first time, the individual's success and status tend to be a function not of age, or parental support, but rather to depend on personal skill, wisdom, and accomplishment.

The primary new roles are marriage and parenthood. These roles combine for the first time many duties and expectations that could formerly be separated into relatively separate and discrete compartments. The spouse is now at one time lover, companion, roommate, coworker, and confidant.

Even when the young adult has learned to cope with these role expectations effectively within separate relationships, their consolidation within marriage compounds difficulties and problems. The individual is forced to meet a multitude of competing and sometimes conflicting needs and expectations within the confines of a single pervasive and emotionally charged relationship. When the parental role is added to the marital situation, life becomes still more complicated.

At the same time, the young adult is also being severely tested within the career arena. The career roles encountered in early adulthood are often quite different than those confronted in earlier part-time or entry-level work experiences. When the career choices made are highly ego-involving and success and progress within the career are central to the individual's self-esteem and satisfaction heavy pressures are imposed.

Almost inevitably career roles and marriage and family roles tend to collide. One of the major tasks of young adulthood involves the managing of career-family role conflicts and competition. This task is even more pressing as very large numbers of both men and women aspire to combine ego-evolving careers with marriage and family responsibilities and relationships. As dual career marriages and families become the norm, successful management of the intricate problems and potential conflicts involved becomes more and more crucial to the development both of marriage partners and their children.

The central developmental tasks of young adulthood involve the attainment of *intimacy* and *commitment*. Intimacy involves the capacity to form concrete and honest affiliations and partnerships and the ethical strength to persist in such close relationships even when they require major sacrifices and compromises. In this sense, intimacy goes far beyond what we commonly think of as sexual intimacy. Intimacy is the ability to put the welfare of a special relationship at the very top of one's personal priorities. Without the ability to attain intimacy, the chances of forming and maintaining a successful long-term relationship such as marriage are diminished.

The concept of commitment which is certainly an essential part of intimacy is, however, generalized to go beyond close interpersonal or family situations to include dedication to ideals or causes and so to organizations and enterprises. The successful implementation of many kinds of higher level career roles requires this kind of commitment.

Commitment in this sense involves the capacity to invest heavily of one's time, energy, and self-esteem in causes, organizations, or institutions. Without the ability to make such commitments, possibilities for higher levels of career development may be very limited. The more commitments that the individual makes in his or her life, the more complex are the problems involved in managing them singly and in relationship to each other.

The competencies of early adulthood can be categorized under three headings.

1. *Sexual behavior.* Taking a traditional view, successful sexual behavior can be defined as:
   - Mutuality of orgasm;
   - With a loved partner;
   - With whom one is able and willing to share a mutual trust; and
   - With whom one is able and willing to regulate the cycle of work, procreation, and recreation;
   - So as to secure to the offspring a satisfactory development.
2. *Risk-taking behaviors.* These behaviors involve the ability to take calculated physical, economic, and psychological risks to reach desirable personal, family, and career goals.
3. *Relationship maintenance behaviors.* These behaviors involve the skills and attitudes necessary to negotiate needs, resolve conflicts, set and

adhere to priorities, and make rational choices and decisions in complex interpersonal situations.

THE REALIZATION STAGE (AGES 30 TO 50)

The realization stage marks the culmination of the primarily formative aspects of human development. Physical maturation is complete and psychological growth through the process of exploration has hopefully laid down a set of personal understandings, attitudes, and skills that can support both stability and a high level of functioning. Levinson (1986) called much of the activity that characterizes this stage the pursuit of one's "dream." During this stage, people tend to invest themselves wholeheartedly on behalf of their most cherished goals or aspirations. While individuals may become very effective in controlling aspects of the environment that are especially significant, this stage may be marked by a narrow focusing of efforts and a closing out of opportunities and areas of living that were highly prized at earlier stages.

In the realization stage, the balancing of family, career, and leisure interests may become especially difficult. Maintaining psychological intimacy in marriage, protecting health and psychological well-being in the face of work commitments, and maintaining open and sensitive relationships with children may constitute formidable challenges. They require attitudes and skills that will support a stable and high level of functioning. The beginning of the realization stage occurs roughly around age thirty and proceeds into the early forties.

Realization is the stage at which individuals are often able to achieve their highest levels of functioning and effectiveness. It is also the period in which people tend to exert maximum control over their environments. In the realization stage, the social role structure of the individual may undergo a subtle, but important, change. In every social role situation there are two aspects to the structured interaction that defines a role. Role expectations are the external determinants of role behavior. The behaving individual, however, also interprets his or her role from an internal perspective. We can term the individual's interpretation of the role and his or her willingness to engage in the role, role conception, and role acceptance.

In the realization stage, people tend to have their best opportunities to interpret their principal roles and to modify or reject roles that are antithetical to their needs or values. This kind of "role freedom" provides the individual with important opportunities for self-expression and self-fulfillment that may be less available in earlier life stages. This increased role freedom arises out of personal power and status and accompanying financial and emotional independence. When individuals do not experience increasing role freedom as they move into the realization stage they may experience gradual loss of self-esteem, with accompanying frustration or even depression.

When individuals are able to achieve a degree of role freedom, they are able to construe and accept roles that provide increased personal satisfaction and self-esteem. These include:

1. *Leadership roles.* These are roles in which individuals are able to make outstanding contributions to group projects and receive personal recognition as especially significant members of an organization.
2. *Helping roles.* These are roles in which individuals are able to make outstanding contributions to the welfare, growth, or development of others and receive recognition and positive responses from them.
3. *Creative roles.* These are roles in which individuals are able to make new and original contributions and be recognized for them.
4. *Accomplishment roles.* These are roles in which an individual has an opportunity to achieve a high level of performance in some personally worthwhile and socially valued activity.

From the standpoint of social roles, then, the realization stage is characterized by efforts to conceptualize role situations in ways that allow the individual to enhance his or her own growth and self-esteem through making contributions that are recognized and valued by significant others and by the larger society. When the realization stage does not bring opportunities for these kinds of roles, we should not be surprised to see mounting frustration or depression. If archaic racial or sexist biases, or other kinds of constrictions of legitimate opportunities for growth, stifle the individual at this stage, we do not need to turn to a deficit model to understand the difficulty. Developmental counseling and life planning aimed at helping the individual to achieve greater role freedom may be more appropriate than psychotherapy aimed at reconciling the individual to the status quo. Some of these problems are discussed further in Chapter 10. Mid-life changes are often aimed at obtaining greater opportunities for self-expression and satisfaction.

The central developmental task at this stage is the ability to harness energy and resources on behalf of major life goals and values. It involves the ability to invest unilaterally, and without immediate reward, when such investment is important for the attainment of long-term goals.

Such investment is required in parenting situations, and in many career situations that involve offering leadership, help, and supervision. Key aspects of this quality are gratification deferral, self-confidence, and self-efficacy.These qualities enable the individual to persist in a consistent and sustained course of action aimed at attaining a long-term goal without being sidetracked or deflected by temporary setbacks or minor failures.

Other important developmental tasks at this stage are:

1. *The development of inner-directedness.* It has been suggested that people may be tradition-directed, inner-directed, or other-directed. The realization stage provides the greatest opportunity for inner-direction and the security and satisfaction that goes with it. When people at this stage are excessively other-directed they may experience being vulnerable and relatively unable to formulate and implement goals of their own.

2. *Development of interdependence.* High levels of development are characterized not by aloofness or emotional separation from others, but by mutually constructive participation with them. Interdependence is defined by participation in a network of mutually rewarding, essentially democratic relationships that are characterized by honesty, respect, and caring among members. Competence in identifying and negotiating such relationships is needed.

3. *Development of emotional control.* Mature adults are able to exert flexible yet effective emotional control. This kind of control is established without having to suppress awareness of feelings. When people feel able to control their level of emotional arousal, they are able to remain aware of the full range of feelings, and are not forced to use energy in denying or suppressing their awareness of their own or others' emotions.

4. *Development of effective problem-solving techniques.* Competence in problem solving involves the ability to perceive and define problems in their entirety, the ability to preserve a tentative outlook while seeking information, and the ability to analyze and compare the probable outcomes of a set of alternative solutions.

The developmental tasks and competencies cited above require openness to new learning, and a willingness to experiment and analyze one's own experiences.

THE STABILIZATION STAGE

The stabilization stage is optimally characterized by the achievement of a sense of unity, stability, and harmony within one's lifestyle, and between the individual and the culture. Such a description is, however, somewhat deceptive. The stabilization stage may begin in the early to mid-forties and run into the late sixties or even beyond. Often by imposing compulsory retirement ages, the society attempts to set an arbitrary upper limit on this life stage.

The stabilization stage marks one of the most complex and almost paradoxical points in the entire life cycle. While most people aspire to a sense of closure and tranquillity marked by completion of childrearing, attainment of financial security, and achievement of career objectives, this stage is also a frequent site for the midlife crisis.

The midlife crisis was first described by psychoanalyst Carl Jung (1933). It is, essentially, a period in which individuals become acutely aware of their own mortality, and tend to reassess life goals. They may make major changes in their careers, marriage, and family relationships and other significant aspects of their lives.

Considerable research has been done on the midlife period. Levinson (1986), in a large scale study of midlife, found that 80% of his male sample reported some kind of tumultuous struggle within themselves. Levinson found that the onset of the midlife crisis occurred most frequently between ages 38 and 43. Thus considerable evidence exists for the operation of some kind of midlife transition phenomenon, although the exact timing and experiencing of the transition may vary widely from one individual to another.

What seems clear is that this transition involves a review and reassessment of one's past achievements and commitments and a reorganization of the priorities with which the individual approaches his or her remaining years.

The midlife transition may be very painful and disruptive for some individuals, while for others it may represent a pulling together or relatively minor realignment of the themes that have characterized their past experiences.

We can define three essential developmental tasks in the midlife transition. These are:

1. To review, reappraise, and move on from early years into a more mature and independent life.

2. To make major decisions about how one's remaining active and productive years should be spent.
3. To deal with major life issues. These polarities are youth vs. aging, destructiveness vs. creativity, masculinity vs. femininity, and attachment versus separation.

These three tasks involve the ability to face the future rather than attempting to recapture the past, to become more fully aware of the manifold aspects of one's personality, and to reassess the significance of important relationships in one's life. During the earlier realization stage, people are apt to concentrate so completely on status and career goals that they tend to take for granted important relationships. Similarly dissonant aspects of their own personality that might make their lives more complicated tend to be ignored. Special interests or talents that lie outside the central focus of their awareness may be abandoned or neglected.

The midlife transition is a time of reawakening and burgeoning awareness of interests, aspirations, and potentials. This reawakening of self-awareness may be accompanied by considerable anxiety, and some individuals may engage in impulsive and irrational efforts to deal with the panic that is engendered by multiple discontinuities in their lives.

Major career changes, divorce, or even problems of alcoholism or depression are sometimes triggered by midlife crises. Working through the crisis in a thoughtful and thorough way, however, can help the individual to attain the sense of unity, coherence, and harmony that is represented in optimal development during the stabilization stage. Failure to work through a difficult midlife transition can lead to a progressive withdrawal from younger and more productive people and pursuits. This kind of developmental arrest leads to an almost mechanical and robotlike existence in which the individual feels increasingly useless, unneeded, and unloved. In a sense, the resolution of the midlife crisis represents a kind of victory of creative and productive forces over resignation and despair.

THE EXAMINATION STAGE

Examination is a final life stage that is characterized by reflection and ultimately by a progressive disengagement from many of the pursuits and activities that marked earlier years. It is a life stage that is typically feared and dreaded by many people in our youth-oriented culture.

Optimal development during this stage is characterized by the attainment of what Erikson (1963) called "ego integrity." People who have achieved *integrity* are able to accept who they are and what they have become. Integrity involves a kind of inner tranquility that includes an acceptance of death as part of the natural order of life.

The great danger in the examination stage is the polar opposite of integrity that is *despair*. Despair is defined as a refusal to accept the reality of one's life. This refusal can lead to an all-pervading sense of fear and depression arising out of the reality that time does not permit going back to live one's life over again.

Research on older populations (Neugarten, 1979) shows that while many aged people do show symptoms of despair, with attendant bitterness and disappointment, many others feel that life has been both good and meaningful, and have a deep sense of satisfaction with their lives.

Even at this final stage the processes and challenges of life go on. As Havighurst (1972) pointed out, this stage is:

> A period of learning, rather than a period when learning is past. It is a period of facing new and unresolved problems rather than a period of floating gently on the surface of familiar solutions to familiar problems. (p. 442)

Developmental tasks in this period include:

1. Learning to cope with the death of friends or spouse.
2. Learning to cope with retirement and reduced income or status.
3. Learning to affiliate with an age group of elders.
4. Learning to cope with reduced vigor and chronic physical problems.
5. Learning to cope with changed living arrangements.
6. Learning to develop new social roles that will bring continued recognition and respect.
7. Learning to use leisure time in constructive and satisfying ways.
8. Learning to relate to younger people within a new age appropriate set of expectations.

The examination stage is one of severe and sometimes unpredictable discontinuities. Precipitating events such as the death of a spouse, or the onset of a debilitating illness may be largely unpredictable and unavoidable. Social norms and conventions governing forced retirements, or general attitudes toward aging and age appropriate behavior may be predictable, but arbitrary and uncontrollable. When such events plunge aging individuals into sudden isolation and create an emotional detachment from the mainstream of life, the resulting discontinuities may precipitate depression, panic, and even death.

When people at this stage can cope by remaining relatively open, flexible, and adaptable, and when they can remain sensitive and aware to the changes at work in their lives, they are much more able to cope with stresses. Perhaps the greatest asset at this stage is a set of well-articulated values and interests of a self-transcending nature that allows the individual to retain a realistic perspective on what is happening within self and within the world.

USING A LIFE-SPAN FRAMEWORK

The framework described above is *normative*. That is, it is based on the generalized experiences of a large number of people, usually those who have been studied or worked with by developmentally oriented clinicians or researchers. That does not make these experiences either *timeless* or *universal*.

For each developing individual, each developmental task, each constellation of social roles and relationships, and each hard-earned set of coping and mastery behaviors is embedded in an idiosyncratic social and cultural *context* woven out of the individual's social characteristics, situations, and circumstances. These contexts are shaped by factors such as gender, religion, ethnicity, socioeconomic background, national origin, health, and a host of other highly personalized and individualized elements. We will discuss cultural factors further in Chapter 11.

For a life-span framework to be useful in working with individuals it can only be seen as the starting point in a process of fine tuning that brings into play all of the crucial factors mentioned earlier. In Chapter 5, we will describe the use of a series of filters or ways of understanding developing people. In Chapter 11, we will go on to examine cultural and social factors that bear upon developmental and counseling approaches in a multicultural society.

We have defined a set of contextual variables that constitute powerful and pervasive influences in the lives of developing human beings. The concept of *life stages* helps us to understand the influence of age related factors. The concept of *developmental tasks* helps to elaborate the basic challenges or crises that they confront. The concept of *coping behaviors* helps us to identify the psychological resources needed at each phase of the life cycle. We can identify sources of stress and support and map the network of social roles and relationships within which people meet needs, encounter problems, and either grow or stagnate. The entire life-span schema is summarized in Table 3.1.

Table 3.1
Principal Developmental Tasks and Relevant Counseling Goals by Life Stages

Life Stages	Social Roles	Developmental Tasks	Relevant Counseling Goals
Examination stage (65+ years)	Retirement roles, nonworker roles, nonauthority roles	Learning to cope with death, with retirement, affiliate with peers, cope with reduced physical vigor, cope with changed living conditions, use leisure time, care for the aging body	Engagement behaviors, productive leisure time behaviors, personal enhancement behaviors
Stabilization stage (50–65 years)	Leadership, helping, managing, creative accomplishments, authority, prestige roles	Ego-integrity; learning to be aware of change, have attitude of tentativeness, develop broad intellectual curiosity, develop realistic idealism, develop time perspective	Coping with mid-life transitions, renegation of relationships
Realization stage (30–50 years)	Leadership, helping, creative accomplishment roles	Ego-integrity; learning to be inner-directed, be interdependent, handle cognitive dissonance, be flexible and effective emotionally, develop creative thought processes, develop effective problem solving techniques	Problem solving, career choices, dual career problems, family and child-rearing relationships
Exploration stage, later adolescence, young adulthood (16–30 years)	Marriage roles, career roles	Intimacy and commitment, generativity; learning to commit self to goals, career, partner; be adequate parent, give unilaterally	Family and child-rearing relationships, sexual behaviors, risk-taking behaviors, value-consistent behaviors, career decision making, mutual decisions
End of organization stage, early adolescence (12–14 years)	Peer roles, heterosexual roles	Identity development; learning to be masculine or feminine, belong in various relationships, control impulses, be positive toward work, study, organize time, develop relevant value hierarchy	Social behaviors, sexual-appropriate behaviors, achievement-oriented behaviors, dating, study skills, emotional independence

(continued)

Table 3.1 *(Continued)*

Life Stages	Social Roles	Developmental Tasks	Relevant Counseling Goals
Later childhood (6–12 years)	Student, helper, big brother, big sister roles	Initiative-industry; learning to read and calculate, value self and be valued, delay gratification, control emotional reactions, deal with abstract concepts, give self to others, formulate values	Environmental mastering behaviors, value-relevant behaviors, work-relevant behaviors, educational skills, relating to parents, siblings
Organization stage begins, early childhood (3–6 years)	Sibling, playmate, sex-appropriate roles	Autonomy, sense of separateness; develop sense of self, sense of mutuality, realistic concepts of world, learning to be a boy or girl, manage aggression and frustration, follow verbal instructions, pay attention, become independent	Cooperate behaviors, control behaviors, substitution behaviors (parental or family counseling)
Infancy (birth–3 years)	Love-object roles, receiving and pleasing	Trust, learning to eat solid food and feed self, control elimination, manipulate objects, walk, explore immediate environment, communicate	Approaching behaviors, receiving behaviors, accepting behaviors (parental or family counseling)

We have organized and integrated these concepts into a life-span developmental framework within which to trace the progress of people through the life cycle. Within this framework we can begin to specify possible goals and objectives that can increase competence, bridge transitions, and reduce discontinuity.

A framework such as that described here also enables developmental counselors to begin to understand the behavior and experiences of clients without *categorizing, pathologizing,* or *stigmatizing* them as sick, deviant, or deficient.

CHAPTER 4

Concepts of
Optimal Development

The good life is a *process* not a state of being. It is a direction not a destination.

—Carl Rogers (1961)

FOR US fully to comprehend and appreciate human development, we must have some understanding of its various levels. When we facilitate the development of a human being what are the directions and distances through which that person grows and changes, and what are the destinations of that developmental journey?

One way of understanding the milestones and endpoints of optimal development is in terms of *human effectiveness*. We defined effectiveness as long-term control over the personally significant aspects of one's life. In this sense, effectiveness is a deeply personal and individualized state of being, and can also vary tremendously from one aspect of a person's life to another.

For centuries, theologians, philosophers, and finally psychologists have endeavored to define a set of positive human characteristics that cut across the many domains and differences that define the human condition. These conceptualizations or "models of human effectiveness" are in essence idealized representations of what is perceived to be good and true and beautiful within ourselves as human beings and what is valued and appreciated in our society.

These models are neither timeless nor universal. They are rooted in changing cultures, in philosophical viewpoints and in ethnic, religious, and social class experiences. When we grasp the limitations of such models, they can however provide a useful jumping off place from which each counselor can begin the career-long quest for a coherent set of goals and priorities with which to orient a professional practice (Gelso & Fassinger, 1992).

THE BAG-OF-VIRTUES APPROACH

One of the first psychologists to attempt a kind of cataloguing of desirable human characteristics was Abraham Maslow (1970). He conceptualized a hierarchy of human needs that provided a pyramid that the developing human being may ascend over the course of a lifetime (Figure 4.1).

At the base of the pyramid, Maslow placed basic physiological and survival needs. Once these are satisfied, the individual next focuses on needs for safety and security. As these in turn are satisfied, they give way to needs for love, then esteem or recognition, and finally at the very top of the pyramid, what Maslow termed *self-actualization* needs.

In Maslow's view, the higher level needs and the individual's striving to satisfy them will only emerge when needs lower in the hierarchy have been reasonably well satisfied.

When we observe the striving of any individual, we are likely to see only behavior that is relevant to the particular needs that are salient or prepotent at that particular point in time.

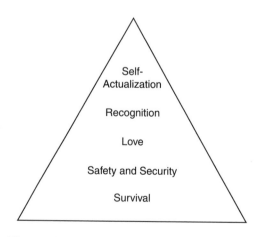

Figure 4.1 Maslow's hierarchy of needs.

Maslow pointed out that the best way to obscure the higher level aspirations and motivations of people is to keep their lower needs chronically unsatisfied, that is, to keep them hungry, cold, insecure, or unloved.

If on the other hand, an individual's developmental history is such that lower level needs are regularly satisfied, the efforts and aspirations of that individual will tend to center around the higher level need for *self-actualization*, and energy and resources will be mobilized toward the full development of abilities and talents.

While the concept of self-actualization is a fascinating one that has commanded considerable attention in American psychology, it is exceedingly difficult to apply in actual life situations.

On the surface, self-actualization means the realization or fulfillment of potentials, that is talents, aptitudes, and capacities. The notion of development as the fulfillment of one's highest potentials is an attractive and compelling one.

Unfortunately, self-actualization is a very global, abstract, and perhaps, idealistic concept. Flesh and blood human beings have many, many potentials, and yet each person must live with the reality of limited time, limited energy, and a finite set of opportunities (Tyler, 1964). Is the youngster with musical talent more self-actualized giving music lessons and playing oboe in a symphony orchestra, or earning 20 million dollars a year plucking an electric guitar in a rock group? Should the girl with budding artistic talent aspire to animate cartoons or paint portraits or both? The concept of self-actualization cannot answer these and other questions that confront counselor and client in a world of finite opportunities and realistic limitations.

Maslow (1968) attempted to flesh out the nature of self-actualization, or high-level human functioning, through studies of biographical materials about people who were commonly judged in the culture to have succeeded at unusual levels. In a sense, they were cultural heroes.

Since Maslow was neither an historian nor a biographer, we should, perhaps, view his methods of compiling a list of optimal human characteristics as both highly selective and subjective. Maslow's list of 15 characteristics of these self-actualized people is:

1. Self-actualizers tend to be *realistic* in their perceptions of themselves and the world.
2. Self-actualizers tend to *accept* themselves and their fellow human beings.

3. Self-actualizers tend to possess a *zest* and *enthusiasm* for living.

4. Self-actualizers tend to focus on real problems that are amenable to solution. They are *effective problem* solvers.

5. Self-actualizers are able to *separate* themselves from immediate situations and casual relationships.

6. Self-actualizers are not *over-conforming* or *other directed*.

7. Self-actualizers have a wholesome, fresh *appreciation* of people and things.

8. Self-actualizers report having experienced some sort of deep *mystical* or *spiritual* experience, in which they feel wonder and awe at the universe.

9. Self-actualizers have a basic feeling of *caring* and *belonging* to humanity.

10. Self-actualizers *share intimate relationships* with a few specially loved people.

11. Self-actualizers tend to show *religious, racial,* and *ethnic acceptance* rather than intolerance.

12. Self-actualizers are able to *distinguish between ends and means* and *pursue ethical ends* with firmness and certainty.

13. Self-actualizers tend to possess a *spontaneous, philosophical sense of humor.*

14. Self-actualizers are *creative, original,* and *divergent* in their thinking.

15. Self-actualizers are *resistant to blind conformity.*

As a set of ideals for the society to strive for, Maslow's list of the self-actualizer's traits is admirable. The concept of a needs hierarchy that should be attended to if we are to tap the best potentials that reside in people again is good *social theory.*

As psychological theory, to be applied to develop a goal structure to use with troubled individuals, self-actualization and its attendant "bag of virtues" seems idealistic and almost patronizing in the glibness with which it details the attributes, accomplishments, and public accolades of these "great" people.

The Maslow list is something of a grown-up version of the Boy Scout Oath and Law. We are tempted to suspect that self-actualizers are, in addition to their other noble virtues, also trustworthy, loyal, helpful, brave, clean, and reverent.

One need not be cynical to suspect that Maslow's list of virtues came more from perusing the history and literature of a culture sadly in need of unblemished heroes, than from careful and systematic observation of flesh and blood human beings.

Other similar if somewhat less grandiose catalogues of human virtues have been compiled by other psychologists.

Jahoda's Concept of Normal Behavior

Marie Jahoda (1958) proposed a simple and common sense definition of adequate personality development or "normal" behavior. She described the normal person as one who actively masters his or her environment, demonstrates a considerable unity or consistency in behavior, and is able to function without making undue demands upon others.

This definition stays rather close to the notion of human effectiveness mentioned earlier. It omits, however, any mention of prosocial behavior or interpersonal functioning.

Shoben's Version of the Normal Personality

Shoben (1957) provided a somewhat similar but expanded version of the normal personality. The concept of "normal" in regard to human behavior is a slippery one. It is sometimes used in a statistical sense to describe what is average or most common, while at other times simply what people find acceptable or expected.

Shoben described four sets of characteristics of a "normal" person that he believed could be defined independently of group norms or statistical averages. He saw these characteristics as those that are necessary for people to function in and contribute to a stable and free society; they are:

1. *Willingness to accept the consequences of one's own choices and behavior.* Basically, this is the idea of personal responsibility.
2. *Capacity for positive interpersonal relationships.* This is the ability to function cooperatively and constructively with others and to maintain close and lasting personal relationships.
3. *Contribution to society.* This characteristic involves the ability to identify as a group member, and to subscribe and contribute to the goals and purposes of a group. This essentially encompasses the duties of good citizenship, and the willingness to nurture and help others.

4. *Commitment to ideals and standards.* This final characteristic relates to the ability of an individual to identify with and commit to ideals, values, and standards that transcend immediate self-interest.

Shoben's simple list of "normal" characteristics really is based upon basic behaviors required for the maintenance of a stable, reasonably democratic society. Certainly without a considerable number of people endowed with these characteristics, a free society would be in grave trouble.

A simple reading of a daily newspaper, however, will convince the reader that these characteristics are far from universal, or perhaps even "normal" in a statistical sense.

More recent catalogues of positive personality traits tend to put greater emphasis on social or interpersonal functioning. Goleman (1998) points out that while IQ scores have apparently been increasing steadily almost since the advent of intelligence testing, what he calls "emotional intelligence," or the ability to control or harness one's emotional life on behalf of goals and values has if anything decreased.

Goleman asserts that intelligent and purposive control of feelings and motivations is the most important ingredient for success in the modern world. Goleman (1998) has constructed an "Emotional Competence Framework" to describe effective human functioning. These competencies are rooted in an individual's inner or emotional life, and are seen to determine how people manage their lives in terms of choices, motivations, and decisions. The Goleman framework includes:

- *Self-awareness,* that is, knowing one's internal states, preferences, resources, and intuitions. This includes recognizing one's feelings and their effects on judgment and reactions. It also includes accurate assessments of one's strengths and limitations, and finally, includes feelings of self-confidence and self-worth.
- *Self-regulation.* Under this category is placed self-control of emotions, trustworthiness, conscientiousness, flexibility, and openness to new ideas.
- *Motivation.* This category includes achievement drive, commitment, initiative, and optimism.

SOCIAL COMPETENCE

Another category of great importance in the Goleman framework is *social competence.* Included in this is: empathy, nurturing others, meeting others needs, accepting and reaching out to diverse groups, and understanding the dynamics of groups in terms of feelings and power relationships.

Under social competence is also included skills in influencing others, communicating, leading, managing conflict, building positive relationships, and working cooperatively with teams.

When we compare Golemans's 1998 list of qualities with the Maslow compendium from 40 years earlier, except for the greater emphasis on social competence, the 1998 model seems to be a little more comprehensive, but to reflect much of the same substance.

Heath (1994), building on thirty years of research on optimal functioning, describes a vision of "human excellence." This vision encompasses a set of virtues that cut across the primary human roles of worker, citizen, spouse, parent, lover, and friend. Heath's list of such characteristics included:

1. Caring and compassion
2. Honesty and integrity
3. Sense of humor
4. Openness and self-disclosure
5. Tolerance and acceptance of others
6. Dedication and commitment
7. Understanding of others
8. Respect for others
9. Empathy for others
10. Adaptability, flexibility
11. Self-confidence

Reviews of qualities of successful professionals in a variety of disciplines produce lists very similar to the Goleman and Heath formulations (Rest & Narvaez, 1994).

Sometimes the lists of virtues invoked to describe optimal development seem to envision an almost superhuman being. They represent an idealized state that all may strive for, but most of us will never reach. Few clients will either enter or leave counseling endowed with all of the virtues.

In many ways, all of these lists are the opposite side of the same intrapsychic approach that has been used to create the lists of deficits and personality defects that have been criticized earlier.

Both the lists of virtues and deficits are couched in terms of *traits,* that is predispositions to behave in given ways through time and across situations. Such trait descriptions may actually tend to obscure the environmental and developmental contexts within which behavior occurs and is maintained (Seeman, 1989). Under varying environmental conditions, the behavior of most human beings changes, bringing out both the best and the worst in people. Few people, for example, retain a keen sense of humor all of the time in all situations.

Total reliance on trait concepts may limit our ability to understand and intervene in positive ways to help individuals grow in effectiveness as they move through the life cycle. These lists often do not help us to iden-tify the specific situational transactions between the individual and the environment that can be used to reach attainable goals for improved func-tioning and a step toward higher level development (Wapner, 1987). It is often also more useful to consider the kinds of organizational and insti-tutional arrangements that *promote* virtuous behavior than to prepare armchair catalogues of what *might* unfold spontaneously from within.

DIRECTIONS OF DEVELOPMENT

Carl Rogers (1964), drawing on clinical experience, tried to enumerate the *directions* of growth, and the values or goals of clients who were success-ful in Client-Centered Therapy. This description of the strivings of imper-fect, but growing people seems a little less pretentious than the list of characteristics that emerged from the "bag-of-virtues" approach.

Carl Rogers.

Rogers' list of directions for development of people moving toward greater maturity included:

1. They tend to move away from facades and pretenses.
2. They tend to move away from "oughts," that is, tasks, obligations, or expectations laid on them by others.
3. They are less anxious to please others and are more concerned with pleasing themselves.
4. Being real and spontaneous, in the sense of being aware of and willing to express one's true feelings, is increasingly valued.
5. Self-direction is positively valued.
6. They tend to value themselves, and to see their own opinions and accomplishments as worthwhile.
7. They find zest and excitement in the very process of pursuing goals, and in discovering new potentials and possibilities in themselves.
8. They become more sensitive and accepting of others.
9. They increasingly tend to value deep personal relationships that allow the sharing of feelings and aspirations.
10. Finally, they move toward valuing openness to the full range of inner and outer experiences.

CLIENTS' OWN VALUES AND ASPIRATIONS

Aside from Rogers' descriptions of these directions for development, the literature of counseling and psychotherapy seems relatively devoid of concern or knowledge about what ordinary people may want, or how they may see progress or growth.

Psychologists have, however, studied quality of life and self-reported happiness or, as it is called, *subjective sense of well-being* for more than 20 years. Large-scale studies of people's perceptions of personal goals and life satisfactions were reported by Andrews and Withey (1976) and Flanagan (1978). Diener (1984) reviewed the research on subjective well-being as did Ryff (1989) and D.G. Myers and Diener (1995).

These studies and reviews have produced some surprising conclusions about the needs, satisfactions, and aspirations of ordinary human beings. First, a higher percentage of Americans report being happy than are estimated to be so by mental health professionals (Brown, Regan, & McPartland, 1996). Next, variables such as age, income, religion, occupation, and other demographic factors are relatively minor determinants of subjective well-being. Self-reported happiness is a *psychological variable* rather than an automatic function of age, wealth, or status. Finally, the experience of stress in one's life is *not* a major impediment to personal happiness.

When people are asked to report the features that are most crucial to quality of life they tend to list the following kinds of factors (not arranged in order of importance):

1. Material comforts and financial security
2. Health and personal safety
3. Relationships with relatives
4. Having and raising children
5. Relationships with spouse (lover, etc.)
6. Relationships with close friends
7. Helping and encouraging others
8. Participating in government and public affairs
9. Learning
10. Understanding self
11. Interesting, rewarding, worthwhile work
12. Expressing self creatively
13. Socializing with others in recreation
14. Reading, listening to or watching concerts or sports, and so on
15. Participating in active recreation, sports, or hobbies

Not surprisingly people tend to place material comfort, financial security, and good health as most crucial to well-being. Beyond these values, however, it is clear that work, close social and family relationships, and opportunities for personal growth and self-expression are very important.

The broad picture that emerges from these studies is that subjective well-being is fairly stable across time and is not radically or permanently affected by single events (Lykken & Tellegen, 1996). People who report high levels of happiness tend to be involved in close, positive interpersonal relationships (Baumeister & Leary, 1995); be actively involved in and committed to work (Evans, Pellizzari, Culbert, & Metzen, 1993); be actively striving toward the attainment of goals and the realization of personal values (D.G. Myers & Diener, 1995); and perceive themselves as making progress in the attainment of such personal goals (Carver & Schier, 1990).

If we take a cue from Carl Rogers' account of the successes of Client-Centered Therapy, we could describe the successful client in *developmental counseling* in these terms: (1) lives within an increasingly caring and supportive network of interpersonal relationships, (2) engages in, or is preparing to engage in work that is personally worthwhile and satisfying, (3) is pursuing a set of consciously chosen goals that are reasonably congruent with personal values and psychological resources, as well as environmental supports and opportunities, and (4) is aware of systematic progress in moving toward the attainment of cherished goals.

If the theory and research cited earlier in this chapter is at all valid in terms of the ingredients of "subject well-being," the successful client in developmental counseling should be on the road to experiencing at least a modicum of that elusive quality.

COGNITIVE DEVELOPMENTAL SCHEMAS

Cognitive psychology also offers a useful set of tools for examining optimal levels of development and effectiveness. Cognitive developmental psychology, has studied changes in human cognitive functioning across the lifespan. Theoretical formulations derived from such studies have generated frameworks that can help us to understand crucial differences in the ways in which individuals grow in terms of their ability to think or process information about themselves and their environments.

Out of cognitive psychology has come a unique view of human behavior. Essentially, this view of human functioning asserts that human beings respond not simply to the stimuli that confront them directly in the environment, but that they also organize, categorize, and process the information contained in these stimuli to obtain their own idiosyncratic "construction" of the stimulus situation. It is to this unique interpretation of the stimulus world that people actually respond and act. This view of cognitive growth is called a *constructivist* position regarding development (Mahoney & Lyddon, 1988).

In this view, the individual is seen not simply as a passive receiver of external information, but as an active and dynamic "maker of meaning." From a constructivist position, to understand the interaction of an individual with his or her environment, we must understand the way in which that individual construes or interprets the information available from the environment.

Cognitive developmental psychology has attempted to describe and explain the growth processes through which individuals acquire higher level cognitive functioning over the life-span. As we noted in Chapter 2, a number of cognitive developmental frameworks have been articulated to describe sequences of cognitive growth. These frameworks have described specific cognitive stages, each of which is seen to be characterized by particular styles of reasoning, judgment, decision making, and interpersonal relating. Each of these stage-specific cognitive styles is seen to be *qualitatively* different from either preceding or ensuing stages of development (Okun, 1990).

It is important to note again that the stage schemas used in these cognitive developmental frameworks are very different from the *chronological stages* described in the psychosocial theories of development. In these cognitive developmental schemas, stages are arranged in *hierarchical* order. They are not normative in the sense that there is an assumption or expectation that all or even most members of the society will eventually pass through them. Indeed, within such hierarchical frameworks, the distinct possibility is seen that many individuals will never reach the upper levels of the hierarchy.

While development is seen to proceed through an invariant sequence, such progress is by no means considered to be inevitable.

One of the first cognitive developmental schemas was proposed by the pioneering Swiss child psychologist Jean Piaget (1929). Subsequently, cognitive developmental schemas have been articulated to describe *moral development* (Kohlberg, 1969), *intellectual and ethical growth* (Perry, 1970), and *conceptual development* (Harvey, Hunt, & Schroder, 1961). Loevinger (1976) viewed the concept of *ego development* to be the most comprehensive of these developmental schemas and maintained that it subsumes the other schemas.

LOEVINGER'S MODEL

Loevinger's system consists of seven more or less discrete stages of development that progress from a very simple, undifferentiated, and unintegrated style of construing events and situations to a complex, highly differentiated level of cognitive development. Because ego functioning or, essentially, cognitive processes, are so central to total personality, each stage has important implications for behavior in a wide range of situations. Understanding the individual stage is an important key to understanding both the client's behavior and the meaning that behavior has. Loevinger's stages of ego development are described next. Table 4.1 summarizes five of the seven levels in Loevinger's system.

THE PRESOCIAL STAGE

In infancy children lack the ability to differentiate themselves fully from their environment. As babies begin to develop a degree of self-awareness and to distinguish themselves from their environment, they tend at first

Table 4.1

Implications of Higher Ego Stages for Counseling

	Ways of Defining Problems	Meaning of Goal-Attainment	Way of Relating to Counselor	Motives for Counseling
Self-protective	Ritualistic actions that yield solutions	Means to concrete ends: used to obtain instru-mental effects in world: education to get *X*	As external authority, asking how to get things, what to do	Instrumental, to satisfy immediate needs
Conformist	Need for general information required for social roles: objective truth, revealed by authority	Social approval, appearance, status used to meet expectations and standards of significant others	As external authority asking how things work	To impress significant others, to gain social accep-tance and entry into social roles
Conscientious	Need for know-how; personal skills in problem solving: divergent views resolved by rational processes	Competence in work and social roles: used to achieve internalized standards of excellence and to act on or change world	As helper in personal integration of information, based on rational inquiry: help setting goals, exploring causal relationships and asking *why* things are as they appear	To achieve competence relative to own standards of excellence
Autonomous	Need for personally generated insight about self and nature of life	Self-knowledge: self-development, used to transform self and the world	As facilitator of personal experience, reflection, and personally generated concepts, insights, judgments	To deepen understanding of self, world, and life; develop increasing capacity to manage own destiny
Integrated	Need for specialized information	Self-development, high level leadership, original contributions	As consultant or resource person	To obtain specialized or expert consul-tation or to help others

Note: Counseling is generally inappropriate for clients below the self-protective stage.

to view others solely as providers who exist only to meet their own imme-diate needs. As a child begins to develop language, the process of self-awareness and social differentiation is rapidly accelerated.

Prior to this process of differentiation the child really does not have an ego, that is a sense of self-awareness and a view of reality through which to construe events and to begin to manage his or her own behavior. Ego development really begins with the end of this stage.

THE IMPULSIVE STAGE

As infants develop, they begin to separate a sense of self from the rest of their world. Along with self-awareness comes an awareness of impulses, that is, tendencies to act on the environment. Because of the relative immobility and helplessness of the small child these impulses are constrained and regulated almost entirely by parents or other caregivers. As the child grows, these older beings begin to regulate and control the child's behavior through reward and punishment. The inevitable result is that the child is heavily dependent on adults both for meeting physical needs and for impulse control. The child is almost totally dependent, and sees other human beings largely in terms of what they can provide. The child soon learns that some kinds of impulses, particularly sexual and aggressive ones, are met with punishment. Because the child is not yet able to control such impulses from within, punishment is often experienced as arbitrary and retaliatory.

At this stage the child's experiencing is almost entirely in the immediate present, and the focus of awareness is upon immediate gratification. When an individual remains at this level past the early years of childhood, he or she is seen as *uncontrollable,* or even as *incorrigible* and *unsocialized.*

THE SELF-PROTECTIVE STAGE

As the young child grows, and particularly as language develops, some inner controls are established. These controls are fragile and under stress the child may still revert to "tantrum behavior" reminiscent of earlier stages. The learning and internalizing of social rules still occurs in a social context where punishment is experienced as arbitrary and retaliatory. The first rule that is generalized from this context is "don't get caught!"

In terms of the child's thinking and experience, the self-protective stage is far from a mature model of moral reasoning. The child may tend to blame circumstances, or other people for difficulties. If this kind of excuse is not available, some arbitrary characteristic of self may be chosen for the displacement of blame.

The self-protective stage is most notable in terms of the way in which the child conceives and structures interpersonal situations. Since he or she is occupied with immediate gratification and sees other people primarily as need-satisfiers, interpersonal relationships may be centered around manipulating and gaining advantage over others. Interactions with others may become win-lose games and winning is always preferable to losing. Behavior is viewed as getting what you want from others.

When this stage continues past middle childhood, the individual is seen as an *operator* or *manipulator*. In adolescence or adulthood, the individual who functions at this level may be seen by others as *ruthless, antisocial*, or *without conscience*.

THE CONFORMIST STAGE

The conformist stage begins with the development of real socialization, that is the child's growing awareness of a basic congruence between his or her own welfare and that of a group. This identification begins in the family and may gradually be extended to other significant groups.

This sense of group identification is based upon trust and a sense of being able to predict and comprehend the behavior of others. The presence of social rules enhances this trust. The child obeys the rules because they stem from the group. Disapproval from others, with the possibility of being rejected is a consequence to be feared and avoided at all costs.

The child is able to differentiate among other people, but they are still often seen as stereotypes derived from their principle group roles. Father, mother, teacher, brother, and so on, may define other people in absolute, simplistic, and final ways.

Individual behavior is perceived in terms of external and superficial appearances. Inner thoughts, feelings, intentions, and motivations are ignored as tools for understanding and construing others' behavior. The individual is preoccupied with appearance, conformity, reputation, and social approval.

THE SELF-AWARE LEVEL

As the individual moves through the conformist stage, he or she *may* enter a transition period that is characterized by an increase in self-awareness beyond that experienced in the earlier phases of the stage.

This is an important phase of the developmental process in that some research suggests that it may represent the most common level for people in our society (Holt, 1967). This phase is marked both by an increase in self-awareness and the ability to consider multiple possibilities and perspectives in making moral and social judgments. At this level, people are able to perceive some exceptions to the rule of group conformity, although such exceptions may be both limited and somewhat arbitrary.

THE CONSCIENTIOUS STAGE

This stage of ego development marks the first presence of a fully adult conscience. It is also marked by the ability to engage in self-criticism and the ability to establish long-term goals and to evaluate them in terms of the individual's personal values rather than on the basis of general social approval. At this stage, individuals are able to accept responsibility for helping others and are more concerned with the consequence of actions on the welfare of others than they are about observing or ignoring abstract or irrational rules.

The central feature of this stage, and the one that gives it its name, is the emergence in the individual of the ability to choose or formulate rules or standards for behavior based on personal values and deeply held convictions regardless of whether these conform to the group opinion.

The people who reach this stage view themselves as the source of their destiny. They are able to measure success, morality, and wisdom in terms of personal rather than merely socially sanctioned standards and criteria. To operate in this self-aware and autonomous way, people must have a rich and highly differentiated inner life. They are able to integrate perceptions, feelings, and experience into principles that can guide and validate judgments.

At this stage, people are able to be aware of deep feelings and convictions not only in themselves, but in others. As a consequence, they are able to form richer and more sensitive relationships. Because they can draw upon greater depths of personal experience, they are able to use longer time perspectives in judging events rather than fixating upon immediate consequences.

Some research indicates that many if not most adults in our society never fully enter this stage. The consequences of this failure are rather obvious for both individuals and the society. Certainly many of our most cherished goals, both in counseling and in education, aspire to this kind of functioning. In some counseling situations, the goal attainment of clients is dependent on the client entering and functioning in this stage.

The end of the conscientious stage is marked by another transition phase—the *individualistic level*. This phase marks a sort of vestibule to the subsequent *autonomous stage*. As developing individuals are able to make personally relevant judgments, set their own goals, and judge for themselves their own successes and failures, they also develop a very strong sense of individuality and emotional independence.

The growing sense of independence is often acquired at the price of heightened awareness of conflict and potential conflict both within themselves and with others. At the individualistic level, people may lack the tolerance and perspective-taking ability to manage conflicts with others constructively and comfortably.

THE AUTONOMOUS STAGE

At this stage of development, individuals acquire the ability to acknowledge and cope with conflicting and competing values and needs within themselves and between themselves and others. Much of this ability results from increased capacity to take multiple perspectives and to abandon simplistic either/or, and absolutistic thinking. As autonomous individuals become more comfortable with their own intellectual and emotional independence, they come to recognize and appreciate others' needs for autonomy and so are less controlling and manipulative. Autonomous individuals have greater tolerance for ambiguity and complexity and are able to set long-term goals based upon self-fulfillment rather than on immediate accomplishment or recognition.

At the autonomous stage, the individual has finally acquired a complex and truly sophisticated cognitive structure capable of handling a wide range of difficult and complicated philosophical issues and personal problems.

THE INTEGRATED STAGE

The seventh and final stage in Loevinger's framework is termed the *integrated stage*. Relatively few individuals have been identified and studied at this stage. In a sense, it remains almost an ideal rather than a tangible entity. It represents the apex of the developmental pyramid.

In the autonomous stage, the individual has developed the ability to tolerate and even appreciate the complexities, ambiguities, and contradictions that abound in the real world. At the integrative stage, the individual fully masters, reconciles, and resolves many kinds of problems and issues and to exert mastery over them. This stage represents a kind of ultimate in intellectual achievement, emotional control, and environmental mastery.

COGNITIVE DEVELOPMENTAL MODELS AND COUNSELING

We have traced Loevinger's developmental model and have examined it as a kind of map that can orient us to optimal paths of human growth and development. The cognitive developmental or constructivist approach deals with the "making of meaning." It is this capacity of the individual to organize, construe, and interpret information from the environment that makes every human life unique. It is the basis of human personality and individual differences. Counseling is inevitably and centrally concerned with the ways in which people form meaning out of their experiences, including the experience of counseling, itself.

Swenson (1980) argues that one of the key issues in modern psychology has concerned the relative importance of personality variables versus environmental forces in influencing human behavior. The ecological approach expounded in this book is at the center of this important controversy.

In a sense, the study of ego or cognitive development is the study of how people, or rather *some* people, are able to liberate themselves from the tyranny of the external reward-punishment cycle that is often represented in their psychological and physical environments. Loevinger (1976) saw this process of liberation through development as one of the great mysteries with which psychology deals. Does continued development lead to increasing autonomy and greater freedom of choice?

If counseling is committed to human freedom through development, as we suggested in Chapter 1, then certainly the cognitive developmental frameworks are very important guides in both understanding where individual clients are as they enter counseling, and in helping to formulate goals with them as they move through counseling.

OPTIMAL DEVELOPMENT IN CHILDREN AND ADOLESCENTS

Identifying patterns of optimal development in children and adolescents is very difficult (Wagner, 1996). Change is very rapid and individual differences in rates of change are great. Efforts to set up criteria to define optimal functioning in pre-adolescents have focused on social functioning, cognitive development, and physical health as primary criteria (Prugh, 1973).

Adolescent development is similarly difficult to identify in terms of optimal functioning. Wagner (1996) posits a model with six basic areas of functioning:

1. Biological development,
2. Cognitive development,
3. Emotional development,
4. Social development,
5. Moral development, and
6. Vocational development.

These areas of development are not necessarily highly intercorrelated and must be considered as relatively independent of each other. At age 18, a given adolescent may vary widely across these domains. Historically, as we noted earlier, psychology has tended to pathologize adolescence and to interpret much of adolescent behavior as symptomatic of underlying disorders (Newcomb, 1996). As we saw, about 80% of American adolescents proceed through this stage and develop into healthy adults (Kaczmarek & Riva, 1996). Probably criteria for adolescent functioning are not very different from those applicable to other life stages. Van Slyck, Stern, and Zak-Place (1996) proposed three key criteria of optimal functioning: resilience, coping, and problem solving as the basis for assessing optimal adolescent development. These are implicit in the integrated life-span model presented in Chapter 3.

HEALTH AND HUMAN EFFECTIVENESS

One of the developments in our thinking about human behavior in recent years is the growing tendency to interrelate concepts of human effectiveness, optimal development, and sense of well-being with a very broad and unifying concept of *health*. The health psychology literature uses the idea of *wellness* to describe and conceptualize "positive health" (Lightsey, 1996). In this notion, health is far more than the absence of identifiable disease (Altmaier & Johnson, 1992).

The expanded definition of health provided by the World Health Organization (1964) exemplifies the broader and more comprehensive view of health. Health was defined as "a state of complete physical, mental, and social well-being" (p. 1). As Seeman (1989) pointed out, such a broadened definition of health requires a truly comprehensive concept of the functioning of human beings within the full context of their interactions with the environment as well as their internal, physiological functioning.

As definitions of positive health and wellness have expanded to become almost synonymous with human effectiveness and optimal human development, boundaries between developmental counseling and health-related specialties in the field of psychology have been blurred. In a real sense developmental counseling has become an aspect of health psychology.

HEALTH AND DEVELOPMENT IN CHILDREN

One of the key issues in the development of children relates to health. Health concerns impact children from the neonatal period on through adolescence. Research has shown that prematurely born infants are perceived differently by parents. Over-protective parents may perceive their infant's growth and development as delayed or deficient even when it is essentially normal (Stern & Newland, 1994). Even health care providers may also tend to have negative expectations for premature or frequently ill infants. Such perceptions may be transmitted to siblings, other relatives, and even to teachers to form what may become self-fulfilling prophecies about vulnerability and inadequacy.

When children in a family are victims of chronic illnesses, the entire family including siblings are affected. Childhood cancer, diabetes, birth defects, and myriad other conditions constitute major stress factors in family functioning, and may inhibit optimal development in both the victim and other family members.

Developmental counselors may work with families and individual children in both preventive and rehabilitative efforts. They may help parents, teachers, and other care-givers to recognize the effects of stereotypic approaches to ill or disabled children as well as the impact on other family members. Such counselors can also function as child advocates in helping to obtain needed services for ill or disabled children. Often access to specialized medical care, rehabilitative services, prosthetic devices and appropriate educational programs can make tremendous differences in the development of children with special needs and their families. The preventive role of developmental counseling is further elaborated in Chapter 13.

Health and Development of Adolescents

Adolescence is both a period of rapid biological development and a period in which the individual is increasingly subject to a wide variety of risk factors that may threaten health, longevity, and optimal development. Adolescence is generally the period in which the foundations for a healthy lifestyle are either formed or forever abandoned. The foundations for such a lifestyle include of course sound dietary and exercise habits and avoidance of tobacco, alcohol, and other kinds of substance abuse.

Research indicates that about 20% of adolescents are obese and about 25% use tobacco regularly (Wagner, 1996). Adolescence is also a period in which experimentation with and eventual addiction to or dependence upon a variety of drugs is likely to occur. Boys are more likely than girls to abuse drugs in adolescence. Excluding extreme poverty, few differences in drug use have been found among different socioeconomic groups. Family influences have been associated with drug and alcohol abuse among adolescents. Those whose parents abuse drugs or alcohol, or who are members of families in which there is discord or disorganization are more likely to abuse substances themselves.

Other threats to adolescent health include sexual promiscuity and result-ing exposure to AIDS or other sexually transmitted diseases, and early, un-wanted pregnancies. Reckless or drunken driving, various other forms of excessive risk taking and suicide are all major risk factors confronting ado-lescents. Finally, exposure to deadly violence is a major cause of death and disability among adolescents. Homicide is one of the five leading causes of death in children *under* 12 years of age (Emery & Laumann-Billings, 1998). One of the sad realities of contemporary American life is that being a child or adolescent is likely to be dangerous to one's health and even life.

Most of the threats to adolescent health cited are part of complex pat-terns of social problems and social disorganization within communities. Counselors may play major roles in community programs aimed at pre-venting or alleviating such problems (see Chapter 13).

Health and Adult Development

As with adolescents, healthy lifestyles are essential to the development of adults. Good dietary and exercise habits, avoidance of tobacco use, re-straint of alcohol use, and participation in a network of positive social re-lationships all contribute to health, longevity, and optimal development.

Family and workplace stress are major negative health factors and probably account for about as many health problems as smoking. Person-ality factors are also important contributors to many kinds of chronic health problems. Stress management approaches are discussed further in Chapter 13.

We have examined a variety of concepts regarding the nature of human effectiveness and optimal development. These ideas have ranged from slightly superhuman catalogues of human virtues based upon idealiza-tions of the presumed characteristics of cultural heroes, to the self-reported sources of life satisfactions of flesh-and-blood "ordinary people."

One of the constructs that we have studiously avoided but that psychol-ogists frequently use to evaluate human behavior is the concept of *mental health*. Actually there are at least four approaches to defining this con-struct that make it difficult to understand the rationale behind its use (Powers, Hauser, & Kilner, 1989). Positive or normal mental health may refer to what is statistically average or most frequent in the majority of the population. In this sense, it may refer to what we *expect* to see in peo-ple's behavior.

The concept of positive mental health may also be used to refer to *optimal functioning,* or to the behavior of an "ideal" person in ideal circumstances.

When the concept of mental health is "pathologized" it may simply refer to the absence of any clinically diagnosed disorder, or the failure of the individual to complain or report symptoms.

Finally, the most rarely used approach to the term is to refer to human functioning within a specific set of cultural, ethnic, or environmental circumstances. In this approach, optimal or adequate functioning might be considered to differ across subcultural groups or even from one generation to another within the same group.

The latter approach is certainly the most difficult and complex. It may, however, be the most useful approach in a rapidly changing multicultural society. We will discuss multicultural issues in Chapter 11.

Each counselor and each thoughtful individual faces the task of framing his or her own conceptions of what is good and true and beautiful in human existence. Each person must finally decide what is worth striving toward and reaching for. The goals of developmental counseling are ultimately valid only as they reflect the hopes and aspirations of individual clients.

Few clients come to counseling and psychotherapy initially able to articulate clearly and concisely what they are seeking. Very few come in to have the "dents pounded out of their psyches." The process of setting goals is generally a collaborative one in which counselors and clients gradually construct and cement a *working alliance* that commits them both to a set of purposes and aspirations that constitute directions for development for that particular individual. In this process, counselors need to be aware of their own value systems, and be prepared to help clients articulate their hopes, fears, and aspirations as they strive to obtain some degree of control over the directions and distances traveled on their developmental journeys.

CHAPTER 5

Developmental Diagnosis

> How queer everything is today! . . . I wonder if I've been changed
> in the night. . . . But if I'm not the same, the next question is,
> "Who in the world am I?" Ah, *that's* the great *puzzle.*
> —Lewis Carroll
> from *Alice in Wonderland*

O NE ACTIVITY that is characteristic of all approaches to counseling and psychotherapy is the effort to understand the client and the client's world. This quest for understanding and empathy is not an easy one. Human beings are forever separated from each other by myriad physical and psychological barriers. Differences in age, sex, ethnic memberships, socioeconomic background, religious beliefs, political persuasions, and personal history make each human being inevitably, to some extent, a mystery to every other human being.

Developmental counselors face the formidable task of attempting to bridge these many barriers to understand, empathize, and intervene in another human life.

The process counselors use to reach out and understand has been the subject of great controversy and not a little confusion and misunderstanding over the years. The earliest attempts to describe this process was, perhaps unfortunately, termed *diagnosis.*

THE QUESTION OF DIAGNOSIS

The question of whether to diagnose or not to diagnose has been around since the beginning of professional counseling and psychotherapy. If we define diagnosis simply as the effort to understand the client, the question becomes meaningless. All counselors or therapists of necessity struggle with the need to understand clients and to communicate that understanding.

In medicine, diagnosis has historically consisted of assigning patients to one or another category of disease on the assumption that each disease entity has an identifiable cause and so requires a different treatment of choice. The assumptions underlying this kind of diagnostic process are seldom relevant to the practice of counseling and psychotherapy.

In developmental counseling, the diagnostic process is a *continuous, tentative,* and *testable* process of understanding the client insofar as it is ever possible for one person to understand another. In developmental counseling, the process of diagnosis *permeates* and *pervades* the whole course of counseling. This ongoing process is concerned with a continuous revision and modification of the counselor's impressions and perceptions of the client.

As we listen to and observe each client, we construct a "hypothetical" client who exists only in our own mind, created and clothed by our limited and possibly flawed impressions. When we are aware of the tentativeness and limitations of those impressions, we constantly endeavor to "check out" our perceptions and interpretations. We do this most frequently simply by asking the client to react to our interpretation of a communication. Sometimes we try to check out our clinical hunches or judgments by making predictions about the client's future reactions. In some situations, we may compare our impressions with those of others. In this sense, we function as scientist-practitioners, testing our hypotheses as we go along (Spengler, Strohmer, Dixon, & Shivy, 1995).

When we treat diagnostic processes as continuous, tentative, and testable aspects of our efforts to understand, relate, and help, we can bridge much of the social psychological distance that separates human beings from one another. We can use our knowledge of human development and our appreciation of contextual factors at work in each human life to relate empathically and effectively to our clients.

UNDERSTANDING DEVELOPMENT
RATHER THAN DEFICITS

As we examine the contextual elements at work in an individual life, we can create a set of lenses or filters through which to understand to some degree the behavior that we observe as we see that person functioning in his or her natural environment. These filters help us to understand the purpose and meaning of behavior and experience to the individual, and to identify those elements in the person-environment situation that may be limiting or facilitating that individual's growth and development. They are the building blocks of developmental diagnosis.

LIFE-STAGE ELEMENTS

The first perspective through which we can understand clients involves the concept of *life stages*. The life-span framework in Chapter 3 is based on life stage concepts.

Some physiological events that are developmental catalysts, such as the onset of puberty, are relatively discrete. Others are very gradual and continuous processes. In complex cultures, however, the society itself structures the environment around what are perceived to be discrete, age-related stages of development. The concept of life stages has a degree of social reality regardless of its relationship to underlying physiological or psychological processes.

One of the cautions in using life-stage concepts is that they, like all diagnostic constructs, can become a rigid way to categorize people. They are useful in understanding as long as we use them flexibly and with an appreciation of the within-stage variability that is inevitable.

Life-stage approaches allow us to establish the kinds of frameworks within which to understand social role expectations, developmental tasks, and transitions that may trigger major discontinuities at particular points in the life cycle.

Chronological stage frameworks share a number of basic premises. All see development as a process of continuous change that pervades the entire life-span. Within an individual's life, stresses, transitions, and discontinuities may occur at predictable or unpredictable points in time. Development tends to be orderly, that is progressive and sequential, following much the same pattern generation after generation.

Within a chronological stage model, we can see several basic types of influences at work in an individual life. Danish (1981) categorized these multiple influences in three areas:

1. Normative influences tend to have biological and environmental determinants strongly related to age. Compulsory retirement at age 65, or the onset of menopause in the late forties are examples of age-related influences.

2. Normative, historically related influences tend to affect most members of a particular generation in similar ways. The Great Depression, World War II, the Korean or Vietnam War, and the Feminist and Civil Rights movements are all examples of historical events that profoundly impacted most of the members of an entire generation.

3. Non-normative life events impact on an individual, but do not occur as a function of either age or of historical events. The loss of a job, an illness, a divorce, or the death of a child or a spouse are events that may occur in any of several life stages. The precise meaning and impact of these events may vary markedly, however, in terms of the specific time or stage in the life cycle at which they occur. A divorce or death of a spouse, for example, may have very different meaning and impact at age 24 than at 48 or 64 years of age.

Okun (1984) listed four basic assumptions that grow out of a life-stage or life-span perspective. They are:

1. Developmental change is a continuous process not limited to any one time of life.

2. Change occurs in various interrelated social, psychological, and biological domains of human development.

3. Change is sequential, and therefore it is necessary to view each stage of life in relation to the developmental changes that precede and follow it.

4. Changes in individuals must be considered in the context both of the prevailing norms of the day and of the historical time within which one lives.

Chronological stages and the life-span frameworks of which they are a part help us to pinpoint crucial issues, problems, and crises in the life of an individual. Often they help us to understand why clients are "stuck," troubled, and frustrated at this particular point in the life cycle. Within and across specific life stages, individuals are challenged by developmental tasks, experience transitions, and are subject to discontinuities. As counselors and clients are able to identify these developmental turning points, they can set realistic goals in order to convert crises to opportunities for further growth (Fassinger & Schlossberg, 1992). The life-stage framework allows the counselor and client to focus not only upon the client's pain, but also to begin to see goals in terms of mastering developmental tasks, bridging discontinuities, and increasing coping resources or competence to resume a positive pattern of development (Schlossberg, 1989). A life stage is the essential context within which each person lives and functions on a day-to-day basis. It is a vivid and ever-present part of each person's identity and reality.

Life-Style Concepts for Understanding Clients

Chronological or life-stage frameworks are useful tools for understanding developing clients. Within any given life stage, however, we see tremendous individual variation in the ways people attempt to cope with or master the specific tasks and challenges that arise at that particular point in the life cycle.

To understand the unique striving of an individual at whatever age or stage, we need a set of concepts that are more finely tuned to the particular developmental history of the individual. The term *lifestyle* was coined by Alfred Adler to identify major themes or motives in an individual's life. Gradually it has been expanded to include characteristic ways of dealing with stress and approaching problems.

We are using the concept of lifestyle in that sense to describe the particular pattern of behavior with which an individual characteristically copes with stress, seeks to satisfy needs, or seeks to understand and master problems within the environment (Terry, 1994). Coping styles are learned patterns of behavior rather than intrapsychic traits. They are tendencies to respond in particular ways to specific situations (Catanzaro, Horaney, & Creasey, 1995).

A concept that enables us to understand the ways in which individuals deal with problematic situations that involve challenges, stresses, or threats is the concept of *coping behaviors*. The concept was originally used to distinguish between rigid and ineffective patterns of behavior termed *defensive* in psychoanalytic theory, and more flexible and effective patterns of behavior. Gradually the concept of coping behaviors as central to the outcomes of counseling and psychotherapy has been given increasing importance (Gibson & Brown, 1992).

It is clear from research (Folkman & Lazarus, 1986) that coping behaviors are complex. They deal both with cognitive appraisal of problems and situations, and with the emotional arousal experienced in the situation. Coping may involve both immediate situations and the threat of future situations.

Generally, when stressful events are predictable and anticipated, the individual is able to prepare, the emotional arousal caused by the event is somewhat reduced. In these situations, the full energy and resources of the individual can usually be brought to bear on the actual problem situation.

An important aspect of coping strategies involves the availability and actual use of important resources. These resources include social support, inner or personality resources such as confidence and optimism, as well as basic life skills, or experience in dealing with similar situations. The availability and use of material resources such as money, housing, and specialized professional assistance including legal, medical, or other technical assistance is important.

A global concept related to successful coping is that of *hardiness* (Kobasa, 1979). This research showed that individuals who are subjected to stressful events and who do not "breakdown" or become dysfunctional tend to experience being in control of situations, experience being challenged rather than overwhelmed and demonstrate commitment to the values and activities central to their lives.

Another somewhat similar construct is *resilience* (Garmezy, 1994). This concept denotes the ability of individuals to cope with stressful situations without experiencing lengthy debilitating emotional breakdown or dysfunctions. No matter what name is given to the ability to cope successfully with problematic and challenging situations, or exactly how it is defined, it is quite clear that coping behaviors are a central ingredient in human effectiveness.

Some coping behaviors are specific to particular situations and are acquired only through extensive training or experience. Others however are more general and are considered part of an individual's personal resources (Long & Schutz, 1995).

COPING STYLES

We know that when children are faced with stressful circumstances they very early develop characteristic ways of coping with stress and attempting to meet needs. As they grow into adulthood, these characteristic coping patterns are refined and strengthened to become important aspects of the individual's interaction with problematic or stressful elements in the environment (P.P. Heppner, Cook, Wright, & Johnson, 1995).

We can identify several specific coping styles that help define patterns of person-environment interaction:

1. *Minimizing and avoiding.* Some individuals attempt to cope with problematic situations through avoiding or minimizing them. Such

an approach may take the form either of physical avoidance by literally moving away from stressful situations as much as possible, or psychological restructuring in which the disturbing situation is minimized by framing it in a larger perspective.

The individual may simply cope by recognizing that "I have a lot of stress and dissatisfaction in my job, but my family life is great and I have several interesting hobbies." While avoidance-minimization is a passive approach it may be effective in situations that are beyond the capacity of the individual to control, or which would be very costly to attempt to change in terms of other values. This coping style verges closely on "defensive" as opposed to "coping" behavior and may move toward defense mechanisms of denial, distortion, and repression. When used appropriately and flexibly, however, it can help an individual to maintain an essentially positive total life perspective in the face of some degree of unavoidable stress and tension.

2. *Impulsive-intuitive.* In this second coping style, the individual responds to stressful situations in a very spontaneous and immediate way. Coping is not consciously planful, but is based upon what "feels right" in an intuitive sense. People react quickly and decisively in problem situations. They may resist using formal problem-solving or decision-making models. To the degree that these people are in touch with and in control of their feelings, and have had successful experience with similar problem situations, this style may be very effective. People who are successful with this style are often seen as very confident, poised, and effective in difficult interpersonal situations. They may also be high risk takers.

   People using this style may have difficulty when confronted with very complex problem situations, or when they are confronted with totally new problems with which they have had little prior experience.

3. *Rational-analytic.* In this coping style, people tend to defer action in stressful situations until they can analyze them carefully and make specific and sometimes detailed plans. The rational-analytic style often focuses heavily upon intellectual aspects of a problem and may ignore or minimize emotional aspects either in self or others. This coping style is most effective in complex situations, and may be least effective in emotionally charged, crisis situations where immediate and decisive action is required. Sometimes people with this style tend to be immobilized when it is difficult to obtain all of the information desirable to make a fully rational decision.

4. *Confrontive-tenacious.* This coping style involves meeting problem situations head on and "hanging in" with a particular strategy or approach until results are obtained or failure is apparent. In interpersonal problem situations, this style may be seen as direct and even aggressive. Sometimes people using this style are premature in defining problems and fail to consider a full range of possible alternatives. They may perseverate on less than optimal strategies. They tend to be effective in dealing with relatively simple problems that require high levels of energy and hard work to resolve.

These four coping styles have both advantages and limitations. In counseling it is helpful to try to understand clients' characteristic coping styles to support those styles with which the client is most comfortable and successful, and also to help the client acquire more flexible ways of coping in situations that demand new approaches.

INTERPERSONAL STYLES

People vary greatly in terms of their interpersonal styles. Much of our interpersonal behavior is learned within the family when we are too young to question or analyze the effectiveness of what we are learning.

Karen Horney (1950) described three characteristic interpersonal styles that people may use in dealing with stressful circumstances or social relationships. They are:

1. *Moving toward other people.* In this interpersonal style, individuals when confronted with stress or tension tend to move toward others in the sense of seeking closer, warmer, or more intimate relationships. In this process, such people are able to self-disclose, discuss their fears and feelings and seek emotional support and practical assistance from others.

   If this interpersonal style is carried to excess or used in rigid ways, the individual may be overly dependent and may be seen as weak or vulnerable. In some situations, moving toward others may actually damage relationships by frightening off people who may fear being "dumped on" or imposed on or exploited by others.

2. *Moving away from other people.* A second interpersonal style involves moving away or distancing oneself from others when in stressful circumstances or situations. The troubled person tends to withdraw from others, resists self-disclosure or expressions of feelings to

others and may even reject and resist offers of help, support, or assistance from family or friends. This interpersonal style is reminiscent of what is often erroneously called the "strong silent type." When used to excess it is likely to be the "broken-and-brittle type."

This style may be effective when the individual is enmeshed in neurotic or exploitive relationships and no genuinely helpful relationships are available. Unfortunately, this style may cause the individual to refrain from reaching out to initiate positive relationships or to fail to explore the environment thoroughly to identify such relationships.

3. *Moving against other people.* The third interpersonal style involves coping with stress by striking out against other people in aggressive or hurtful ways. Since people generally retaliate against this kind of behavior, this style may simply add to the tensions already felt. The individual may alienate key support people in the environment at the very time they are most needed. This style is an example of the frustration-aggression phenomenon in which the frustrated individual strikes out against available bystanders rather than dealing with the real source of the frustration.

This interpersonal style may be very destructive when it is characteristic of the most powerful person in an authority hierarchy. When this style becomes characteristic of an entire family or group in any stress-laden situation, hostility tends to be displaced downward to the least powerful and often most vulnerable members of the group. This interpersonal style is characteristic of the rigid authoritarian parent or leader who is unable to delegate anything except blame.

Life Space Contexts

Human beings do not live in a vacuum; every individual lives within a physical, social, and psychological context or setting. Human beings are not passive recipients of information or stimulation from the environment. They actively organize, construe, and interpret events and situations in the world around them.

When we as counselors endeavor to understand clients, we must also try to visualize and conceptualize the world in which they live. In this process, we use the concept of *life space*. Life space is as much a psychological concept as a physical one. It encompasses both the physical environment and the ways in which that environment is perceived and experienced by each individual interacting with and within it.

In this sense, a room full of a dozen people represents a dozen different life spaces, not only because each individual occupies a slightly different physical position in the room, but because each perceives, organizes, and construes the total situation differently. Consider a crowded courtroom at the climax of a dramatic trial. Each of the principal participants or spectators is certain to have a very different and unique conception of the scene.

The sheer physical aspects of life space and their physiological and psychological consequences are important in themselves. For some children, for example, the physical environment maybe constantly filled with danger or the threat of danger to their very lives. Other environments may be dull, dreary, and without positive stimulation.

The geography of life space from a social psychological standpoint is mapped in terms of the roles and relationships within which people interact with and influence each other. The rivers and mountains of life space are the expectations, conceptions, and perceptions of self in relation to others. Interpersonal space is organized and construed in a wide variety of ways that essentially define the life experience of each individual personality (Forsyth & Leary, 1997). Most of the situations that bring clients to counselors arise out of the ways in which they function or fail to function in their fundamental social roles and interpersonal relationships.

Human beings are social animals. They are innately programmed to meet or attempt to meet myriad needs with and through other people (Lopez, 1995). Human interaction is structured and regulated through the establishment of social roles. A role is a more or less clearly defined way of participating in the life of a group or organization. Roles arise out of social participation and group membership. Roles may be defined within very small face-to-face or primary groups such as the family, or may be defined by the larger society and its social, political, or economic institutions.

As Super (1980) pointed out, a career is essentially a collection or series of social roles enacted over the life-span. One of the most prominent and psychologically significant features of the life space of most adults is the particular interwoven set of evolving vocational roles than over time we call a career. Because developmental counseling is centrally concerned with helping people function more effectively within social roles and with utilizing those roles to nurture the fulfillment of potentials, developmental counseling inevitably includes vocational counseling. This topic is elaborated in Chapter 9.

Social roles have several dimensions. Four significant aspects of social roles exist and together determine how individuals will construe and begin to organize their life space:

1. *Role expectations.* These are the cultural prescriptions that are generally assigned to the role by the group or society that invented or attempted to define it.
2. *Role conceptions.* These involve the way the individual performing the role actually perceives or interprets the expectations.
3. *Role acceptance.* This entails the willingness of the individual to accept or become involved in the role as interpreted.
4. *Role performance.* This deals with the way in which the individual actually behaves in the role situation.

When sharp differences exist between role expectations and role acceptance or performance, conflicts usually arise between the individual and other members of the social group. Many family conflicts are of this kind. One role for developmental counselors is often to help a client attain the necessary skill to perform adequately in terms of role expectations, or to renegotiate those expectations. When role expectations are clearly arbitrary and unreasonable in a family, for example, the counselor may undertake to work with the whole family unit.

Conversely autonomy in a job or career is the relative freedom to conceptualize one's own role within an organization, or even to invent a new role that is needed in the organization, but represents greater opportunities for growth and development for the worker. Sometimes vocational planning involves helping clients to seek out or negotiate such opportunities. Much of what we call freedom and autonomy arises out of our opportunities to negotiate and redefine our most significant roles. Role conflicts and role rigidity are at the core of many of the problems that bring clients to counseling. Even though we see client's individually, the geography of that client's life space in terms of roles and relationships is always present. We cannot understand clients without understanding their roles and relationships.

STRESS AND LIFE SPACE

An individual's life space also involves the presence, nature, and intensity of stressors. The term *stress* was first used in engineering to refer to force or pressure applied to metals and other structural materials (Matheny, 1988). One of the engineering problems related to stress is the amount of stress a given material can withstand without permanent damage. This is called the *elastic limit* of the material. Many of the stress-related problems with which counselors deal are somewhat similar.

Some of the stressors that operate in the life space of an individual may be properties of the physical environment. We know, for example, that excessive heat, cold, noise, crowding, or pollution in an environment all induce stress. Similarly physical exhaustion, continuous repetitive or exacting tasks, sleep deprivation, or even stimulus deprivation can induce stress. Natural disasters, violence, or fear of violence or other victimization produce stress reactions.

It is important for counselors to recognize the existence of these kinds of stressors in the life space of an individual and to understand their impact. Psychologists define stress very broadly and do not confine the concept to the kinds of physical or environmental conditions mentioned.

Stress Factors

We can define stress simply as any threat to the satisfaction of a fundamental need. In this sense, every new venture into the unknown or any uncertain outcome may be stressful to some degree. Stress is not always harmful. The presence of stress within an individual's life space, in fact, triggers new behavior and new learning. Healthy development involves learning to cope with and manage stress factors as well as learning to avoid them. Prolonged exposure to relatively high levels of stress or short-term exposure to intense levels of unpredictable and uncontrollable stress may be physiologically and psychologically damaging, however.

We can examine several major aspects of stress situations within an individual's life space. These include, intensity, length of exposure, and the health and resources of the individual. These three factors influence the probable effects of the stress on the individual and the nature of the coping reaction with which he or she seeks to manage or modify stress levels.

Intensity

The most immediate and obvious factor in stress reactions involves intensity. When any creature encounters an intensely stressful stimulus, the reaction is generally overt and unmistakable. The child who puts his hand on a hot stove, for example, responds quickly and audibly. We, as observers, usually have no difficulty in understanding what happens.

Reaction to intense stress usually involves a strong physiological component characterized by rapid breathing and heartbeat, increased blood pressure, sweating, and increased secretions of adrenalin and other chemicals. People experiencing intense stress, such as fear or pain, typically suffer decrements in all kinds of task performances. These decrements are most severe in performances of complex tasks. People under intense stress may be accident prone or unable to perform adequately even routine duties or functions.

Intense stress is most damaging and debilitating when it is experienced as unpredictable and/or uncontrollable and it may trigger panic reactions or moderate to severe physiological dysfunctions of many kinds.

Wartime battle experiences, accidents, natural disaster situations, sudden illness, or contact with criminal violence including assaults, rapes, or homicides are all examples of events that trigger very powerful stress reactions.

Helping people to predict, appraise, or control stressful situations that cannot be totally avoided helps them to manage stress reactions. Such interventions are sometimes called *stress inoculation.* Stress management programs are described in Chapter 13.

Intense stress produces not only strong immediate reactions, but also triggers significant after effects. Such after effects can be produced both by the kinds of situations described earlier and by excessive task demands in a working or family situation. Providing care for a very ill or disturbed family member, or dealing with a business crisis or failure even on a relatively short-term basis of several weeks or months, for example, may produce severe after effects.

The likely after effects of intense stress include decreased sensitivity to people, irritability, decreased task performances, disturbed sleep or digestive problems, and severe mood swings. These effects may persist for relatively extended periods if help is not provided. Again, symptoms of such disturbance in people whose life space has included intensely stressful situations such as fear, pain, danger, violence, conflict, or other intense stressors need not be accounted for on the basis of presumed intrapsychic deficits or psychopathology.

LENGTH OF EXPOSURE

A second major factor in determining the effects of stress exposure is duration. Contrary to what we may believe intuitively, relatively long exposure to moderate or even low levels of stress may be even more damaging than short periods of high intensity stress. This may be especially true for children. Research evidence (Lazarus, 1966) suggests that coping strategies for dealing with short-term intense stress are learned earlier than are coping behaviors for managing chronic low-level stressors.

While reactions to short-term, high-level stress are immediate and overt, as we noted, reactions to chronic low-level stress may be much more subtle. Even the individual who is experiencing chronic stress in his or her life space may have little awareness or understanding of either the sources of the stress or its immediate and long-term effects.

Symptoms associated with exposure to chronic stress may be similar to those triggered by intense levels of stress, but may be relatively less severe and produce an onset only after prolonged exposure over a period of many months or even years. In addition to irritability, insensitivity to others, sleep disturbances, digestive disorders, or mood swings, prolonged chronic stress may also be implicated in a variety of serious illnesses.

Identifying sources of chronic low-level stress within the life space of a client may require considerable exploration of roles, relationships, and tasks in which the client is involved. Too often this kind of exploration is not done and disturbances or symptoms are attributed primarily to intrapsychic deficits.

HEALTH AND PERSONAL RESOURCES

People respond to stress as total organisms. Attempts to understand stress reactions in terms of single components such as emotions, cognitions, or physiological reactions as though they were separate and isolatable lead to misunderstanding. The general health of an individual is an important determinant of reaction to stress. Habits of eating, sleeping, and exercise are important aspects of stress management. General physical condition, age, and medical history are also very important factors.

To a considerable extent reaction to stress is influenced by the individual's prior learning history and record of personal perceived successes and failures. When this history has built up a sense of confidence and self-efficacy people are able to tolerate and to learn to predict and control many stress factors (Lightsey, 1996).

In attempting to understand a client's life space and the sources of stress that may be contained in it, counselors need to obtain data about both the client's general health and well-being and his or her prior learning history.

While we have focused in this discussion primarily on the negative consequences of stress, we should note that some degree of stress is an inevitable and not altogether undesirable part of the life space of every developing individual.

Some degree of stress accompanies every new challenge and opportunity. Confrontation with stress mobilizes our full physical, cognitive, and emotional resources on behalf of the needs, goals, or aspirations that are at risk. A life lived totally without any element of stress would tend to be unproductive, unchallenging, and above all uninteresting. The very factors that induce stress within life space are the same ones that provide interest, adventure, and challenge.

The elements in any stimulus situation that attract our attention and actively involve us are those that can potentially induce stress. These factors include novelty, intensity, ambiguity, complexity, and uncertainty. Some common sources of stress are listed in Table 5.1.

When we are highly ego-involved, that is, when important personal values are at risk in such situations, the potential for stress is apparent. When we are totally uninvolved in the events around us, or if the elements of novelty, intensity, ambiguity, complexity, and uncertainty are entirely missing, the potential for apathy and indifference is also apparent.

SUPPORT AND LIFE SPACE

The second major variable that can help us understand the life space of an individual is that of support. The concept of support includes both material and relationship factors. Material support involves adequate provision for food, clothing, shelter, and other basic needs. While many of us take the resources that supply this kind of support for granted, we unfortunately find that many clients do not (McCloyd, 1998). In assessing the life space of any client or potential client, one of the first tasks is to ascertain the degree to which a reasonable level of material support exists. Clients who do not have reasonable levels of material support are likely to have little energy or concentration available to invest in meeting longer term needs or coping with long-range problems in counseling.

The second aspect of support can be called *social* or *emotional* support. This kind of support comes from the presence of a network of positive and caring human relationships within the individual's life space. When such a network is completely missing, or if, for some reason, the individual fails to utilize it, alienation and apathy or panic are likely results.

When individuals feel genuinely cared for, understood, respected, and trusted, they experience social support. The presence of social support is

Table 5.1

Stress Assessment Checklist

I. Novelty Factors

In the last year has the client . . .

_____   1. Married or remarried?
_____   2. Divorced or separated?
_____   3. Changed employer?
_____   4. Changed career field?
_____   5. Received a major promotion?
_____   6. Changed residence to a new city or region?
_____   7. Assumed primary care for an infant?
_____   8. Assumed primary care for an aged, ill, or disabled person?
_____   9. Experienced a chronic illness, disability, or long hospitalization?
_____ 10. Begun a major educational or training program?

II. Intensity Factors

Presently is the client . . .

_____   1. In a marriage or other relationship in which he or she engages in at least one major quarrel or argument per week?
_____   2. Working in an environment in which there is excessive heat, cold, noise, or pollution?
_____   3. Working in an environment in which there are frequent and intense emotional outbursts?
_____   4. Working or living in an environment in which there is frequently real physical danger?
_____   5. Working in an environment in which there is boring and monotonous repetition and routine?
_____   6. Working or living in an environment in which members express chronic and open hostility to each other?
_____   7. Working in an environment in which special and high-level public performances are frequently required?
_____   8. Working in an environment in which unpredictable but frequent overloads of required overtime are demanded?
_____   9. Working more than 48 hours per week?
_____ 10. Involved in primary care of one or more seriously disturbed individuals?

III. Ambiguity Factors

Is the client presently . . .

_____   1. Involved in an emotional relationship in which the future course of the relationship is in doubt?
_____   2. Engaged in a relationship in which the role expectations are constantly shifting and unclear?

Table 5.1 *(Continued)*

_____ 3. Engaged in a work or study situation in which the expectations and feedback about performance are shifting and/or unclear?

_____ 4. Unclear about future plans with regard to work, living arrangements, or major roles and relationships?

_____ 5. Seriously contemplating marriage or remarriage?

_____ 6. Seriously contemplating divorce or separation?

_____ 7. Seriously threatened by loss of job?

_____ 8. Seriously contemplating a major career change?

_____ 9. Engaged in major litigation or legal problems?

_____ 10. Experiencing uncertainty regarding a major health problem?

IV. Complexity Factors

Is the client . . .

_____ 1. Holding two or more jobs?

_____ 2. Combining major homemaking or child-rearing responsibilities with a full-time career?

_____ 3. Engaged in working for three or more supervisors?

_____ 4. Engaged in direct supervision of more than eight workers?

_____ 5. Engaged in work demanding accurate collating, computing, or compiling of diverse and extensive data or information?

_____ 6. Engaged in work that requires frequent and important judgments based on complicated and extensive sets of information and data?

_____ 7. Engaged in providing leadership to a diverse and sometimes conflicting group of people?

_____ 8. Engaged in parenting in a complex family situation involving children from two families or origin, or children with special problems or handicaps?

_____ 9. Engaged in work that requires creative, original, or unusual productions or solutions?

_____ 10. Engaged in a wide variety of social, volunteer, or community service activities in addition to a demanding career?

V. Involvement Factors

Is the client presently involved in a competitive, risky, or highly uncertain situation in which there is a distinct possibility of an unfavorable outcome that could . . .

_____ 1. Result in the complete loss of financial security?

_____ 2. Damage self-esteem as a spouse or parent?

_____ 3. Undermine career aspirations?

_____ 4. Damage confidence in basic intelligence or competence?

_____ 5. Result in a loss of independence?

_____ 6. Destroy trust in a loved one?

_____ 7. Hurt someone who he or she loves?

_____ 8. Make him or her appear foolish and incompetent.

_____ 9. Disappoint those who depend on him or her?

_____ 10. Let down the people whose respect is most important?

an important ingredient in managing stress and in taking risks. When individuals do not feel social support, they experience alienation, insecurity, vulnerability, helplessness, and loneliness. Often the counselor begins working with a client who has little support in his or her life space by providing a supportive relationship directly. One of the goals of developmental counseling is to help clients to build long-term supportive relationships into their life space.

An exploration of a client's life space involves a consideration and appraisal of the individual's role structure, relationship network, and crucial sources and levels of both stress and support. When we are able to understand the factors at work in a client's life space, we are able to understand more thoroughly the meaning and effectiveness of the individual's patterns of coping and mastery behavior. We are thus better able to establish goals and to design counseling interventions or strategies. Techniques for managing stress and utilizing support are discussed in Chapter 13.

We have introduced three sets of variables that combine to explain and elucidate much of the behavior of individuals. The concept of life stage helps to shed light on the impact of age-related variables that change as people move through the life cycle. They arise from the progressive interaction of forces within maturing individuals and forces that stem from the environment.

We also examined lifestyle variables as these arise from the unique pattern of the coping behavior of the developing individual. We saw that an individual's thinking, feeling, and acting are based on unique styles and tendencies that define how he or she copes with and relates to the world.

Finally, we looked at a set of life-space variables that represent the fundamental interactions between the individual and the world in which he or she lives. The impact of stress and the role of support in dealing with that world were discussed.

These three facets of human experience and functioning can be combined to provide a rich and comprehensive view of clients as they live within a physical, social, and psychological context. Such an understanding or diagnosis can be achieved without invoking or applying a set of labels based on presumed intrapsychic deficits, or fanciful and untestable personality theories. These concepts can enable the developmental counselor begin to understand clients and help to facilitate growth and build on assets. This kind of understanding enhances opportunities rather than attempting to prescribe nonexistent cures for dimly defined illnesses and aberrations. Taken together they help to define the process of developmental diagnosis.

LEVELS OF IMMEDIATE FUNCTIONING

We conceptualized human effectiveness as the ability to exert more or less long-term control over significant aspects of the environment. Effectiveness is not an intropsychic trait or characteristic of an individual because we recognize that such control is likely to vary from time to time, from one aspect of the environment to another, or from one social role to another. It is rather a *pattern of interaction* or transaction with the environment. For example, a successful business executive operating at a high level of effectiveness can see a business merger or downsizing wipe out 30 years of effective control in a matter of hours. Similarly, a divorce, bereavement, or catastrophic illness can disrupt lifelong patterns of coping and control in an instant.

Every individual no matter what the history of effectiveness has been, can be overwhelmed by sudden and drastic changes in the environment. The degree of resilience that we discussed earlier may help to determine the length of time and resource needed for the individual to bounce back to former levels of effectiveness.

Even though we are always aware of a client's potential for growth, it is important to conceptualize the *immediate* level of functioning of an individual at a given time and in a specific set of circumstances.

We can categorize this kind of person-environment interaction within a unitary model that specifies five levels of effectiveness in terms that include the cognitive, affective, and behavioral components of that interaction (Blocher, 1987). Figure 5.1 illustrates the levels.

Panic

The lowest level of human effectiveness is aptly described by the term *panic*. This level is characterized by a major loss of control over the individual's affective responses, and by significant loss of control over even the immediate and short-term environment. In situations of extreme panic, the individual often requires hospitalization or careful supervision for his or her own protection.

People in extreme panic may be suicidal or even violent. Panic is characterized by intense feelings of helplessness or being out of control and at the mercy of random or malevolent forces in the environment. Panic may be accompanied by crying, rage, or intense physical symptoms such as hyperventilation, rapid pulse, increased blood pressure, frequency of urination, faintness, sweating, and shaking.

Figure 5.1   A Unitary Model of psychological diagnosis.

Panic is heavily a reaction to intense, uncontrolled or uncontrollable stress. Panic is not automatically an indication of an intrapsychic deficit or inadequate personality development. Almost any individual can be reduced to panic if stressful stimuli are intense and prolonged, and if no control of the situation is perceived as possible.

Panic is the lowest level of human effectiveness precisely because the individual's affective arousal is so high that cognitive functioning, including problem solving and actual coping behaviors, are severely impaired. When in panic states, individuals may be unable to operate simple safety devices, may become disoriented in time and space, and be temporarily unable to accomplish previously learned skills such as driving an automobile, using machines, or operating other equipment.

Panic reactions are frequently triggered by exposure to extreme danger in natural disasters, wars, victimization, or accidents. Panic can also occur in response to prolonged exposure to moderate stress levels when these are perceived as totally uncontrollable. Providing constant care for an emotionally disturbed or acutely ill person, performing very demanding or complex tasks for long hours or under very adverse working conditions, or experiencing chronic pain, discomfort, or danger for long periods can all trigger panic.

In counseling situations, when dealing with panicked individuals, rational or highly introspective counseling approaches will be ineffective until panic has subsided. Withdrawing the individual from the stressful situation, providing positive reassurance and support in a calm and composed way, and offering direct, structured advice or instruction on how best to control the situation may be helpful.

In cases of extreme panic, sedation by a physician and even short-term hospitalization may be indicated.

People in panic states seldom approach professional counselors directly and voluntarily. Often panicked people are referred to counselors by others. Clients who are victims of rape, assault, or other violent crimes are frequently referred for counseling. Sometimes people facing surgery, life-threatening illnesses, or who are suffering from very painful or disabling injuries or illnesses are referred. People who are experiencing bereavement are also often referred. Frequently people who have attempted or threatened suicide are referred for psychological counseling or therapy. Victims of natural disasters or survivors of other catastrophes are similarly referred.

Counseling with clients who are, or have recently been in panic states, or who are on the verge of such states is often called *crisis intervention.* Crisis intervention focuses upon helping people to cope with extremely stressful or crucial short-term situations. It generally involves helping individuals to deal with affective arousal and to acquire immediate coping strategies. Allowing the client to cathart or express strong emotion in a safe and supportive setting is also often helpful.

APATHY

The second level of human effectiveness can be called apathy. At this level, there is some control of very short term and immediate aspects of the environment. In comparison to panic, the immediate level of affective arousal is much lower and obvious symptoms of emotional arousal are often reduced or absent. At this level, individuals often attempt to exert environmental control largely by avoiding stressful or threatening interactions, even when these might lead to greater long-term control. While the individual may not require institutionalization, he or she is unlikely to be economically or socially self-sufficient or independent. Planfulness is almost totally absent, and even the degree of organization required to hold a low-level job is often missing.

At the apathy level, the individual tends to avoid or ignore long-term demands from the environment. The emphasis is on avoiding immediate punishments or obvious failures. The individual is often unable or unwilling to follow through on even carefully structured plans.

At this level, the individual may have difficulty in accepting responsibility for his or her own behavior and its consequences. Blame may be projected upon others and a wide variety of excuses used to rationalize lost opportunities or failures. Typically, individuals at this level experience very low self-esteem and often feel at the mercy of fate or luck. In interpersonal relationships, such individuals may show distrust and indifference.

Like people at the panic level, individuals at the apathy level may be very hard to reach. They are unlikely to self-refer. They are often referred by relatives or others who simply do not know how to cope with them.

People at the apathy stage often have histories of long-term hospitalization, imprisonment, unemployment, invalidism, or have experienced a long series of tragedies or failures that have led to the abdication of efforts to control the environment. They respond in lethargic ways and often show a flattened affect in response to either positive or negative stimuli from the environment. At deeper emotional levels, there may be feelings of despair, alienation, and abandonment.

This type of client is often referred involuntarily by courts, probation or parole services, or welfare agencies. This type of client is even more difficult than the panicked individual. Clients at the apathy stage typically require a great deal of counselor-initiated structure, even to the point of setting and reminding the client of specific times and places for appointments. When goal-setting is accomplished, goals, and action plans must be very explicit and short term. Often this means breaking down goals into a series of very short term closely supervised and readily accomplished objectives.

STRIVING

At this level of human effectiveness, the individual is able to maintain control over most of the short-term transactions with the environment and is actively engaged in seeking more long-term control. The individual has considerable control over affective responses, but may vacillate between feelings of hope and confidence and feelings of resignation and despair.

The striving individual is capable of a limited amount of planning and gratification deferral, but is easily discouraged by failure to attain results quickly. Often this kind of client tends to set goals and objectives that are unrealistic in either time or magnitude, and then becomes discouraged when they are not attained. The individual's life is likely to be characterized by a series of crises and emergencies that are preventable with more consistent and careful planning.

At this stage clients may self-refer, but may also have unrealistic and grandiose expectations for immediate results. Clients at this stage frequently withdraw from counseling prematurely. Clients at the striving level are frequently referred by teachers or supervisors because of inconsistent performances or underachievement in school or on the job.

Clients at the striving level may want considerable counselor initiated structure, but are usually able to accept a gradual increase in responsibility. They may be able to profit from cognitive approaches when these move very slowly and are accompanied by considerable support. Sudden attempts at confrontation with these clients may result in premature termination of counseling.

COPING

At this level of human effectiveness, the individual has control over large segments of long-term transactions with the environment. Behavior is planful and very largely goal-oriented. The individual reacts more to life problems as challenges than as intense threats to psychological integrity.

Problems and difficulties tend to be readily identifiable within specific roles or relationships, or centered around particular developmental tasks.

Clients at this level tend to self-refer and to provide fairly well-articulated presenting concerns and problems. Clients at this level may also have considerable anxiety about the outcome of ego-involving problems and situations. The anxiety is not crippling, however, and provides motivation for them to work actively in behalf of goals.

Clients generally have fairly realistic perceptions of themselves and their life situations. They may, however, have blind spots around specific relationships or situations.

At the coping level, clients are able to take considerable responsibility for choosing goals and setting directions in the counseling process. The counselor is able to utilize a rather wide range of counseling approaches. Once a reasonably good relationship has been established, an effective alliance between counselor and client usually results.

MASTERY

This level of person-environment transactions represents the highest category of effective functioning. The individual is in active control of large and important segments of the environment on both a short-term and long-term basis. Such people typically enter into active, planful, and proactive interaction with the environment, anticipating rather than merely reacting to events.

At the mastery level, people tend to experience feelings of adequacy and self-confidence in most of their roles and relationships. They experience problems or obstacles as challenges and may show real zest and enthusiasm in goal-setting and planning activities.

Clients may self-refer or be referred by others, often for specific kinds of information or assistance. They may seek counseling help in doing educational and vocational planning prior to graduation from school or college, or at the point of major life transitions. Such transitions of course may temporarily move such a client back to lower levels of effectiveness. Similarly catastrophic events may move such individuals to lower levels.

DEVELOPMENTAL COUNSELING AND DIAGNOSIS

When the counselor is able to assess the client's level of functioning and modify counseling approaches accordingly, the probability of obtaining an effective working alliance is greatly increased. The first three or four sessions are often a *negotiation phase* of therapy in which both therapist and client are attempting to find a common ground on which to establish a working relationship. The counselor's sensitivity to client expectations, characteristics, and immediate functioning is especially important at this time.

By combining and integrating concepts of life stage, life space, lifestyle, and stages of cognitive development with the levels of immediate effectiveness, counselors can form comprehensive and coherent albeit tentative impressions of clients. From these they can form useful clinical hypotheses that can then be tested, modified or discarded as more information is generated in the counseling process itself. Table 5.2 demonstrates such an integrated diagnostic framework.

We have sketched out a comprehensive framework within which a developmental counselor can assemble and organize initial impressions and data about relevant client characteristics. These in turn can be used to generate a set of tentative clinical hypotheses to be tested in the course of counseling. They can then be revised and new impressions and hypotheses developed.

It is out of this kind of process that a more and more accurate, comprehensive, and clinically relevant picture of the client can grow. That is the process of developmental diagnosis. For an example of this process, see the vignette on pages 113–115.

Table 5.2
An Integrated Framework for Developmental Diagnosis

I. Level of Immediate Functioning (see Figure 5.1)

Panic	Apathy	Striving	Coping	Mastery

II. Life Stage Factors (see Table 3.1)

    A. Principal social roles and relationships

Present Functioning	Family	Social	Career	Other
Adequate				
Problematic				
Distressed				

    B. Key developmental tasks

Mastered	Problematic	Failed or Avoided

    C. Major developmental transitions or crises (See Chapter 1)

III. Ego Developmental Stages (see Table 4.1)

Self-Protective	Conformist	Conscientious	Autonomous	Integrative

IV. Life Space Factors

    A. Source of stress (see Table 5.1)

    B. Sources of psychological support

(continued)

Table 5.2 *(Continued)*

C. Level of material support (Housing, health care, financial, etc.)

V. Lifestyle Factors

A. Coping style(s)

Minimizing-Avoidant	Impulsive-Intuitive	Rational-Analytic	Confrontive-Tenacious

B. Interpersonal style

Moving toward Others	Moving away from Others	Moving against Others

VI. Other Clinical Impressions

VII. Tentative Overall Assessment as of _____
Clinical Hypotheses to Be Tested

VIII. Revised Assessment as of _____

Vignette: A Developmental Diagnosis

David is a 25-year-old high school graduate who has one semester of work in a community college. David came to a career development program and job fair accompanied by his mother. He completed a work history and goal statement. He indicated an interest in computers. David was interviewed by representatives from a computer manufacturing firm and a computer sales and services company. Both interviewers told him rather bluntly that he was not qualified for the kinds of technical positions that he sought.

After the second interview, David and his mother engaged in a rather heated exchange. One of the community college counselors helping to host the program intervened to suggest that David take advantage of free counseling being offered to program participants.

The next day David appeared at the Community College Counseling Office for an intake interview. He completed a Personal Data Sheet and a brief interview, was assigned a counselor and given an initial appointment.

David's counselor assembled the following information from the materials filled out by David and from the folder from his college enrollment seven years earlier.

David's employment history indicated that he had 11 different jobs in the last six years. All of these were entry-level positions in the fast-food or retail sales areas. In two of the positions he had lasted for nearly a year and had been promoted to an assistant manager position. He left both of these within two months after being promoted.

David gave a variety of reasons for leaving these jobs, generally saying that he was underpaid, unappreciated, and that supervisors "had it in for him." His job history was interspersed with long periods of unemployment.

David's high school records showed that he had above average intellectual ability, but below average grades, barely meeting graduation requirements. A letter from his high school counselor described David as an underachiever, popular with classmates, and something of a class clown. That counselor felt that David had much more ability than his record suggested.

In his semester of work at community college David had an A in math, a C in English Composition, and two incompletes in history and chemistry. He dropped out midway in the second semester.

On the Personal Data Sheet David indicated that he was currently unemployed and living with his parents. David's father is a foreman at an automobile factory and his mother works part-time as a supermarket checkout clerk. David has one brother, a year younger, who graduated from the university and is employed by an East Coast insurance company. David indicated that his reason for coming to counseling was "to get his parents off his back."

In his first counseling session, David denied needing help. He spoke of several grandiose but nebulous plans involving establishing web sites and selling several unnamed products. He indicated that he had few social relationships because most of his high school group had married or moved away. He spent most of his time "surfing the net." He insisted that all he needed was a little money and a "couple of good breaks."

The counselor was somewhat surprised that David returned for a second interview. As the second session progressed, David dropped much of his bravado. He acknowledged that his relationships with his parents were increasingly strained. His father was especially impatient with him, and periodically threatened to throw him out of the house. Twice they had nearly come to blows. David felt that he was constantly being compared with his younger brother. David described his brother as a "nerd" who was not popular in high school and "sucked up" to his teachers. The brother however was now making "big bucks" and on his "way up."

As he continued, David admitted that his real problem was that his father had recently accepted early retirement at the auto plant, and that his parents were planning to move into a retirement village in Florida. They had informed David very emphatically that he was not going along. At his mother's insistence, the parents had agreed to support David for one year *if* he entered and persisted in some kind of vocational education or training program.

At this point, David acknowledged that he was frightened at the prospect of being "abandoned by everyone."

In preparing for the third session, David's counselor decided to organize the information available together with his clinical impressions. The counselor felt that his third interview would be crucial to setting goals and building a working alliance. Using a worksheet similar to Table 5.2 the counselor developed a set of *tentative* working hypotheses about David as follows:

1. David seems to be functioning at the *striving* level. His planning is loose and often grandiose, but he has continued to seek employment.
2. At the present time, David's only active social role is in the family where he is functioning more as an adolescent than an adult. His relationship with his mother is strained, while that with his father is distressed. He has no close relationship with his brother, but appears threatened by his success. His career roles have been fragmented, brief, and unsuccessful.
3. David has apparently been unable to deal with developmental tasks involving commitment to any clear goals in career or even in social relationships. He seems unable not only to give unilaterally, but even to engage in cooperative relationships. He may have difficulty dealing with authority figures. At this point he seems to be functioning more as an early adolescent than as a young adult.
4. The major developmental crisis confronting David now is the forthcoming departure of his parents and their material and emotional support. He is now forced to begin thinking of himself and acting as an independent adult. He is struggling with the "breaking away" transition.
5. David seems to be moving out of the *self-protective* stage of ego development and into the *conformist* stage. He wants social approval and status, but is so far unable to earn it. Helping him to find ways to earn

approval and respect of family and others may tap his strongest current motivations.

6. The threat of being left on his own, or as he puts it "abandoned" is currently the greatest source of stress.

7. David has attempted to cope primarily by *minimizing, avoiding,* or *denying* problems. When faced with problems in jobs he has typically cut and run. In his two most successful job experiences he left shortly after being given more responsibility. Is fear of failure a dominant theme?

8. On the surface, David's interpersonal style seems to be moving against others. When at all threatened he seems defensive and almost belligerent. Underneath that, however, seems to be some emotional dependence and fear of rejection and abandonment.

9. David has the promise of one year of financial support if he returns to some kind of schooling and succeeds. He feels very little emotional support at this time except perhaps from his mother.

After collecting and organizing these impressions and hypotheses, the counselor began to seek ways to test out his perceptions in subsequent interviews and to develop a tentative treatment plan. He had begun the process of developmental diagnosis.

- How would you go about testing your hypotheses about David?
- What would be your plan for the next counseling sessions?
- What further information would you want?

CHAPTER 6

Counseling Theories as Sources of Gain

Nothing is as practical as a good theory.

—Kurt Lewin (date unknown)

THE FIELDS of counseling and psychotherapy have spawned so many approaches that as practitioners we are confronted with an embarrassment of theoretical riches, while suffering from a scarcity of empirically proven and undisputedly effective interventions. We tend to term all of these varied approaches *counseling theories*. That is, however, a somewhat loose usage.

Most of our approaches are theoretical only in the sense that many of their central tenets are still not fully supported by empirical evidence. A scientific theory is a way of organizing what is known about some phenomenon in the natural or empirical world in order to discover more of what is unknown. A theory, then, organizes what is known about a phenomenon to generate a set of *interrelated, plausible,* but *refutable* propositions about what is unknown regarding the phenomenon in question (Blocher, 1988).

Theories are tested through rigorous empirical research. Their central propositions are convertible to research hypotheses to be tested and possibly refuted through experimentation. The process of scientific inquiry through theory building and research is analogous to the process of diagnosis that we described in Chapter 5. Scientific inquiry like diagnosis is a continuous process of generating *tentative* hypotheses and subjecting them to rigorous *testing*.

Scientific theories are not really intended to be used directly as a basis for professional practice. Theories are, rather, intended to generate research that, in turn, produces a firm body of *knowledge* upon which we can base professional practice as we intervene in the lives of clients and client systems.

What we call counseling theories have tended to proliferate rather than converge over the years precisely because they are not really theories. Most of what we call counseling theories are, in reality, *recipes* or *prescriptions* about how to approach clients in various situations and conditions. Sometimes we have limited research evidence about what happens when the prescription is applied in practical situations. Too often, however, that evidence only indirectly addresses the basic tenets around which the so-called theory is organized (Borgen, 1992).

Counseling and psychotherapeutic approaches have tended to proliferate rather than be reduced and reconciled by the steady accumulation of research evidence. Adherents of particular approaches have tended to coalesce into competing camps, rather than to seek out common areas of inquiry and agree on appropriate rules of evidence and designs for experiments through which to reduce differences.

Our counseling theories may have heuristic value even though they do not meet the qualifications for formal scientific theories. A heuristic is a way of narrowing a search by suggesting important factors or variables to be considered. Many of our counseling theories make this kind of contribution much more effectively than they function as sources of formal research hypotheses.

If we view most of our counseling theories as *heuristics* that call attention to important factors and variables to be considered, we do not have to view such variables as the basis for fixed prescriptions, or catalogs of techniques to be applied blindly or in rigid ways. Instead, we can conceptualize variables drawn from quasi-theoretical approaches as possible "sources of gain" to be explored and exploited as they prove relevant to the problems encountered in professional practice. Such a view is the basis for eclectic and integrative formulations.

Counseling theories or approaches are sets of interrelated ideas. Like all ideas, they have a specific and limited range and focus of convenience. That is, they are more useful in certain situations than in others. Counseling theories can be likened to lights playing upon a many-faceted surface. Some of these spotlight and illuminate certain facets while leaving others in shadow or darkness.

Today, after many years of searching for panaceas and broad-spectrum prescriptions, we know that it is both fruitless and frustrating to ask questions like "Does counseling or therapy really work?" or even "Which is the best theory?" Instead, we have finally come to realize that we must ask more intelligent and sophisticated questions. We must ask *what* treatments with *which* clients in the hands of *what kinds* of counselors will produce which *specific results* under a given set of circumstances.

This leaves the formidable task of choosing treatments and evaluating theoretical approaches in the hands of the practicing counselor. Unfortunately, there simply is not a single, well-unified, and easily interpreted body of scientific knowledge about counseling or therapeutic interventions upon which the counselor can confidently base his or her professional practice. Instead, the counselor is faced with the challenge of building a personal theory, or point of view and carefully, systematically, and sometimes, even painfully, shaping, and sharpening it out of the facts and wisdom gradually acquired and accumulated during the course of his or her career.

The task of building such a personal theory and constantly shaping, modifying, and modernizing it is far from easy. It requires a sharpened sense of self-awareness so that the counselor's own knowledge and understanding of self can be an active ingredient. The challenge also requires a willingness to continue the process of professional development long past the period of formal graduate training. It means continued reading, reflection, and examination of one's professional practice. Most of all, it means an unflinching courage in examining closely and systematically both the successes and the failures that inevitably arise in professional practice. The process of professional development is discussed further in Chapter 15.

COUNSELING MODELS AND SOURCES OF GAIN

We can help the reader begin this deeply personal process by introducing a number of models that emphasize and build on one or more specific sources of gain. Each model has been researched to a greater or lesser extent. None, however, is presented as a final, ultimate, or even fully comprehensive approach to the practice of counseling and psychotherapy. They are to be viewed as heuristics, designed to help the counselor to begin and perhaps to focus a deeply personal search for answers that are relevant to his or her own development and professional practice.

THE RELATIONSHIP MODEL

The relationship model is an approach that has grown largely out of the work of Carl Rogers and his associates. The approach was first called *nondirective counseling* and later *Client-Centered Therapy.*

PHENOMENOLOGY

Client-Centered Therapy has its scientific and philosophical roots in phenomenological psychology. *Phenomenology* is a philosophical concept that holds that since the perceptions and experiences of each individual are essentially unique, each person exists at the center of his or her own idiosyncratic and largely private world of reality. This reality, then, is unique to the person and can be shared only in partial and imperfect ways. This view is similar to the constructivist position described earlier.

Phenomenology, when applied to perceptual psychology, held that all behavior was a function of the individual's *perceptual field* and is a function of the individual's perceptions at the moment of behaving. In other words, people tend to behave according to how the world *seems* to them, rather than according to some objective or consensually shared view of a public reality.

According to a phenomenological psychology, as perceptions change, so does behavior. When people perceive their world differently, they behave differently. When perceptions are confused, ambiguous, and vague, behavior is likely to be equally confused and uncertain. Where perceptions are clear and sharply defined, behavior is likely to be equally purposeful and goal-directed in terms of the person's own experienced needs and aspirations.

Since behavior is viewed as emanating from the perceptions of the individual, it seemed to follow that the goals of any effective approach to counseling must be aimed at helping the individual to perceive self and environment more clearly. To behave effectively, a person must perceive his or her world accurately and with as little distortion as possible. To some degree, Client-Centered Therapy acknowledges the existence of an objective world of reality that exists apart from the individual's perceptions of it. A major purpose of such therapy is to help the client perceive that world more accurately.

Perception, according to this view, is a function of several aspects of the individual. It is related to the health of the person, his or her needs and aspirations, and finally to concepts of self. Perceptions are seriously affected by threats to the individual. People tend to perceive what is *appropriate* and comfortable for them to perceive in terms of their self-concepts. Events and facts that are discrepant from, or inconsistent with, concepts of self may be distorted or denied to protect the existing self-structure. We should note that the term *perception* is used in similar ways to the term *cognitions* in the constructivist view.

The self-concept or self-structure is seen as the core around which all of the individual's perceptions are organized. When a person's self-concepts are seriously threatened, his or her perceptual field is narrowed and perceptions are distorted. Everything in the perceptual field except the threatening stimulus may be ignored, and relationships among events and aspects of the situation may be distorted as the individual reacts only to the perceived threats to the existing self-structure.

From this view, it follows that if counseling or therapy is to result in better and more accurate perceptions, it must *reduce threat,* and so remove the primary obstacle to perceiving more clearly and hence to more effective behavior. The most important aspects of threat that counselors must seek to reduce are threats to the self-concept.

In early formulations of Client-Centered Therapy and the psychological foundations that supported it, Rogers (1951) listed a number of crucial assumptions on which his approach was based. These assumptions are still basic to the relationship model, although, there have been a number of later modifications or refinements to his position.

ROGERIAN CONCEPTS

Several of the key propositions of Rogerian counseling are:

1. The individual exists in a continually changing world of experience of which he or she is the center. This world is not completely known to any other person. It is the individual's private world and constitutes reality for him or her.
2. Each individual responds to this private world as he or she experiences it. The individual reacts to what is perceived as true as though it were true.
3. Individuals react to their perceptual fields as organized wholes. They do not respond in purely intellectual terms, or in purely emotional terms, nor do they act mechanically.
4. Every human being has within one basic tendency or striving. He or she is constantly struggling to enhance and maintain the *self.* This inner growth force is fragile and weak, but, when freed, will

unerringly direct the person along paths of development that are desirable for both the individual and society. When an individual perceives choices clearly, he or she will always choose to *grow.*

5. People behave in purposeful, goal-directed ways, according to how they perceive the world and experience their needs. Behavior is rational and purposeful when seen from the perspective of the behaving person.

6. Emotion accompanies and generally facilitates goal-directed behavior. The intensity of emotion is related to the degree of investment or ego involvement of the individual.

RELATIONSHIP CONDITIONS

Out of these propositions Carl Rogers and his followers developed a tremendously influential approach to counseling and psychotherapy. Most of these propositions are, indeed, assumptions. They tend not to be easily tested or refutable propositions.

For our purposes, in examining sources of gain in therapeutic approaches, the Rogerian movement has clearly pointed to the relationship as the ultimate, if not only, crucial variable in counseling and therapy.

This notion of the overriding importance of the counseling relationship is derived logically from the basic assumptions listed. That logic proceeds like this: When persons are not threatened, they perceive clearly; when they perceive clearly, they *always* choose the right path; the purpose of counseling is to remove threat; the counselor removes threat by forming a very special and therapeutic relationship.

Early in the development of ideas about Client-Centered Therapy, Rogers (1957) articulated the fundamental importance of the counseling relationships in what he termed the "necessary and sufficient condition for therapeutic change." Basically, Rogers and a number of other researchers in the area of Client-Centered Therapy have endeavored to identify and describe a specific set of relationship conditions within counseling and psychotherapeutic processes that work to induce positive change in all sorts of clients under a wide variety of circumstances.

Originally Rogers (1951) postulated that progress in client movement or counseling outcome would be bound to occur if:

1. The counselor or therapist is *congruent* or *genuine* in the relationship;
2. The counselor experiences *unconditional positive regard* for the client; and

3. The counselor demonstrates *accurate, empathic understanding* of the client's own internal or frame of reference.

When the client experiences high levels of these conditions in the counseling relationship, while feeling vulnerable or anxious, the conditions will reduce threat, help to clarify perceptions, releasing the client's own creative growth forces and so lead to positive outcomes.

Over the years as Client-Centered Therapy has been influenced by related ideas from other fields, the list of facilitative relationship conditions has to some extent been lengthened and amended. Carkhuff (1969) listed six basic relationship conditions that should be established within a helping relationship: (1) empathy, (2) respect, (3) concreteness, (4) genuineness and self-disclosure, (5) confrontation, and (6) immediacy.

Probably the most important change that has marked the development of the client-centered approach has been the more direct active and even confrontive role assigned to the counselor in the more recent formulations.

Originally, at least as the approach was widely interpreted, the nondirective therapist assumed a rather passive, almost reactive role, serving as a sort of sounding board or mirror through which the client came to express a deeper and wider range of feelings. Techniques of restatement of content, reflection of feelings, and clarification of meaning tended to constitute a very high percentage of the nondirective counselor's responses. Self-disclosure on the part of the counselor, or confrontations between the counselor and client were considered unproductive.

As Client-Centered Therapy was influenced by existential psychology, the role of the therapist and the nature of the therapeutic relationships was broadened. Existential psychotherapy was an outgrowth of the existential viewpoint in philosophy. The existential view of the human condition is that people respond to and are influenced primarily by their *own* direct and immediate experiences. Elaborate philosophical or ideological frameworks through which to analyze or "philosophize" about the nature and meaning of life are considered less relevant to human beings than is their *own* personal and immediate experience. The existential philosopher Kierkegaard is said to have remarked that people who construct such complex philosophical systems are like a man who builds a magnificent castle and then goes to live in the adjoining barn.

To the extent that theories of personality or of psychotherapy and the world view that accompanies them are similar to such systems, they are seen to have little relevance or meaning to troubled clients. The kind of therapeutic intervention that is seen to be helpful is what is called an *encounter.* The purpose of therapy in the existential sense is to help clients reestablish the unity and intactness of their experiencing and so help them to find full meaning in their lives. This is most likely to occur when they engage in a deeply genuine and spontaneous "encounter" with the therapist.

In such an encounter, the therapist does not supply ready-made meaning to the client through interpretation, but rather helps the client to abandon facades and formulas in dealing with others and instead take responsibility for choosing the direction for the course of therapy, and finally for regaining contact with his or her own experiences.

The emphasis in this kind of therapeutic relationship is on the ability of the therapist to be *genuine, spontaneous,* and at times, *confrontive.* Responding to the client in a deeply empathic and caring way is important, but in being authentic, the therapist may well confront the client with his or her own perception and feelings about the client and their relationship. At such times, therapist and client may talk candidly and extensively about the "here and now" aspects of their relationship or encounter.

As ideas from existential psychology blended with those drawn from earlier formulations of Client-Centered Therapy, the final emerging view of the therapist shifted from an essentially passive and reflective, almost shadowy presence, toward an active, dynamic, and sometimes confrontive posture. In terms of the relationship as a source of gain, this emphasis shifted to include the importance of communicating with clients in *deeply honest* as well as in caring and empathic ways.

RESEARCH ON COUNSELING RELATIONSHIPS

A great deal of research on relationship conditions has emerged from what we now call humanistic psychology. This research is not without methodological problems. Elements as fragile and ephemeral as empathy, authenticity, and positive regard are very difficult to operationalize, and even harder to control for experimentation (Duan & Hill, 1996).

Reviews (Lambert & Bergin, 1994) of the effects of relationship conditions on counseling outcomes have been much less convincing in terms of empirical supports than were some of the earlier assessments. We have certainly been unable to find firm research evidence to support Rogers' original position that the counseling relationship constitutes the necessary *and sufficient* ingredient for all kinds of counseling or therapeutic gains or outcomes. Some more recent research does support the effectiveness of modified experiential therapies (Greenberg, Elliot, & Lietaer, 1994).

Even though little research evidence exists to support the notion that the relationship as a source of gain in counseling operates as a panacea, some research evidence (Sexton & Whiston, 1994) does link the kinds of relationship conditions discussed with client improvement in a variety of clinical situations. Essentially, this research suggests that high levels of basic relationship conditions tend to be associated with client improvement on a variety of criteria, while low levels of the conditions were associated with deterioration in client functioning.

Quite apart from research evidence, it is obviously very difficult to ignore or oppose basic conditions within any kind of relationship that are described by labels such as empathy, respect, concreteness, genuineness, confrontation, and immediacy.

Many of these elements have been prized in interpersonal relationships long before Carl Rogers sought to identify them as crucial variables in counseling and psychotherapy. In considering relationship factors as sources of gain in psychotherapy, however, we must do more than give a nod of approval and commendation to a set of labels.

According to Rogers' theoretical formulation the crucial factor is that the client *experience* high levels of the core conditions. It is not easy to specify a set of therapist behaviors that we can guarantee will be experienced by every client as empathic, genuine, respectful, and so forth.

Despite the difficulty in defining the elements of therapeutic relationships and the even greater difficulty in researching and specifying its effects, the concept remains at the heart of the psychotherapeutic enterprise. More recent formulations of relationship phenomena conceptualize it as the *therapeutic bond*. These approaches define the therapeutic relationship or bond more broadly than in earlier formulations. Gelso and Carter (1994) conceptualized three basic relationship elements: the *real relationship* that includes the core conditions described earlier, the *working alliance* that is essentially the therapeutic contract or joint commitment within which therapist and client work toward mutually defined goals, and finally the *transference relationship* that includes irrational elements in the client's perception of the therapist. *Transference* is essentially a psychoanalytic concept that as defined today holds that long-term, emotionally charged relationships including therapeutic ones are inevitably colored by irrational elements drawn from previous experiences that may distort or color them.

Hill (1994) includes four basic elements in the therapeutic relationship: (1) the feelings and attitudes the participants have toward each other; (2) the conditions contributed to the relationship by the therapist including empathy, warmth, expertness, attractiveness, and trustworthiness; (3) the client's perceptions, previous experiences, reaction, and intentions; and (4) the *interactions* between the two including the working alliance.

This very comprehensive definition includes concepts such as the core conditions drawn from Client-Centered Therapy, concepts like expertness, trustworthiness, and attractiveness drawn from social influence therapy and the concepts of working alliance and transference drawn from psychoanalytic theory (Bordin, 1994). It is essentially an *eclectic definition*.

What seems abundantly clear from these contemporary views is that relationship-building within counseling and therapy cannot be reduced to a simple set of techniques or formulae. The exact nature of the therapeutic bond or relationship will inevitably vary across therapists, clients, cases, and situations. Each therapist in each case is faced with the task of helping to build a unique, nonrecurring relationship with each new client.

COGNITIVE MODELS

Since Breuer and Freud developed the talking cure in Vienna over a century ago, one of the major sources of gain for virtually all types of psychotherapy has been derived from changes in the client's ways of thinking about self. The process of developing new ways of thinking was originally called *insight*. Today, insight is considered a sudden flash of discovery that results in a relatively major change in understanding. Clients may speak of it as "a light going on," or "all the pieces suddenly fitting together" (Elliott et al., 1994). In psychoanalytic terms, insight usually meant the recall of formerly repressed material or the role of defense mechanisms in protecting from anxiety.

In modern cognitive therapies, many kind of cognitive changes are considered evidence of therapeutic success or progress. Clients may begin to accept the ownership of problems or shift from a blaming to a problem-solving focus. They may recognize that certain beliefs or assumptions about self or others are irrational or patently inaccurate.

All of the cognitive approaches are based upon the belief that the greatest resource available to people in dealing with problems or challenges lies in their ability, or potential ability, to *think*, clearly, and rationally about themselves and their situation. These approaches also recognize the fact that for a variety of reasons human beings frequently have great difficulty in doing that.

Cognitive therapists generally focus on the client's thinking processes and serve as a kind of teacher who helps the client to build sets of logical and rational conclusions and generalizations around their experiences and circumstances (Beck, 1976).

Often cognitive therapists help the client to engage in logical problem solving or decision making, and to test out new approaches based upon new sets of assumptions about themselves and others.

Generally, cognitive therapies assume that thinking, feeling, and acting are closely interrelated aspects of human functioning. When people change the ways in which they *think,* corresponding changes occur in their emotional life and in their behavior. The goal is to help clients become *aware* of self and the world, *think clearly* about both, and in the process gain greater control over *feelings* and *behavior.*

BEHAVIORAL AND COGNITIVE-BEHAVIORAL MODELS

Behaviorism as a movement in American psychology was a reaction against a science that dealt almost exclusively in untestable inferences about what supposedly went on *inside* human beings. Behaviorism is a point of view in the philosophy of science that maintains that psychology as a science must deal with *observables,* that is, data that are directly and publicly available to the observer. These actions or movements are *behavior,* hence the name behaviorism. For many years, behavioral research was confined primarily to the laboratory and focused on experimental studies with animals.

For about the past 30 years, a great deal of interest and inquiry in the behavioral mode has focused on research and clinical applications with humans. Three principal lines of behavioral research have been applied to psychotherapy. Operant conditioning, or what is called the experimental analysis of behavior, classical conditioning, and social learning have all furnished bases for psychotherapeutic approaches.

OPERANT CONDITIONING

The operant approach to the study of behavior change was pioneered by B.F. Skinner. Operant research has demonstrated the fact that certain stimuli called *reinforcers,* increase the probability of responses that immediately precede the reinforcer. Laboratory studies done with rats and pigeons, for example, have demonstrated the ways in which the responses of an organism can be brought under the *control* of a reinforcing stimulus. Reinforcers used with animals are primarily food, but a reinforcer is defined by its effect on behavior not by its substance. The ways in which the stimulus is presented in relation to the organisms response is called the *contingency of reinforcement.*

Contingencies for reinforcement do not pertain only to lower organisms. Let us think for a moment of a gambler operating one or more slot machines in a casino. The gambler approaches a row of machines. Two of these have lighted dials, the third is unlit and hence is out of order. The gambler proceeds to play the lighted machines for several hours. In both practical and operant terms, his behavior has come under the control of the reinforcers, in this case by the coins delivered by slot machines.

We have not really explained or demonstrated much that is very new, original, or earth-shaking about human behavior. It is probable that in the ten thousand years or so of man's linguistic history, few neurologically intact human beings have failed to understand intuitively that much of human behavior is controlled or influenced by the administration of rewards and punishments. The *law of effect* is a pretty obvious statement of the operation of a familiar and easily understood phenomenon.

BEHAVIOR MODIFICATION

The application of reinforcement techniques or the experimental analysis of behavior to human problems and therapeutic or educational settings has been termed *behavior modification.* That specific term is no longer particularly useful in that the approach has spread to a wide range of settings and has been subsumed in a variety of other kinds of treatment. Behavior modification approaches have been used in hospitals, penal institutions, special education, and rehabilitation settings.

IMPLICATIONS OF THE OPERANT MODEL FOR PSYCHOTHERAPY

The central idea in the operant model is that much human behavior is under the control or influence of specific reinforcing stimuli operating in the environment. Behavior is thus seen to be maintained by its *consequences.*

When the principles of operant conditioning are applied as a source of gain in therapy it is necessary for the therapist to specify very clearly and explicitly the precise goals of treatment. The specific behaviors that therapist and client want to strengthen (increase in frequency) or weaken (decrease in frequency) must be carefully specified along with the precise settings and situations in which the behavior change is intended to occur.

When using operant principles as a source of gain, the therapist is thus forced to think very carefully about goals before beginning treatment.

Indeed, one of the real strengths of behavioral approaches lies in their emphasis on setting goals and objectives.

It is often not easy to go from a client's statement of a presenting problem, or a vague description of needs or difficulties, to a specific set of target behaviors that should be increased or decreased in frequency.

Once this difficult task has been accomplished, however, it may be equally hard to select a set of reinforcers that will effectively influence the frequency of the target behaviors. Outside of residential settings, it may also be difficult for the counselor to establish and administer a schedule of reinforcement for the client. Many times counselors invoke the cooperation of parents, spouses, teachers, friends, or roommates in assisting with establishment of a behavioral counseling program.

Self-Management Programs

One of the most remarkable and serendipitous findings to come out of operant research with human beings, has been the fact that to a considerable degree people can use operant principles to obtain greater control over their *own* behavior. This approach does, to some extent at least, raise the question of whether in such programs the source of gain is really in the external reinforcement, or involves cognitive mediation. The practical advantages of self-management programs are so obvious, however, that they have been widely and successfully employed in a variety of situations.

Like other operant-based treatments, self-management involves the specification of behavior goals, the identification of antecedent cues and environmental consequences, and the implementation of an action plan that alters these antecedents and consequences. In a self-management situation, however, the action plan is administered directly by the client. The client generally defines the behavioral contingency, selects one or more reinforcers, and then administers his or her own schedule of reinforcement.

In self-management programs, clients are often taught to record target behaviors carefully using counters such as those used in keeping golf scores. Daily totals of the target behaviors are then graphed so that progress can be monitored. In such a program, for example, a client may decide to attempt to improve study habits and academic performance by rewarding himself or herself for completing homework assignments. Such assignments may be defined behaviorally in terms of number of pages read, or trial tests over material passed, and so on. The client chooses a small reward such as taking a coffee break or making a phone call to a friend as a reinforcer contingent upon completion of the target behavioral task. Progress is carefully monitored and reinforcers or contingencies changed to involve larger and larger target behaviors.

It is often found that the simple act of recording and monitoring behaviors is helpful in inducing behavior change. Self-management strategies may also be framed in terms of changing environments. A client who wishes to quit smoking may make a list of specific places to be avoided. These are places where the antecedent cues that precede "lighting up" are prevalent.

On the whole, self-management strategies involving self-reward or punishment, or environmental strategies, have become important adjuncts and aids to counseling treatments.

OBJECTIONS TO OPERANT APPROACHES

Perhaps because much of the basic research on which operant treatments are based came from animal laboratories rather than from clinical settings, many people, both professionals and others, have very negative views about their employment with human beings. The term *behavior modifier* seems to conjure up images of the white-coated, cold, distant, and uncaring technician who manipulates people with no more warmth than might be shown in removing a rat from a Skinner box.

Such images and the feelings they connote are nonsense. The effective behavior therapist *is* quite concerned with relating to clients in warm, empathic, and caring ways. To use operant principles effectively, the therapist must understand the client and the client's environment very thoroughly. If the therapist wishes to use social reinforcers such as praise, encouragement, or support, then developing a warm and close relationship with the client is essential.

Similarly, many people have an equally unrealistic picture of the behavioral counselor as a kind of subtle, Machiavellian manipulator who manages to control people without their awareness or knowledge. Again, on the contrary, the behavior modifier who did not utilize the awareness and cooperation of clients in every way possible would simply be *inefficient.*

The experimental literature is divided on the *necessity* of subject awareness and cooperation if behavior change is to occur. Indeed, it is exceedingly difficult experimentally ever to be sure that a subject is *not* aware of target behaviors and reinforcement contingencies. There is ample evidence to show however, that behavior acquisition is very much enhanced when subjects or clients *are* aware of contingencies and *decide to cooperate.*

As we saw in self-management situations, clients, themselves, learn to specify contingencies and administer reinforcements. For the most part, the use of operant principles as a source of gain in psychotherapy simply consists of helping a client to specify clearly and carefully a set of behaviors that are goal oriented. The therapist then assists the client to pair these behaviors with a set of rewards that the client has helped to choose, under conditions that will enhance the efficiency and effectiveness of the new learning (Emmelkamp, 1994).

THE CLASSICAL CONDITIONING MODEL

Another aspect of behavioral approaches involves the use of the so-called classical conditioning paradigm pioneered by Ivan Pavlov. He was concerned with responses that are directly triggered by some stimulus event occurring in the environment. Emotional responses tend to be of this kind. A pedestrian narrowly missed by a speeding taxi experiences a strong fear response. The individual's breathing, pulse rate, perspiration, and other smooth muscle responses are quickly and powerfully affected.

Research has shown that many of these kinds of responses and the ways in which they are interpreted can be changed through learning. They can be weakened or "extinguished" through appropriate recall or re-exposure. A variety of treatment approaches have been used particularly with cases of irrational fears or phobias, or with problems of anxiety.

To some extent, conditioning phenomena occur naturally in many therapeutic situations. When the therapist provides a secure and comfortable environment in which clients can talk about frightening or painful situations, that alone may help alleviate some of the fear or pain associated with the traumatic events. Many times, however, therapists attempt to use classical conditioning principles in more systematic and intensive ways. Such techniques are widely used and have been found to be effective especially in the treatment of irrational fears or phobias (Deffenbacher, 1992).

Treatments involving *systematic desensitization, implosive therapies,* and other arrangements have been widely used. In systematic desensitization, a gradually more intense exposure to a threatening stimulus, or the recall of a threatening situation is arranged while the client is in a relaxed state. Over time the client is able to tolerate more and more intense exposure or recall while remaining relaxed.

In *implosive* therapy or flooding, the exposure is sudden and intense and the client emotional discomfort is allowed to build. After such exposure and discomfort, the intensity of the reaction tends to fade.

The crucial variable in all of these treatments for fear or anxiety is continued contact with the offending stimuli (Lambert & Hill, 1994). Both systematic desensitization and flooding have achieved successful results in a variety of situations (Emmelkamp, 1994).

Various kinds of conditioning procedures have been used successfully to help victims of rape or assault, with cases of post-traumatic stress disorders, with generalized anxiety and panic management. Obsessive-compulsive behavior has also been helped by a combination of in vivo exposure and prevention of compulsive responses (Emmelkamp, 1994).

THE SOCIAL LEARNING MODEL

Another behavioral model that offers a potential source of gain in counseling has been derived from research on social learning. By social learning we mean, essentially, learning through contact with or observation of others.

People obviously learn from each other in a variety of informal ways. Much of the research in social learning has focused upon the effects of modeling specific behaviors in the presence of a learner, who then initiates the modeled behavior. Modeling effects can occur under a variety of conditions and circumstances.

A subject can follow the example of a leader, and then be rewarded for an accurate performance. Sometimes the observer watches the performance and sees the model being rewarded. This vicarious reinforcement may then influence the observer to imitate the modeled behavior. Sometimes two people are involved in a shared or cooperative task and learn by observing each other. At other times, the subject simply observes the model and then attempts the new behavior without any reward being administered.

Social learning is a very prevalent form of learning. Much of the human socialization process is accomplished through modeling procedures. Children constantly learn new behavior by observing role models and trying out the observed behavior. Modeling is also very widely used in advertising and propaganda campaigns in which observers are expected to imitate the behaviors of various celebrities and high prestige models.

In many complex learning situations, modeling is used to show a complete performance that would be difficult to communicate accurately in any other way.

Research has shown that a number of specific factors tend to influence the success of modeling procedures in effecting behavior change in the subject or observer. These factors include:

1. *Characteristics of the model.* Generally, models who are at least moderately similar to the subject are more effective. Models who are high in status or prestige in the eyes of the subject are also more effective. Finally, models who are seen to be rewarded for their performance are still more effective.

2. *Characteristics of the performance.* In many situations, coping performances in which the model overcomes some of the common problems
associated with a beginner are more effective than are mastery performances which reflect a very high level of ease, skill, or expertise.

3. *The orientation of the subject.* Subjects are more likely to attempt the
modeled performance and if they have a sense of self-efficacy, or in
other words, confidence in their ability, eventually to learn the modeled behavior.

APPLICATIONS OF SOCIAL LEARNING

Social learning principles have been utilized as sources of gain in psychotherapy in a variety of ways. In some situations, the therapist is a
model for the client. When counselors model honesty, trust, confidence,
and willingness to self-disclose in the counseling situation, itself, these
behaviors may be, in turn, attempted by the client. In group counseling
situations, the group leader often models a variety of helping or leading
behaviors in the beginning of the series of meetings that then are gradually adopted by other members through social learning processes. Sometimes, especially in group approaches, clients are given precounseling
orientations that involve watching videotaped or filmed simulations of
group sessions.

Many times, however, therapists are not particularly good models because of age or sex differences or other dissimilarities with clients. In such
situations, counselors may utilize others who make better role models.
Again group sessions in which members vary in terms of mastery or coping skills in regard to relevant skills or competence may provide a variety
of modeling opportunities. Sometimes special film presentations can utilize high status models to demonstrate desirable behaviors.

Other social learning approaches use behavioral rehearsals or role plays
to learn specific responses, to discriminate between appropriate and inappropriate strategies or techniques, to increase self-awareness, and to
develop clients' confidence in performing in difficult situations. Research
on work with children and adolescents has shown modeling procedures
to produce changes in behavior (Kazdin, 1994).

More recent research and theorizing about the social learning approach
has stressed the importance of the client's feeling of *self-efficacy* in regard
to performing the target behavior. Client attitudes of "agency" or power
and responsibility are considered crucial (Bandura, 1982). The more recent findings regarding the relationship between client attitudes and

thoughts and social learning have led to a merger of cognitive and behavioral models that is called *cognitive behavioral therapy.*

We have briefly examined a variety of behavioral principles that may be utilized as sources of gain in counseling. There is nothing particularly new or revolutionary about any of these principles. They have probably been intuitively understood by most human beings for many hundreds of years.

The teacher who affixes a gold star to the spelling paper of a proud second grader has a working understanding of the law of effect. The ubiquitous and banal commercial on television that features the football hero sipping beer surrounded by admiring followers and a bevy of eager beauties, demonstrates much of what there is to know about modeling techniques. The politician practicing an acceptance speech in front of the mirror, or with a tape recorder, understands behavioral rehearsal. The race driver who gets behind the wheel immediately after a near crash, and the young woman who puts a drop of her favorite perfume on a note to her wavering lover, both understand the practical applications of classical conditioning principles.

Behavioral principles and their intelligent application in counseling are neither menacing nor magical. They offer valuable sources of gain to the counselor and can be incorporated into professional practice without compromising any commitments to human freedom and dignity. They can and should be utilized with the full awareness and cooperation of clients.

Behavioral approaches do not necessarily detract from the establishment of warm empathic, caring relationships, and, in fact, are undoubtedly most effective when used in conjunction with such relationships. Clearly behavioral principles can be used to advance humanistic goals.

COGNITIVE-BEHAVIORAL APPROACHES

Many of the differences between the so-called counseling theories are largely cosmetic, superficial, and semantic. If, for example, we substituted the word cognition for perception in the phenomenological approach so dear to humanistic psychology, much of the difference between it and several of the cognitive approaches would be vastly narrowed. In practical terms, it is virtually impossible to distinguish between a raw percept and a cognition. As soon as we try to communicate or comprehend perceptions, for example, they are transformed into cognitions.

Similarly, the various behavioral approaches generally prefer to ignore the role of cognitive mediation in human clients even though it is significant in virtually every aspect of learning.

One of the reasons that it is more useful to think of these counseling approaches as general models that emphasize and explicate a particular source of gain, rather than as discrete and formal theories, is this kind of semantic overlap. Too often psychological theories have tended to magnify differences and to mask similarities by using obscure or esoteric labels for familiar ideas and concepts.

In recent years, we have finally achieved a sort of breakthrough in the area of counseling theories in the sense of a genuine attempt to combine and integrate different approaches. This relatively new effort at achieving some kind of unity within the field is termed *cognitive-behavioral counseling*. Cognitive-behavioral theorists have attempted to use techniques and approaches drawn from cognitive psychology and to utilize them within what is generally a behavioristic language and conceptual framework (Hollon & Beck, 1994).

Cognitive-behavioral counselors or therapists generally accept the importance of cognitions or "self-talk" in both triggering emotional responses and in intervening between environmental stimuli and behavioral responses. Sometimes these efforts at integration strain the behavioral data language. Cognitive-behavioral writers frequently use terms such as *covert behaviors* that have no real meaning in strictly behavioral terms.

It should be recognized that cognitive-behavioral approaches, to the extent that they depend upon explanatory constructs about what goes on inside clients, are operating on the basis of inferences just as much as do relationship-oriented, psychoanalytic, or purely cognitive frameworks.

The use of inferences in any of these models may be perfectly appropriate and useful, as long as the user is aware of the limitations and pitfalls associated with untested inferences or untestable assumptions. When behavioral language is used loosely, it has the ability to lull the user into believing that he or she is really dealing with objective information, or observable data.

A number of specific cognitive behavioral counseling treatments have been developed. One of these is termed *stress inoculation*. The importance of helping clients to manage stress in their environments is discussed further in Chapter 13.

Stress inoculation training combines cognitive and behavioral principles to allow a client to deal with threatening stimuli or situations in a sequence of graduated steps. During the first phase, the counselor provides a general conceptual framework to the client that is couched in terms he or she will be able to understand. This framework helps the client understand the nature of reactions to stressful situations.

The logic of the stress inoculation program is then explained in terms of helping the client to deal both with heightened physiological reactions, and in helping to avoid thoughts or self-statements that would be counter-productive in simply increasing emotional upset.

The client is taught to think about four aspects of a stress situation. These include: (1) preparing for a stressor, (2) managing the stress situation, (3) the possibility of being overwhelmed by the stressor, and (4) reinforcing oneself for having coped successfully with stress.

In the next phase of the training program, the client is taught a variety of specific behavioral techniques and cognitive strategies. These may include the use of progressive relaxation, avoidance of catastrophizing, and refraining from making negative self-statements. The client is helped to develop examples of positive self-statements that can be used in the stressful situation.

In the final phase of training the client practices the techniques learned in simulated stress situations, or tries them out in a series of graduated, real situations that approach the intensity level of the anticipated stressful experience.

Stress inoculation training represents a practical example of an approach to treatment that systematically endeavors to draw upon multiple sources of gain.

THE SOCIAL INFLUENCE MODEL

One of the relatively recent approaches to counseling and psychotherapy is the *social influence model.* This approach has been explicated and researched by Stanley Strong and his associates (Strong, 1997). In a sense, the social influence model cuts across the relationship, behavioral, and cognitive approaches in that it deals directly with a phenomenon that is of central concern in each of the other models.

Research in social psychology has shown for many years that people tend to be influenced in their judgments, opinions, and behaviors by the influence attempts or persuasive appeals of others. Writers such as Jerome Frank (1961) and Strong and Claiborn (1982) have pointed out that this phenomenon is relevant, if not central, to the process of counseling.

They see the counseling process as a social situation in which one person, the counselor, seeks to exert influence on the behavior of the second person, the client, in a variety of ways. These influence attempts may be directed at either the final outcomes of counseling such as decisions or commitments made by the client, or may be directed to obtaining client cooperation in aspects of the counseling process, itself, such as self-disclosure, homework assignments, acceptance of responsibility, or tryouts of new behaviors.

Research on social influence has focused on several factors that are related to the effectiveness of a social influence attempt: (1) the perceived attractiveness of the influencer, (2) the perceived expertness of the influencer, (3) the perceived trustworthiness of the influencing person, (4) the influencer's legitimate status, and (5) the influencer's control of resources.

Adherents of this approach maintain that since the counseling situation is one that inevitably involves social influence, it is incumbent upon the counselor to learn to recognize and maximize his or her social power on behalf of professional goals. This social intractionist view of counseling has led to a large number of research studies that have attempted to identify influence factors and study their effects on counseling process and outcome. Much of this research has been done in counseling analogue situations that attempt to simulate counseling dynamics in the laboratory, rather than to observe them in field settings. Most of the studies have also dealt with initial interview situations rather than sustained counseling relationships.

Generally (Corrigan, Dell, Lewis, & Schmidt, 1980) this research supports the view that variations in perceived counselor characteristics do affect client responses to counselor influence attempts. Exactly how this occurs, or the nature of its effects on counseling outcomes in the natural environment, is not entirely clear (P.P. Heppner & Claiborn, 1989).

Counselor credibility in terms of trustworthiness, expertness, attractiveness, and legitimate status are concerns to professional counselors across all theoretical persuasions. Beyond behaving in a professional and ethical manner, operating within the limitations of one's professional training and experience, and communicating genuine concern and respect for the client, we are unable to specify a set of *counselor behaviors* that are guaranteed to enhance the counselor's influence.

Many counselors are genuinely concerned about attempts to maximize counselor power or influence in the counseling relationship. How does one influence a client, directly, to accept more responsibility for his or her own behavior, or to be more original, spontaneous, assertive, or autonomous?

Social influence phenomena are clearly relevant and inevitable aspects of counseling. They continue to pose knotty problems for the counselor at both philosophical and practical levels.

We have described a number of specific psychological models for the practice of counseling. Each specifies and emphasizes at least one dominant source of gain to support its claims for effectiveness. Each one also undoubtedly draws upon several other such sources, whether by intention or circumstance.

At this point, we can specify several sources of gain in counseling processes that research evidence indicates contribute to positive outcomes. These are *not* sharply discrete or mutually exclusive variables. None has been shown to operate in isolation from other sources of gain, or in the total absence of a variety of nonspecific factors.

None of these variables is morally or philosophically objectionable or incompatible. As Truax (1966) showed many years ago, even Carl Rogers selectively reinforced some kinds of client responses, while not attending to others. We can point to six basic and fairly well-supported sources of gain, or behavioral change models, that can influence specific counseling outcomes. These are:

1. Relationship conditions involving characteristics such as warmth, empathy, genuineness, respect, positive regard, and immediacy.
2. Cognitive restructuring or "insight" including increased self-awareness, self-understanding, appropriate self-statements, and use of problem-solving and decision-making frameworks.
3. Direct acquisition of new behavior through careful specification of goals and the manipulation of reinforcement contingencies and schedules including self-management techniques.
4. Weakening of emotional arousal through relaxation, graduated or vicarious re-exposure.
5. Modeling of target behaviors by high similarity, high status, or well-rewarded models.
6. Social influence factors such as direct persuasion or use of suggestions from a credible source who is perceived as expert, attractive, and trustworthy.

None of these sources of gain is new, revolutionary, or magical. Together, they constitute the basic ingredients or raw materials with which the counselor works. The lack of comprehensive, fully tested, and carefully organized bodies of either scientific theory, or proven knowledge, means that to a very considerable extent the individual therapist must organize, integrate, apply, and evaluate these sources of gain within his or her own professional practice.

CHAPTER 7

Eclectic-Integrative
Therapies

No clinical theory has a monopoly on truth or utility; clinical
realities have come to demand a pluralistic, if not an integrative
perspective.

—Norcross and Arkowitz (1992)

FOR MOST of its history, the field of counseling and psychotherapy
has looked like an assemblage of facts, findings, and formulations
frantically searching for a unified and coherent theory or framework. There has been no shortage of theories waiting in the wings to vie
for the dubious title of "theory of the year." New philosophies, world
views, ideologies, and prescriptions have burst upon the scene with all of
the subtlety and humility of a Fourth of July fireworks display. Most have
lasted about as long.

More than four hundred distinct, if not distinctive, separate therapies
have been identified (Karasu, 1986). There are literally more brands of
psychotherapy actively competing for the counselor's attention and commitment than there are remedies for the common cold. With so many
brand names, no one can recognize, let alone remember all of the competitors (London, 1988). Practitioners have gradually wearied of being
first dazzled then disappointed as each new promised panacea has collided with the sobering realities of rigorous research and the exigencies
of full-scale professional practice. The cries of Eureka! have been heard all
too frequently throughout the land.

The search for more flexible and credible approaches to counseling and
psychotherapy is by no means a new one. A half century ago Williamson

(1950) defined four basic intellectual tasks that are involved in the search for new approaches. Such a search should, in his view, attempt to reconcile conflicts and points of view. It should bring out into the open and examine critically unrecognized assumptions underlying current theories and practices. It should reveal commonality in different approaches and seek to weld them into a broader synthesis of disparate points of view. Finally, it should produce emerging values and emphases and problems to be explored.

Similarly, psychotherapy researchers such as Jerome Frank (1971) pointed out that results of therapy evaluation studies pointed consistently to the effects of nonspecific factors that cut across theoretical lines as those responsible for a major part of therapeutic effectiveness. Hobbs (1962) in a landmark paper coined the term *sources of gain* and questioned the role of insight as the sole source of therapeutic change. Shaffer and Shoben (1956) pointed to common factors in all approaches to psychotherapy. Carkhuff (1966) called for the development of "systematic eclectic" models that consciously capitalized on common factors and utilized specific sources of gain from a variety of theories. He cautioned that this must be done in a systematic rather than a haphazard way.

Studies done of the self-reported theoretical orientations of therapists (Garfield & Kurtz, 1977) showed that more than 20 years ago a majority of therapists considered themselves to be "eclectic." Watkins et al. (1986) in a study of counseling psychologists found that eclectic was the most frequently endorsed theoretical orientation. Norcross, Prochaska, and Farber (1993) found similar results among psychologists engaged in psychotherapy.

To a considerable extent, psychotherapy integration has been a response to the findings of outcome research and to the lack of strong evidence to support the existence of differential effectiveness of existing approaches. Along with these findings has come a growing consensus that no one approach is clinically adequate for *all* problems, clients, and situations (Norcross & Arkowitz, 1992). Despite the persistent demand by practitioners and researchers alike for systematic eclectic or integrative models, these have been slow in coming and even slower to be recognized. The search for grandiose and global "theories" and prescriptions has continued unabated until quite recently. It has been suggested somewhat facetiously that psychology's preoccupation with "grand designs" is due to "physics envy." In the case of counseling and psychotherapy, it has been a search for what promises to *explain* everything, rather than for what *works* with specific clients in specific situations. As Jerome Frank (1971) noted a quarter century ago, features that are shared by all approaches have been relatively neglected since little glory derives from showing that one's own specific method may really be indistinguishable from another in terms of its practical effects. Zeig (1985) described the theoretical biases of therapists this way:

> Actually all theories of therapy are adventures in extremism . . . I think it is most interesting how tenaciously theorists and students become committed to their own models. Probably it is twice as effective to have the courage of one's fantasies as to have the courage of one's convictions. (p. xxi)

Wolfe and Goldfried (1988) noted that the field of psychotherapy was then not ready for full scale integration of approaches, but rather should be concerned with breaking down barriers between therapeutic schools and orientations. Much of what holds back such a desegregation is social and political rather than scientific in nature.

Goldfried (1980) observed that the popularity of a therapy school is often a function of variables having nothing to do with the efficacy of its procedures. It often depends on the charisma, energy level, and longevity of the leader; and the spirit of the times.

At the present state of integration (or lack thereof in counseling and psychotherapy), it is most instructive to examine carefully a few of the eclectic/integrative models that have been recognized. There are undoubtedly many more such models developed by effective counselors that have never been published.

ECLECTIC-INTEGRATIVE
THERAPEUTIC FRAMEWORKS

Some 20 years ago Goldfried (1980) wrote that to be eclectic was to have a marginal professional identity. Clearly, that is no longer the case. Eclectic-integrative approaches and their proponents are visible though journals, professional associations, handbooks of research and practice, and a rapidly developing professional literature both in this country and abroad. The eclectic therapy movement has even been characterized as a "revolution" in mental health (Norcross & Arkowitz, 1992).

Approaches to systematic eclecticism and integration vary widely. Norcross and Arkowitz (1992) distinguished four quite different approaches: (1) theoretical integration; (2) the common factors approach; (3) technical eclecticism; and (4) the integration of psychotherapeutic theory with basic psychological theory and research.

The cognitive-behavioral model described in Chapter 6 was an early effort to meld therapeutic approaches at the level of theory, combining major emphases from cognitive therapies and behavior therapy into a new theoretical formulation. This rather reluctant marriage combines approaches that are based on largely incompatible scientific assumptions. It has however resulted in the creation of exciting new approaches to treatment albeit at the cost of fracturing the conceptual integrity of the underlying theories. The approach has been called "theory smashing" (London, 1986). Similar approaches to theoretical integration have been proposed by Wachtel (1997) and Prochaska and DiClemente (1984).

The return to basic psychological theory and research as the font of wisdom on which to base psychotherapeutic approaches has to some extent been the orientation of the social influence model also described in Chapter 6. Basic social psychological research on persuasion and social influence has been applied to the therapeutic situation by writers such as Jerome Frank (1961), Strong and Claiborn (1982), and Strong (1997).

In any systematic eclectic or integrative approach, two major tasks must be accomplished. The process or *rationale* for selecting the techniques or clinical strategies to be drawn from various other theories must be specified. Similarly, the therapeutic factors that are presumed to cut across theoretical frameworks must be identified. These tasks are the major challenges confronting *technical eclectic* and *common factors* approaches.

TECHNICAL ECLECTIC APPROACHES

LAZARUS' MULTIMODAL THERAPY

One of the first systematic eclectic approaches to psychotherapy to gain wide recognition was Multimodal Therapy developed by Arnold Lazarus (1976). To a considerable extent, *Multimodal Therapy* or *technical eclecticism* as it is sometimes called was an outgrowth of Lazarus' work as a more traditional behavior therapist.

The multimodal orientation goes beyond conventional behavior therapies by adding a set of distinctive assessment procedures and by dealing in great depth with factors such as imagery, cognitions, and interpersonal relationships and their interactive effects (Lazarus, 1995).

A basic premise of the multimodal approach is that clients are typically troubled by many kinds of specific concerns or problems, and that the many and varied sources of difficulty should be helped through an equally wide variety of specific therapeutic techniques. According to Lazarus' *Multimodal Therapy* is *not* a separate or unique *theory* about psychotherapy.

There is a distinct relationship between the rationale for multimodal therapy and the psychological theory of functionalism put forth early in the history of American psychology by William James and W.H. Burnham. Both viewed human behavior and experiencing as multidimensional and many layered. Essentially, all of these approaches viewed behavior, affect, and cognition as *interrelated* and *interactive* aspects of overall human personality functioning.

Lazarus began to evolve his ideas about psychotherapy while a student in South Africa. He was exposed to the Freudian and Rogerian approaches, but tended to reject them as unscientific and untestable. Lazarus helped to legitimize behavioral approaches to psychotherapy and claims credit for introducing the terms *behavior therapy* and *behavior therapist* into the literature (Eskapa, 1992).

After practicing as a behavior therapist, Lazarus became discontented with the kinds of results obtained with strictly behavioral techniques and began to explore the use of other techniques and approaches. So was born what he chose to call *Multimodal Therapy.* The approach is based on social learning theory and to a lesser extent on general systems theory. It draws upon other therapeutic models for specific *techniques* or *strategies,* not for a general therapeutic orientation or basic psychological theory.

The systematic emphasis in *Multimodal Therapy* is based on a way of conceptualizing and assessing various areas of client functioning and dysfunction. This assessment model is represented by the acronym BASIC ID. These letters stand for the following aspects of client functioning:

Behavior
Affect
Sensation
Imagery
Cognition
Interpersonal Relationships
Drugs/Biology

Therapy begins with a careful assessment of the client's functioning in each of these seven areas. Upon completing the initial assessment phase the therapist is in a position to develop a personalized and individualized approach to treatment plan with the client. This plan may draw upon techniques selected from a variety of other approaches tailored to the assessed needs of each individual client.

As Lazarus (1995) put it:

> Clinical effectiveness is predicated on the therapist's flexibility, versatility, and technical eclecticism. The technical eclectic uses procedures drawn from different sources without necessarily subscribing to the theories that spawned them. (p. 323)

Multimodal Therapy draws heavily from other systems of psychotherapy, especially behavior therapy, rational emotive therapy, and cognitive therapy. The most distinctive feature of *Multimodal Therapy* is the specific attention and focus given to the BASIC ID which is seen to be a comprehensive and coherent model of personality functioning.

The BASIC ID model is assumed to account for the full scope of human thinking, feeling, and acting. Virtually the whole range of human experience and reactions are seen to be understandable in terms of this framework. Individual personality styles are explained in terms of "firing orders," that is the particular sequences of imaging, feeling, thinking, or behaving occurring in various situations.

Contextual elements in the client's life such as cultural or social situations are recognized as realities to be considered, but the focus is clearly on the *internal* personality functioning of the client. Lazarus (1995) noted that regardless of an individual's background, detailed descriptions of behaviors, affective responses, sensory reactions, images, cognitions, interpersonal styles, and biological propensities will provide the principle ingredients of his or her psychological makeup.

Assessment using the BASIC ID framework is a *continuous* process in therapy and furnishes an ongoing guide for the therapist's approach and behavior. Therapists may adopt quite different patterns of relating across different clients, depending on their assessment of client expectations and personality characteristics. A therapist may attempt to be warm and personal with one client and relatively formal and detached with another. No particular style or type of therapeutic relationship is seen as desirable across all clients. Indeed, since the therapeutic approach is determined by the clinical assessment process, what Lazarus described as therapist "flexibility and versatility" might be viewed as role-playing ability.

Lazarus (1995) consistently plays down the importance of common factors and refers to attempts at integration of therapeutic approaches that end up with conglomerates of logically incompatible or contradictory ideas and assumptions as *multimuddle* therapies. He views relationship factors such as empathy, warmth, wit, and wisdom as elements to be taken for granted in the same way that the absence of tremors in a surgeon might be considered a given.

Despite the emphasis on continuous assessment and the comprehensiveness of the BASIC ID schema as a unifying framework, the precise selection and employment of techniques and therapeutic strategies seems to be heavily a function of clinical judgment based on the therapist's *interpretation* of formal assessment results and clinical impressions. The clinician evolves a therapeutic strategy or *process model* for each individual client.

To the extent that treatment focuses directly on the elements of the BASIC ID model, techniques are drawn from other approaches in a rather straightforward and logical manner.

When the therapist works to change *behavior,* the first item in the BASIC ID checklist, approaches drawn from traditional behavior therapy such as *counterconditioning, flooding, positive or negative reinforcement,* or *punishment* are employed.

Changes in affect are dealt with through *abreaction* or helping the client to recount or re-live painful emotions in a secure and comforting setting. At times owning and accepting feelings that were outside of the client's awareness is a process goal.

Sensation may be dealt with by providing *tension release* through the use of biofeedback, relaxation techniques, or exercise.

Imagery is worked with in helping a client to visualize self-control or achievement in problematic situations, or to change self-images after achieving success in coping.

Cognition is changed through conventional cognitive therapeutic techniques of challenging illogical conclusions, generalizations, or irrational expectations.

Interpersonal relationships or behaviors are often worked with through social learning techniques with the therapist as role model during role reversal exercises or behavioral rehearsal. Relationships are analyzed to examine unhealthy or unproductive stances or alliances.

Drugs/biological factors are attended to by urging physical examinations, prescribing dietary or exercise programs, helping with withdrawal from substance abuse, and prescribing psychotropic medications. The latter can be done only in medical settings or with referrals.

Evaluation of therapy is accomplished by setting and monitoring goals in each of the relevant BASIC ID areas. Lazarus claims a 75% success rate with very low relapse rates on follow-up. A complete course of Multimodal Therapy often takes a full year with an average of about 50 weekly one-hour sessions.

BEUTLER'S SYSTEMATIC ECLECTIC PSYCHOTHERAPY

Larry Beutler's model of eclectic therapy is simply termed systematic eclectic therapy (sep). This approach was developed out of a careful review of comparative psychotherapy studies. According to Beutler and Consoli (1992), an eclectic therapy must address three basic defining rules or principles. First, most of the well-defined approaches to psychotherapy must be viewed as potentially helpful to some clients. Second, an eclectic model must assume that worthwhile therapeutic approaches can be successfully implemented *independently* of their originating theories. This is the basic assumption of technical eclecticism. Finally, the specific eclectic approach must operate from a theory of change that provides a clear basis for and gives credence to a variety of technical procedures, that is the systematic aspect of the approach.

Systematic eclectic therapy approaches these problems by addressing the concept of therapist-client compatibility, essentially the personal characteristics of both therapists and clients that will best combine to allow for the formation of a therapeutic bond.

In approaching this problem, sep draws on social influence theory. Therapy is assumed to represent a social influence situation in which one member, the therapist, draws on personal life experiences to develop an explanatory philosophy or world view that is then taught to the second member, the identified client. In this view, one theory or philosophy of life is considered as "true" as another. The value of the philosophy rests more on its believability and usefulness than on its truth. This view of the nature of psychotherapy is by no means new or original to Beutler. Shoben (1962) and Hobbs (1961) articulated this view of counseling theories, while Frank (1971) conceptualized therapy as an exercise in social influence or persuasion. As we saw earlier, this is also the essence of Strong's (1997) approach.

In general, sep advocates a rough matching of therapist-client pairing on demographic and background variables where this is feasible and points to research that suggests that at least moderate perceived similarity facilitates progress in relationship development early on in therapy.

CRITERIA FOR SELECTION AND APPLICATION

Most of the rationale for selecting and applying techniques or procedures is based on an assessment of client characteristics. Four basic sets of client dimensions are emphasized: *problem severity, problem complexity, reactance level,* and *coping style.*

Problem severity is a concept used to refer to the ways in which the client's existing coping behaviors have or have not been able to maintain anxiety and distress within manageable limits. Severity is conceptualized as a continuum, ranging in extremes from mild expressions of distress to totally incapacitating symptoms. This concept is very similar to the "levels of human effectiveness" model discussed in Chapter 5. Severity is indicated both by level of emotional arousal or distress, and by impairment in the client's capacity to function in meeting the social, occupational, and interpersonal demands of daily life, that is the client's principal roles.

Problem complexity refers to the degree to which client dysfunctioning is pervasive across principal roles or areas of life space. Such pervasive dysfunctions are symbolized by recurrent themes or patterns of behavior that recur over time and intrude into a wide range of social roles, settings, and situations.

Beutler and Consoli (1992) state that the concept of problem severity captures the acute, intense, situation-specific aspects of the patient's difficulties that require immediate attention, while problem complexity addresses the enduring, less situation-specific characteristics of the patient's complaints—those that require long-term attention.

The concept of *reactance level* is drawn from research on persuasion. It essentially refers to the amount of opposition an individual exerts against external suggestions, demands or other influence attempts. The concept is very similar to the concept of resistance, although reactance may include rational as well as irrational responses to influence attempts and may be evoked by suggestions or advice as well as by interpretations about the client's symptoms or reactions.

Coping styles have been discussed in Chapter 5. The sep approach recognizes four such styles that are considered important variables in designing therapeutic approaches: *internalizing, externalizing, repressive,* and *cyclic.* The internalizing and externalizing styles are defined by the assignment of blame or responsibility for difficulties on self or others. The repressive style is based on ignoring or denying crucial factors in a problematic situation. Cyclic styles are characterized by instability and rapid changes in coping behaviors.

Selection of Techniques

The combination of client characteristics and problem categories constitutes a sort of mini personality theory with which to match techniques drawn from other approaches to the individual case and client. Since the characteristics and problem categories interact with each other the matching process is based largely on complex clinical judgments. Further, as clients change and progress in therapy the matching process must be continuously revised.

In a very general way when dealing with complex and pervasive problems, insight-oriented approaches tend to be utilized. Severe problems are dealt with by establishing sequences of intermediate objectives and utilizing behavioral or directive techniques such as direct instruction or advice.

When dealing with internalizing coping styles, procedures are used that facilitate emotional arousal and awareness. Procedures that facilitate uncovering and insight are used with repressive coping styles, while procedures that facilitate cognitive control and focusing are used with cyclic styles. Externalizing coping styles are met with behavior change procedures. The strength of influence attempts is matched to the level of reactance or resistance observed in a client.

In general, procedures are chosen that help clients to be more flexible and effective in coping, and which preserve the therapeutic bond between therapist and client.

Use of Common Factors

Beutler and his colleagues do not disdain common factors such as relationship enhancement techniques as does Lazarus. Relationship enhancement and maintenance are seen as crucial to the social influence process. The philosophic orientation to which the therapist is committed is seen as part of the therapist personality functioning and is seen to occur independently of the specific techniques selected and applied.

Systematic Eclectic Therapy in the Beutler model typically requires about 20 sessions and might qualify as brief therapy compared with other traditional therapies.

THEORETICAL INTEGRATION

Prochaska and DiClemente: The Transtheoretical Approach

An approach to psychotherapy integration is found in the *transtheoretical* approach articulated by Prochaska and DiClemente (1984; Prochaska, DiClemente, & Norcross, 1992). Transtheoretical therapy represents a step beyond typical systematic eclectic approaches, and is an effort to create a higher order theory of therapy that cuts across and transcends existing theories, it essentially attempts to discover or create a set of *interrelated concepts and processes* that can subsume existing theories and serve to integrate them under a coherent, unifying, and systematic umbrella.

The focus of this approach has been on identifying the *stages of change* that mark the progress of clients as they move successfully through counseling and psychotherapy regardless of the particular theroretical orientation represented. In studying psychotherapeutic processes, Prochaska and DiClemente and their associates found that while different theoretical approaches varied in terms of the kinds of "content" discussed, there was a surprising degree of *convergence* in the stages of change that occurred across theoretical orientations.

According to the transtheoretical approach and the considerable research done by its adherents, clients typically go through five stages of change in the course of successful psychotherapy. In making these stages the focus around which the process of psychotherapy can best be understood and techniques and strategies applied, transtheoretical therapists assume that the problems or dysfunctions that clients bring to therapy are generally characterized by a lack of *autonomy*. That is, clients lack the ability to make changes in their own behavior even when it is apparent that such changes would be in the client's own self-interest. Much of the research done on transtheoretical therapy has been in clinical settings working with substance abuse and addiction. The fit between the transtheoretical approach and that kind of professional practice is readily apparent.

After careful observations and analyses, Prochaska and DiClemente and their associates postulated the existence of five basic changes in the process of successful client movement through many forms and approaches to psychotherapy: *Precontemplation, Contemplation, Preparation, Action,* and *Maintenance.* The process of moving through the sequence of stages was called a "spiral pattern of change" (Figure 7.1).

PRECONTEMPLATION

At this stage, a prospective client really has not even considered changing. There is no intention to change in the foreseeable future. Clients who are pressured to enter therapy by family, courts, employers, or other outside forces may actually enter therapy at this stage. Such clients often deny the existence of personal problems or blame others for their difficulties.

CONTEMPLATION

The client or prospective client has become aware that a problem exists and is seriously thinking about working on it, but has not yet made a firm commitment to such a move. Sometimes clients come into counseling or

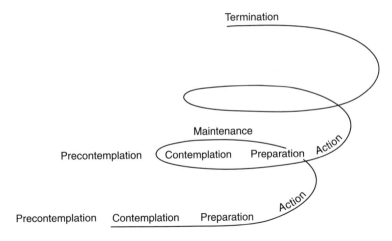

Figure 7.1 A Spiral Model of the stages of change.

therapy on a pretext to obtain information or work on a very minor problem while considering whether to make a commitment to work on something that is really troubling them. At times, clients will weigh the pros and cons of taking action during the early stages of counseling or therapy. Some very passive or conflicted clients may stay in the contemplation stage for years.

PREPARATION

Clients *make a decision* or commitment to take action. Clients in this stage may have made previous unsuccessful attempts to deal with a problem, or have stated intentions for future action while procrastinating about an actual beginning. This could be called "the-next-week-I've-got-to-get-organized stage."

ACTION

Clients actually *begin to modify* their behavior, experiences or environment on behalf of their goals and commitments. Sometimes counselors mistake the action stage with full and complete change. The action stage is generally greeted with praise and recognition from the therapist and from significant others. It does not mean that the change process is complete or final. Relapse or backsliding is still a very real possibility.

MAINTENANCE

Clients work to *consolidate* and *integrate* gains made in the action stage. Sometimes this involves adopting a new lifestyle, entering new roles and relationships, or making new coping behaviors a well-established part of interpersonal or problem-solving behavior. Often the client is able to generalize and transfer new coping behaviors to new settings and situations and attain higher levels of development.

INTERRELATIONSHIPS AMONG STAGES OF CHANGE

Transtheoretical researchers have identified 10 basic therapeutic processes that help to move clients through the stages to successful goal-attainment and termination of therapy. Each of these therapeutic processes can be facilitated by specific therapist interventions, drawn from a variety of theoretical approaches.

The interrelationships among *stages of change, change facilitating processes,* and *therapeutic interventions* shown in Table 7.1 represent the essence of

Table 7.1

Titles, Definitions, and Representative Interventions of the Processes of Change

Process	Definitions: Interventions
Consciousness-raising	Increasing information about self and problem: observations, confrontations, interpretations, bibliotherapy
Self-reevaluation	Assessing how one feels and thinks about oneself with respect to a problem: value clarification, imagery, corrective emotional experience
Self-liberation	Choosing and commitment to act or belief in ability to change: decision-making therapy, New Year's resolutions, logotherapy techniques, commitment enhancing techniques
Counterconditioning	Substituting alternatives for problem behaviors: relaxation, desensitization, assertion, positive self-statements
Stimulus control	Avoiding or countering stimuli that elicit problem behaviors: restructuring one's environment (e.g., removing alcohol or fattening foods), avoiding high risk cues, fading techniques
Reinforcement management	Rewarding one's self or being rewarded by others for making changes: contingency contracts, overt and covert reinforcement, self-reward
Helping relationships	Being open and trusting about problems with someone who cares: therapeutic alliance, social support, self-help groups
Dramatic relief	Experiencing and expressing feelings about one's problems and solutions: psychodrama, grieving losses, role playing
Environment reevaluation	Assessing how one's problem affects physical environment: empathy training, documentaries
Social liberation	Increasing alternatives for nonproblem behaviors available in society: advocating for rights of repressed, empowering, policy interventions

the transtheoretical system of therapy intervention. The stages at which each kind of intervention is emphasized is shown in Table 7.2.

The transtheoretical approach views interventions drawn from diverse theoretical approaches as compatible and complementing when they are applied at appropriate points in the overall change process. Change processes traditionally associated with experiential, cognitive, and psychoanalytic approaches such as consciousness-raising through confrontation or interpretation are considered most useful at the precontemplation or contemplation stages.

Self-reevaluation through clarifying thinking and feelings is used as the client approaches preparation. Building commitment and making decisions readies the client for action. Behavior management and supportive relationship building are utilized during the action stage. At the maintenance stage, the focus is on developing alternative responses understanding environmental forces and becoming the kind of person one wants to be.

The transtheoretical approach is perhaps the most elegantly articulated and thoroughly researched of the eclectic-integrative systems. It utilizes a conceptual model of sequential steps and stages in the typical pattern of behavior change, together with a specification of the probable psychological processes that underlie each phase of the pattern. Seemingly diverse and incompatible interventions drawn from a variety of theoretical sources are then utilized at specific points in the overall change process.

Research and evaluation of this model in the treatment of addictions has demonstrated its usefulness in that area. The model, itself seems to have a wide range of applicability to other therapeutic problems and

Table 7.2
Stages of Change in Which Particular Processes of Change Are Emphasized

Precontemplation	Contemplation	Preparation	Action	Maintenance
Consciousness raising Dramatic relief Environmental reevaluation				
	Self-reevaluation			
		Self-liberation		
			Reinforcement management Helping relationships Counterconditioning Stimulus control	

situations (Koraleski & Larson, 1997; Satterfield, Buelow, Lyddon, & Johnson, 1995; Smith, Subich, & Kalodner, 1995).

Wachtel's Cyclical Psychodynamics

One of the earliest attempts to integrate theoretical formulations about psychological development and functioning was undertaken by Dollard and Miller (1950). In a book entitled *Personality and Psychotherapy: An Analysis in Terms of Learning, Thinking and Culture,* they attempted to translate and integrate concepts taken from psychoanalytic and behavioral approaches.

Dollard and Miller wrote that their ultimate goal was to combine the vitality of psychoanalysis, the rigor of the natural science laboratory, and the facts of culture. Their book, which was dedicated jointly to Sigmund Freud and Ivan Pavlov marked the beginning of an effort to integrate psychotherapeutic theories that is very much alive a half century later. Paul Wachtel, one of Dollard and Miller's students has designed an approach to psychotherapy that builds upon fundamental concepts drawn from these two very different theoretical positions (Wachtel, 1997).

Wachtel accepts the psychoanalytic notion that personality is largely formed out of early developmental experiences, but rejects the idea of early fixations as the fundamental cause of psychopathology. Instead, he sees early experience as simply shaping patterns of interpersonal behavior that tend to persevere across the life-span and often lead to the individual to engage in a series of self-defeating roles and relationships. They are not replaced by new or more adaptive responses because the anxiety associated with the dysfunctional responses causes the individual to avoid new learning. These maladaptive patterns of behavior tend to cycle through the individuals life causing the same self-defeating scenarios to be acted out over and over. Wachtel (1987) called this view *cyclical psychodynamics.*

Wachtel sees psychotherapy as an intervention aimed at breaking these "vicious circles" of maladaptive behavior. Like other psychodynamic approaches, Wachtel sees the development of insight as the key to changing neurotic behavior patterns and acquiring effective coping behaviors.

Wachtel's view of the nature of insight and the varied paths that can lead to its acquisition is much broader than that seen in traditional psychodynamic approaches. Fundamental to Wachtel's view of insight is the notion that it can be acquired through direct *action* or *experiencing* as well as through the tedious and time-consuming process of interpretation in therapy. Essentially this means that *changing behavior* can lead to changing *cognitions* and so to *insight* that allows the client to recognize, understand, and modify self-defeating patterns of interpersonal behavior. Before behavior change and insight can be accomplished, however, excessive anxiety must be extinguished.

Wachtel also departs from psychodynamic approaches in emphasizing the importance of contextual or situational factors in behavior including patterns of reinforcement and neurotic interactions maintained by members of a "system."

In cyclical dynamic therapy, the process begins by examining the nature of the client's presenting problem in terms of its relationship to early family experiences. As possible causal links or themes are identified and explored, the therapist begins to examine the present situations in which these are played out, together with their consequences. At this point, a variety of behavioral or cognitive-behavioral approaches may be introduced. These may include systematic desensitization, graduated exposure or other anxiety extinguishing techniques, role playing, behavioral rehearsal, homework assignments, and coaching in social skills. As anxiety is reduced, the client is able to try out and test new behaviors that then lead to new insights.

The use of behavioral approaches is based on clinical judgments regarding the material elicited from the client. The integrative nature of cyclical psychodynamic therapy lies primarily in the willingness to accept the notion that direct behavior change can lead to emotional re-learning, and to changes in cognitions, that is to "insight." Insight in turn leads to lasting changes in client functioning.

COMMON FACTORS APPROACHES TO ECLECTIC-INTEGRATIVE THERAPIES

GARFIELD'S ECLECTIC-INTEGRATIVE THERAPY

Sol Garfield (1995) bases his approach to psychotherapy on the view that despite the rapid proliferation of presumably unique and different therapies much of the positive results obtained can be attributed to the effects of a finite number of curative factors or sources of gain, that are neither unique nor specific to any single theory or framework. No single approach is seen to emphasize and consciously capitalize on more than a few of these factors. In operating from an eclectic-integrative approach, the therapist has the opportunity to "bring on line" most or all of these factors.

Garfield defines a set of therapeutic variables that can be utilized in all psychotherapy to facilitate client change, including:

- *The Therapist-Client Relationship.* Garfield describes relationship factors in broad terms that include affective factors of warmth, empathy, and respect; social influence factors of trust and credibility, as well as the therapeutic alliance. He makes clear that the formation of a positive therapeutic relationship is a major source of gain in most or all forms of therapy.
- *Interpretation, Insight, Cognitive-Modification, and Understanding.* Virtually all therapies bring about some degree of new insight or understanding to the client. All therapists whether explicitly or implicitly communicate to the client some consistent way of understanding self and the world. Changes in client's thinking and understanding lead to a variety of other changes in feelings and behavior. Garfield treats the formation of "insight" as separate from "cognitive modification" but acknowledges that they overlap.
- *Catharsis, Emotional Expression, and Release.* One process that occurs frequently in almost all therapies is the release of strong emotion. In early psychoanalytic therapy this kind of catharsis was identified. The simple expression of very strong and long-suppressed feelings to a listener who reacts in a nonjudgmental, accepting, and understanding way can provide a sense of relief and help a client move on to begin to cope more effectively.
- *Reinforcement.* While reinforcement is employed systematically in a variety of behavior therapies to shape desired client behaviors, all therapists tend to reinforce those responses of the client that they view as desirable and to extinguish those responses not so viewed. Simply giving attention, responding nonverbally, or changing the content of conversations are all potentially reinforcing or extinguishing therapist interventions. Since reinforcement is bound to occur in the therapeutic situation, Garfield points out that it behooves the therapist to be aware of its effects and to utilize them wherever possible on behalf of therapeutic goals.
- *Desensitization.* The very process of discussing troubling concerns causes them to lose some of their threatening quality. Bringing matters out into the open and sharing them with a therapist may help to reduce crippling anxiety and so help the client be more realistic and rational in defining and solving problematic situations.
- *Information.* Many people who enter psychotherapy are, among other things, poorly informed or misinformed on many topics that influence their everyday lives. People often confuse painful or emotional reactions to situations as abnormal. They may have unrealistic

expectations of themselves or others. Providing accurate information can be of therapeutic value.

- *Reassurance and Support.* These are certainly not factors exclusive to psychotherapy, but for many clients may reduce tensions to manageable levels and so facilitate coping.
- *Positive Expectancies.* Therapists almost inevitably communicate hope and optimism. These reduce the sense of helplessness and hopelessness that lead to apathy, avoidance, or withdrawal.
- *Confronting Rather Than Avoiding Problems.* The act of seeking and receiving help is in itself a step toward confronting and owning problems. All therapies tend to move clients toward active, direct exposure and coping with troubling or frightening aspects of their situations.

This list of curative factors or sources of gain is in a way based simply on common sense analyses of the therapeutic process and situation. To the degree that the eclectic counselor or therapist is aware of their importance and their operation, they can be built upon as central elements around which a counselor or therapist can develop a helping stance or style.

The eclectic counselor or therapist is able to draw on these elements without being blinded by the rigid adherence to pat prescriptions or formulas that are characteristic of many theoretical frameworks.

JEROME FRANK'S COMMON FACTORS APPROACH

As noted earlier, Jerome Frank was one of the earliest advocates of eclectic approaches to psychotherapy. His 1961 book *Persuasion and Healing* made a compelling case for the proposition that psychotherapy was essentially an example of social influence processes applied in a professional setting. He believed that much could be learned about change processes in psychotherapy by studying other types of persuasive and social influence activities.

Frank examined basic similarities among psychotherapy, placebo-effects in medicine, brainwashing, and faith-healing in both technological and primitive cultures. Frank concluded from his review that the basic ingredients in all such procedures included:

1. Instilling new hope and confidence in the client.
2. Mobilizing and arousing appropriate emotional reactions in the client.
3. Encouraging new goal-oriented patterns of activity and effort outside of the therapy sessions.

4. Promoting new *self-understanding* and understanding of problems through interpretation and explanation.
5. Corrective emotional experiences that allow the client to *manage fear and anxiety* without being immobilized by them.

Frank believed that all of these factors are common to all forms of psychological healing, and that modern psychotherapy represents merely an elaboration of age-old principles and procedures for treating psychological problems.

In later expositions, Frank (1982) focused on the goal of restoring morale of clients as a major common factor in all therapies. He pointed out that many if not all people who enter therapy present a common picture of loss of self-esteem, subjective feelings of inadequacy and incompetence, alienation from others, lack of positive relationships, and general feelings of helplessness and hopelessness.

Frank suggested that all forms of therapy may be helpful in dealing with "demoralization" even though they may approach the problem in a variety of ways. Common to all such therapeutic approaches, however, according to Frank were a number of common therapeutic ingredients that include:

1. An emotionally charged relationship between therapist and client
2. A secure and benign setting
3. A conceptual schema, ideology, or myth to explain symptoms or distress
4. A ritual engaged in to dispel symptoms and alleviate distress

In Frank's view, the scientific validation of a personality theory or therapeutic procedure is not as important as is the *credibility* of the entire process to the client. The really essential elements of therapy, as seen by Frank, are: a therapist seen as caring and trustworthy; operating in a safe and benign setting; explaining the client's experience in a consistent and understandable way, and helping the client to engage in a set of activities that are seen as reasonable and effective in relieving distress and attaining goals.

UTILIZING ECLECTIC-INTEGRATIVE THERAPIES

If we examine the basic concepts that provide systematic rationales for each of the various eclectic-integrative therapies, we can come up with a set of principles that can guide therapists in choosing specific techniques or strategies from the vast array of approaches that exist. The principles include:

- The first general principle that unites all eclectic-integrative approaches is that specific techniques can be applied successfully independently of the particular theoretical framework from which they were derived or emphasized. Therapeutic techniques or strategies help clients, theoretical frameworks endeavor to explain why they help.
- From Arnold Lazarus we can receive the basic principle that client problems, concerns and dysfunctions are widely varied, and that the identification of the domain of functioning with which the client needs help is a major factor in choosing the type of therapeutic techniques or approaches that are most appropriate.
- From Beutler comes the principle that the severity and complexity of a client's presenting problems and the client's style of coping are important considerations in choosing a therapeutic approach.
- From Prochaska and his colleagues comes the principle that the client's stage of involvement in the change process is a major factor in designing and applying a therapeutic approach.
- From Garfield and Frank comes the principle that general, common factors that cut across theoretical frameworks are the bases for much of the effectiveness of counseling and psychotherapy and are not to be ignored or taken for granted.
- Finally, the most important maxim of all is the one of open mindedness. All major approaches have important values and assets to offer.

In most of the eclectic-integrative approaches that were discussed the actual selection and application of techniques and approaches are based on *informed clinical judgments*. Assessment processes that are *continuous, tentative,* and *testable* provide the therapist with needed information about clients, but the final choices and applications are a function of the therapists own personality, training, and experience. In one sense the eclectic-integrative counselor or therapist develops a personal approach that can be fine tuned to each new client based on assessment and clinical judgment. Eclectic-integrative approaches place a considerable burden on the individual counselor to be able to utilize a wide range of techniques, and above all to be able to select, combine, and integrate them effectively.

In Chapter 8, we examine an eclectic-integrative model based on the definition of a sequence of basic counseling or therapeutic tasks that help provide a focus for applying specific techniques.

CHAPTER 8

Applying an Eclectic-Integrative Approach

[T]here is no *one* "right way" to treat a client, no *one* "right theory" to explain a client's problems, and no *one* "right therapist" for a particular client. Each of the major models of psychotherapy has something of value to contribute to our understanding of clients and our efforts to help them.

—Barbara Okun (1990)

I N THE preceding chapters, we examined major theoretical models of counseling and psychotherapy and noted that each tends to specify and emphasize its own "sources of gain" that account for its therapeutic effectiveness. We also examined a number of eclectic-integrative approaches that draw on selected sources of gain across the theoretical frameworks out of which they originated.

To utilize any or all of these sources of gain in working with actual clients, the counselor or therapist must be able to integrate them into a logically consistent and systematic way of proceeding. Such a *process model* is essentially a pattern or template that guides the counselor through the maze of possible alternatives to choose the path that is most consistent with treatment goals with a given client.

One such process model is described next. It is eclectic and integrative in that it draws upon multiple sources of gain derived from a variety of sources. It is systematic in that it is based upon a sequence of specific therapeutic tasks that define the work of the counselor at each stage of treatment. Each such task draws upon a specific set of techniques or "gain-producers." This model is consistent with the goals of developmental counseling as these have been defined earlier.

In describing this process model, we will refer to it simply as developmental counseling while realizing that other process models could also be employed to facilitate developmental goals.

SOURCES OF GAIN IN DEVELOPMENTAL COUNSELING

The philosophical assumptions on which developmental counseling is based relate to a commitment to helping each individual develop his or her fullest potentials through establishing a growth-producing, dynamic set of interactions with the physical and social environment. These value commitments also extend to helping individuals increase their awareness of both self and crucial forces and opportunities in the environment. Out of this kind of awareness comes the possibility of freedom and choice.

The scientific theories that are most relevant to developmental counseling are those that bear upon the processes involved in human behavior change. The formulations and findings derived from these bodies of theory and knowledge are seen as sources of gain to be integrated and organized into a systematic approach to working with clients, that is a process model.

Developmental counseling derives sources of gain from several different domains of psychotherapeutic theory that will be briefly discussed next.

RELATIONSHIP CONDITIONS AND THE WORKING ALLIANCE

The voluminous theoretical and research literature on the role of relationship conditions and working alliances on counseling process has been ably reviewed by Gelso and Carter (1994). A number of basic propositions regarding counseling process can be derived from this literature. These include: (1) It is important that a positive relationship between counselor and client develop early on in the sequence of interviews; (2) Positive relationships are characterized by openness, empathy, and genuineness; (3) Counselors vary in the ways in which they develop relationships and this variability increases across individual clients; (4) The strength of the relationship in successful counseling tends to increase and deepen across the duration of counseling; (5) The ability to develop effective relationship conditions cannot be reduced solely to proficiency in a selected set of techniques or communication skills.

In terms of the working alliance, a similar set of propositions can be drawn from the literature. The working alliance has three basic aspects: an emotional bond between the participants, an agreement about the goals of counseling, and an agreement about the basic processes or tasks that lead to successful outcome (Bordin, 1979). The strength of the working alliance is a primary contributor to positive outcomes in counseling. A strong working alliance must be established relatively early in the counseling process. The strength of the working alliance required for successful outcomes depends on the difficulty of demands posed by the goals and tasks involved.

The establishment of positive relationship conditions is closely related to the development of the working alliance. The development of a strong emotional bond between counselor and client is related to conditions such as mutual warmth, empathy, genuineness, and respect. Relationship conditions and the working alliance involve both counselor and client, and their perceptions of each other and of the counseling process. There are no pat formulas or simple techniques that guarantee success in relationship building. Each counselor must develop his or her own approach to initiating positive relationships and strong working alliances. Even then successful approaches may vary with different clients.

Since the development of the working alliance is, at least in part, a negotiation process involving the mutual definition of goals and the selection of methods for goal-attainment, the effect of social influence factors are also significant (Strong, 1997). In developmental counseling, the counselor seeks to be, and be seen as, caring and supportive, and also as expert and reliable. The working alliance, which is seen as a crucial factor in the counseling process, represents a partnership based both on caring and emotional support, and on the added resources that the expertise and experience of the counselor brings to the client.

INSIGHT AND COGNITIVE RESTRUCTURING

One of the major goals of developmental counseling is increased client awareness and understanding both of self and of the external environment. The acquisition of insight has been a goal of many approaches to psychotherapy since the advent of psychoanalysis. In developmental counseling, insight or increased self-understanding is not necessarily focused on the resurfacing of repressed material, or on the recall of traumas in childhood or other family experiences. Occasionally this kind of material is dealt with when it is clearly germane to the client's present situation.

In developmental counseling, insight or self-understanding includes knowledge about self in terms of interests, abilities, aspirations, and achievements. Self-understanding often involves a realistic yet positive appraisal of the personal resources that a client is potentially able to bring to bear on his or her immediate and future problems and opportunities. Cognitive approaches to counseling and psychotherapy and the sources of gain they represent rest upon the view that the greatest assets of people for growing and coping lie in their abilities to think rationally and realistically about themselves and the world.

A fundamental psychological principle on which most cognitive approaches are based is that *awareness* leads to *cognition* and that cognition leads to increased *control* of both behavior and emotion. When utilizing cognitive sources of gain the developmental counselor often functions as a mentor who helps the client to become more fully aware of and able to analyze aspects of self in order to develop more sensitive and accurate perceptions of situations and relationships. The client is then able to follow more logical and valid reasoning processes in drawing conclusions and framing generalizations.

Another cognitive aspect of developmental counseling involves cognitive re-structuring. Often the client's ways of construing both self and the external situation are self-defeating. The client is often helped to reframe his or her situation by moving from a blaming or self-pitying stance to an active problem-solving or decision-making focus. The latter framework offers opportunity for constructive action rather than apathy or despair.

Most therapeutic approaches focus on how clients *think* about their situations and how these ways of thinking affect their feelings and actions. In the cognitive therapies, a major emphasis is given to helping the client to reason logically and rationally. Many of the strategies or techniques used in these approaches are relevant to eclectic counseling. Indeed, as Beck (1991) suggests, the rapid expansion of applications of cognitively focused therapies and the increased range of techniques adopted make the cognitive therapies themselves, virtually part of the eclectic movement.

Developmental counseling also draws upon constructivist approaches especially the cognitive theory of George Kelly (1963). Within a constructivist view, people are seen quite literally to manufacture meaning and seek to understand the world in consistent ways (Mahoney & Lyddon, 1988). This view is akin to the phenomenological and existential notion that each individual constructs his or her own world of reality. The counselor attends to and attempts to understand through active listening the ways in which the client construes both self and the world and how the meanings derived from personal experience color or limit what is seen as both possible and desirable in the future. Sometimes the counselor uses techniques such as "fixed role" assignments in which the client behaves as he or she perceives a respected or admired character to act. Such assignments help to test the adequacy of current constructions of self and of role situations.

Developmental counseling deals heavily with the ways in which clients think. Very often the counselor is concerned with helping clients to think, plan, and act in more clearly rational and logical ways. Rational problem-solving or decision-making frameworks are used where appropriate. Irrational and self-defeating thoughts and over-generalizations are sometimes pointed out to the client.

Developmental counseling constitutes more than a lecture on logic, or an exhortation on the powers of positive thinking, however. The ways in which human beings think about themselves and construe events around them are shaped out of their prior experiences and are not easily altered. Changes in thinking usually accompany changes in experience. These changes occur both in and out of the counseling situation. Clients are often given homework assignments and are asked to try out new patterns of behavior in order to test assumptions about themselves and others.

Developmental counseling focuses around several basic kinds of change processes that are cognitive in nature or have major cognitive components. These are: (1) The arousal of hope about the future and the revival of positive goals and aspirations. (2) the analysis and reframing of beliefs about the world and the possibilities it offers. (3) The examination of beliefs about self and a constructive re-appraisal of personal resources. (4) The active pursuit of new or increased competence in dealing with the demands and opportunities in the environment. (5) These changes interact with each other in a dynamic and synergistic way.

LEARNING AND BEHAVIOR CHANGE

Developmental counseling is concerned with both helping clients to increase self-understanding and helping them to *act* upon that knowledge. A major contribution of behavioral approaches to psychotherapy has been an insistence upon framing the outcomes of therapy in terms of observable behaviors or actions. Only when counseling goals are so defined is it really possible to evaluate counseling process and outcomes empirically.

Modern approaches to behavior therapy are no longer based exclusively on experimental paradigms drawn directly from the learning laboratory. Rather, the recent literature acknowledges that factors such as cognitive processes play an important part in behavior change and the persistence of those changes (Emmelkamp, 1994).

The essence of behavioral approaches to psychotherapy appears to lie primarily in an insistence upon empirical verification of the results of therapy as these are observed with actual clients. To the extent that behavior therapies are this broadly defined, developmental counseling can draw heavily from them.

Behavioral approaches are efforts to study and improve the interaction between organisms and their environments. In this approach, the focus is on the organism's responses to rewards or punishments occurring in that environment. Developmental counseling is likewise concerned with the interaction between the client and the environment. The counselor is keenly interested in the effects of rewards and punishments on the client particularly as they affect the maintenance of newly acquired behaviors. Developmental counseling, however, is also heavily concerned with how affective and cognitive processes mediate the client's responses. The ways in which clients interpret environmental events and how they feel about them are seen as just as important as are the client's overt responses or the nature of the specific external stimuli.

Several basic propositions derived from behavioral approaches are utilized in developmental counseling: (1) The goals of counseling should be framed in terms of client *actions* and should permit both client and counselor to recognize clearly when successful outcomes have or have not been achieved. (2) Where feasible the client should make public to significant others his or her goals, and seek encouragement from a support network. (3) Clients should be encouraged to use self-management techniques such as charting the frequency of target behaviors and giving themselves rewards for achievements. (4) Counselors should attend carefully to and actively help to build the client's sense of self-efficacy, or confidence in attaining goals and overcoming obstacles. (5) When clients transfer new behaviors to their natural environments, every effort should be made to ensure supportive and encouraging conditions in that environment.

PROCESS MODELS

Developmental counseling is not a narrowly prescriptive approach. One of its principal virtues is the latitude that is provided for the individual counselor to adapt, integrate, and synthesize from a wide range of sources concepts and techniques in terms of that counselor's own values, personality, and clientele. The danger in that freedom is that the resulting formulation may be so loosely organized and dimly articulated that it cannot be replicated or evaluated, and so cannot provide a vehicle for the improvement of the counselor's own professional skills and effectiveness. Developmental counseling is not a license for "flying by the seat of one's pants!"

A process model is a way for the counselor to make explicit to self and others what he or she actually does or attempts to do in counseling situations. All counselors have implicit approaches that provide some degree of consistency to their behavior. To be without any such a model would be to behave mindlessly and capriciously. The articulation of a process model is an exercise in personal and professional self-awareness (Blocher, 1987).

The first step in the articulation of a professional process model is the definition of general counseling goals, as these are derived from the philosophical assumptions and value system of the counselor. Such general goals and values have been described earlier in this book. While it is necessary to conceptualize general counseling goals to design or articulate process models these general goals must inevitably be fine tuned in terms of the needs and characteristics of individual counselors, clients, and service delivery systems. A general process model must be flexible enough to encompass the full range of clients and counseling situations encountered in the counselor's professional practice.

BASIC THERAPEUTIC TASKS

After general goals are defined, a kind of task analysis may be performed that allows the counselor to specify those essential steps that must be accomplished to attain the goals defined (Blocher, 1987). A basic set of tasks for developmental counseling includes:

1. *Developing* an initial working relationship with a client that will support and encourage appropriate levels of self-exploration and self-disclosure in the early phases of counseling.
2. *Arriving at a mutually defined* and accepted view of the client's life situation including problems, concerns, and aspirations. These encompass both cognitive and emotional components, that is where, how, and why the client hurts or yearns for more or better satisfactions. This is the first step in building a working alliance.
3. *Obtaining* a mutually agreed upon statement of counseling goals and specific objectives, that is, desired outcomes to which both counselor and client are willing to commit themselves vigorously and wholeheartedly. This is the second phase of the development of the working alliance.

4. *Developing* cooperatively with the client a plan or strategy through which the goals of counseling can be achieved. This is the third phase of the evolution of the working alliance. This may involve establishing a problem solving or decision-making framework and a new set of causal attributions about important aspects of the client's situation.

5. *Helping* the client to assess the personal and environmental resources available to be brought to bear on behalf of his or her goals. This process may include using psychological tests or inventories examining self-estimates, and self efficacy, analyzing the kinds of emotional or material supports available, and even examining the strength of the working alliance established with the counselor.

6. *Specifying* the needed changes in the client's, thinking, feeling, and acting that are required to attain the agreed upon goals.

7. *Providing* a climate of support and encouragement for the client in modifying, thinking, feelings, and actions, and providing or arranging for practice and tryout of new behavior in relatively safe and reinforcing settings and situations.

8. *Planning* with the client for the maintenance and transfer of the newly acquired concepts, attitudes, and competencies as they are applied in the natural environment on behalf of the client's personal goals and continued development.

9. *Evaluating* counseling outcomes and processes and using the results systematically to enhance the quality of the counselors own professional practice and to enrich the knowledge of the profession, itself.

After identifying a set of basic counseling tasks, the counselor is prepared to develop a cognitive map that will specify more clearly what is actually done to accomplish these crucial tasks. At this level of specificity, it is not possible for anyone to prescribe exactly what the individual counselor should do or say. The counselor's personality, values, and interpersonal style are essential elements in the counseling situation. The counselor's personality is the primary therapeutic tool in the counseling process. Similarly the needs and characteristics of each individual client are unique and represent essential variables in the counseling situation. Brammer, Abrego, and Shostrum (1993) put it this way:

> [E]ach counselor and psychotherapist ultimately must develop a point of view that is uniquely his or her own. Freud was not a Freudian, Jung not a Jungian, and Rogers not a Rogerian. Each of them was himself most fully and completely, while building on the wisdom of the past. (p. 19)

BUILDING ON COMMON ELEMENTS

Developmental counseling does not prescribe a specific and highly styl-ized or artificial pattern of interaction for the counselor to emulate. Rather, developmental counseling draws on a set of generalizations or principles derived from research on the counseling process. These are seen as common elements in effective counseling that may hold across a variety of theoretical models or orientations. The following generaliza-tions are adapted from comprehensive reviews of counseling process re-search such as that done by Orlinsky, Grawe, and Parks (1994). These principles are based on factors that have been frequently or consistently found to be associated with successful outcomes of counseling and psy-chotherapy with a large and wide ranging set of problems and clientele. They are framed here as a set of basic propositions to guide the develop-mental counselor in developing a personal process model:

1. The way we begin to help a client is to listen to the client and to help the client listen to himself or herself.
2. Structuring with the client the expectations and responsibilities of both parties is helpful early in the counseling process.
3. The more the counselor and client collaborate in sharing initiatives and responsibilities, the better the outcome is likely to be.
4. It is important for counselors to attend to and facilitate the expres-sion of clients' affect. The expression of negative client affect is es-pecially important early in the counseling process.
5. Client self-exploration is an important factor in successful counsel-ing. Generally, the more a client talks about self, explores feelings and articulates fears, hurts, hopes, and aspirations, the better the probability of successful outcome.
6. The more the client discusses and defines problematic issues and is willing to accept responsibility for them, the better the prospect for success.
7. The more the client perceives the counselor to be deeply interested, caring and actively engaged in helping, the better the prospect for success.
8. Mutual client-counselor warmth and acceptance is positively re-lated to outcome.
9. Client trust and openness in working with the counselor is very im-portant to success. The overall quality of the emotional bond be-tween client and counselor is similarly important to success.

10. The more the client and counselor are able to develop a mutually agreed upon and reasonably specific plan of action to attain goals and resolve problems the better the outlook for success. The more the client clearly and publicly accepts responsibility and expresses willingness to undertake that action, the better the prospects for success.

11. The more the client experiences a sense of self-efficacy and realistic confidence in his or her own inner resources, and in the possibility of mastering necessary competencies, the greater the probability of successful goal-attainment.

These propositions are a guide to the nature of effective counseling process. As the individual counselor develops and refines a personal process model these principles provide a set of criteria or process goals against which to evaluate the effectiveness of particular techniques, strategies, or approaches.

Probably the most important resource available to counselors in developing a process model is simply to listen to and learn from clients. When a large group of clients who had experienced success in counseling and psychotherapy were asked to list the factors that contributed to positive outcomes, the following factors were most frequently mentioned (Lambert, Shapiro, & Bergin, 1986): (1) the personality of the therapist, (2) receiving help in understanding the nature of problems, (3) receiving encouragement to gradually practice facing the things that bothered them, (4) being able to talk to an understanding person, and (5) receiving help toward greater self-understanding.

The responses of these successful clients who had experienced therapy from a variety of therapists and orientations strongly suggest that the personality of the counselor, and the patience and persistence with which the counselor works to promote increased client self-understanding and constructive action are highly important factors in counseling processes.

FUNDAMENTAL INGREDIENTS OF EFFECTIVE COUNSELING

Why does counseling work when it works? Why do clients change their ways of thinking, feeling, and acting as a result of counseling interventions? It is possible to identify a number of factors that are probably common to many forms of psychotherapy including developmental counseling. These include:

1. The first and perhaps the most important ingredient in client change is the arousal of hope in the future, and in the possibility of obtaining some greater degree of control over one's own life. People are unable and unwilling to mobilize energies, abilities and other resources on behalf of desirable changes unless they see these changes as possible. Indeed, simply having goals and aspirations is an affirmation of hope.

2. Counseling helps clients to change or correct maladaptive, erroneous and self-defeating beliefs and assumptions about the world. As these beliefs change, new opportunities, choices, and possibilities emerge.

3. Counseling actively *teaches* clients new information, attitudes, and skills. These new competencies allow clients to accomplish tasks, achieve success, and to cope with and master challenges and opportunities in the environment.

4. Counseling changes clients' basic beliefs about *themselves.* Counseling helps clients to discover and utilize strengths, including interests, abilities, and energies, that they had not recognized and utilized before.

5. Counseling helps to mobilize clients' energies through the arousal of emotion. As clients get in touch with feelings, they also discover and clarify needs and motivations that can be harnessed to sustain and focus efforts and support active involvement with essential tasks.

6. Counseling helps to enhance clients' sense of self-efficacy or self-confidence. Obstacles that once seemed insurmountable are seen as amenable to rational problem-solving strategies. Hurdles are approached in step-by-step sequences of attainable objectives. Both inner assets and environmental resources are inventoried and mobilized. The realm of the *realistic* and *possible* in the client's life is expanded.

Developmental counseling works because it promotes greater self-awareness including increased awareness of needs and aspirations and the feelings attached to them. As these needs and feelings are recognized they are attached to a set of personal goals. The client then mobilizes newly recognized personal strengths and environmental resources on behalf of those goals and deals with obstacles to goal attainment in rational and effective ways. Awareness leads to *understanding,* and understanding leads to *control* of emotions and to effective *action.*

ACCOMPLISHING THERAPEUTIC TASKS

Developmental counseling services are delivered in both one-to-one and in group situations. In individual counseling, the most common arrangement is the traditional weekly, one-hour session. In some situations where constraints or availability of client and counselor time exists, sessions may be scheduled more or less frequently.

Counseling typically begins with relationship-building and structuring of mutual expectations about the counseling process. Direct and candid discussions are held about the division of responsibility for both process and outcomes of counseling, and about the client's role in the process. Ethical considerations in regard to confidentiality, conflicts of interest or dual relationships, and informed consent are thoroughly discussed. Other considerations such as fees, scheduling of sessions, and other practical considerations are discussed. Client questions and concerns about the nature of counseling are invited and dealt with honestly and in a matter-of-fact manner. The client may be asked to complete an intake or personal data sheet for the agency's records. Some of this intake procedure can be accomplished prior to the first actual counseling session.

The first counseling session does not begin with a barrage of factual or narrowly focused questions. The client is invited to talk about those topics that are of most current concern. The counselor listens actively and responsively, endeavoring to communicate interest, caring, and concern for the client. The counselor is tentative and honest about the extent of his or her understanding of the client, and of the client's experiences and life situation.

The counselor may employ a variety of interview techniques as these are useful and are integrated into his or her own interpersonal style. It is not considered useful to adopt a mechanical or highly artificial pattern of interaction. The overriding purpose of the early counseling sessions is for the counselor to communicate a genuine interest in the client, together with a desire to help. In the early sessions, this is communicated to the client largely by the counselor's consistent effort to *listen and understand* the client's thoughts and feelings about self and life situation.

Out of this kind of interaction, a relationship of mutual trust and concern is built that will sustain the client's serious efforts at self-exploration, and the self-disclosure that these efforts require. This trust will also sustain the counselor's effort to understand and help the client to gain increased awareness of hurts, fears, hopes, and aspirations.

As the client's increased self-understanding and self-awareness develops, the counselor and client are able to begin the goal-setting phase of counseling. Goals help the client to set directions and to focus efforts. They are also an affirmation of hope for the future, and evidence of an increased sense of self-efficacy.

In the goal-setting phase, the counselor may make a variety of contributions. The counselor may supply relevant information about possibilities and opportunities in the environment. The counselor may utilize assessment data, or information about the client's past performances that may help in goal-setting. The counselor may help to identify recurring themes in the clients perceptions and experiences, and help the client to explore these in terms of both their positive and negative implications.

Often the goal-setting process, itself, results in a reframing of the client's perspectives and the development of new attributions about the causes and forces that have influenced the client's past development. As goals are articulated, obstacles to those goals are recognized. This is the beginning of the process of *problem sensing*. Problems are defined as obstacles to goal attainment and continued growth.

The counselor attempts to help the client to get in touch with feelings about problems and to accept ownership of those problems. This often involves helping the client to move from a blaming or denying posture in regard to the problem to one of the accepting ownership of the problem.

The most crucial phase of the entire process of developmental counseling comes as the client's goals are specified and a series of steps or objectives on the way to attainment of those goals are specified. As this mutual goal-setting process is accomplished, the working alliance really comes into being, and the energies and resources of both counselor and client are meshed toward a common purpose.

Obstacles to goal attainment are recognized and carefully defined as problems to be resolved. Two crucial aspects of problem definition must be recognized. The problem must be defined accurately in terms of the removal of the obstacle that is actually blocking progress to the goal. The problem must also be defined in terms that make it solvable through changes in the client's own behavior or actions.

After the goals are specified and the problems are defined, a set of action plans are developed that involve the client directly and actively in the problem-solving and goal-attainment process. Individual counselors often have special expertise and experience in helping clients with particular problem-solving plans. Such expertise may be in fields such as educational and vocational planning, academic improvement, rehabilitation, conflict resolution, or interpersonal skill development. At this point, counselors use their expertise and experience in active teaching or coaching of clients. They help the client to recognize successes and the good feelings attached to them. The counselor may help the client to build or enter support networks to provide added and continued reinforcement and encouragement for newly acquired skills and attitudes.

The counselor utilizes at least three very distinct sources of gain throughout the counseling process. The counselor develops a relationship of trust and caring with the client that will facilitate client self-exploration and self-awareness in terms of both feelings and cognition. This relationship provides support and encouragement to the client in exploring painful or threatening feelings and perceptions. It culminates in the development of a strong working alliance based on a positive emotional bond and a clear commitment to mutually defined goals and problem-solving strategies.

The counselor also helps the client to reframe and restructure *ways of thinking* about self and situation. These cognition are based upon new information about possibilities and opportunities in the environment. They are also based on more rational and coherent reasoning processes and logical analyses. Finally, these cognition arise out of increased self-awareness and self-understanding, particularly as these relate to inner strengths and resources.

The counselor also uses as a source of gain, basic learning principles to facilitate the acquisition, transfer, and maintenance of new patterns of client behavior. The counselor functions as a behavioral coach helping the client to organize action plans into manageable and attainable steps that can be reinforced by the counselor, by other supports in the environment, and by the client's own recognition of and satisfaction in success.

When counseling is delivered in a group format, the total process is somewhat similar. The counselor functions as a group leader in addition to other responsibilities. The counselor attempts to create a total group climate that will provide a relationship network analogous to the one-to-one counseling relationship. Group members help each other in self-exploration and self-awareness tasks. Often counseling groups are formed around a set of common issues and concerns. The group format is particularly useful in supplying a supportive and reinforcing setting in which action plans can be tried out and new behaviors practiced in a safe and encouraging atmosphere.

At this point it may be helpful to look at a typical case of developmental counseling. The case that follows arises out of the transition between adolescence and young adulthood. It involves the acquisition of a new set of coping behaviors to deal with changing roles and relationships in both family and peer settings. The case illustrates the utilization of multiple sources of gain in the counseling process and a method of evaluating the outcome of counseling.

A CASE EXAMPLE OF
DEVELOPMENTAL COUNSELING

Lynne was a 20-year-old college student in a large state university. She was referred for counseling by a residence hall advisor. The referral indicated that Lynne had frequent episodes of crying, had chronic difficulty in getting along with roommates and other residents, and seemed negative and "turned off" about virtually all aspects of her college experience. The advisor felt that Lynne was on the verge of a serious depression.

Lynne completed a personal data sheet and had a brief interview as part of the intake procedure. She was an only child. Her father was a lawyer and her mother a high school teacher. Lynne had grown up in a small town in a rural area of the state. She volunteered that she had been valedictorian of her high school graduating class, and that she and her parents had always looked forward to her coming to the University. Both parents had graduated from the University, and had very fond memories of their college experiences.

Lynne listed as her presenting problem that she "hated the University, hated the residence hall in which she lived, and could find nothing interesting or worthwhile in her academic studies."

Early Sessions

After a brief structuring statement by the counselor, Lynne began the initial session by saying "I don't know why I am here at the University." Lynne went on to describe in a very articulate way what she saw as the emotional emptiness and intellectual superficiality of student life. She reported that she had chosen and abandoned three different college majors, and had dropped or taken incomplete grades in more than a dozen courses in her three years at the University. She had come to the University with very high expectations about both the intellectual and social facets of college life. After three years, she felt totally disillusioned about both.

In the first three counseling sessions, Lynne went on in a similar vein describing her feelings of frustration, anger, and disappointment. The counselor attended to her negative feelings and communicated understanding of her perceptions and feelings. Gradually through the early sessions, Lynne's emotional expressions deepened from childlike anger and frustration to communicate an almost tragic vision of life, characterized by loneliness, meaningless rituals, and growing despair. As she talked about her deeper feelings, her speech was much less fluent, and her nonverbal expressions conveyed very strong emotional arousal.

At this point, Lynne began to shift from feelings about life as a student to deal with other aspects of her experience. Since early adolescence she had experienced growing dissatisfaction about her relationships with her parents. Lynne saw her parents as very successful, well-organized, but emotionally cold and self-contained people. She understood that her parents loved her, but increasingly saw herself as simply a mechanical cog in their well-ordered and predictable world.

Lynne felt that her parents were unwilling to acknowledge her growth and maturity. When she attempted to discuss her feelings and view of life with them, she felt either dismissed as immature, or "humored" rather than understood, or even seriously listened to. On most of these occasions she either went into a childish, emotional outburst, or retreated into the submissive "parent-pleasing" role that they seemed to expect. In both situations, she felt ashamed and inadequate.

Lynne also began to talk about her relationships with peers. In high school she had a reputation as a "brain." She felt that she was an effective student leader, but that she intimidated other students, particularly boys, and that she was not really liked for herself. She had dated very infrequently in high school.

Upon entering college, Lynne had attempted to continue in leadership roles in the residence hall and in several student organizations. In these situations, she felt that she had been rebuffed as dominating and "bossy." Her experiences with roommates was very similar, with frequent outbursts and bitter arguments over relatively trivial incidents.

Finally, Lynne talked about two very painful romantic experiences. In her first year in college she had "gone steady" with a boy for the first time. She also had her first sexual experiences in this relationship. After an almost euphoric several months, the boy abruptly stopped seeing her saying that their relationship was becoming too intense and demanding. Lynne was deeply hurt in this relationship and did not date again for over a year. She had entered a second relationship a few months before beginning counseling and it had ended very recently in almost the same way as the first.

LATER SESSIONS

As Lynne talked about her feelings of hurt, disappointment, and rejection, the counselor helped her to make connections among these experiences, and to trace patterns that seemed to recur in various relationships. Several times the counselor asked Lynne to recall critical incidents in her relationships and they role-played these. Sometimes the counselor played Lynne's part while she put herself in the role of parent, friend, or lover.

Gradually Lynne began to move away from the stance of seeing herself as the passive victim of rejection, betrayal, and abandonment by others. She began to recognize patterns of interaction that were initiated and at least partially maintained by her behavior. She particularly was struck by her use of sarcasm when fearing rejection. She also began to recognize the absolute and non-negotiable nature of the demands and expectations she put on others. She summed up her new awareness and self-understanding in the exchange below:

COUNSELOR: How does it seem to you that all of these relationships we've talked about fit together?

CLIENT: It seems like I always come on real strong with people. . . . From the very beginning I want to be recognized and taken seriously. I want the relationship to be important to both of us. I think sometimes I try too hard and scare people away . . . or maybe I just ask too much from them too soon. . . . When I feel like I'm being ignored or taken for granted, I lash out and hurt someone.

As Lynne increased her self-awareness and moved toward greater self-understanding, two specific goals began to emerge. First, she wanted to improve her relationship with her parents. She wanted to learn to deal with them as younger adult to older adult. While she hoped that this would lead to greater acknowledgment of her adult status from them, Lynne recognized that the only parts of the relationship that she could control was her own behavior and emotions.

Second, Lynne wanted to learn to build more satisfying and less turbulent relationships with other young people, both men and women. She decided that this goal involved learning to communicate herself more clearly and more patiently to others. It also involved learning to listen to others and to show more sensitivity and concern to their needs.

At this point, the counselor sought to assess the quality of the working alliance being established:

COUNSELOR: How do you see the way you and I are relating right now?

CLIENT: I think its pretty good. You listen to me and seem to understand where I'm coming from . . . how I see things. I've never had anybody do that before.

COUNSELOR: How does that make you feel?

CLIENT: It feels really good! I don't feel so alone anymore. I feel like I can do something. I don't have to just lie around and feel sorry for myself, and be mad at the world all the time.

At this point, Lynne and the counselor developed two action plans on behalf of her counseling goals. The first of these involved returning home the following weekend to begin a process of renegotiation of her relationship with her parents. She planned this meeting in some detail and role-played the session with the counselor. Lynne also decided to keep a log or diary to record her efforts in improving her interpersonal relationships.

At the first counseling session after her weekend at home, Lynne reported on her progress. For the first time in memory she had been able to talk with her parents about her own feelings and issues without being interrupted with unsolicited advice from her father and empty reassurances from her mother. While somewhat shocked by the fact that she had entered psychological counseling, they agreed to continue a series of family sessions devoted to better understanding and appreciation of her development as a person.

The counselor discussed with Lynne her feelings about the conferences with her parents.

COUNSELOR: How do you feel about this past weekend?

CLIENT: It was great! For the first time I was able to talk to them about *me* without having to keep saying to myself, they're my parents, I know they love me even if they don't act like it . . . I feel good about myself. I know that I can explain myself to others. . . . I'm not a child anymore.

Lynne's second action plan involved working on a set of new interpersonal relationships skills. She decided to focus on allowing others to choose topics of conversation, listening attentively without interrupting or giving opinions, and checking out with others whether she fully understood their ideas and wishes.

In this action plan, the counselor asked Lynne to identify someone whom she knew well and whose interpersonal skills she admired. Lynne chose her favorite high school teacher whom she saw as a warm and interested friend and confidante. She role-played with the counselor how she saw this woman's interpersonal style. Lynne then undertook to tryout new skills within the "fixed role" inspired by her former teacher.

Lynne tried out her new skills by visiting a childhood friend who was enrolled at a nearby liberal arts college. She shared with the friend her goals and spent a weekend as her guest in the college dormitory. She was introduced to a variety of new acquaintances. Each evening she discussed her progress with her friend and received support and encouragement. She also recorded her experiences in her diary.

At the subsequent counseling session, Lynne reported positive feelings about her tryout, but felt that her success was limited. The counselor discussed and role-played some difficult situations and provided encouragement.

Lynne and the counselor then proceeded to break down the new interpersonal skills that she hoped to acquire into two sets of target behaviors. She compiled a list of distancing behaviors that she hoped to reduce or eliminate, and a set of welcoming behaviors that she wished to acquire. Lynne set up a self-management program in which she charted the frequency of each set of behaviors. To help with the self-management program she enlisted the help of the residence hall advisor who had made the original referral to counseling. This woman observed Lynne in a variety of situations, went over her progress charts and provided support and encouragement.

Lynne continued to work on both her relationship with parents and her new interpersonal skills. Her counseling sessions were gradually more widely spaced and were devoted primarily to monitoring and supporting progress on her goals.

The counselor and Lynne agreed on three success indicators to determine the outcome of counseling. First was the elimination of explosive conflicts in the residence hall, second was the continuation of successful family conferences on a monthly basis, and third was the resumption of casual dating. These success indicators were to be reviewed six months, after the beginning of her action planning program. At the end of six months, all three success indicators were achieved. Although not included in her formal goal selection, Lynne's academic achievement and satisfaction also showed marked improvement.

EVALUATING COUNSELING OUTCOMES

The global question of does developmental counseling or any other approach to psychotherapy, work is largely meaningless. To ascertain the effectiveness of any approach, questions must be asked in considerably more sophisticated and specific ways. In most cases, the question must be put in this way: What results are obtained by this counselor, using these procedures, with this client, presenting these problems or concerns?

For counselors to evaluate their own effectiveness and improve their own professional practice it is necessary to evaluate the outcomes of counseling at the level of the individual and the kinds of clients and client concerns with which he or she works.

Counselors can accomplish this kind of evaluation process utilizing the five basic steps described below:

1. Accomplish some rough grouping of clients by demographic characteristics and by the nature of the presenting problem. This grouping can be quite simplistic in the beginning since it will be continuously and systematically refined in the evaluation process itself. The counselor might begin such a grouping, for example, by including adolescent females presenting family conflict issues.

2. For each individual case, the counselor determines from case notes the specific goals mutually determined by counselor and client in the process of building the working alliance. The goals must be specific and behavioral in order to serve as "success indicators" or criteria for satisfactory case outcomes. They are in a sense behavioral objectives.

3. At the point of termination of each case, the success criteria are reviewed carefully and a decision is made to record the case as "successful" or "unsuccessful." This decision may be made by the counselor, by the counselor and client together, or by an objective third person. If the success indicators or criteria have been well-defined this decision should not be difficult.

   When several cases with the selected type of clients and problem have been completed, it is possible to calculate a success ratio. For example, the counselor might record successes with 6 out of 10 adolescent females presenting family conflict issues.

4. The counselor now carefully analyzes both successful and unsuccessful cases in terms of the basic processes and procedures that were employed in each instance. This analysis may be done using case notes, recordings, assessment, and other personal data about clients. In some situations, the counselor might use client logs, or data from significant others such as parents, spouses or friends. (This is only done with the client's knowledge and consent.) The counselor also carefully examines his or her own reactions and attitudes toward each client for clues to the ingredients of both success and failure.

5. The information in this analysis of successful and unsuccessful cases is then carefully fed back into the counselors own professional development process. For example, the counselor may find that five out of the six successful cases involved clients from relatively intact and stable family situations. In all four of the unsuccessful cases, the client lived in a relatively disorganized family situation in which a single custodial parent or parent figure was also severely stressed.

Another similar set of clients may be counseled and results analyzed to see if they are replicated. If the results are repeated the counselor now separates these clients into two groups on the basis of family support and stability, and seeks to develop an improved treatment protocol for these clients that were not successfully counseled. Such a treatment might, for example, involve creation of peer support groups, or efforts to work jointly with custodial parents. In-service training for the counselor in working with culturally different clients might be indicated as well. This evaluation model is shown in Figure 8.1.

The point of this type of evaluation process is that it generates the kind of information needed to begin to improve the quality of professional practice, and to guide the course of the counselor's own professional development.

SCOPE AND APPLICABILITY OF DEVELOPMENTAL COUNSELING

Developmental counseling is practiced effectively with a very wide range of clients and presenting problems. Since developmental counseling has a psychosocial rather than a purely intrapsychic orientation and emphasis, it is able to focus on the immediate level of social functioning of the client. The quality and effectiveness of the client's current transactions with the

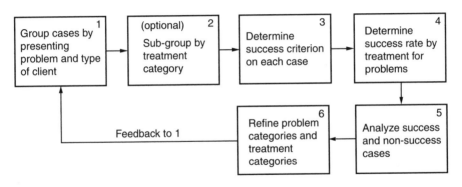

Figure 8.1   Evaluating process and outcome.

environment, as these are part of the client's pattern of daily living, represent the starting point for developmental counseling.

Clients who are unable or unwilling to explore extensively their past traumas, or who are in a state of crisis, are able to begin to deal with the immediate concerns that brought them to counseling very early in the counseling process. It is not necessary for the client to engage in a lengthy and often painful exercise in retrospection before sensing any attempt to focus on immediate practical concerns. Clients who might not persist in other courses of psychotherapy because of frustration with the process are often able to work effectively in developmental counseling.

Developmental counseling is used frequently to provide services for hard to reach clients who do not utilize other psychotherapeutic services. Such counseling services are offered in a variety of outreach settings such as day hospitals, half-way houses, and "storefront" counseling centers. Clients with histories of chronic dysfunctions, alcohol or drug abuse, or victimization are frequently treated successfully by developmental counselors in such settings.

One major advantage of developmental counseling in working with relatively low functioning clients is that very immediate and practical goals clearly related to the client's immediate quality of life can be negotiated. Similarly very small increments of client progress can be noted, encouraged, and reinforced. With such clients, counseling may begin with very practical and immediate goals involving basic material needs, employment, or social support.

Developmental counseling often includes or is supplemented with training or coaching in basic life skills. These might include basic literacy or completion of high school equivalence, self-care and grooming, assertiveness, job seeking, or other practical skills needed in daily living. Developmental counseling is offered in a wide variety of community human services programs and agencies.

Developmental counseling is offered extensively in a wide range of educational settings from elementary schools to universities. Counselors offer educational and vocational counseling, academic improvement counseling, and developmental counseling around a wide range of problems frequently encountered by children, adolescents and young adults.

Many approaches to counseling and psychotherapy are inappropriate for work with children and early adolescents (Stern & Newland, 1994; Wagner, 1996). Developmental counseling is based on a conceptual framework that allows counselors to employ treatment strategies across the life-span.

For example, a developmental counselor working with at-risk children in either elementary school or community settings can build treatment packages that include support groups for children from broken or dysfunctional families, design mentoring, tutoring, or peer counseling programs, engage in whole family counseling, or deliver parent education programs as well as working directly with an individual child (Blocher, 1987).

Another major advantage of developmental counseling is that it offers psychological assistance without stigmatizing or labeling people as mentally ill or socially deviant. Many potential clients who would avoid psychiatric treatment will seek counseling through employee assistance programs, through churches or community centers, or as part of school systems or community colleges.

The developmental and preventive emphasis of developmental counseling treats many troubling and distressing situations as developmental crises or problems of living in a stressful and often chaotic world. This approach makes it possible for people to receive help with problems such as marital or family discord, stress symptoms, depressive reactions, or interpersonal conflicts without the added anxiety of being labeled as abnormal or deviant.

Developmental counseling does not prescribe a narrow and rigid set of techniques, nor does it rely on a single mechanism or source of gain to accomplish its purposes. Such counseling draws upon a variety of concepts, techniques, and research findings. The approach places considerable responsibility on the individual counselor to refine, synthesize, and integrate these sources of gain into a flexible, yet systematic approach that is compatible with that counselor's interpersonal style and professional values.

CHAPTER 9

Career Counseling

> Vocational planning is a quest for self-fulfillment and its
> resolution represents one way in which a person comes to terms
> with himself.
>
> —Henry Borow (1959)

THIS BOOK adheres to two truisms: Change is inevitable and empowerment comes to those who plan. A basic aspect of developmental counseling is assistance with life planning. In the early years of the counseling profession, although vocational counseling was a core activity in the development of the profession, sharp lines were often drawn between vocational counseling and so-called personal counseling.

No distinction could be more misleading. Most adult human beings spend almost one half of their waking hours engaged in work. Most have spent almost that much of their childhood and adolescence preparing themselves for work. Work is one of the major structuring forces in most people's lives. Where we work, whom we work with, what our working hours may be, and how we are paid all constitute major determinants of both our quality of life and our lifestyles. Of just as great significance is the direct psychological impact of work. Work plays a crucial role in attaining and maintaining self-esteem, in acquiring a sense of autonomy or empowerment, and in achieving a sense of purpose and meaning in life. One of the most devastating sources of stress in our society is that of chronic unemployment (Reynolds & Gilbert, 1991).

It has been said that if in some future world, technology made work economically unneeded, its psychological necessity would force us to reinvent it as a social institution. For more than 65 years in the face of mind-boggling changes in technology, social mores and economic circumstances, the standard work week has stayed at about 40 hours, or one half of an individual's waking hours over the five-day week. Yet, work remains very much a double-edged sword that holds both the spice of life and the kiss of death.

Any attempt to divorce vocational life from personal problems clearly ignores reality. The National Institute for Occupational Safety and Health (NIOSH) has listed the 10 most important work-related diseases, injuries, or disorders. The list was based on both the frequency and severity of these conditions. High on the list along with lung disease and cancer are psychological disorders, such as neuroses, personality disorders, and alcohol and drug abuse (NIOSH, 1988).

One estimate is that about one-half of the entire working population is unhappy in their jobs, and that as many as 90% may be spending much of their time and energy in work that brings them no closer to their life goals. According to this estimate, about 75% of those who seek psychiatric help are experiencing problems that can be traced in part at least, to a lack of job satisfaction, or an inability to manage work-related stress (Levi, 1990).

Surveys have shown that in the United States nearly 11 million workers report health-endangering levels of mental stress at work (Sauter, Murphy, & Hurrell, 1990).

The reasons behind these sobering statistics are not really mysterious. When people are unable to cope adequately with the stresses and strains of vocational life, when they fail to achieve any degree of success or recognition, or are unable to find any intrinsic satisfaction in the ways in which they spend almost half their waking hours, it is naive indeed to expect that the remainder of their lives will be tranquil, fulfilling, or harmonious.

Many of the problems of alcohol or drug abuse, domestic violence, child abuse or neglect, and anxiety and depression are in themselves either triggered by, or exacerbated by problems that originate in the workplace.

Yet, as we saw in Chapter 4, satisfaction from work remains a primary life goal across almost the whole population and through the entire lifespan. A student of happiness or "optimal experiences" (Csikszentmihalyi, 1990) concluded that happiness, or what he describes as a sense of "flow" comes from the combination of the feeling of *control* or mastery over key aspects of one's life, and a deep sense of *involvement*, or indeed, virtually *immersion* in deeply valued activities. Not surprisingly, many of his subjects found this kind of "flow" in work.

Despite the overpowering array of evidence supporting the psychological significance of work in people's lives, many counselors and counseling theorists continue to see vocational planning as essentially nonpsychological in nature. In this intellectually anemic view, vocational planning merely requires supplying information, relaying test scores, or occasionally dispensing advice. In this view, vocational counseling can be relegated to public libraries or employment agencies that dispense pamphlets, college catalogues, or transcribe "want ads" onto computer discs.

Although Sigmund Freud is reported to have declared that the two great arenas of personality development and conflict were love and work, many contemporary counselors and personality theorists seem to be in love with love and oblivious to work. Some studies of counselors' involvement and priorities continue to show decreasing interest in vocational counseling (Blustein, 1992).

Some of this lack of commitment to vocational counseling stems from a set of profound and long-standing misconceptions about the activity, itself. Nearly a century ago, when vocational guidance was in its infancy, Frank Parsons, who is sometimes erroneously referred to as the Father of Vocational Guidance, enunciated a simplistic formula to describe the vocational guidance process. Parsons had no psychological education (he was a lawyer, social philosopher, and would-be politician). After less than six months of professional counseling experience, he pronounced that counseling consisted of information about the client, information about the occupation, and true reasoning about the relationship between the two (Parsons, 1909).

The notion that people make simple, totally rational, and once in a lifetime vocational choices probably deserves a place in the *Guinness Book of World Records* as a masterpiece of oversimplification. Even more amazing is the fact that the myth has persisted for almost a century.

In a recent qualitative study of the career paths of prominent women psychologists, the authors expressed surprise that almost all of their subjects credited important aspects of their career development to "serendipitous" events, that is, essentially unplanned for circumstances or situations (Nutt Williams, Soeprapto, Tourodji, Hess, & Hill, 1998).

Rather clearly the authors' view of vocational development and life planning still reflects the century-old Parsonian paradigm (Krumboltz, 1998). Life planning is just that—life-long planning. Intelligent life planning recognizes that life is full of unpredictable events, and that every human life is greatly influenced by these. We described some of these in the discussion of developmental influences in Chapter 2.

Intelligent planning helps people recognize, comprehend, and take advantage of unforeseen opportunities. Intelligent plans usually contain options and alternatives rather than rigid and inflexible pseudoprescriptions etched in stone, or rather in ignorance. Until recently, many vocational theorists treated this kind of flexibility as indecisiveness, an almost pathological condition, in their eyes, rather than as open-mindedness and intelligent cooperation with the inevitable (Krumboltz, 1998). Having Plan A and Plan B is a mark of an intelligent assessment of reality.

As it became clear that vocational life did not consist of single, simple decision-making situations, the term *vocational development* was substituted for vocational choice as the crucial process with which counseling was concerned. Similarly the term *career* came to be used rather, than simply vocational since it was also clear that people typically moved in and out of many different jobs and even occupations in the course of a working lifetime. The notion of work as a "divine calling" that is implicit in the notion of "vocation" did not seem either realistic or relevant to life in the late twentieth century.

It has been harder to shake the notion that career choices are often no more or less systematic or rational than are any other of the major life decisions confronting human beings. Simple observation shows us that most people do not choose spouses, houses, automobiles, or underarm deodorants, for that matter, on the basis of pure logic and systematic analysis. If that unlikely situation suddenly came to pass, the world of marketing and advertising would collapse in an instant, and a thousand romantic novels and motion pictures would have to be rewritten.

THE CONCEPT OF CAREER

The term *career* as opposed to vocation connotes a dynamic but coherent process that operates in the life of an individual through time and across specific jobs. People take, keep, or change jobs and employers for a variety of reasons. Wages, hours, working conditions, economic circumstances, and family roles all influence these kinds of immediate and short-term choices. Careers, however, are relatively stable and represent *psychologically* coherent patterns of person-environment interaction (Holland, 1996).

The terms *career* and *work* are not synonymous. For many people, a career may represent a pattern in which regular, paid work may be less central or psychologically compelling than is the search for fulfillment and recognition represented in musical, artistic, religious, or political aspirations and commitments. The starving artists, actors turned taxi drivers,

THE CASE OF FRANK

Frank Hanley is a 49-year-old college graduate who has worked for the past 26 years as a cost accountant for a manufacturing firm. After graduation from college, Frank and Marcia were married. She teaches English at the local high school. They have three children two of whom are their own, while the third will graduate from college in the spring.

For the past 10 years, Frank has been increasingly absorbed in his hobby of painting. He has been president of the local art society and has exhibited his work in a number of local art shows. Two of his seascapes have been sold through a local gallery.

A few months ago, Frank's firm merged with a West Coast manufacturer. He was recently told that his department would be moved to the corporation's Los Angeles headquarters. Frank was offered the choice of taking an immediate retirement with a severance package equivalent to two years of salary, or moving to Los Angeles with no promises about his future with the company.

Frank has decided that this is an opportunity to start a new career. He wants to sell the family home, study with a famous teacher in an art colony on Cape Cod and then embark on a new career as an artist.

Marcia is horrified by the idea. She says that he is simply going through a mid-life crisis. At her insistence they have gone to see a counselor in private practice in the community.

How should the counselor approach the case? Is it a marriage counseling situation, a career planning case, or an adult transition?

---

or sopranos waiting tables *do have careers.* So too do dedicated volunteers, from hospice workers to Scout Masters.

A career is not simply a series of jobs, or even necessarily a persistent engagement in one or more occupations. A career is rather a long-term, psychologically compelling quest for a degree of personal fulfillment, continuing development and social contribution. A career is not simply climbing a ladder toward higher pay and promotion. In our changing work world, that notion is increasingly unrealistic.

A successful career is not measured just by the award of a pension and a gold watch, but by a long-term pattern of person-environment interaction that leads to growth, satisfaction, and personal empowerment.

THE MEANING OF CAREER DEVELOPMENT

As career counseling was seen to embrace far more than a set of one time interventions at the approach of graduation from high school or college,

Henry Borow.

the term "career development" came into wide use. Unfortunately, as a field of inquiry career development has proved something of a disappointment. Early theorists clearly saw developmental psychology as the discipline that would help to elucidate patterns of change in vocational behavior and indeed hoped for the eventual merger of vocational psychology with the mainstream of developmental psychology (Borow, 1959). Donald Super (1990) proposed a life-stage, life-space model that could provide a relevant framework for the interface of the two disciplines. The full fruits of such an interface are unfortunately still to be hoped for rather than celebrated (Richardson, 1993).

We can examine what is known about "career development" under the same rubrics that we used to look at general development. Indeed, it seems clear what we call career development is a subset of general human development.

CHRONOLOGICAL ASPECTS OF CAREER DEVELOPMENT

Several chronological or life stage frameworks to describe career development have been proposed. Super's model is the most comprehensive and most widely researched (Super, 1985). Super (1957) adapted a model by Buehler (1933) in proposing a five-stage framework with stages labeled (1) Growth, (2) Exploration, (3) Establishment, (4) Maintenance, and (5) Decline. The reader will note the similarity between Super's model and the general developmental framework described in Chapter 3.

The first two stages, Growth and Exploration have been the most intensively studied. Originally it was hypothesized that the Growth period would end with the beginning of adolescence, while the Exploration phase would terminate at about age 25.

Longitudinal research has shown that exploratory behavior for many people continues well into the thirties and, as we suggested earlier, early termination of this stage, that is the suspension of tentativeness and closing off of alternatives, may actually lead to undesirable outcomes (Phillips, 1982).

CHILDHOOD

There is much that is not known about career development in childhood. It is clear that by about 9 years of age children have already developed concepts of sex-appropriate and sex-inappropriate roles. They are able to play out with considerable fidelity familiar occupational roles of parent, spouse, teacher, physician, nurse, policeman, fireman, and so on. They clearly possess at least rudimentary occupational stereotypes. Beginning with fantasy-based activities, children form images of high status or heroic occupational roles as well as of low status or socially disapproved ones.

Similarly, children are in the process of forming self-concepts, including academic self-estimates and estimates of athletic ability, social attractiveness, and other characteristics. They are influenced by the responses of significant adults and by social comparisons with other children. The foundations for perceptions of self-efficacy or lack thereof are already in place. All of these factors affect the hopes, fears, and aspirations of developing children. Developmental theorists have listed numbers of career-relevant developmental tasks in childhood.

Generally, these involve developing stable and realistic concepts of self in relation to work and preparation for work. They also include continuously enlarging knowledge about work and developing the ability to plan, that is set goals and develop and follow through on strategies for attaining them. The development of "initiative and industry" that was described in Chapter 3 is obviously a crucial factor in childhood career development.

In later childhood, the process of *crystallizing* or evaluating various kinds or aspects of work in relation to self is seen as an important developmental task. Crystallization requires an accompanying development of personal identity. In a sense, this process involves the beginning of seeking answers to the question of "who am I" in terms of work.

Donald Super.

ADOLESCENCE

The process of exploration is seen to begin in early adolescence and continue into young adulthood and even beyond. Much of the early phases of exploration involve specifying possible options. This may involve learning to cluster related occupations into job families or narrowing options by ruling out certain occupations or clusters of occupations.

According to Super, the primary compass used in the initial phases of exploration is compatibility with an emerging self-concept. Other theorists see the influence of social role models as a major factor in the narrowing process (Krumboltz, 1996).

In later adolescence, the process of implementation may begin as the individual tries out various options through part-time or entry-level employment, or in choices of college majors or vocational training programs. All of these early attempts at implementation tend to remain tentative and exploratory and, as we noted, may persist well into the thirties. Actually, a danger to optimal career development in the exploration stage may come from pressures from family, teachers, or counselors who push the individual into premature closure of the exploration process.

ADULTHOOD

The later stages of establishment, maintenance, and decline involve further and more finalized implementation followed by stabilization and consolidation. The latter processes are almost self-explanatory. These later stages as outlined in career developmental theories imply a kind of neat linear progression that is probably not realistic in today's work world or in terms of varied contemporary life styles. Considerable research on mid-life suggests that linear progression in a simple, single, life-long pattern is no longer the rule, but that many paths and much variability are frequently found (Lachman & James, 1997). Similarly, existing career developmental theories may not adequately reflect the differing career influences and experiences of men and women. These differences will be discussed more fully in Chapter 10.

Several efforts have been made to define and measure career maturity. Usually, they involve attempts to measure factors such as extent of planning, sophistication of decision-making processes, general world of work information, and specificity of information about preferred occupations. Generally, these approaches and instruments have not been very useful to practicing career counselors (Super, 1985).

COGNITIVE APPROACHES

The process of career development and subsequent life planning involves learning—learning about self, work, occupations, and the people in them. Frank Parsons was right about that much of the equation. *How* people learn and how they come to think, feel, and act in regard to work is considerably more complicated than Parsons and many of the vocational guidance workers who came after him appreciated. For many years, it was assumed that the panacea for problems of educational-vocational choice or planning lay in giving the client more and better information about self and occupations.

Information about self was to be derived from test scores. In these years, vocational counseling was dominated by the use and misuse of psychological tests and inventories. It was the age of the "test-them-and-tell-them" approach to vocational counseling. Paralleling this aspect of vocational counseling was the overriding emphasis on occupational information. Students in schools were bombarded with pamphlets and brochures. Counseling offices were often mini-libraries of mostly unread and greatly unappreciated blurbs of information pouring from the printing presses of commercial publishers.

Gradually, we have come to realize that effective life-long planning requires that people not only *acquire* facts about self and others, environments and occupations, but that they also *organize* and *integrate* such information into a coherent, and fully conscious set of self-estimates, values, goals, and strategies.

The processes by which information is translated into understanding and action is, as we saw in Chapter 2, the subject of cognitive psychology. The constructivist or cognitive developmental view that was discussed earlier also has profound implications for career counseling.

In career counseling and life planning, we do not expect to be able to plan for or predict all of the client's future choices or behaviors. No amount of counseling or planning enables anyone to write his or her autobiography in advance. Within the kind of ecological framework discussed in Chapter 1, we expect that all human behavior will be a product of the *interaction* between psychological processes within the person, and the environmental events and changes that are continually occurring in the surrounding world.

Developmental career counseling deals with how people *think* and *feel* about their lives and the role of work in those lives. Counseling deals with how clients set long-term goals, how they develop the value systems that underlie those goals, and how they mobilize energy and resources on behalf of those goals. In this sense, career counseling, like other aspects of developmental counseling, centers around how clients "make meaning" out of their experiences.

Cognitive psychology has focused upon the cognitive structures or *schemas* within which people organize information about a particular area of experience or field of knowledge. Schemas are seen to influence the selection, organization, and recall of available information. One aspect of cognitive schemas is "personal constructs" (J.G. Kelly, 1955). Constructs are bipolar dimensions that people use to describe or analyze various objects, people, or events. Vocational constructs are used to describe various characteristics of people and occupations. They may help the individual to assess an occupation in terms of high or low status, indoor versus outdoor work, working alone or with people or any other relevant dimensions.

Construct systems function as maps or templates for organizing impressions and information from which individuals interpret events, predict future events, and determine actions to be taken. In other words, they are used to make meaning.

A key assumption of the psychology of personal constructs is that meaning is made out of contrasts or the comparison of opposites. *Strong* has meaning only in terms of *weak* and hot has meaning only in terms of cold. As people develop personal constructs they are *differentiating* more and more relevant factors or facets to weigh and consider in planning or goal setting.

Early research in cognitive career development (Bodden, 1970) indicated that high levels of differentiation were related to more appropriate vocational choices.

Since career problems and plans generally involve a number of relevant factors the planner must also be able to *integrate* a number of such factors into a single coherent yet comprehensive impression. The combination of abilities to differentiate and integrate is, as we saw in Chapter 2, generally called cognitive complexity.

DEVELOPMENTAL SELF-CONCEPTS

As people vary in terms of cognitive complexity in perceiving other people as well as external events and situations, they also vary in terms of their views of self, that is *self-concepts*. Mature individuals have a variety of self-concepts, rather than a single, simplistic view of self. They have impressions of interests, tastes, and preferences drawn from a variety of sources. They recognize in themselves a variety of abilities, strengths, and weakness. These all change over time with experience and like other aspects of personality are largely a product of person-environment interaction. As individuals grow in experience and cognitive complexity, their self-concepts become more stable. Indeed, the stabilization stage in Super's developmental stage schema discussed earlier represents among other things an increasingly stable set of self-concepts formed out of increasingly consistent patterns of person-environment interactions. Even in mid-life, however, major changes in these interactions can produce corresponding changes in self-perceptions.

To the degree that people are able to be aware of increasing numbers of characteristics in themselves, and these self-perceptions are reasonably stable, they are able to set long-term goals and consequently more comprehensive and long-term plans. Both external events and perceptions of self can and do change so that effective life planning is always *continuous, tentative*, and *revisable* in terms of a changing self in a changing world.

Self-Efficacy

An important concept in cognitive approaches to career development is that of *self-efficacy*. The concept was invented by Bandura (1977) to help explain why people often make little or no attempt to perform certain tasks or behaviors even when rewards are clear and desirable. Self-efficacy expectations refer to an individual's beliefs about the ability to perform a given task or behavior.

Self-efficacy expectations have been found to be limiting factors in academic achievement (Lent, Brown, & Larkin, 1986). Extensive research on vocational self-efficacy indicates that many people in a wide variety of career-relevant situations tend to respond to new, nontraditional or unusual challenges or opportunities with a simple and untested "I can't do that." This reaction closes off further exploration or consideration even when factors of interest and rewards are positive (Hackett, 1995).

After more than 30 years of research on cognitive career development, we are able to specify a set of general principles that are relevant to career counseling and life planning. These include:

1. Giving clients more information about occupations does *not* necessarily increase complexity (Neimeyer, 1988).

The Case of Alice

Alice graduated from high school as the class valedictorian. Although she was encouraged by teachers and counselors to attend the university, she decided to enter the local community college, and to pursue a business course. After graduation from the community college, Alice took a position as a clerk in the payroll section of a large manufacturing firm. Two years later she was promoted to be the head of the payroll department. Alice had almost immediate problems as a department head. She found it difficult to supervise her staff members, especially to delegate responsibility to others. At the end of each pay period when the deadline for the payroll approached, Alice was stressed out almost to the point of being physically ill. After six months, she resigned her position and left the company. She moved to another company in a similar position and the same scenario was repeated.

Recently she took a position at a local branch bank as a teller. Again she did well and was again soon offered a promotion. She refused the promotion. After a long conversation with the bank manager, Alice decided to seek counseling at the Community Counseling Center.

How should the counselor approach the situation?

---

2. Generally, information that challenges existing perceptions increases complexity, while information supporting existing impressions decreases complexity (Moore & Neimeyer, 1992).

3. Generally, men are better *differentiators* and women are better *integrators* in terms of cognitive complexity in career situations (Neimeyer, Metzler, & Bowman, 1988; Parr & Neimeyer, 1994).

4. Generally, when people furnish their own set of constructs about highly relevant career alternatives, these are used in more complex ways than when the constructs are supplied or suggested by others (Parr & Neimeyer, 1994).

5. Readiness to make decisions or engage in active career planning is related to ego-identity development or, in other words, general maturity (C.R. Cohen, Chartrand, & Jowdy, 1995).

6. Clients perceptions or impressions about people *in an occupation* may be at least as important as perceptions of the actual duties or activities involved in the occupation (Winer, Cesari, Haase, & Bodden, 1979).

7. The level of complexity in person perception may affect the career preferences, exploration, and choices of clients. Low levels of complexity may cause clients to summarily reject careers that are seen as unusual or nontraditional (Capurso & Blocher, 1985).

8. The readiness of a client to engage in active life planning and career exploration is a function of the client's confidence or self-efficacy in regard to the exploration process (Solberg, Good, Fischer, Brown, & Nord, 1995).

9. Career exploration is largely limited to those areas in which the client has some degree of self-efficacy. Clients are unlikely to seriously consider or even to explore options or alternatives for which they have no sense of self-efficacy (Hackett, 1995).

10. Concepts about self differ in cognitive complexity as much as do impressions of others. Stable highly differentiated and reasonably well-integrated self-concepts are important in goal-setting and long-term planning (Super, 1990).

PERSON ENVIRONMENT FIT (OR FLOW)

The purpose of modern career counseling is not simply to fit the client neatly into a pre-existing, permanent occupational niche. The only such niches that exist in the real world are those marked *Rest in Peace*. The old square peg analogy has very little real meaning in today's world.

The goals of career counseling are much broader and indeed more ambitious. Krumboltz (1998) described the goals of modern career counseling as facilitating the learning of "skills, interests, beliefs, values, work habits, and personal qualities that enable each client to create a satisfying life within a constantly changing work environment" (p. 31).

Creating a satisfying life, however, presupposes the presence of certain long-term patterns of interaction between growing and therefore changing human beings and environments that are also constantly evolving. The time honored concept of "person-environment fit" is better replaced by the more dynamic notion of *person-environment flow.*

Person-environment flow describes the growth-enhancing patterns of interaction between a developing human being and a responsive environment. We discussed the nature of this kind of interaction in Chapter 2. By abandoning the static notion of "fit" in person-environment interaction, however, we do not have to move to a "one-size-fits-all" position.

Models of Person-Environment Interaction

A number of models for describing and analyzing work environments and people's responses to them have been advanced. Pervin (1968) hypothesized that people seek out and perform best in environments that are congruent with their personality needs. They are particularly receptive to those that help them to implement their "ideal self concepts," that is help them to be more like the person they are striving to become. People with large discrepancies between self and ideal self-concepts may seek *support,* while those with more congruent self-perceptions may seek greater *challenges.*

Analyses of environmental factors by Barker and associates have developed the principle of "optimal manning" (Bechtel, 1977). This line of research indicates that opportunities to perform responsible and growth-enhancing roles in a given environment are a function of the number of people available or competing for such roles. This idea is similar to the concept of "opportunity structure" described in Chapter 2. When the manning situation allows ample opportunity for people to engage in attractive and rewarding activities researchers found that people tend to:

1. Work harder and do more important work.
2. Engage in a wider range of activities.
3. Are given greater recognition by others.

4. Are given greater autonomy and personal responsibility.
5. Have a greater sense of identification and belonging to the organization.
6. Are more ego involved in work.

Thus, important differences were found between people engaged in essentially the same kinds of activities in different environments. These were differences not of basic personalities, but of different patterns of person-environment interaction.

By far the most intensively researched model of person-environment interaction is that proposed by John Holland (1992). Holland's model hypothesizes the existence of six major personality types and a corresponding typology of work environments. One of the interesting aspects of the Holland personality theory is that it proposes that the six personality types, realistic (R), Investigative (I), artistic (A), social (S), enterprising (E), and conventional (C) can be arranged in a hexagonal fashion based on decreasing similarity (see Figure 9.1). Holland also proposed that a corresponding set of work environments can be identified and arranged accordingly.

Holland's theory, which has been supported by many studies (Holland, 1996), suggests that people seek environments that are compatible with their abilities, allow them to express their attitudes and values and permit them to engage in intrinsically interesting tasks.

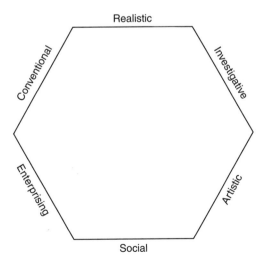

Figure 9.1   Holland's Person-Environment Model.

According to Holland's theory an individual of a given personality type is more likely to choose, persist in, and have greatest satisfaction in an environment that corresponds with that personality type.

Holland's theory is essentially a matching model. According to his position although people clearly do enter and leave vocational situations for a variety of reasons, and specific environments provide greater satisfaction for some people than others, it is still important for people to consider matching and mismatching factors in both choices and rejections.

Most working environments are complex, containing elements such as physical characteristics, tasks and duties, social climates, as well as hours and working conditions. Similarly, work environments are variable in terms of the characteristics of the people who inhabit the environment. According to the theory and supporting research however, similar work environments should be populated to some extent by similar people (Wampold, Mondin, & Hyun-nie, 1999).

The Holland model of person-environment interaction has the problems inherent in any matching model. A great variability exists within categories, both in terms of people and environments. People change with time as do environments. Organizational climates change as do job descriptions. Engineers may become salesmen, accountants become managers, lawyers become politicians, and so on. To a considerable degree, people create their own social and psychological environments out of their own perceptions and behaviors (Schneider, 1987). A worker at the service desk in a large department store, for example, may view the role as one of social service in helping people with problems, while another sees it as one of enforcing rules and regulations.

Despite the weaknesses inherent in any matching model, Holland's theory and the tools derived from it, are useful in career counseling. It has far more empirical support than most psychological theories. Holland (1996) reports that 79% of a large sample men 30 to 39 years of age, despite a large number of job changes stayed within a single category in the six-category system. Stability within a category also tends to increase with age as one would expect from developmental stage theory.

The Holland scheme is a very useful approach in helping clients to explore the world of work. It is a valuable heuristic in narrowing and focusing exploratory activity. Attempting to explore any domain of knowledge as vast and as amorphous as the work world is confusing and discouraging without some kind of structuring process. The Holland scheme is an effective, logical, and empirically tested way of beginning career exploration. It need not be used in a rigid or mechanical way, but rather as a way of organizing information and impressions.

WORK AND LEISURE

If we apply George Kelly's notion of personal constructs to the term *work* then the dimension that apparently gives meaning to work is *leisure.* Work and leisure are very closely related concepts. The term leisure is derived from a Latin verb meaning "to be permitted." In a literal sense, then, leisure activities are those that we are free to do, while work consists of what we are required to do.

In the postmodern world, from a psychological standpoint at least, the work-leisure dimension may not always have much meaning. As we noted, one definition of "optimal experience" equates happiness or "flow" with the condition of being fully involved or immersed in an activity. If an individual is fortunate enough to be paid for such activities then rather clearly the work-leisure dimension has relatively little meaning. Some psychologists have suggested that the most important area of study for counseling psychologists is the role of work in people's lives (Richardson, 1993). Certainly work and leisure are psychologically related concepts that connect to the ways in which people construe themselves and interpret their world.

The concept of *career* goes well beyond paid work to represent the ways in which people strive to meet psychological needs and to give meaning to their lives. We need to understand the ways in which work and leisure interact to help define an individual lifestyle. Career counseling, in the sense in which we have discussed it, often includes planning for both work and leisure and in the process carefully considering the meaning that each has in the client's life. Leisure activities are also often important in managing unavoidable stresses in the workplace. That aspect of leisure will be discussed in Chapter 13.

COMPLEMENTARY WORK-LEISURE PATTERNS

As we look at the ways in which work and leisure interact within an individual's total lifestyle, several frequently occurring and psychologically relevant patterns can be observed. One pattern of work-leisure relationships can be termed *complementary*. In this pattern or style, a close relationship exists between the actual activities performed in paid work and in leisure. The two sets of activities may be very similar in terms of intrinsic satisfaction or interests.

The auto mechanic may build or race automobiles, or the music teacher may compose songs or perform in a variety of settings. In some cases, the overlap may be so great that it is difficult to identify where work ends and leisure begins. Indeed, this whole pattern illustrates why the concept of career has more utility than the term *occupation*. In the complementary pattern, we might expect that work and leisure activities would both fall into identical or adjacent Holland categories.

A second type of complementary work-leisure pattern involves the types of social relationships that accompany the two sets of activities. We noted earlier that an individual's perceptions of the kinds of people in an occupation are at least as important as are the actual activities performed. In this pattern, work and leisure activities may be quite different, but the common factor is in the consistency between the people and the social relationships involved.

A worker may bowl with the company team, attend office parties and company picnics, or spend Friday nights drinking with the gang from the department. Business partners may play golf together on Saturday mornings, belong to the same country club, or have season tickets together at the game.

In some managerial, sales, and professional occupations social life revolves around contacting clients. Joining social groups such as clubs, lodges, country clubs, and alumni associations is an essential part of promoting the firm or building a clientele. Again, the distinction between work and leisure at least from a psychological standpoint is blurred.

Similarly, in family-operated businesses or in some company towns, whole extended families representing several generations may be closely involved in work as well as family relationships. For some families, choosing an occupation may simply mean carrying through a family tradition in law, medicine, police work, the military, or a host of other professions and businesses.

In these examples, the concept of career involves work, leisure, and often family and social life. Paid work is inseparable from many other ingredients that constitute a lifestyle. Certainly, the notion of a neat separation between personal counseling and career counseling is ridiculous in these situations.

Although complementary work-leisure patterns may be satisfying and rewarding in many instances, they may not always afford either the degree of novelty and variety necessary to stimulate intellectual growth, or the privacy and separation from workday stress that allows for relaxation and real recreation.

SUPPLEMENTARY WORK-LEISURE PATTERNS

A second psychologically significant work-leisure pattern can be called *supplementary*. In this pattern, the psychological meaning is in the degree to which the leisure activity presents a set of opportunities not easily available in the work situation. In this kind of pattern, work and leisure combine to round out and balance an overall lifestyle. In such patterns, sharp contrasts may exist between work and leisure activities and between accompanying social relationships. The sedentary office worker may seek recreation in mountain climbing or distance running. The professor who deals in abstract ideas may restore antique cars or refinish furniture. The police officer who faces danger and witnesses violence every day may sing in a church choir or grow prize roses.

To the degree that work is experienced as constraining, monotonous, or stressful, leisure may provide vital opportunities for doing new and different things with new and different people in novel and stimulating or conversely relaxing situations. Often when economic, family, or other circumstances seem to compel compromises in career preferences and aspirations supplementary work-leisure patterns can help to provide a reasonably satisfying overall lifestyle.

COMPENSATORY WORK-LEISURE PATTERNS

A third work-leisure pattern can be called *compensatory*. To a degree it can be considered an extension of the supplementary patterns. Sometimes, however, compensatory patterns have a driven and urgent sense to them that can lead to irrational, self-defeating, or even self-destructive behavior. They can involve activities and social relationships that are either similar to or dissimilar to the work situation. Sometimes they represent rigid and maladaptive defenses against stress or aversive conditions in a work situation. Extreme frustration, boredom, or lack of recognition on a job may be associated with patterns of heavy drinking, drug abuse, sexual promiscuity, reckless driving, or even criminal activity, for example. Chronic frustration in a subordinate relationship at work may be associated with abusive family relationships or aggressive behavior in social settings. Compensatory patterns may be involved in many cases of marital discord, substance abuse, accident proneness, or even child abuse.

Not all compensatory patterns are unhealthy or destructive. Some that are well-controlled may provide a healthy relief from boredom. Competitive or contact sports and sensation-seeking activities such as sky-diving or auto racing may be healthy outlets when done under controlled conditions.

Often when compensatory activities do verge on being self-defeating or reaching destructive levels, counseling focused on career issues and work-leisure relationships may be more effective than traditional psychotherapy.

CAREER COUNSELING AND THE USE OF TESTS

Probably no topic in the whole counseling literature has aroused more controversy than has the question of when, how, or whether psychological tests and inventories should be used in counseling. Some of this controversy stems from the period in which career counseling was, as we noted earlier, practically swallowed up by the obsession with psychological testing. The day of the testing-and-telling approach to career counseling is, or should be, long past. Today, the basic question that defines the use of tests in counseling is whether they can help us as counselors to understand clients more fully, and in turn help those clients better understand themselves and plan more effectively.

Much of the controversy that surrounds the use of tests focuses on *feelings* about tests rather than upon their practical *utility* in the career counseling process. Various opinions have been expressed about tests for nearly a century, characterizing them as good, bad, unfair, immoral, prejudicial, useless, or infallible.

Actually, the correct answer is *none of the above*. A psychological test or inventory is nothing more or less than a sample of behavior taken under standard conditions from which we *infer* other behavior. Most of the problems or controversies that surround psychological testing center around the kinds of inferences drawn from those observations.

For more than a century psychologists, and indeed much of the rest of society, have waged heated debates about the nature of intelligence and other psychological constructs. The nature-nurture debate about human abilities has gone on and on, and will probably continue to go on for another century. The definition of *intelligence,* its origins in terms of genetic versus environmental influences, and the nature and causes of individual and group differences have polarized the field of psychology, and at times almost the whole society.

These controversies have little to do with the utility of tests or inventories in practical career counseling situations for the simple reason that we are not called upon to make inferences about the underlying *causes* of individual differences. Standardized test scores allow us to make, where it is appropriate and helpful, comparisons between one person's behavior in the testing situation and that of others. In some situations, we may compare that behavior to some external criterion such as the ability to read and understand certain material or to perform given mathematical operations.

One of the basic tenets of developmental counseling is that virtually all human behavior including aptitudes, interests, and other personality traits or tendencies arise out of the *interaction* between predispositions within the individual and influences operating in the environment. All people change all of the time. The basic goal of developmental counseling is to help individuals channel those changes in a valued direction, that is, to facilitate development. Few human beings ever approach the upper limits of their potential in any area of endeavor. The potential for further growth and development is always present and is the primary focus of developmental career counseling.

Using tests or inventories in career counseling is really no different than making any other kind of observation and drawing any other kind of inference. If we set up a structured interview asking a specific set of questions, or ask a client to complete a Personal Data Sheet, we have created something that closely resembles a psychological measurement situation.

The use of tests, inventories, questionnaires, and interviews to *assess* aspects of a client's behavior involves the fundamental scientific processes of observation and inference. We all make such *observations* and *inferences* constantly both in and out of counseling situations. The important consideration is that we remain *aware* of our inferences, *conscious* of the limited observations on which they are based, and always keep in mind *the limitations* that are imposed by all of the circumstances and factors involved.

Most of the misuses of tests and other observations come from lazy, sloppy, and erroneous use of inferences about people. Tests results may be a little more vulnerable to such errors because to the naive user or consumer they have an mistaken aura of "scientific" respectability. The usefulness or misuse of psychological tests is almost always a function of the *user*, not of the instrument.

When we give a client a scholastic aptitude test, for example, we observe a *performance.* When we use the score obtained to make an estimate of the client's ability to succeed in a given school we *infer* the presence of an *aptitude* that is a psychological construct that can never be measured directly, and which carries meaning that goes far beyond the observations on which

it was based. In given situations, it may be helpful to a client engaged in educational planning to consider the results of a scholastic aptitude test and
incorporate that information into his or her planning. It is always the responsibility of the counselor to be sure that the test results are fully understood in terms of both their usefulness and their limitations.

In developmental career counseling, test information is not used to
classify or categorize people. Rather, psychometric information is used
where relevant to help a client better understand the kinds of experiences
and environments that may be most likely to support life goals and nurture further growth and development.

When psychometric data are interpreted to clients, the most important
consideration is that the information never constitutes an end in itself. It is
always used to further the client's planning, and its value is determined
solely by the *meaning* and *relevance* the information has for that client.

Psychometric results should always be interpreted in the context of a
client's own concern, or as an aspect of a client's plan or problem. A few
simple cautions that career counselors should keep in mind when interpreting psychometric data to clients are:

1. Psychometric data should be interpreted in the context of *all* available information regarding the client. Information regarding the
   cultural background, health, aspirations, anxiety and educational
   and linguistic skills of clients, among other variables, are essential
   factors in establishing the meaning of scores or results.
2. Predictions drawn from test scores and obtained through use of ac-
   tuarial or expectancy tables are always based on *groups,* not specific
   individuals. Such predictions are generalizations about groups of
   people with similar scores.
3. Success in any endeavor is influenced by a complex set of factors
   that include motivation, emotional control, and social support as
   well as aptitudes. Aptitude may be a necessary factor, but is never a
   sufficient factor for successful implementation of plans.

Psychometric instruments are useful tools in career counseling in many
situations. The nature of inferences that can be legitimately made about
clients from such data, as from any other single sources, is necessarily limited. No human being can be fully understood or adequately described on
the basis of psychometric data alone. Tests and inventories are most useful
in career counseling when they are selected in close collaboration with the

client, are directly relevant to a client's plans or problems and are carefully integrated with other available information. Both clients and counselors should recognize that inferences made in an effort to understand self or others are most useful when they are *continuously* revised in the light of further information, recognized as *tentative* hypotheses, and *tested* against real world criteria wherever and whenever possible.

THE EFFECTIVENESS OF CAREER COUNSELING

The effectiveness of career counseling has been questioned for many years. It is very difficult to define clearly the nature of the outcomes that we would expect to result from the many kinds of career interventions. We no longer believe that one-time vocational choices are the most relevant outcome, or that it is even easy to classify such choices as good or bad. Comprehensive career counseling goals such as those listed by Krumboltz (1998) are much more relevant, but difficult to measure. Studies using a variety of criteria have generally found that career counseling is effective in producing desirable changes in the career behavior of clients (Holland, Magoon, & Spokane, 1981; Phillips, 1992).

Two systematic reviews of the evaluation research have been undertaken using the meta-analytic approach. In this way of reviewing research, different studies using a variety of specific criteria can be thrown together, and questions answered about their general effectiveness in producing intended results. One of these, Oliver and Spokane (1988), defined career interventions as any treatment or effort to enhance an individual's career development, or to enable the person to make better career-related decision. This definition can subsume a wide range of specific criteria and particular methods. These researchers combined 58 studies that included individual counseling, group interventions, computer-assisted methods, and even self-administered approaches. All of the studies together involved more than 7,000 subjects.

Oliver and Spokane's analysis indicated that career-related interventions were on the whole highly effective, that individual counseling approaches were the most effective, and that the more intensive the treatment, the greater the effects. A replication of Oliver and Spokane's earlier study, which had used only studies completed prior to 1983, was reported by Whiston, Sexton, and Lasoff (1998). Generally, their results were similar to the Oliver and Spokane analysis. Again, individual career counseling produced the greatest impact.

LIFE-STAGE CONSIDERATIONS IN CAREER COUNSELING

Developmental career counseling must be carefully attuned to the developmental level of clients. Many developmental career interventions with children are aimed at facilitating their general development and are focused around the kinds of developmental tasks and coping behaviors outline in Chapter 3.

Career Interventions with Children

In addition to facilitating general developmental tasks and educational development, several specific kinds of career developmental emphases can be identified from the approaches described earlier, including:

1. Children can be helped to access a *variety* of career role models who are similar to themselves in gender and ethnic background, and who have positive status in the community.
2. Children can be helped to grasp the very wide range of vocational opportunities that exist in the world of work.
3. Children can be helped to begin to develop simple age-appropriate ways of structuring work roles and opportunities. These may include for example, working with people, working with ideas, working with tools, or with machines or electronic devices, working in the outdoors, or work involving travel and adventure.
4. Children can be helped to understand the work-related aspects and applications of basic school subjects including mathematics, science, art, music, communications, and so on.
5. Children can be helped to develop a positive sense of self-efficacy in regard to school achievement, social skills, creative expressions, and physical activities.
6. Children can be helped to engage family members, friends, and neighbors in conversations about work experiences and opportunities.
7. Children can be helped to distinguish career-related aspects of their developing concepts of self. They can be helped to understand the relationship between personal characteristics such as responsibility, caring for others, truthfulness, honesty, curiosity, energy, and enthusiasm to success as a worker.

CAREER COUNSELING WITH ADOLESCENTS

Career counseling with adolescents centers around the exploration process. Much of that process involves developing personal constructs that are relevant to self, jobs, and workers. Counselors can provide cognitive structures such as the Holland schema to help reduce the enormity of the exploration task. To a considerable extent exploration for adolescents necessarily involves a narrowing process. One of the pitfalls in the early exploratory process is prematurely ruling out options and possibilities simply because they are unfamiliar, or because the occupational stereotypes held of workers in such fields do not fit immature self-concepts of masculinity, femininity, or social status. Self-efficacy expectations may similarly unduly limit the exploration process or even cause the adolescent to focus only on the safe, secure, and familiar. Self-efficacy expectations of girls for mathematics and science fields may be particularly limiting in closing off exploration.

Face-to-face contacts with a wide variety of workers in different fields is an important aspect of early exploration as are part-time and entry-level work experiences. Career counseling can contribute to the integration of impressions, feelings, and facts acquired in exploratory experiences into conscious and rational aspirations, preferences and rejections.

Planning activities can be built around relatively short-term goals of gaining relevant exposure and experience. The *continuous, tentative,* and *reality-testing* aspects of planning can be emphasized. As planning for post-high school education begins, this too can be seen as continued exploration rather than one of closure.

CAREER COUNSELING WITH YOUNG ADULTS

As we saw in Chapter 3, the young adult stage is one of pulling together and reconciling competing roles and expectations. From a career standpoint concepts of self as a worker and developing career aspirations must be integrated with self as spouse, parent, lover, friend, son, or daughter and so forth.

The young adult transitions are difficult and career counseling often involves supplying emotional support. Career decisions must often be made in the context of family responsibilities. The major career developmental transition is the move from exploration to implementation. Family, economic, and social pressures often combine to push the client to close off exploration prematurely. The role of general maturity is very important at this stage and career counseling and general developmental counseling are frequently closely intertwined.

The central focus in career counseling in young adulthood is often on *compromise.* In many career counseling situations, compromise and the nature of those compromises are the crux of the problem. The ability to accept compromises is a crucial part of both personal and career maturity.

Counselors often facilitate the compromise process by helping to "frame" the compromise situation in terms of outlining options and alternatives, or helping to identify the relevant aspects of the situation to be considered. (Gati, Houminer, & Aviram, 1998).

CAREER COUNSELING IN MID-LIFE

The mid-life stage is not always one of increased stability and tranquillity. Actually research does indicate that people in mid-life report increased self-confidence, greater warmth in relationships, and a greater sense of commitment to both work and relationships (Lachman & James, 1997). The mid-life crisis often portrayed as a sudden and frantic "kicking over the traces" is actually more often a reflective and thoughtful re-examination of personal values and goals.

Part of this kind of review is a re-examination of the downside of the kinds of inevitable career compromises described earlier. At mid-life, people often review long dormant career aspirations and decide to pursue them again. Completion of child-rearing responsibilities or the attainment of some degree of financial security often make this kind of return to a second round of career exploration possible. Unplanned-for crises such as those caused by divorces, unemployment due to corporate downsizing, or career changes dictated by failing health also bring about the need for career counseling.

Two issues that are frequently emphasized in mid-life career counseling are those involving self-efficacy questions and problem solving. Mid-life career changes often require further education or specialized training. A return to school is often threatening. Generally career changes in mid-life are also accompanied by a variety of practical problems that must be solved.

Similarly, mid-life career changes usually involve a renegotiation of close relationships, and the ability to communicate changes in goals and aspirations. The ability to reassure partners and offspring that these changes do not threaten emotional bonds is also important.

Career counseling with mid-life clients often means giving emotional support, offering help with practical problem solving and teaching of personal communication, negotiation and conflict resolution skills.

CAREER COUNSELING AND RETIREMENT

Career counseling with retirees and preretirees would have seemed absurd within the narrow concepts of career as concerned only with paid work. The concepts of career as a psychological quest across the life-span and concerned with all aspects of an individual's life space means that career counseling for retirement or preparation for retirement is very relevant.

The needs to *grow,* to *contribute,* and to *remain* in the main stream of human existence does not end at age 65, or whatever age the society arbitrarily decides that people should quit work. Career counseling with retirees may involve helping to review areas of expertise and the fruits of experience that can be employed in volunteer efforts. It may involve selecting leisure activities or even a return to schooling.

Career counseling may help clients to cope with feelings of rejection and abandonment. It may involve support and reassurance about self-worth and helping to restructure an identity that was built around position and status in the workplace. As one retiree put it, "retirement means going from *Who's Who* to who's that?"

COUNSELING PROCESSES IN CAREER COUNSELING

One of the most pernicious misconceptions in the field of counseling is the notion that career counseling requires less attention to relationship factors, less sensitivity to feelings, or less focus on personality dynamics or developmental crises than does so-called personal counseling. The process of career exploration and career planning causes clients to bring into question fragile concepts of self, put at risk cherished relationships, and make disappointing and painful compromises with reality.

A study of process and outcome in career counseling (Kirschner, Hoffman, & Hill, 1994). examined counselor intentions and client perceptions of helpfulness. Along with information-giving, the most helpful counselor activities as perceived by both counselor and client were support, clarification of feelings, helping to promote insight, bringing about and reinforcing behavior change, challenging misconceptions, and providing a warm and caring relationship.

Clearly, effective career counseling is effective psychological counseling.

CHAPTER 10

Gender Issues in Developmental Counseling

> The essential fact about the *New Women* is that they differ among
> themselves as men do, in work, in play, in virtues, and in rewards
> achieved. They are *Women* not *Woman.*
>
> —Leta Hollingsworth (1927)

IT SEEMS unlikely that in the past few thousand years of recorded human history that many postpubertal individuals have failed to notice that men and women are different, both anatomically and psychologically. The nature of those differences, their origins, magnitude, and significance have been sources of wonder, speculation, and controversy for most of that time.

Three-quarters of a century ago, Leta Hollingsworth, a pioneering student of the psychology of women and one of the principal founders of professional psychology, rebuked attempts to stereotype women as they began to enter the mainstream of political, intellectual, and economic life in America.

Most of what has been written about gender in our efforts to understand the lives, development, and experiences of both men and women has centered around differences and contrasts between the two. The apparent fixation in both psychology and the larger society with searching for differences between men and women rather than focusing on the much larger domain of shared characteristics is perhaps indicative of the uneasy and usually unfair balance of power between the sexes (Hare-Mustin & Marecek, 1988). If men and women are really so different then

208

perhaps all of the inequities in pay, promotions, privileges, and opportunities might be justifiable after all. Meanwhile disagreement continues around the question of the magnitude and meaning of sex differences.

GENDER DIFFERENCES

Much of the recent research on gender differences seems to have as much of a political flavor as it has the aura of sober scientific inquiry (Eagly, 1995). Studies have been done to show that men touch women more frequently than women touch men, that women smile more than men, that in conversation men interrupt women five times as often as women interrupt them, and that men and women have very different conversational styles (Hyde & Plant, 1995). At a casual glance, much of this research seems to reflect a dedication to trivial pursuits.

One of the first and most widely quoted reviews of research on psychological differences between men and women was done more than 25 years ago (Maccoby & Jacklyn, 1974). The reviewers concluded that most of these differences between men and women were relatively small and probably not of much practical consequence (Maccoby, 1990). Since that time, continued research has focused on several areas of personality development where differences have been generally perceived to exist (Jacklyn, 1989).

MALE VULNERABILITY

One consistent finding is that males are physically more vulnerable than females and that these differences are particularly pronounced at the beginning and end of the life-span. More males are at risk in infancy than females and differences in longevity persist. Males are also disproportionately represented in mental retardation, attention disorders, dyslexia, and speech problems (Halpern, 1997).

The degree to which these factors affect life-span development and behavior is largely unknown. We might speculate that men's self-protectiveness, tradition of "macho-toughness," and worship of physical prowess are related to feelings of vulnerability.

COGNITIVE AND INTELLECTUAL DEVELOPMENT

One of the most widely researched areas in gender differences concerns cognitive development. Earlier reviews of research concluded that there were gender differences favoring girls in verbal ability, while differences favoring boys were found in quantitative and spatial abilities. Some more recent studies suggested that these cognitive gender differences were shrinking or disappearing (Feingold, 1988), while others continue to report such differences (Halpern, 1997). One of the frequently cited gender differences relates to performance in mathematics. A number studies were reviewed in the 1980s indicating that boys consistently scored higher on standardized tests of mathematics ability or achievement. A variety of explanations were advanced to explain these results including the possibility of biological differences. Further research has suggested that differences may be due to a combination of socially mediated factors such as math anxiety, attitudes of parents toward mathematical achievement of girls, and girls' own perceptions of the value of mathematics in terms of plans and aspirations (Jacklyn, 1989).

Further support for social learning explanations in regard to mathematical achievement and self-efficacy have been found in more recent research (Farmer, Wardrop, Anderson, & Risinger, 1995; O'Brien & Fassinger, 1993). At this point, little credible evidence exists to support the notion of biological differences in *general* cognitive or intellectual functioning between men and women (Halpern, 1997). Observed differences in levels of aspiration, education, and achievement are largely explainable in terms of differences in socialization, opportunities, and social support. Even the context in which tasks are presented in testing situations is important. In some studies, when the same task was presented to boys and girls as either a measure of needlework skills or electronics, sex differences were reversed (Archer, 1996).

SOCIAL BEHAVIOR

Differences in social behavior have been found in a wide variety of studies (Archer, 1996). Generally, women have been found to be more likely to engage in personal helping behavior, be less aggressive, less assertive, and more nurturant than men. Men are also found consistently to be less emotionally expressive and less self-disclosing than women. These differences have been subsumed in terms of two clusters of behavior tendencies called *communal* and *agentic*. As translated into general social roles, the communal role emphasizes nurturant, socially sensitive, and often compliant behavior, while the agentic role stresses assertive behavior and direct action to control situations or environments.

These behaviors reflect traditional sex roles and socialization experiences of men and women in Western cultures. Major questions exist around whether these behaviors simply reflect historical differences in social learning and opportunities, or the degree, if any, to which they are genetically linked to the evolutionary history of the human species.

As research into gender differences has become more sophisticated, it is clear that rather than defining differences as general *traits* residing *inside* men and women, the origin of differences in social behavior are considerably more complex. Sex differences in a variety of behaviors reflect the gender-relevant beliefs that people bring to a social interaction situation, and the extent to which the situation activates those beliefs. Sex differences are now seen as flexible, *context dependent* outcomes of social processes (Archer, 1996). The differences do *not* imply, for example, that women are unable to be assertive or action-oriented, or that men cannot be nurturant and emotionally expressive.

SOCIAL RELATIONSHIPS

In terms of relationship development, children generally begin by preferring same-sex partners in play situations. Play activity also involves more social interaction in same-sex pairs of preschool children. Same-sex preferences in social activities continue to grow throughout childhood. Gender segregation or same-sex preferences are very strong, stable, and widespread determinants of social behavior and development through childhood and into adolescence. Both boys and girls have difficulty forming or engaging in groups that include children of both sexes. Some of this may be due to the reluctance of boys to accept influence from girls and may relate to observations of power differentials in family and community situations (Maccoby, 1990).

In same-sex social situations, girls are more likely than boys to resolve conflict with verbal negotiation, while boys are more likely to engage in competitive or aggressive strategies. These differences and difficulties in childhood interactions go a long way in explaining problems of communication and cooperation between the sexes in interpersonal situations throughout the life-span.

One interpretation of those findings is that facilitative styles of communication and interpersonal problem solving enable women and girls to form more integrated and more intimate social relationships than do men. It may also help to explain why men are relatively less emotionally expressive and self-disclosing (Maccoby, 1990).

In group problem-solving situations, men are more likely to engage in task behavior and women are more likely to engage in group maintenance activities. Friendship patterns in men and women also show sharp differences. Men tend to form less disclosing relationships and to form relationships based primarily on shared activities such as work or recreation. In some studies, most of the men were actually unable to name a best friend. Men who do report having close friends often tend to avoid discussing personal concerns with them to avoid appearing vulnerable or dependent.

Women on the other hand, tend to form close, more intimate friendships that are based on shared feelings and experiences. Most women are able to name a best friend and to report instances of sharing feelings and problems. These kinds of differences have been found consistently in many studies (Archer, 1996).

In play and recreational activities, boys and men are likely to establish and enforce rules as ways of preventing or resolving conflicts. For males "fairness" is a matter of rule-following. Women are more likely to negotiate differences on the basis of enhancing or protecting relationships.

DIFFERENCES IN MORAL REASONING

Much of the early research on moral development focused on a model of development based on the issues of fairness and justice (Kohlberg, 1984). The Kohlberg model posited the existence of ascending levels of moral development that reflected increasing complexity and autonomy in moral reasoning. Early research on the Kohlberg model rather consistently showed men to be at higher stages of moral reasoning than women. More recent research suggests that sex differences in reasoning on a justice and fairness model are not as great as previously supposed.

Gilligan (1982) criticized the Kohlberg model as unrepresentative of the moral concerns and experiencing of women. She argued that women's concepts of morality focus more on considerations of caring and maintenance of relationships with others, while men's concepts have more to do with justice, fairness, and individual rights and responsibilities.

In Gilligan's model, the orientation to individual survival is the lowest level of moral reasoning, and as moral development proceeds, women acknowledge the importance of self-sacrifice and move on to emphasize the importance of truthfulness, and finally to incorporate a morality of nonviolence. Values that become increasingly important as the woman grows, include increased respect for truth, caring for self and others, and an obligation to avoid and prevent hurting others. In this model, the moral imperative is to *care* and take responsibility for understanding and alleviating the suffering and troubles of the world.

The Gilligan model makes intuitive sense in terms of the differences between men and women's social development described earlier. The emphasis is more on the preservation of social conscience and sense of community and responsibility than on the formation of formal rules and abstract principles.

THE MEANING OF *LES DIFFERENCES*

While we might join the French in simply rejoicing about the nature of sex differences, it is abundantly clear that major *psychological* differences do exist between men and women. It is also clear that these are of far greater consequence than a few points on a standardized mathematics test, or a disparity in who interrupts whom in social conversation.

To a very large degree, these differences are the product of patterns of social role-taking and socialization processes deeply embedded in our culture. It is also possible that these differences have some origins in the differing problems and challenges confronting male and female human beings from the very beginning of human history, and so have become a part of human evolution (Buss, 1995). Whether the origins of these differences are traceable in terms of centuries or millenia is not really the question of most concern to developmental counselors.

What is of greatest significance to developmental counseling is that to a considerable extent men and women have different patterns of thinking, feeling, and acting in response to many of the developmental transitions, crises, and problems that confront them as they move through the life cycle. What are also of great concern are the injustices, limitations of opportunity, and psychological burdens placed on human beings as a result of the ignorance, confusion, and ambivalence that surround issues of gender in interpersonal relationships.

GENDER AND PSYCHOLOGICAL WELL-BEING

Women are referred and diagnosed with depression about twice as often as men. The lifetime risk factor for depression is about 10% for men and more than 20% for women. Married women are more frequently diagnosed with depression than single women, and those with children are still more frequently diagnosed as depressed (Culbertson, 1997). The onset of depression in women tends to be later than for men.

More men than women ages 20 to 30 are seen as depressed, however, while more adolescent girls than boys are diagnosed as depressed. There is some indication that depression in men is increasing relative to women and that the above ratios may be changing. The figures cited above seem to hold true generally for all of the Western industrialized nations (Culbertson, 1997).

Sex differences in rates of depression have long been cited as both evidence for and consequences of sex discrimination and social injustice. As we noted in Chapter 4, the assessments of mental health workers vary considerably from those directly reported by general populations in terms of subjective well-being or happiness. To judge from self-reports, more people are happy than mental health professionals estimate.

While depression has been seen historically as a major problem of women, alcohol abuse has been seen as a primary problem of men. Large differences between men and women have been found both in alcohol consumption and in problem drinking. Men begin drinking earlier than women, drink greater quantities of alcohol, and drink more frequently. Estimates put the ratio of male problem drinkers as compared to women at between three and four to one (Lemle & Miskind, 1989). These estimates have been fairly stable over time. Some researchers have suggested that alcohol consumption and even abuse is virtually part of the male gender role in the United States (McCreary, Newcomb, & Sadava, 1999).

The suicide rate for men is about three times as great as for women. The rate rises rapidly for men from adolescence to about age 35. Both men and women with a history of alcohol or drug abuse are at greater risk for suicide. About one-third of suicides are associated with alcohol use (Corey, Corey, & Callanan, 1993).

Men use mental health treatment facilities less frequently than do women (Leaf & Bruce, 1987). The differences in self-disclosure and emotional expressiveness discussed may help to account for this difference. Because men are less likely to self-refer for treatment, their rate of psychological disturbances and distress may be underestimated.

GENDER AND LIFE-SPAN DEVELOPMENT

The question of whether existing theories of life-span development adequately represent the experiences and challenges facing women has continued for many years. The model of chronological or life-stage development proposed by Erik Erikson, which forms the basis for the developmental framework outlined in Chapter 3, is a case in point. Ironically, Erikson's first statement of his scheme was in a paper titled "The Eight Stages of

Man." The use of the male gender was more a function of contemporary grammatical form than one intended to limit its applicability, however.

At this point, the answer to the question of whether psychosocial theories such as Erikson's adequately describe women's development is a resounding "yes-maybe." Recent research (Lachman & James, 1997; Parker & Aldwin, 1997; Stewart & Ostrove, 1998) suggest considerable similarity in the experiences of men and women as they move through developmental transitions from young adulthood into mid-life and suggest reasonably high congruence with predictions drawn from psychosocial theories.

Both men and women experience a degree of stabilization in their sense of personal identity and tend to move into a period of "generativity" or peak productivity and contribution to others and to society. Both men and women tend to grow in self-confidence and self-esteem after this transition. Both men and women apparently go through a mid-life crisis in which they re-examine aspirations and values and frequently make midcourse corrections in life planning. For women, this re-examination may be somewhat less tumultuous than for men, but the changes made may be even more drastic.

Most of the research on the adult development of both men and women has been done on college-educated people. Most has also been done on essentially two generations: those who grew up during the Great Depression and World War II, and the subsequent generation of Baby Boomers born in the 1940s and 1950s.

We know now that the young adult experiences of these two groups has been considerably different. For example, a study done of the 1964 women graduates of an Eastern liberal arts college showed that virtually 90% of these graduates married and had children soon after graduation. They were very similar in this regard to graduates from 20 years earlier. Slightly more of the 1964 graduates entered professional occupations, had slightly fewer children and considerably more were divorced. Only 11 years later a similar study of 1975 graduates showed that three years after graduation only 13% were married and none had children. Eighty percent of the 1975 graduates were pursuing careers, and more than one-half were in graduate school. These statistics reflect a major social change (Stewart & Ostrove, 1998).

Studies of mid-life women, particularly those who are college educated, show that most have an increased sense of personal identity and confidence in personal self-efficacy, paralleled by a somewhat increased preoccupation with aging, itself. The pattern of feelings found were *not* consistent with popular stereotypes of middle-aged women as discontented, depressed, or down-trodden. As Stewart and Ostrove describe it, "there is an exuberance in these women that is hard to miss, along with a sense of personal authority and personal agency" (1998, p. 1191).

The mid-life women in these studies tended to be those whose education, planning, and social support had prepared them to take advantage of the rapidly opening windows of opportunity made possible by the social and economic changes occurring over the past 30 years. Unfortunately, there are doubtless many more who were not able to share in such opportunities. As we move into the twenty-first century an important role for developmental counseling is to help insure that opportunities for both women and men continue to widen and that more and more young adults are able to seize them, and so move along the paths of optimal development.

GENDER AND CAREER DEVELOPMENT

One area in which gender differences and gender-role expectations have been enormously important is in career development. Traditional concepts of sex-roles and gender appropriate behaviors have undoubtedly contributed to a constriction of opportunity for women, to their economic exploitation, and to a tremendous waste of human resources. To a less obvious extent, such expectations have also chained men to a rigid and often debilitating and constricting concept of what it means to be a man.

THE CAREER DEVELOPMENT OF WOMEN

Over the past quarter century, a voluminous literature has pointed up the many inequities within the society that have tended to inhibit the career development of women. That literature is much too extensive to relate here. It has, however, sparked the development of a very vigorous and creative body of theory and research around the area of women's career behavior and development (Hackett, 1997).

The degree to which this new body of knowledge has been translated into improved career counseling and more efficacious career planning for young women is not yet entirely clear. A study of the career-planning behavior of high school girls done in 1975 found that almost one-fourth of the 200 junior and senior girls in the study were unable to specify any even tentative or rudimentary post-high school educational or vocational plans (Rapoza & Blocher, 1976). The authors called this unfortunate phenomenon the "Cinderella Effect," that is the tendency to await the arrival of a "Prince Charming."

A 1993 study (O'Brien & Fassinger) done in an admittedly more selective high school setting showed that 98% of the adolescent girls planned to attend college, more than 60% had already chosen a college major and more than one half had already made a tentative career choice. This study found that one of the major influences in career planning involved the attitudes and values of mothers toward careers. If these results are at all representative of the general population, progress has indeed been made.

Theory and research on women's career development have focused on several key concepts that appear to have crucial significance in women's career development. One of these that was mentioned earlier in the chapter is the concept of *agency* which is similar to White's concept of competence discussed in Chapter 2. It is interpreted, however, as a *trait* rather than an inherent drive, and has been construed to be a characteristic of men and to be weaker or absent in the personality makeup of women. The trait has been defined as a tendency to seek independence and autonomy, to master the environment, and to exert power and influence over others. In terms of aspirations, agentic goals are seen to focus on prominence and status as marks of success.

Traditional sex role concepts of women, which as we noted, seemed to center around communal facets of personality development such as nurturance, self-effacement, and compliance to other's needs or wishes, have been seen as almost antithetical to agency, and have often been perceived as being sources of disadvantage in a male-dominated and competitive world of work.

Sex differences in social behavior are *not* immutable tendencies locked into human personality, but are themselves products of social learning, social expectations, and concepts of self and others. It seems clear that an increasing emphasis in personality development in the direction of a greater sense of agency and wider repertoire of agentic behaviors and motivations might enhance the career capabilities of many women. Studies of highly successful women support this position (Fassinger & Ritchie, 1994).

A second key concept related to women's career development is the idea of *multiple role planning*. One of the basic propositions on which developmental counseling is based is the view that human effectiveness and resulting life satisfactions are products of the successful implementation of the variety of social roles that provide structure and substance to every individual life. All human beings engage in a variety of life roles and in so doing pursue many different sources of fulfillment and satisfaction.

The successful implementation of multiple social role opportunities is much more difficult for most women than for most men. Success and satisfaction in career, marriage, family, and community participation represents a daunting if not impossible challenge for most women. Even with the significant changes in male and female role concepts and responsibilities that have occurred over the past 30 years, the burden of parenting, homemaking, care of aging or infirm relatives, and other responsibilities still falls more heavily on women than men. For women to enjoy the multiple role opportunities that men have tended to take for granted requires careful planning and high levels of energy and commitment.

Since women's career patterns are often interrupted, and career and family priorities are frequently shifted, planning often has to incorporate the acquisition of portable and storable skills, and the utilization of opportunities for continuing education, part-time employment, flexible hours, job sharing, or working out of the home. Planning thus must be continuous, complex, and pervasive.

A third key concept in the career development of women is *connectedness*. One of the major developmental assets of women is their ability to form close relationships, facilitate the development of others, and resolve and manage interpersonal conflicts. Although flexibility in the employment of some of the agentic behaviors mentioned above may help women to succeed, these should not be acquired through the sacrifice of the interpersonal skills, social sensitivity, and sense of social responsibility that distinguish and illuminate women's lives. A qualitative study of the career development of highly successful women showed that in addition to the passion and commitment with which they pursued their dreams, these women were also deeply conscious and concerned with the social contribution and sense of relatedness to others that gave added meaning to their careers. The researchers (Richie et al., 1997) put it this way:

> The women in this sample tended to see merit in the people around them. They tended to think from a collective rather than individual perspective about work and personal life. . . . The essence then of the core story is persistence, connection, and passion. (p. 139)

MEN'S CAREER DEVELOPMENT

Research on gender differences in career development have generally shown the kinds of results that might be expected from the discussion of agentic behavior and aspirations given earlier. Generally, men have been found to attribute high importance to instrumental factors such as job security, possibilities for advancement, compensation packages, authority, prestige, and autonomy. Women on the other hand were seen to be more concerned with working hours, working conditions, and relationships with people (Goldin, 1990). Most recent research suggests that some of those differences may be lessening (Gati, Osipow, & Givon, 1995).

The emphasis in career decision making is a product of the traditional male role in American society. The traditional view of the male as the family breadwinner, and the fixation upon male dominance and autonomy are reflected in these preferences.

It is likely that these preferences are also reflected in the notoriously low relationship found between job satisfaction and general life satisfaction. Satisfaction with work does not seem to be a major source of life satisfaction for American men (R.A. Myers & Cairo, 1992). For most American men, success in work seems to reflect external rewards rather than those intrinsic satisfactions that are major ingredients in overall happiness.

Much of the tumult associated with the male mid-life crisis may be a function of a growing sense of disappointment and desperation with the psychological emptiness of their work lives. Research has shown that middle-age men are less conflicted about success, power, and competition than are college-age men, but are more concerned about conflicts between work and family (Cournoyer & Mahalik, 1995). In a strange and ironic way, men seem to be hostages to their own sex-role conceptions, and to make career choices that provide relatively little lifelong satisfaction even though the external aspects of success in terms of pay, prestige, and independence are central to their choices.

GENDER ROLE CONFLICT IN MEN

One of the ironic and irrational aspects of gender issues in psychology is that while male development and male gender roles have often been assumed to represent the appropriate *norm* for both sexes, the traditional male role is associated with its own set of psychological problems and pitfalls. In the past, the masculine role has been seen as fostering psychological well-being in terms of assertiveness, self-confidence, self-esteem, and decisiveness. The concept of *agency* which has been conceptualized as a primarily masculine trait rather than as a general human need and tendency is a case in point.

More recently, it has become clear that there are definite liabilities associated with rigid adherence to stereotypic male roles (Cournoyer & Mahalik, 1995). Popular conceptions of male sex roles and male personality development propagated by the media and represented by a motley collection of cultural heroes have helped to create a maladaptive set of so-cial norms for adolescent and young adult men. These norms have often translated into behavior tendencies associated with thrill-seeking, exces-sive risk-taking, substance abuse, and sexual promiscuity, as well as ac-tive aggression and sometimes deadly violence.

In adult men, similar role concepts have been associated with excessive stress, anger proneness, and Type A behavior associated with heart dis-ease. Problem drinking has also been associated with strong adherence to traditional masculine sex roles involving beliefs that men should always be in high status positions in terms of occupational success, act in ways that show physical and emotional toughness, and avoid anything remotely as-sociated with feminine activities (McCreary et al., 1999). The John Wayne role is not always one that leads to health, fame, fortune, or even sobriety. The strong silent type is too often the brittle and broken type.

As these research findings have become widely recognized, a specific syndrome of male psychological dysfunction called *Gender Role Conflict* has come into prominence. Gender role conflict in men is seen to occur when men are socialized to hold a set of rigid, sexist, or restrictive beliefs about the nature of sex-appropriate behavior. When these beliefs are rigidly held or extreme, they may constrict personal development, inhibit the range of choices, and cause devaluations of the worth of self and oth-ers. In situations where environmental pressures impel men to act or con-sider acting in ways that threaten stereotypic beliefs or self-concepts, they may react with anxiety or even aggression.

Considerable research has demonstrated the connection between gen-der role conflict and psychological dysfunction and distress across the life-span (Cournoyer & Mahalik, 1995). Much of the fear of intimacy, emotional constriction, and social isolation in men discussed in this chapter has been attributed to gender role conflict. Gender role conflict may complicate various developmental crises and transitions confronting men across the life-span by constricting the range of options available in problem-solving situations and also by depriving them of needed social support (Wang, Heppner, & Berry, 1997).

Other studies have suggested that masculine ideology helps to foster emotional inexpressiveness, which in turn negatively affects shyness and interpersonal competence (Bruch, Berko, & Haase, 1998). Interper-sonal skills and effectiveness relate to a host of developmental tasks and transitions.

It seems abundantly clear that both men and women can be victims of rigid and irrational sex-role socialization experiences. For all clients, a primary task of developmental counseling may be to help them loosen the bonds of constricting beliefs about their nature, potentials, and possibilities as fully human and actualized men and women.

GENDER AND THE COUNSELING PROCESS

Although there are probably situations and circumstances in which same-sex matching of client and counselor is desirable, the nature of those situations is not at all clear. Research indicates that men and women with both traditional and nontraditional sex-role concepts report choosing competence in counselors in preference to same-sex matching with a less competent counselor (DeHeer, Wampold, & Freund, 1992).

Research relating counseling outcome to same-sex matching for female clients has been largely inconclusive (Nelson, 1993). At this point, we have little evidence either to support or reject the notion that same-sex matching is generally desirable for either male or female clients. One model of psychotherapy intended for women has been developed and widely practiced.

FEMINIST THERAPY

For many years, models of psychotherapy, particularly those with roots in psychoanalysis, have been seen as sexist in terms of assumptions about appropriate sex roles, and a lack of understanding about the extent, origins, and nature of the psychological problems and concerns of women (Hare-Mustin, 1983). Some of this distrust of traditional psychotherapy stems from cases described by Sigmund Freud. One of these, "The Case of Dora," suggests an insensitivity and possible sex bias on the part of Freud in working with a depressed young woman who was the apparent victim of a pattern of family intrigue and betrayal. Freud's attempt at psychoanalysis was unsuccessful and in case descriptions the blame for failure was put on the patient. Dora's premature termination of treatment by walking out on the eminent Dr. Freud was probably testimony to her good judgment and resilience.

Considerable distrust of traditional counseling and psychotherapeutic procedures in regard to women continues today. Women are generally the most frequent consumers of mental health services. A strong belief persists that women are often mistreated in the therapeutic relationship (Denmark, 1994). Evidence suggests that much psychotherapeutic practice and the intrapsychic theories on which it is based serves to perpetuate the status quo in terms of sex roles and other social issues by labeling and treating resistance to, or even discontent with, unjust and irrational aspects of the social order as evidence of psychopathology. This tendency holds true for both men and women and may be particularly destructive for gay or lesbian clients.

As the feminist or women's movement developed in the 1960s, a reaction to perceived sex biases in counseling and psychotherapy produced what is termed *feminist therapy*.

Feminist therapy is a method of treatment that takes into account the discrimination against women contained in traditional social role concepts and institutional practices. The underlying philosophy is drawn from the values of feminism as a social movement. These stress the ideas that men and women must be given equal opportunities for gaining personal, political, and economic power. Feminist therapy further holds that traditional sex-role differences should not be perpetuated in the counseling relationship itself. Dependency, passivity, and helplessness on the part of female clients is discouraged.

Feminist therapy tends to attribute many of a client's personal problems to social factors that are external rather than intrapsychic. One of the goals of feminist therapy is to empower women to become more independent and socially and politically active on behalf of the rights and welfare of women (Denmark, 1994).

Most of the values and philosophical orientation of feminist therapy are fully compatible with the perspective of developmental counseling. The

---

The Case of Miriam

Miriam and her family came to America from the Orient when she was 3 years old. Her father is a professor of mathematics at the state university. She attended public schools, graduating from high school with honors. She is attending a liberal arts college for women where she will receive her BA degree in the spring. She has been seeing her college counselor as she plans for her application to graduate school.

Last week she came to her appointment in tears. Her parents informed her that she is to wed a young man from her native country who will arrive next week. The wedding was arranged between the two families many years before.

If Miriam refuses to go through with the wedding, she will be ostracized and shunned by her entire family. Quite apart from her apprehensions about marrying a man she does not even know, Miriam is afraid that she will be expected to be totally submissive, and to subordinate all of her own aspirations to those of her husband.

How should the counselor approach the situation? How would a feminist therapist approach the case?

emphasis on *empowerment, advocacy, personal development,* and *social interactionism* are all tenets of developmental counseling. To the degree that feminist therapy is seen as primarily a political and social movement (Fitzgerald & Nutt, 1986), it goes beyond the aims of developmental counseling.

PRINCIPLES FOR COUNSELING WOMEN

For more than 20 years, the Division of Counseling Psychology of the American Psychological Association has enumerated a set of basic principles that are intended to guide the ethical and professional practice of counseling with women (Division of Counseling Psychology, APA, 1978). These principles have since been endorsed by the parent organization and by several of its other divisions. The full text of these principles appears in Figure 10.1.

These principles call on counselors to be knowledgeable and well informed about biological, psychological, and social issues affecting women. Much of psychological theory and research has in the past tended to focus on male issues and male experiences. An inspection of the professional and scientific literature of counseling psychology today suggests that this balance has at least in part been redressed.

The principles also call on counselors to be aware of the implications of various theoretical points of view in terms of their impact on women. The principles also call for both preservice and continuing education of counselors to deal with issues and knowledge domains relevant to the counseling of women. These principles should be read and heeded by every counselor. They are part of the ethical framework within which all professional counseling must operate to deserve the name.

Unfortunately, many of the most important aspects of counseling with women concern not only the knowledge and skills of the counselors, but also their beliefs, values, and attitudes regarding men and women and the essential relationships between them. These principles emphasize the need for counselors to be aware of and to continually review their own values and biases, and the effects of these on their women clients. This injunction is probably the most important, but the least attainable goal reflected in the APA principles.

Many of the implicit beliefs and values around gender issues are formed early in an individual's developmental history and are held at very low levels of self-awareness. Many gender-relevant beliefs are inextricably intertwined with deeply held and emotionally charged social, political, and religious convictions.

Although competent counseling/therapy processes are essentially the same for all counselor/therapist interactions, special subgroups require specialized skills, attitudes and knowledge. Women constitute a special subgroup.

Competent counseling-therapy requires recognition and appreciation that contemporary society is not sex fair. Many institutions, test standards and attitudes of mental health professionals limit the options of women clients. Counselors/therapists should sensitize women clients to these real-world limitations, confront them with both the external and their own internalized limitations and explore with them their reactions to these constraints.

The principles presented here are considered essential for the competent counseling/therapy of women.

1. Counselors/therapists are knowledgeable about women, particularly with regard to biological, psychological and social issues which have impact on women in general or on particular groups of women in our society.
2. Counselors/therapists are aware that the assumptions and precepts of theories relevant to their practice may apply differently to men and women. Counselors/therapists are aware of those theories and models that proscribe or limit the potential of women clients, as well as those that may have particular usefulness for women clients.
3. After formal training, counselors/therapists continue to explore and learn of issues related to women, including the special problems of female subgroups, throughout their professional careers.
4. Counselors/therapists recognize and are aware of all forms of oppression and how these interact with sexism.
5. Counselors/therapists are knowledgeable and aware of verbal and non-verbal process variables (particularly with regard to power in the relationship) as these affect women in counseling/therapy so that the counselor/therapist-client interactions are not adversely affected. The need for shared responsibility between clients and counselors/therapists is acknowledged and implemented.
6. Counselors/therapists have the capability of utilizing skills that are particularly facilitative to women in general and to particular subgroups of women.
7. Counselors/therapists ascribe no pre-conceived limitations on the direction or nature of potential changes or goals in counseling/therapy for women.
8. Counselors/therapists are sensitive to circumstances where it is more desirable for a woman client to be seen by a female or male counselor/therapist.
9. Counselors/therapists use non-sexist language in counseling/therapy, supervision, teaching and journal publications.
10. Counselors/therapists do not engage in sexual activity with their women clients under any circumstances.
11. Counselors/therapists are aware of and continually review their own values and biases and the effects of these on their women clients. Counselors/therapists understand the effects of sex-role socialization upon their own development and functioning and the consequent values and attitudes they hold for themselves and others. They recognize that behaviors and roles need not be sex based.
12. Counselors/therapists are aware of how their personal functioning may influence their effectiveness in counseling/therapy with women clients. They monitor their functioning through consultation, supervision or therapy so that it does not adversely affect their work with women clients.
13. Counselors/therapists support the elimination of sex bias with institutions and individuals.

Source: "Principles Concerning the Counseling and Therapy of Women," *The Counseling Psychologist*, vol. 8, no. 1 (1979), p. 21. Copyrighted © 1979 by *The Counseling Psychologist*. Reprinted by permission of Sage Publications, Inc.

Figure 10.1 APA principles concerning the counseling and therapy of women.

There is little reason to believe that gender-relevant biases can be eliminated even in same-sex counselor-client pairings. A simple reading of a daily newspaper or attentive listening to the six o'clock news report will convince one that the issues around abortion, sex-education, birth control, premarital sex, treatment of sex offenders, domestic violence, divorce, and even equal pay and promotion continue to divide America along ethnic, generational, political, economic, and religious lines. Those divisions do not simply pit women against men, but are indicative of deep-seated cultural and historical influences.

At this point in our development as a society, it is probably most useful for both male and female counselors to examine their own gender-relevant beliefs, and to discuss these with clients as openly and candidly as possible in all of those many counseling situations in which gender is an important factor.

COUNSELING MEN

Informal observation and research findings indicate that men are considerably less likely than women to seek or persist in psychological counseling or other forms of psychotherapy. Reluctance to self-disclose, emotional inexpressiveness, and rigid and maladaptive sex-role concepts all mitigate against men seeking or profiting from professional psychological help. The combination of these factors is sometimes called the *masculine mystique* (O'Neil, 1981).

The masculine mystique can be summed up as the following beliefs:

1. Power, dominance, competition, and control are essential in proving one's masculinity.
2. The expression of negative feelings and emotions other than anger is a sign of weakness, vulnerability, and femininity and is to be avoided at all costs.
3. Control of self, others, and the environment is essential for personal security and discharge of masculine responsibilities.
4. Seeking help in managing feelings or fears is a mark of weakness and incompetence and is unmanly.
5. Persistence and blind courage in the face of overwhelming odds and obstacles are the highest marks of manliness.

The masculine mystique is an age-old cultural product celebrated and reaffirmed in history, art, literature, music, and drama. It is widely

The Case of Chuck

Chuck is 41 years old. He is married and has one son in college and a daughter who is a senior in high school. Chuck has a degree in business education. He taught in high school for three years and hated it.

Sixteen years ago Chuck went to work for a family-owned company that manufactures and distributes supplies for the food service industry. He now manages their shipping and delivery operation.

Until recently, Chuck reported directly to the CEO of the company who is also the son of the founder. Chuck has a close personal relationship with the CEO. They frequently lunch together, play golf, fish, and have season tickets to the university football games.

A few months ago, the CEO had a minor heart attack and decided to retire. The family decided to sell the company to a large conglomerate corporation.

The new CEO was sent out from the company's New York office. The new CEO is 29 years old with a Harvard MBA and was described by Chuck's former boss as being on the fast track to move up the corporate ladder in the parent company. She is also African American.

Chuck has never worked for a younger person or for a woman. He has never even known an African American person socially. Chuck is nervous and ill at ease in the new CEO's presence. He finds himself reacting defensively even to simple questions about his department. Twice he has stalked out of meetings when he felt his department was being unfairly criticized.

Chuck is losing sleep, drinking too much, and is irritable to everyone. He is afraid to talk to anyone about the situation, even his family, because he fears that they will accuse him of being racist and sexist, things that he vehemently denies to himself.

After stopping at a neighborhood bar one Friday evening, Chuck had a serious automobile accident. Although he was not tagged for drunk driving, Chuck's wife insisted that he see a counselor at their HMO. He finally shared his feelings and situation with the counselor.

How should the counselor deal with the situation? Is Chuck an example of the masculine mystique? Is he sexist and racist?

---

recognized and supported by the attitudes of both men and women, and is learned and relearned from infancy to adulthood and old age. It is a part of our basic concept of human nobility, heroism, and patriotism. It is also responsible for an incredible amount of misery, suffering, illness, and premature death.

Most of the social interaction processes that are inherent in counseling are almost directly antithetical to the masculine mystique. Many approaches require that clients come to counseling in touch with their feelings and able to define problems in terms of their own behavior. Many men are socialized to swallow their feelings and to ignore or deny them. Counseling also often requires clients to engage in an emotionally wrenching process of self-exploration, and to share that process with a relative stranger, the counselor. In this process, the client risks the loss of self-control, is forced to depend on the emotional support of the counselor, and to acknowledge the possibility of failure and loss.

It is not really remarkable that many men fail to see psychological counseling as a viable source of assistance. Research has shown that traditional sex-role concepts are related to men's negative attitudes toward counseling (Roberts & Fitzgerald, 1992).

Several possibilities exist to make counseling more palatable and accessible to men. One is a matter of simple labeling. Counselors have often sought to mystify and medicalize their services, sometimes to enhance their own prestige. Describing counseling programs in terms of seminars, classes, workshops, training sessions, or consulting services may elicit less resistance than terms such as psychotherapy, personal counseling, support groups, encounter groups, or other terms drawn from medical or psychological jargon.

Counselors may use techniques of introducing an emotionally loaded topic with discussions of problems facing well-known public figures, or dilemmas facing a given group of men before personalizing the discussion to the particular client. Similarly, topics drawn from books, films, plays, or the experiences of friends or relatives may be used to initiate self exploration in a relatively safe way. Leads such as "How did your father handle that problem?" or "Are your friends dealing with this kind of thing too?" may begin the process. Using mechanical or hydraulic images and illustrations to describe psychological phenomena may be less threatening than using psychodynamic jargon.

Perhaps the most important aspect of counseling men is in sharing control over the process of counseling with the client in a genuine rather than a manipulative way. Traditional male clients are not the only control freaks. Many counselors unwittingly indulge their own needs for power and control by playing subtle and not so subtle manipulative games with clients. One of the surest ways to lose a male client is to win such a game.

Gender issues are inescapable elements in counseling. Nothing is more fundamental to an individual's identity or more central to his or her hopes and aspirations than gender. For many years relationships between men and women have been described as those of lover, mate, and rival. The ways in which these fundamental relationships and the multitude of roles that surround them are conceived, internalized, and acted on are basic to full human development.

CHAPTER 11

Counseling in a
Multicultural World

Like Job of old we protest the inevitable . . . we protect ourselves
from the disturbing reality of change by surrounding ourselves
with a cocoon of pretended reality. . . . This is "cultural
encapsulation," an encapsulation within . . . our culture and
subculture, within a pretense that the present is enduring.
—C. Gilbert Wrenn (1965)

"ASK NOT for whom the bell tolls, it tolls for thee." So wrote the poet John Donne some four hundred years ago. Ernest Hemingway used the phrase to title his novel about the Spanish Civil War that warned of the creeping tide of hate and bigotry oozing across Europe on the eve of the Second World War. Donne went on to declare that "no man is an island." An examination of human history of the past four hundred years is likely to convince the reader that it has taken a long time for the poet's message to sink in, if indeed it has been heeded at all.

The reasons for our human tendency to weave personal and cultural cocoons or to retreat onto fantasy islands of presumed isolation are not always clear. Some of our encapsulation is a product of the tragedies of our history. War, exploitation, and the evil of racial divisions and attendant bigotry have scarred us all.

At an individual level, our isolationist tendencies seem more understandable if not more palatable. No human being ever fully and finally understands, appreciates, or comes to know another. Because we are all constantly changing, we often do not fully know or understand ourselves. Even people who have shared a warm, loving, and deeply committed relationship for more than half a century continue to surprise and even to astound each other with their opinions, reactions, and feelings. If this were not true, relationships and life itself would be pretty boring and monotonous.

We are separated from each other by a host of differences that tend to create the gulf that divides our little island from all of the others. Age and generation, gender, religion, family background, wealth, and education all set us apart. In our society with its long history of racial and ethnic strife, the color of one's skin or differences in ethnicity and national origin deepen and widen the chasms that separate and divide us. Often these differences and the way we regard them seal us off from much of the richness that we can enjoy. Far too often we regard diversity with fear and suspicion rather than as a vast storehouse of varied treasures. Strangely enough, at one level we know that each of the world's cultures and peoples constitutes a veritable cornucopia of wonderful sights and sounds, tastes and images. We yearn to travel to exotic places, eat ethnic foods, buy the art, and adopt the fashions from faraway places.

At the level of human relationships, however, we seem to perceive differences as a source of danger and to view anything unfamiliar with distrust and suspicion. We allow differences and presumed differences to set us apart from interesting and rewarding relationships. We are reluctant to look past the superficial and insignificant to find what is real and wonderful in others.

We can call the aggregation of all of these many differences and the feelings that accompany them *social psychological distance*. It is this kind of distance that isolates us and cuts us off from others whose different views and experiences could enrich our lives.

One of the many paradoxes that confounds the study of human nature is that even though we often help to create and maintain the social psychological distance that separates us from others, we cannot really live comfortably for long without the very people that we tend to wall out. We are after all gregarious, interdependent, and fundamentally social creatures. What is more we live in a constantly shrinking, ever more interdependent world. That is the essence of what the poet was trying to say 400 years ago.

We are constantly reaching out and pulling back from others as we try to build relationships while preserving our petty and childish prejudices. We live in a world in which the cost of distancing oneself from others is higher and higher. Reaching out to people of differing backgrounds today is an essential part of psychological, social, and economic survival. For counselors, it is virtually the essence of their professional existence.

Studies show that the tendency for most people is to reach out first on the basis of what is called *assumed similarity;* that is, we reach out primarily to those who seem to be much like ourselves, or at least like the way we see ourselves or hope ourselves to be. We pull back from those who appear to be different even in the most superficial ways.

DEVELOPMENTAL PERSON PERCEPTION

One of the interesting things about the way we look at others is that the process of *person perception* usually reveals far more about the perceiver than it does about the person that he or she attempts to understand or describe. The process of perceiving others is a function of one's own personal development. As we grow and mature in the ability to understand the world, we may also grow in the ability to grasp the full richness and complexity in our fellow human beings. For counselors, the process of developmental person perception is an essential part of their professional growth.

At the very lowest levels of intellectual development, people perceive others almost purely on the basis of *stereotypes.* A stereotype is a way of perceiving and construing others that focuses on only one or two characteristics of another person, usually membership in a particular group or acting in a particular social role. When people focus only on these superficial aspects of another person, they begin to attribute all sorts of *presumed* characteristics, motives, or beliefs to that person regardless of the individual's actual behavior, accomplishments, or intentions. This kind of sloppy and primitive thinking creates a kind of interpersonal myopia that allows us to begin to believe that all men or women, or teenagers, or members of a given *ethnic* or *cultural* group are actually alike and can be treated as interchangeable types rather than as unique, complex, thinking-and-feeling human beings. Stereotyping is a destructive way of distancing one's self from others and alienating ourselves from the best that is within us, that is, the capacity to empathize and to feel with and for one another.

As people grow intellectually and emotionally, as they begin to be able to deal with more and more of the complexity and ambiguity that resides in the real world. They may also become more and more sophisticated perceivers of other human beings. As they grow, they may be able to abandon stereotypes and see more and more of the uniqueness and complexity that is found in every personality and every individual life.

At higher stages of development in person perception, people can begin to understand the behavior of others in the context of varying social situations and personal circumstances. They do not have to rely on initial and superficial impressions that presume the existence of fixed and rigid traits or tendencies "etched in stone" within the individual's character or personality by virtue of age or sex or ethnic origin.

They can, for example, come to understand that an individual who feels insecure in a novel or challenging situation may react defensively or withdraw into self, while in a more familiar and comfortable setting, the same person may be charming, friendly, and outgoing. As people move up the ladder in person perception they are able to reconcile and integrate seemingly incompatible aspects of another's behavior into a varied and comprehensive picture that captures the full humanity and distinctive uniqueness of others. It is at this point that people are able to go beyond *tolerating* human diversity to *celebrating* it. They are able to form positive social relationships with people clearly unlike themselves. Also at this point, they begin to think about *inclusion* rather than *exclusion* as a social style.

Such people begin to see others as *multidimensional*, with multiple potentials, hidden talents, and subtle facets that make them all the more interesting, enjoyable, and rewarding to know and to care about. At this point, people are potentially able to function as helpers or counselors.

Unfortunately, development in person perception is not inevitable. Some people remain chained to the bottom rungs of the developmental ladder for a lifetime. Some who succeed in moving up the ladder are perched there precariously. We know that any of us can be bumped from our perches by at least two ugly but ever-present realities: *prejudice* and *power*. When prejudice and power push us down, we may not even be aware of our decline.

Racism, sexism, ageism, and all of the other forms of prejudice are social diseases based on irrational and destructive social norms (Duckett, 1992). That is, they are transmitted socially and mark or scar virtually every person who lives in a plague-ridden society such as ours. As with diseases like tuberculosis in the past, today almost everyone in our society "tests positive" for racism, sexism, or other forms of prejudice. Their lives have been twisted and their relationships have been crippled to some degree by the social pollution around them. Even though we may consciously abhor bigotry and all of the evil, cruelty, and stupidity that it represents, few of us have been able to escape completely the contagion that permeates a society torn by hundreds of years of racial conflict, exploitation, and intolerance. The essence of prejudice in all of its manifestations is the belief that one group of people is *morally* superior to another, and therefore deserves to be heard, respected, and ultimately given power over others.

Sometimes when we are least aware, the residual germs of prejudice stir and drop us back down the ladder to a world of stereotypes, primitive thinking, irrational fears, and ancient animosities. Then, despite all our sophistication and good intentions, we retreat to our illusional castles and fancied isolation, pull up the drawbridge and become prisoners to fear, fantasy, and ignorance.

Along with prejudice, the second factor that eats away at our veneer of enlightenment and sophistication is the presence of power differentials that are often based on vested privilege rather than upon competence and social responsibility.

In terms of complexity in person perception, the powerless attend to the powerful, who may come to control their destinies, far more carefully than they are attended to by the powerful. Each person tries to "psyche out" the "boss," anticipate mood swings, avoid his or her irritability, and generally preserve an uneasy peace.

The powerful tend to listen less, be more oblivious to the subtleties and nuances of communication, and on the whole be less sensitive and complex in their perceptions of the less powerful. This is one of the reasons that even unconscious attitudes of superiority, entitlement, and privilege may poison relationships and perpetuate misunderstanding (Fiske, 1993).

Counselors are as fully human and therefore just as flawed or fallible as other human beings. As counselors, we too, are products and victims of a society torn and tortured by centuries of bigotry and deep-seated traditions of ethnocentrism. Yet, as counselors our very professional identity rests on our desire and ability to bridge the chasms of social psychological distance that separate each human being from every other.

Each time we initiate a counseling relationship, we endeavor to cross over and touch at least a part of the client's psychological world. Social psychological distance is represented in every counseling situation by differences between counselor and client in terms of age or generation, of gender, education, religious beliefs, political convictions, socioeconomic backgrounds, regional origins, and the host of other characteristics that define the uniqueness of each human personality.

As counselors, we consciously employ a set of interviewing techniques and interpersonal skills and attitudes in an effort to bridge social psychological distance. We try to open ourselves to the client's unique experience. We frame our impressions as tentative hypotheses to be continuously checked out. We listen attentively and above all we try to convey our respect for the client, and our deep interest and appreciation for all that is unique and special in the client and the client's world.

Yet, despite all our counseling skills and good intentions we are sometime unable to build those bridges across the gulf that separates us from

THE CASE ANALYSIS

A group of counselor education students took a comprehensive, written examination to complete their master's degree requirements. Part of the examination required them to analyze a set of case materials and to make recommendations for directions to be pursued in counseling.

The students taking the examination were young, very intelligent men and women with high social service interests. They were predominantly white, anglo, and middle class. In the case analysis, the students were asked to read a case description containing a large amount of assessment data and personal information about a hypothetical client. The counselors-in-training were asked to organize the material to provide an accurate and clear picture of the client, form clinical hypotheses, and indicate directions for counseling.

The case was a 39-year-old woman who requested vocational counseling. The client was married and had three grown children who were no longer at home. She had been married for 22 years, ever since leaving high school in her junior year.

Assessment data indicated above average intellectual ability and that the client had artistic, musical, and verbal-linguistic interests.

Two additional pieces of information were included. The client was described as the daughter of Hispanic immigrants and that her husband was upset that she was considering returning to work or further education. Virtually all of the counseling students reacted very directly to the latter information. In many of the analyses, they gave elaborate descriptions of a lower class Puerto Rican or Mexican American woman with a dominating "Macho" husband. The client, herself, was described as coming from a family in which women were traditionally devalued or oppressed. In almost every analysis, the descriptions went far beyond the data given in the case materials. For example, the client's father, who was not even mentioned in the case materials was frequently described as domineering, uneducated, and lower class.

Most of the descriptions were not couched as tentative *hypotheses*, but rather as self-evident facts. Many of the students' *assumptions* had clearly assumed the character of reality.

Because the client's parents were Hispanic immigrants and she had not completed high school, it was assumed that she was from a lower class family and from a culture that devalued women.

Stereotypic thinking had intruded into the perceptual processes of these intelligent and well-meaning people. How can these counselors learn to counsel in a multicultural world?

specific clients or potential clients. Often, we are not even able to understand why our effort to reach out failed or was rejected. In some situations, we fail to recognize or fully appreciate the impact of cultural differences on our ability to communicate and comprehend another's world.

THE CONCEPT OF CULTURE

The concept of culture is an anthropological notion invented to describe the multitude of differences in language, customs, mores, religions, family practices, and so forth that characterize various groups of people. It is a useful concept in describing relatively small groups of people living in simple societies in comparative isolation. The term *culture* is so broad and pervasive, however, that when it is applied to complex, postmodern societies in a shrinking world the concept tends to encompass everything and actually explain very little.

Contemporary societies tend to be very complex and to consist of many different subcultures—each with customs, mores, values, and practices derived from a common heritage and history, but also continuously modified out of contact and interaction with all of the other subcultures that share its geographical and psychological space (Hermans & Kempen, 1998).

From the standpoint of counselors trying to bridge social psychological distance, part of the problem is that it is misleading and indeed destructive to try to classify people into neat sets of discrete categories called cultures, or even subcultures and pretend to be able to understand or predict

C. Gilbert Wrenn (Archives of the University of Minnesota).

their behavior on that basis alone. That kind of categorical approach is the very essence of stereotypical thinking.

A related concept that is more useful is that of the *process of acculturation*. People are not simply neatly packaged, clearly labeled products of either culture or socialization. Particularly in a multicultural world, people accept some aspects of various subcultures, adopt some, and reject others. The key aspect of the acculturation process from a psychological standpoint is that it is largely *unconscious*.

To a considerable degree, the process of acculturation is one of moving patterns of thinking, feeling, and acting from a level of self-awareness and conscious choice to one that is deeply ingrained, but only dimly conscious. Within a given culture or subculture patterns of thinking, feeling, and acting that began as one way of responding or adapting, gradually become *our way, the best way*, and finally *the only way* to believe or behave. Counselors are just as profoundly affected by acculturation as are their clients. It is the mostly unconscious aspects of acculturation that divide people and make bridging social psychological distance so difficult. The first step in learning to counsel in a multicultural world is to begin to understand one's own history of acculturation.

The Reality of a Multicultural World

Multiculturalism is frequently described as a social or political philosophy (Fowers & Richardson, 1996). The growing recognition of cultural diversity and its significance in the lives of individuals may well have contributed to a more enlightened awareness of the moral questions confronting the social sciences and helping professions. The existence of a multicultural world and a multicultural American society is not a point of view, it is a simple *reality*. The impact of cultural influences on human development will not go away whether or not social scientists and counselors choose to recognize it or continue to ignore it. When all of the sciences and professions finally take into account the effects of cultural factors on human behavior, terms like cross-cultural research or cross-cultural counseling will probably no longer be needed (Segall, Lonner, & Berry, 1998).

The New Diversity

Cultural diversity in the United States is a reality that is now and will continue to impact the practice of counseling as it does all of society. As the twenty-first century begins, about one-third of the U.S. population are

---

The Case of Ellen

Ellen is a recent graduate of a prestigious liberal arts college. Her parents are both scientists who teach at the state university. Ellen grew up in an intellectually rich environment. She traveled widely with her parents and met a host of interesting and successful people from all over the world.

In college, Ellen was active in groups committed to social causes. She was determined to devote her life to promoting social justice and equal opportunity. Ellen took her degree in elementary education and began her career teaching sixth grade in an inner city school. She found that 19 of her 34 students spoke little or no English. Most were recent immigrants from Africa, Asia, or Latin America. Almost all of her pupils were from poverty-stricken families. Many were from single-parent families and lived in neighborhoods torn with crime and violence.

After eight months in her teaching job, Ellen is close to a breakdown. Worst of all, her idealism and optimism are withering. Several times she has been brought to tears when a student she attempted to discipline accused her of racial bigotry. Other teachers and counselors she has asked for help seem cynical, emotionally exhausted, and burned out.

In desperation, Ellen returned to the counseling center at her former college. How should her counselor approach the situation?

---

people of color. By 2050, this number is expected to reach 50% (Hall, 1997). In many inner cities in the United States, nearly one-half of the elementary school children have English as a second language.

The range of cultural diversity in the United States is increasing very rapidly. Only a few years ago the term *diversity* was widely interpreted to mean differences among African American, Hispanic Americans (largely those with roots in Mexico or Puerto Rico), and so-called "white Americans," primarily those whose roots emanated from Europe. Occasionally the term diversity included Native Americans.

Differences in religion were talked about primarily in terms of Protestant, Catholic, and Judaic. Linguistic differences were considered to be between English and Spanish.

Today, most of our large metropolitan centers host sizable communities of people representing all of the world's major religions, literally dozens of languages and dialects, and scores of nationalities from every geographic region of the world.

Many of these people are recent immigrants, often refugees fleeing wars, revolutions, hunger, and poverty. Spanish-speaking immigrants may include origins in Central America, the Caribbean, or South America.

African American may mean Somalian, Sudanese, Ethiopian, or Haitian. Asian may mean Cambodian, Laotian, Taiwanese, Filipino, or people with any of a dozen other ethnic or national origins. European may include Moslems from Bosnia, or people from a dozen different ethnic regions of the former Soviet Union.

Diversity is a reality the breadth and scope of which we have never before seen. We are quite literally part of a world community in which the movement of populations across the globe is a norm not an exception.

For all of our diversity, social, cultural, and environmental forces continue to shape who we are, how we develop and ultimately how we function and live together in the everyday world. The cultures we come from, the neighborhoods we live in, the social and ethnic composition of our communities, and the kinds of opportunities open to us, all profoundly affect our lives and the future of our society.

All of these diverse forces are contextual factors that constantly interact with individual biological and psychological characteristics to form the fabric of each human life. Counseling in a multicultural world means constantly striving to understand and appreciate the human diversity that we encounter in our professional practice. It also means constantly searching within ourselves to understand how our own experiences help or hinder our efforts to reach out to others.

RACE AND ETHNICITY

Racism and all of its attendant evils have been an ever-present part of American history. The very concept of race as it is used and thought about in contemporary American life is essentially a mythology born out of tragic historical circumstance.

The notion of race, or so-called racial groupings has been used historically as a biological classification system (Yee, Fauchild, Weizmann, & Wyatt, 1993). A half century ago, race was defined as a subgroup of people possessing a specific and definite combination of physical characteristics of genetic origin, that clearly distinguish them from other groups (Linton, 1943). Such a definition fails in most of the situations in which the term is currently used.

The basic rules in science for the classification of either people or things are relatively simple. The main requirements are that the classes formed must be exhaustive, that is, all instances encountered must fit into one of the classes, and that the classes themselves must be mutually exclusive, that is, no case encountered must fit into more than one category

(Kipnis, 1997). The concept of race as it is used in American society simply does not meet these requirements. The notion of race is not a scientific term or concept.

The scientific basis for using the concept of race to look for statistical differences between so-called racial groups is exceedingly dubious. The explanation of such differences in biological or evolutionary terms is not only questionable, but basically unscientific (Zuckerman, 1990). Fundamentally, the notion of racial groups is of little use in explaining or even studying group variations. In most situations, the variations within such groups are greater than the variations between groups (Betancourt & Lopez, 1993).

Differences such as skin pigmentation, hair or eye color, facial features, height, weight, body types, and so forth tend to vary both within and across various groups. Such characteristics are generally not purely genetic in origin, but are very often the result of complex interactions between biological and environmental factors. The widely noted tendency toward hypertension in African American men in America, for example, has been found to vary markedly across various social and physical environments and geographic regions (Cooper, Rotomi, & Ward, 1999).

The preoccupation with issues of race in American society and unfortunately also in American psychology is virtually unparalleled in modern history. Some observers of American life have referred to the United States as a nation obsessed with race (Yee et al., 1993).

As one examines the history of the concept of race in American history, it is difficult to escape the conclusion that the concept is a pseudoscientific term that has survived in both the popular and scientific literature largely because it serves a sociopolitical purpose (Gossett, 1963). That purpose has been to distance individuals and groups from each other and to perpetuate oppression and injustice.

CULTURE AND ETHNICITY

Concepts that are much more useful in studying and understanding differences between groups are *culture* and *ethnicity*. The concept of culture is so broad that it is often difficult to focus upon those specific aspects of a culture or subculture that are most relevant to psychological differences and to interpersonal and social relationships.

From a psychological standpoint, a culture or subculture refers to a group of people who share a set of *common meanings* or ways of construing or interpreting events and situations. These in turn affect belief systems, ways of life or world views that are transmitted through learning across generations.

This psychological component of culture creates subjective elements that distinguish its members from other groups. These may include a wide range of beliefs and values that affect communication patterns, affective styles and beliefs about personal control, family relationships, definitions of success, concepts of mental health and optimal development, and values regarding spirituality and religion.

It is these subjective and psychological aspects of culture and cultural differences that most concern counseling. These are the kinds of differences that extend social psychological distance between individuals with different backgrounds. To a considerable degree, these subjective cultural differences exist within people at a relatively low level of awareness. We are seldom fully aware of *how, where,* and *why* we come to think, feel, and act as we do in these areas, or why others differ widely from us.

The concept of *ethnicity* is closely associated with culture and the terms are often used interchangeably. The term ethnicity is most precisely used to refer to groups that share a common language or national origin. At times, the distinction between the two terms can be confusing. Although cultural background can help to determine ethnicity, in some cases, major cultural differences can exist between groups that share both language and national origins. Protestants and Catholics in Northern Ireland, for example, may share language and nationality while representing distinct cultural differences. In a multicultural world and a nation of rapidly increasing diversity like the United States, common languages and national origins do not automatically mean cultural similarity. Even the term ethnicity is best understood as a set of dimensions along which individuals and groups vary rather than as categories within which to classify people (Phinney, 1996).

Cultural factors like all other individual and group differences interact so that individuals are always complex and unique composites of many environmental and genetic factors. Age, gender, socioeconomic background, education, and many other factors help to define and shape each human personality. The most egregious error in any cross-cultural situation is to assume that cultural similarity means individual homogeneity. Counseling in context means focusing on all that is special and unique about each client as well as those background factors that tie the client to others.

BUILDING SOCIAL PSYCHOLOGICAL BRIDGES

The development of a helping relationship between any two people involves the bridging of differences and a coming together of at least some common perceptions, interpretations, and meanings regarding people, events, problems, and circumstances. Social psychological distance is a concept that embraces the sum total of differences in cultural, social, and individual perspectives that separate any two people, make communication difficult, and hinder the attainment of shared meaning around crucial life experiences.

A voluminous literature about the problems involved in cross-cultural counseling exists. Unfortunately not much of it offers immediate help to the practicing counselor. Generally, research shows that clients prefer ethnically similar counselors when they are available (Coleman, Wampold, & Casali, 1995). This is not surprising in terms of the tendency already noted for people to initiate relationships based upon assumed similarity. The strength of this preference and its effects when counselors and clients are not matched is still not clear.

Some evidence suggests that when clients and counselors are matched, better outcomes are obtained and premature termination is less frequent. The effects were found to be largest with Asian clients, somewhat lower for Hispanic clients, and still less for African American and European American clients (Sue, 1998).

Some of the differences found in studies of the relationship between outcomes and ethnic matching may be in the degree to which clients identify with or are acculturated into their culture of origin versus having come to terms in a positive way with the larger multicultural society.

STATES OF ACCULTURATION

Atkinson, Thompson, and Grant (1993) have proposed that such differences in acculturation are important in counseling. They point out that in a multicultural society it is possible for individuals to be bicultural, that is, to be comfortable and competent in the predominant or larger cultural milieu without sacrificing or devaluing their ethnic-cultural origins.

The acculturation model proposed by Atkinson and associates suggests that people may adopt any of several basic sets of attitudes toward the relationship between their ethnic and cultural origins and what is perceived as the dominant culture. In the United States, that dominant culture may be seen as "Euro-centered." Five attitudinal states or stages are proposed in this model. They are:

1. *Conformity:* One may devalue one's own ethnic or cultural heritage while appreciating the dominant or majority culture.
2. *Dissonance:* Conflict or ambivalence in regard to one's own and other ethnic or cultural groups.
3. *Resistance and Immersion:* Valuing, defending, and supporting one's own ethnic heritage and championing other minority or oppressed groups. It may include resentment toward dominant groups.
4. *Introspection:* Continuing re-evaluation of one's own cultural and ethnic values, attitudes, and assumptions.
5. *Integrative Awareness:* Realistic appreciation of all cultural and ethnic groups, and an objective view of relationships among groups.

There is no evidence that these attitudinal states represent developmental stages that all or most individuals pass through. The introspective and integrative categories or stances seem highly desirable for counselors, themselves. If counselors are in these stances, then ethnic and cultural mismatches with ethnically different clients who are also in these same stances may not prevent the development of helping relationships. The formation of helping relationships with clients in the conformity, dissonant, and resistance and immersion stances may be more problematic.

THE EMPLOYEE ASSISTANCE PROGRAM

After Steve graduated from the counseling psychology program at the state university, he worked for three years in the community mental health center where he had done his practicum and internship.

Two years ago, Steve decided to enter private practice. He has struggled financially in getting his practice going, but recently got his big break. Steve got a contract to provide counseling services for the Employee Assistance Program for a large corporation that had just moved its warehouse and shipping facility to the city.

Steve is responsible for providing counseling and psychological services to 800 employees and their families. As Steve became better acquainted with his new role, he found some surprising facts. Eighty percent of the employees do not speak English as a native language. More than one-half are recent immigrants from Africa, Asia, Latin America, and Eastern Europe. The workforce represents virtually all of the world's major religions and cultures.

Steve has good Spanish language skills and has had experience working with African American clients in his former position. How should he handle this new challenge?

Approaches to Cross-Cultural Competence

The literature on multicultural counseling speaks volumes about the *necessity* for cross-cultural competence, but is often exceedingly vague about the paths that lead to such competence. An analysis of this literature suggests several avenues for counselors to travel in their quest to become effective in bridging social psychological distance.

Cultural Expertise

Knowledge and understanding of other cultures is an obvious asset to any counselor. When a counselor's practice is heavily involved with clients from one or two specific subcultures knowledge of the history, language, values, and customs of the cultural group is an essential part of professional competence.

When we think in terms of the new diversity that was described earlier, it is obvious that few counselors will have detailed knowledge of all of the cultures from which clients may come. Another limitation on cultural expertise is that knowledge about a cultural group does not always translate into the kind of understanding that is useful in a counseling situation. As one writer on cross-cultural counseling put it, knowing *that* is not the same as knowing *how* (Johnson, 1987).

Probably the best way of acquiring cultural expertise is through close, positive social relationships with members of an ethnic or cultural group. Attending and discussing together a play, movie, concert, athletic contest, or political speech may be more enlightening than reading a book or attending a lecture.

Positive Attitudes

We discussed earlier the fact that our society's history of racism and ethnocentrism has scarred all of its members. Attitudes toward other ethnic and cultural groups are obviously important factors in cross-cultural counseling. Several psychometric instruments have been devised to measure constructs such as "white identity," and related concepts. It is not entirely clear what these kinds of instruments actually measure and how they relate to cross-cultural competence (Behrens, 1997; Helms, 1997).

A factor analytic study of two such instruments found that they tend to measure attitudes of racial comfort and attitudes toward racial equality. Essentially, these scales seem to measure ethnocentric attitudes that support racial discrimination versus those that describe attitudes of comfort and affiliation with minority members (Pope-Davis, Vandiver, & Stone, 1999). Whether these scales measure anything as comprehensive or diffuse as "racial identity," the attitudes tapped are clearly relevant to cross-cultural counseling situations.

The literature of multicultural counseling abounds with appeals for cultural sensitivity. Unfortunately the concept is hard to define. Cultural sensitivity is one aspect of person perception processes. People vary developmentally in the complexity with which they are able to perceive and so understand themselves and others. When counselors are able to perceive the full richness and complexity of a client's experiencing, they are at the threshold of cultural sensitivity.

Cultural sensitivity, then, is a perceptual and cognitive process through which one person, the counselor, comes to understand the unique meanings that another person, the client, has derived out of cultural experiences and memberships (Ridley, Mendoza, Kanitz, Angermeier, & Zank, 1994). Since in a multi-cultural society people may have been members of or influenced by more than one culture, individual patterns of meaning may be very complex.

As counselors develop cultural sensitivity they acquire culture-relevant *schemas* or cognitive-perceptual frameworks that enable them to recognize and assess the significance of culturally significant messages and meanings from clients. Culturally relevant schemas may include ways of recognizing and checking out client meanings in areas such as cultural identity, family relationships, meaning of work, definitions of success, sex-appropriate roles and many other patterns of meaning derived from cultural membership or influence.

Culture sensitivity also includes applying the same kinds of schemas to one's own beliefs and assumptions regarding the kinds of topics mentioned above. Cultural sensitivity is made possible by relatively high levels of cognitive development and self-awareness, but is also a product of extensive personal and professional experience with culturally diverse people.

KEYS TO CROSS-CULTURAL COMPETENCE

Cross-cultural competence in counseling involves at least four major components. These include:

1. Knowledge and understanding of the history, language, customs, and values represented in other cultures and how they impact

members. This includes an understanding that a Euro-centered history and corresponding set of world views is incomplete and may be misleading in understanding the experience of other cultures.

2. Attitudes toward equality and social justice. These include recognition of the effects of oppression and exploitation. These attitudes also include a degree of comfort in psychological closeness with people from other cultures, and a genuine belief that trying to understand and share their experiencing will enrich one's own life.

3. Cultural sensitivity in recognizing and exploring the varying perceptions and world views of members of other cultures. This involves a commitment to one's own continuing cognitive-perceptual development and continuing intellectual and emotional contact with diverse cultures and their members. Such a commitment mandates a social style based on *inclusion* of people from all cultures and walks of life.

4. Continuing self-awareness and self-examination in regard to values, assumptions and attitudes relevant to one's own cultural heritage and place in the multicultural world.

The keys to bridging social-psychological distance are not easily attained. In some ways, they do not represent final destinations, but rather are direction for life-long learning and personal as well as professional development.

Achieving multicultural comfort and competence means transcending without denigrating one's own cultural background and heritage. Cultural identity is usually a warm, comfortable, and familiar security blanket that enables us to ignore much that is different, dissonant, or even threatening to our assumptions about self, society, and the world. When we begin to transcend our own culture, we reach out to touch perceptions, ideas, and emotional contacts that are disturbing and unsettling. We are forced to bring back into consciousness judgments, choices, and encounters that are more comfortably ignored or repressed.

Enhancing awareness of cultural diversity has value for understanding not only another person's culture, but also helps us to understand our own. Such awareness facilitates what can be called *psychological decentering*, or being able to take multiple perspectives about ideas and issues (Ho, 1995). It is this decentering process that liberates people from their comfortable but limiting cultural cocoons.

To come to understand more about another person's culture is to come to know more about one's own world and ultimately to understand more about oneself. The goal of both liberal education and counselor education should be one of cultural liberation and cultural transcendence. To some degree, all counseling is cross-cultural, all counseling involves bridging social psychological distance and all effective counseling leads to greater self-understanding for both counselor and client (Pederson, 1991).

After more than 30 years of studying cross-cultural counseling, psychologist Stanley Sue (1998) asserts that one of the primary ingredients in multicultural competence is scientific mindedness. By this he means forming *tentative* hypotheses rather than jumping to unsupported conclusions, seeking creative ways to test hypotheses and acting on the basis of evidence rather than on assumptions and suppositions. An essential part of a counselor's multicultural competence is a continuous re-affirmation of one's professional identity as a scientist. As in all scientific pursuits, most mistakes are made by assuming that we know too much, rather than acknowledging that we understand too little.

CHAPTER 12

Working with Families

> Over the years I have developed a picture of what human beings
> living humanly are like. They are people who understand
> value. . . . They are real and honest. . . . They are kind to
> themselves and others. . . . When you add all this up you have
> loving . . . creative, productive, responsible human beings.
>
> The family is the context in which a person with such
> dimensions develops . . . and the adults in charge are *people
> makers.*
>
> —Virginia Satir (1988)

O F ALL the environments within which people interact in the
course of a lifetime, clearly family is the most potent, both in
terms of the growth of human effectiveness, and for its ability to
place a virtual minefield of obstacles in the path of developing human beings. The awesome effects of family dynamics are almost as powerful and
pervasive in the lives of adult members as they are for children.

HOW FAMILIES FUNCTION

No institution in American society has undergone as much change or
been the subject of as much scrutiny and soul-searching as the family.
The traditional and heavily idealized model of family life in twentieth-
century America has been the so-called "nuclear family." As idealized in
television and motion pictures, it consists of husband and wife living
happily, humorously, and permanently in the big white house on Maple

Street, complete with porches and picket fence. The nuclear family came into ascendancy around the beginning of the twentieth century with the decline of the multigenerational extended family as urbanization and social and geographic mobility rapidly increased.

The nuclear family merged into what can be called the *conjugal family*, a pattern of family functioning based almost solely on the quality of the emotional relationship that exists between husband and wife. The conjugal family is a fragile and ephemeral model that provides great personal satisfaction and opportunities for growth of members when it works well. It has in the past promised to furnish a kind of emotional sanctuary of support and security in the midst of a depersonalizing and isolating urban-industrial environment.

The fragility of these patterns of family organization is seen in the steadily rising rates of divorce, serial remarriage, and long-term nonmarital relationships. The child-centered "traditional" family with its emphasis on socialization and achievement of family members has become an endangered species in contemporary American life.

What has become pre-eminent is a *multiplicity* of types and patterns of family organization. Developmental counselors seeking to understand how families nurture or negate the optimal development of members are forced to attempt to understand a very wide variety of living arrangements and relationship patterns existing in the community and, indeed, often in the life experience of individuals.

Since families vary so widely on so many different dimensions no single criterion can come close to defining either adequate or optimal family functioning. It is useful to identify a set of issues and variables that seem to operate in all kinds of family environments.

CRUCIAL FACTORS IN FAMILY FUNCTIONING

Studies of family functioning (Olson, 1970) have tended to identify two principal variables that seem to be crucial to functioning across a wide range of family patterns and situations.

The first of these crucial factors is *cohesiveness*. Cohesiveness refers to the extent to which members are committed to the family and are willing to be helpful and supportive to each other. Cohesiveness in the family, as in any other human system, is the psychological glue that holds the group together.

Because family members depend so heavily on each other, cohesiveness within a family needs to be very high. On the other hand, as cohesiveness increases, it necessarily begins to intrude upon needs for autonomy, separateness, and privacy of family members.

At very high levels of cohesiveness, a family may become *enmeshed*, that is, literally so over-involved with each other that they leave little room for personal growth and the development of an individual's uniqueness and autonomy. Some theorists believe that either enmeshment or low cohesion can inhibit the development of coping behaviors in children (Nichols & Schwartz, 1998).

A second crucial variable in family functioning is *adaptability*. Families must cope with a very wide range of stresses, problems, and obstacles as they accompany members through the life cycle. At the same time, families provide structure, order, and security to their members.

Families thus face a constant set of tensions between very high levels of structure and rigidity that may impede problem solving, innovation and creative expression, and low levels of structure or order that can create chaotic and disorganized responses to problem situations. Effective families apparently face constant readjustment and renegotiation of roles and responsibilities as they attempt to balance and manage factors of cohesion and adaptability while avoiding extremes of enmeshment versus disintegration and rigidity versus disorganization.

Themes in Family Functioning

As families grapple with problems, move through the life cycle and endeavor to provide support, nurturance, and security to members, a number of themes can be identified that tend to play out in many situations.

The ways in which individual families tend to cope with these themes or issues often reflect the central dynamics of the family's psychological life.

Several specific and crucial issues in family functioning include:

1. *Cohesiveness.* We noted earlier the importance of this variable and some of the complications that arise from it.
2. *Expressiveness.* This dimension refers to the extent to which members are allowed to express feelings and opinions directly and openly in the family.
3. *Conflict.* This issue refers to the ways in which the family manages disagreement and discord among members.
4. *Independence.* This factor deals with the ways in which the family permits members to develop autonomy, to think through and act upon their own opinions, and to assert their individual needs.

5. *Achievement.* This aspect involves the ways in which the family deals with work, schooling, and issues of personal accomplishment and interpersonal competition.
6. *Leisure and Recreation.* This aspect relates to how the family plays and relaxes together.
7. *Moral and Religious Values.* This dimension deals with the ways in which moral, ethical, and religious questions are handled and how children are socialized with respect to such issues.
8. *Structure and organization.* This issue refers to the ways in which roles are assigned to family members and to how responsibilities are divided.
9. *Control.* This final factor involves the ways in which the family influences members, exerts authority and induces conformity to family norms and values.

As counselors work with families, these factors tend to be the areas in which conflict and competition tend to emerge and in which negotiation and renegotiation are necessary to preserve a degree of harmony and cooperation.

FAMILY FUNCTIONS AND OPTIMAL DEVELOPMENT

Research and theory on family influences on child development have tended to emphasize the importance of parental warmth and emotional support, together with moderate and flexible degrees of parental control or discipline (Becvar & Becvar, 1993). A theory of stage-environmental "fit" has been proposed (Eccles et al., 1993) that views each stage of development of children and early adolescence to require a readjustment of parental roles to nurture optimal development at that stage.

Eccles et al. put it this way:

> There is a . . . need for developmentally responsive family environments. Existing research suggests that there is variability in how families adapt to their children's movement into adolescence and that adolescents fare best in family environments that provide a good fit to their increasing needs for autonomy. Adolescents fare more poorly in families that respond to their development either by throwing up their hands and relinquishing control or by cracking down too much. Families . . . are confronted with a difficult problem providing an environment that changes in the right way at the right pace. (p. 99)

Some ecologically oriented approaches to the study of family functioning (Jessor, 1993) suggest that the ways in which families relate to and interact with the larger community have a major impact on the lives of developing children. Many disadvantaged families desperately need to access and utilize community services and resources. The strategies that such families use or fail to use to deal with schools, police, health care providers, welfare agencies, or housing authorities may be just as crucial to the development and well-being of children as are intrafamilial factors.

CHILDREN IN NONTRADITIONAL HOUSEHOLDS

Family life presents a daunting series of problems under the best of conditions. One very large population of children who may face special developmental problems consists of children living in disturbed, disorganized, or what in the past we would have called "broken homes." The frequency and variety of these living arrangements is so great that it is probably more appropriate simply to refer to them as *nontraditional households*.

In the past 30 years there has been a significant decline in the proportion of two-parent families in first marriages. This is accompanied by a corresponding increase in the numbers of both single-parent families and stepfamilies. These changes are the result of both a rapid rise in the divorce rate and an increase in births to single mothers (Hetherington, Bridges, & Insabella, 1998).

Although divorce rates have declined slightly over the past 20 years, about one million children experience their parent's divorce each year. It is projected that more than one-half of the children born in the 1990s will live at some point in single-parent situations. About one in six of two-parent families with children under 18 years of age are stepfamilies or blended families, that is, having children from two or more marriages or relationships (Hetherington et al., 1998).

The high divorce rate that is indicative of the failure of about one-half of all marriages has not discouraged people with the institution itself. About three-fourths of men and two-thirds of women who divorce will eventually remarry. Divorce rates are, unfortunately even higher in remarriages than in first marriages.

The results of this rather perplexing profusion of marital misadventures is that more than one-half of the nation's children grow up in family situations that are very different from those considered either typical or appropriate a generation ago. Not all of these children are at risk for developmental problems. The quality of family environments varies in nontraditional settings as it does in so-called "intact" families. Marital discord, child abuse or neglect, and effects of poverty and community disorganization can occur in either kind of family environment.

As marriage and family patterns become more varied, however, it is clear that children from all ethnic groups, social classes, and geographical settings are encountering stresses and challenges associated with their parents' marital transitions and lifestyles. Children from divorced or remarried families tend to exhibit more problem behaviors and lower psychological well-being than children from never-divorced families (Hetherington et al., 1998). No clear consensus exists to explain the specific sources or nature of problems in nontraditional families. Probably several sources of stress combine to produce problematic situations.

FAMILY COMPOSITION

The commonly accepted assumption regarding family composition in Western culture has been that two biological parents living together provide the most appropriate psychological environment for optimal development of offspring and for each other. This view is by no means timeless. Until about the beginning of the twentieth century, the multigenerational extended family was very common, and caregivers and authority figures involved in child-rearing often included grandparents, aunts or uncles, older siblings, and "hired help" as well as parents. As the conjugal family pattern was threatened by divorce and single parenting, much of the theorizing about family problems centered around the missing father figure (Kingsbury & Scanzoni, 1993).

PARENTAL DISTRESS

Divorce, single parenting, and stepfamilies all present potential sources of stress on principal family caregivers, usually mothers. This stress is frequently exacerbated by the necessity for paid work outside the home. Single parents must often cope with great personal stress while providing nurturance and economic and emotional support to growing children. The probability of chronic problems is all too apparent. Great individual differences exist in responses to negative life changes associated with separation, divorce, loss of income, remarriage, and step-parenting. Some parents may cope admirably while others are physically and emotionally overwhelmed.

INDIVIDUAL CHARACTERISTICS

Both parents and children possess psychological characteristics that profoundly affect family life. In one sense individuals, including children, help to shape their own environments (Scarr, 1993). Differences in intelligence, temperament, and general health among both parents and children may produce vastly different family environments.

When marital and family transitions are complicated by socioeconomic disadvantage, physical or psychological impairments, criminality, and alcohol or drug abuse, patterns of child neglect or abuse and even domestic violence can ensue. Many of these very serious threats to children's development can be ameliorated by access to appropriate community and educational programs and services.

DEVELOPMENT OF CHILDREN FROM NONTRADITIONAL HOUSEHOLDS

General agreement exists among researchers that children, adolescents, and adults from divorced and remarried families as compared with those from two-parent families are at greater risk for a variety of problems and challenges. Those who have undergone multiple divorces or separations are at even greater risk. Children from divorced or remarried families are more likely to have academic problems, to present behavior problems, be more withdrawn, less socially responsible and competent, and to have lower self-esteem (Hetherington et al., 1998).

CHILDREN HAVING CHILDREN

One of the major problems in American families is that of adolescent pregnancy, literally children having children. Although adolescent birthrates have actually declined in recent decades, they remain high in contrast to other industrialized countries. In 1990, the rate of births to teenagers in the United States was twice as high as in Great Britain, and four times greater than in Sweden and Spain and 15 times greater than in Japan. Although some researchers suggest that these differences are in part due to greater ethnic diversity, the birthrate among white adolescent Americans still easily surpasses that in any other industrialized nation (Coley & Chase-Lansdale, 1998).

Although the total rate of births to teenagers has declined since 1950, the rate of nonmarital childbearing has soared. In 1960, only 15% of births to teenage mothers were out of wedlock. In 1995, 75% of such births were nonmarital. Strong links between teenage births and poverty and welfare dependency exist (Coley & Chase-Lansdale, 1998).

Teenagers who give birth during their adolescent years tend to function less effectively in numerous areas than their peers who delay child-bearing. Many of the negative outcomes associated with adolescent motherhood such as low educational achievement and poverty tend to be causes as well as consequences of adolescent pregnancies. Teenage childbearing tends to add to the problems of already disadvantaged adolescents. Teenage mothers tend to experience poorer psychological functioning, lower rates of school completion, lower levels of marital stability, less stable employment, greater welfare use, and higher rates of poverty (Coley & Chase-Lansdale, 1998).

TEENAGE PARENTING

Teenage mothers have been found to be just as warm but less verbal, less sensitive, and less responsive to their infants than older mothers. These factors may be related to depressive reactions that have been found to occur frequently in adolescents the year following child-bearing. Adolescent mothers also tend to provide a less stimulating home environment, to perceive their children as more difficult, and to have unrealistic expectations of them (Coley & Chase-Lansdale, 1998).

Few differences are found in infancy between children of teenage versus older mothers. Cognitive differences begin to appear among preschoolers as do behavior problems. Adolescence children of teenagers experience higher rates of grade failure, delinquency, incarceration (for males) early sexual activity, and pregnancy as compared to peers with older mothers. The patterns of dysfunction among children of teenage mothers suggests

---

THE CASE OF DENISE

Denise is a 20-year-old single mother of two children, a 4-year-old boy and a 3-year-old girl. Denise lives in public housing on public assistance. She was referred to the community mental health center by a welfare case worker. Denise shows signs of depression and stress and her children are completely out of control. At times Denise locks herself in the bedroom while the children rampage through the house. Denise's mother, who had helped her through the first few years of parenthood, now refuses to babysit or even to visit. Denise and her children are isolated and alone.

How should the counselor approach this case?

---

that parental effectiveness declines as children get older and as more children are born (Coley & Chase-Lansdale, 1998).

All of these findings discussed are clearly confounded with the effects of poverty, lack of education, and general disorganization. These kinds of factors are also closely related to the frequency of child abuse and neglect among parents of all ages (Emery & Laumann-Billings, 1998).

Adolescent mothers and their children are in need of a variety of special services including vocational education, parent education, early childhood education, and family planning as well as prenatal care, continuing medical care, and a variety of other social services.

MEN, WOMEN, AND CHILD CARE

One of the paradoxes in traditional American cultures is the fact that men typically *talk* about the importance of family cohesion and the nurturance of children while women are left largely unassisted to do something about it. The tendency to blame mothers for the social and psychological problems of children is a well-documented and readily apparent phenomenon in popular perceptions, public policy pronouncements, and even in the social scientific literature (Phares, 1992).

In single-parent situations, it has been estimated that families headed by mothers outnumber those headed by fathers by a ratio of better than seven to one. In situations where children live with their biological mother more than a third have no contact with their biological father, and such contact tends to be brief and irregular for most of the others (Phares, 1992).

In two-parent situations, mothers typically spend significantly more time with children than do fathers even when both spouses are employed. Because relatively little research has been done on the parenting role of fathers, paternal influences on the development of children have often been underestimated or de-emphasized in discussions of family life.

There is evidence that fathers influence children in ways that are very similar to mothers. Infants show very similar patterns of attachment to fathers as to mothers when the fathers are available as caregivers. Paternal warmth and attention has been found to be similar to maternal warmth and attention in terms of beneficial effects on children's psychosocial development, achievement, and sex-role development (Phares & Compas, 1992). Overall, the potential effects of fathers on either the optimal or interrupted development of children is about as great as that of mothers.

Very often counselors in school and community settings contribute to the de-emphasizing of the paternal role by tacit acceptance of the notion that mothers have primary responsibility for the child's achievement and development. Counselors and other human services professionals can also advocate for greater roles and involvement of fathers in family life in terms of joint custody arrangements, visitation rights, and participation in both financial and emotional support.

CHILDREN'S DAY CARE

One of the most vexing problems in American family life is the availability of affordable, dependable quality day care for children of employed parents. Out-of-home day care is the normative experience for contemporary American children, the vast majority of whose mothers and fathers are employed. More than one-half the mothers of infants under 12 months of age are in the labor force, while three-quarters of school age children's mothers are working (Scarr, 1998). When day care is safe, healthy, and dependable, little evidence exists regarding major effects on children's development as compared to parental care. Unsafe and unreliable or nonexistent day care often poses very dangerous problems for already disadvantaged children in poverty-stricken and socially disorganized situations. Much child abuse and neglect stems from inadequate day-care arrangements in the lives of such children.

Many of the threats to optimal development in family life that were discussed earlier result from major social and economic problems over which counselors have little control. When counselors are aware of these problems, they can act in advocacy roles to help our communities and our society to act responsibly.

UNDERSTANDING FAMILY INTERACTION

One of the most profound and far-reaching findings in the study of family life has been the realization that family communication and indeed most family interaction patterns tend to *stabilize* over time and then to *recur* across situations and circumstances. Further, these patterns tend to be *homeostatic,* that is, to re-establish and re-affirm themselves when temporarily disturbed or altered by outside influences or events.

These tendencies have profound implications for those who intend either simply to understand families, or who intend to intervene in their functioning. The first of these implications is encouraging to counselors. There is a kind of consistency and regularity in the functioning of every family that makes it potentially understandable. Often when we stand outside a dysfunctional or distressed family, its operations seem chaotic and confused. At first glance all that we may see is a display of persistent and pervasive cruelty and self-defeating and poisonous relationships. Upon careful analysis, we come to find that even these dysfunctional relationships operate according to rules, principles, and boundaries that are understandable if not desirable.

The second implication of the apparent regularity and consistency of behavior within a given family is that each family is unique in terms of its own intricate and complex combination of tendencies. Finally, the least palatable implication of all of this is that families, whether functional or dysfunctional, are very hard to change. The stability and consistency overtime and across situations that makes a family potentially understandable, also makes it very resistant to change.

As students of family life struggled to understand its intricacies, they came to draw on a way of thinking about complex, interrelated phenomena that had been developed to deal with problems in the physical world.

General Systems Theory and Cybernetics

General systems theory was developed out of the need to understand, communicate about, and eventually to innovate, sets of extremely complex and closely interrelated functions. These may exist in nature, be the product of human inventions, or a combination of the two. In early chapters, we discussed the concept of ecosystems as a way of understanding the relationships between a developing human being and the environment. A systems approach can help us to understand the development of a child living within ever-widening circles of influence in family, neighborhood, school, community, society, and so on. We can zoom in or back off to focus on what seems most significant at any given time or in any particular situation.

Using the same kinds of conceptual tools engineers and scientists can solve potential problems in technology that are as mind-boggling as the space program, or they may wrestle with the potential effects of something as pervasive and mysterious as global warming.

Cybernetics

One aspect of general systems thinking as a field of inquiry and innovation is called *cybernetics*. In a technical sense, cybernetics involves the study of how human intelligence can be simulated by computers. The term was coined some 50 years ago to describe the study of control and communication problems between human being and computers. All of the almost miraculous and mysterious capabilities for "surfing the

Internet," and traveling the information highway that we are in the process of coming to take for granted began with the science of cybernetics. The word itself was made up as a derivation of the Greek word for steersman, and is indicative of the problems that are involved in maintaining full human control over powerful and complex processes. When we have complex processes impacting our lives, our most significant problems concern first understanding, and then getting control of those processes. In one sense, that set of problems in individual lives defines the role of developmental counseling.

FEEDBACK

One of the crucial concepts to come out of cybernetics, at least for counselors, is the notion of *feedback*. Feedback describes the exchange of information that occurs between the interrelated parts of a functioning system. In systems analysis, we look for feedback loops, or connections that make the exchange of information possible. When such loops or connections are joined, some of the output of one part of the system becomes available as information to another part of the system. The operation of a simple household thermostat is an example of this kind of arrangement. When the furnace is turned on, heat is circulated throughout the cold house. A heat sensor or thermometer keeps track of the rising temperature, and at a pre-set point, controlled by the occupants, the thermostat automatically turns off the burner. Human beings have exerted control over a chemical and mechanical system.

In human systems, closing feedback loops and exerting conscious control over a system may be much harder to achieve. In a distressed or dysfunctional family, for example, certain aspects of communication between a husband and wife in conflict may be shut off almost entirely. "Why are you upset?" "What did I do to hurt you?" "How can I make amends?" are questions that remain unanswered. As intense feelings and frustration build up, both spouses may feel helpless in controlling the escalating pattern of conflict as it heads relentlessly toward dissolution of the marriage, or even toward domestic violence. Arresting such an escalating pattern of miscommunication may mean closing feedback loops by opening up jammed channels of communication long inoperative in the relationship.

FAMILY SYSTEMS THEORY

Students of family life were quick to realize the significance of conceptual tools drawn from general systems theory to their own concerns and problems. The approaches that have emerged from this development are called *family systems theory* (Kerr & Bowen, 1988). Various versions and variations of family systems theory have been pioneered over the past 30 years by people such as Murray Bowen, Donald Jackson, and Virginia Satir. In its various forms, the systems approach to family functioning has revolutionized and redefined both the study of family life and the process of family counseling.

Family systems theory or what is often called the systematic approach has a number of key concepts that distinguish it from psychodynamic, experiential, or behavioral points of view (Becvar & Becvar, 1993), including:

1. *Reciprocal Causality.* (It takes two or more to tango.) In a systematic approach causes and effects are not seen to exist in a simple linear way. People and events are seen in the context of mutual interaction and mutual influences. Rather than examining individuals or specific incidents in isolation, a systematic approach focuses on relationships and how each individual affects and is affected by all of the others. Meaning is derived out of interactions. Causality becomes a reciprocal concept. The approach does not attempt to isolate either first or final causes or effects. Similarly, persons are not blamed or assigned total responsibility for either positive or negative events. Family roles and relationships are seen as *mutually* defined by two or more members.

2. *Rules and Boundaries.* (Who we are and who they are.) All families are seen to have rules that define their various roles and relationships. Sometimes these represent taboos or things not to be discussed even within the family. Sometimes they legitimize the exercise of authority, or the appearance of authority. Rules express the values, fears, hopes, and aspirations of members. They are often dimly perceived and vaguely articulated by members of the family, but they are always enforced in one way or another. Rules help set the boundaries of the system—that is, they help to define "us and them." Even a person living in the same household and related by blood may sometimes be excluded and left outside the boundaries. Often boundaries isolate families and prevent them from obtaining needed resources or support.

3. *Openness and Closedness.* (Don't listen to them.) This refers to the number and nature of messages exchanged between members of a family and the outside world. It refers to the exchange of information across boundaries with outsiders. When communication is

closed and little outside information is exchanged, maladaptive family norms go unchanged and unchallenged. For example, within some dysfunctional and isolated families spouse or child abuse, or even incest may be viewed as normative.

4. *Entropy.* This concept denotes the tendency of any system to run down or stagnate. It is the process by which all systems undergo progressive deterioration with time and gradually fail to operate in the ways and for the purposes for which they were originally intended.

In purely mechanical systems, entropy is easy to understand. Clock springs unwind and dust, dirt, and corrosion clog the delicate works. Even the finest timepiece finally grinds to a stop. Entropy in human systems such as the family, while just as real, is often much more subtle and insidious. In human systems such as the family, entropy is often caused by the gradual erosion of faith and trust in the ability of the family to meet the legitimate needs of family members. Faith and trust in relationships are, as we noted earlier, the basis for cohesion, the psychological glue that holds families and most human systems together. Many times in families we see once vital relationships turn to apathy, indifference, and disillusionment.

Reversing entropy in a marriage or family involves renewal, a reopening of channels of communication and a deepening of emotional expression. It may also mean reawakening awareness of positive experiences and sources of satisfaction and support to be found in family relationships.

MODELS OF FAMILY COUNSELING

In many ways, the rapid social changes that were described earlier which have produced so many different types of family organizations and environments have outstripped our theoretical advances. Many of our approaches to marriage and family counseling seem more suited to repairing damage to traditional conjugal families rather than dealing with the realities of single parent families or serial marriages and live-in relationships.

The Family Communications Approach

Perhaps the most influential approach to marriage and family counseling over the past 30 years has been the communications approach (Satir, 1988). This approach to counseling focuses on the task of improving the quality of communication among family members, primarily husbands and wives.

Family counseling processes using this approach utilize structured communications exercises, direct analyses by the counselor of member's typical communication patterns within sessions, and active teaching of new communication styles that facilitate open, honest, and clear ways of communicating feelings and frustrations.

A central focus of this approach involves identifying and correcting patterns of dysfunctional communication. Many of the basic concepts utilized in this approach are related to family systems theory discussed earlier. Dysfunctional communication patterns are considered to be those that impede the ability of family members to work together cooperatively, to solve problems effectively and to meet the legitimate needs of members.

The communications approach employs several key concepts:

1. *The impossibility of not communicating.* An axiom of this approach is that when two or more people are in sensory contact they cannot avoid communication. Even when people in a relationship are physically separated a failure to communicate overtly often communicates something. Communication problems arise then not because communication is cutoff, but because of what *is* communicated, how it is communicated, and how the messages are received and interpreted. Miscommunication arises when two or more conflicting and unclear messages are sent.

2. *Dysfunctional mixed messages.* Often the direct verbal message is accompanied by voice qualities, inflections, or nonverbal signals that send quite opposite messages. The receiver may be puzzled or confused in terms of responding. Sending such mixed messages may be a way of controlling or punishing another person in a passive-aggressive way.

3. *Over-generalizing statements.* Another kind of dysfunctional communication involves making sweeping generalizations that are in reality final, absolute, and unsubstantiated pronouncements about people or relationships. These leave the receiver unable to identify or discuss the specific incident or situation that triggered the statement.

4. *Mind reading as a style of communicating.* In this pattern, one person assumes the ability to tell another person what he or she is thinking or feeling without any attempt to check out the impression and often rejecting the other person's efforts to correct the impression.

The kinds of dysfunctional communications patterns described along with many others found in distressed or disrupted family relationships are the central focus of this approach to family counseling. The basic assumption is that when family members learn to communicate clearly, openly, and honestly about their opinions and feelings they will be able to function effectively in family relationships, and the emotional bonds that provide cohesion will be strengthened.

This approach may, for example, be very relevant to the needs of a middle class, two-career family struggling to accommodate to the competing or conflicting aspirations of two self-aware and ego-involved spouses. It may be considerably less relevant to the needs of a 17-year-old single mother of two living on public assistance in an urban ghetto.

STRUCTURAL FAMILY THERAPY

Another major approach to family counseling is termed "structural." In a sense the structural approach views the family as an organization designed to meet a complex set of purposes. Structural family counseling draws heavily upon family systems theory, in that it views the behavior of family members to arise out of a complex set of interactions and transactions (Nichols & Schwartz, 1998).

The role of a structurally-oriented family counselor is much like the role of an organizational consultant. The counselor attempts to analyze various patterns of family functioning, including decision-making and problem-solving processes, and to help to improve them in order to facilitate the overall functioning of the family organization. The counselor analyzes and intervenes in the pattern of roles, relationships, rules, and boundaries defined by the family as it deals with tasks and problems.

Often, prior to direct intervention, the structural family counselor arranges to observe the family as it goes about the performance of tasks or deals with problems and decisions. The counselor then develops a set of working hypotheses about the relationship between family interaction patterns and problematic behaviors of particular members.

Structural interventions tend to emphasize the hierarchical structure of the family. They emphasize the role of parents or parent surrogates in terms of their responsibilities for the managerial or executive functions in families. Many family problems are seen as the result of parental failure to exercise authority and responsibility appropriately. When parental roles and responsibilities are unclear and confused, chaotic patterns of family interaction are set in motion that threaten the basic security and stability of the family environment for both adults and children.

Disorganized families are often seen to involve children in decision-making processes in inappropriate ways. Children may be used as pawns in dealing with marital conflict and dissatisfaction.

In the structural approach, the counselor often attempts to help a troubled family to identify sources of conflict and to help parents to deal directly with these without involving children in ways that are detrimental to their emotional well-being. Such involvements by children may also diminish the overall effectiveness of the family organization.

Counseling often involves setting up semistructured situations that elicit typical decision-making and problem-solving styles in the family. Parents are then taught family management and parenting techniques and attitudes that clearly differentiate between *parental* roles and responsibilities and those of children. Children are further encouraged to operate within age-appropriate roles and to stay out of parental conflict situations as much as possible.

Structural approaches to family treatment have been used with success in a rather wide range of situations with a variety of families. Structural interventions can be used to some extent with single-parent situations and with quite disorganized families. Its success is dependent to a considerable extent on the adequacy of parents in learning to perform responsible adult roles.

Family Networking

A third important approach to working with families is called *family networking*. This approach is again based on the systems view that families, like individuals, function with a social context that inevitably influences much that goes on within the family, itself. The family networking approach is based on the assumption that every family is to some degree dependent upon the array of opportunities and services available in the larger community.

The growth of children is obviously affected by the quality of schools and other educational opportunities within the community. Resources to enhance the quality of life reside in churches, neighborhood associations, friendship groups, extended families, community agencies, and a wide variety of other social institutions. In a very important sense, the well-being and nurturing potential of a family is determined by the ways in which it accesses these important resources and makes them available for use by family members.

Research (Jessor, 1993) has found a negative relationship between family isolation and the growth and development of children. The unfortunate fact seems to be that often highly stressful and traumatic events within families that increase the vulnerability of children, also tend to be accompanied by a relative disengagement of the family from the larger community. Events such as a breakdown of psychological functioning in a parent, a criminal conviction, an incident of child abuse or neglect, desertion of the family by a parent, or even separation or divorce may be accompanied by an increasing isolation of the family from the very supports and services most needed to cope with the current crisis.

Sometimes the nature and the quality of the transactions between the family and outside resources are affected by a variety of family characteristics including ethnic origin and membership, immigration status, religious affiliations, or family beliefs and values. The danger of family alienation may be drastically increased where negative patterns of community attitudes are directed toward families because of their racial, ethnic, political, or socioeconomic status.

Groups such as recent immigrants, migrant workers, political refugees, and non-English speaking families may be particularly prone to alienation from community resources because of experiences with systematic biases and discrimination.

The family networking approach is based on efforts to break down barriers between families and community supports and services. It often involves efforts to build positive relationships between parents and schools or between neighborhood groups and police, for example.

Networking may help to organize support groups or social action groups around the specific needs of single parent families, tenants, or minority groups. Such groups may be organized to cope with street crime, combat juvenile delinquency, or cope with drug-related problems within a neighborhood.

The approach may also be utilized to help alienated families make contact with community service groups such as Big Brother or Big Sister, Parents without Partners, Parent-Teachers Associations, Alcoholics Anonymous, or other resources.

The essence of the family networking approach is on the development of a set of resources aimed at improving the nurturing capacity of a troubled or disrupted family. As such, this approach may be particularly relevant

THE CASE OF CHRIS AND LISA

Chris and Lisa were married shortly after graduating from college. Chris has a degree in business administration, while Lisa's degree is in medical technology. Lisa took a position with a local hospital and progressed rapidly. After four years, she was promoted to head the hospital laboratory.

Chris took a sales job with a large insurance company but was not particularly successful or satisfied. After two years, he entered a management training program with a large department store chain. Two years ago, the couple had their first child.

Recently, Chris's department had an opening for the department manager position. Chris applied and was sure that he would get the promotion. When he was passed over in favor of a person with less experience in the organization, he resigned in anger.

After searching for a job for several months, Chris decided to return to his home town to work in the family business, a farm implement dealership. Lisa was opposed to the move, but reluctantly resigned her hospital job. In the small town, the only position she could get was in a doctor's office some 20 miles away.

After six months, both Chris and Lisa are unhappy with their jobs. Lisa hates both her job and the commute. Chris feels that he has been given little authority in the business and is essentially a glorified computer operator. Both feel that Chris' parents constantly are interfering in their lives. Lisa is now pregnant with their second child.

Their relationship has become more and more strained. Lisa blames Chris for the move and the loss of her hospital position, and accuses him of being weak and immature. Chris blames his wife for being less than supportive or understanding.

They have sought counseling at a local family services center.

How should the counselor approach their case? What family counseling approach would you use? Is it a family problem or a career problem or a developmental problem?

to the kinds of problems mentioned earlier in this chapter. Family networking, insofar as it involves strengthening the umbrella of resources and services available to all members of a community, should always be a priority of the developmental counselor.

FAMILY CONSULTATION AND TRAINING

The simplest and most effective approach to working with families on behalf of children and adolescents in terms of empirical evaluation involves direct consultation and training with parents (Kazdin, 1994). One of the most effective ways to help distressed or disturbed children is through working with parents in terms of imparting knowledge about child development and giving practical training in childrearing and child management skills. Where such direct contact with parents is feasible it is virtually an indispensable part of most developmental counseling with children and young adolescents.

Parent consultation and training often involves teaching parents behavior management skills that utilize positive reinforcement rather than punishment. These may include using praise and expressing love and concern in conjunction with discipline. Other programs stress parental listening skills, two-way communication, the benefits of quality time together, and techniques such as the use of family conferences.

To a considerable extent developmental counseling involves understanding family life and helping to strengthen family relationships. The family is still probably the most potent growth-producing or growth arresting force in the lives of most people in our society. The tremendous changes in family living arrangements and relationships over the past few decades does not change that fact. "People making" to use Virginia Satir's term goes on even as traditional family roles, relationships, and values change.

CHAPTER 13

Counseling as Prevention

> If our goal is the reduction of emotional disorders . . . a major
> social revolution is required. . . . No mass disorder has ever been
> eliminated by treating one person at a time.
>
> —George Albee (1999)

No single proposition in the whole field of human services commands a more solid level of consensus than the conviction that the most humane and cost-effective way to protect and enhance the psychological well-being of people is through *prevention*. Despite the almost universal support for concepts of prevention among human services professionals and researchers, from a public policy perspective at least, prevention frequently remains the issue that everybody talks about, but nobody does anything about.

In Chapter 1, we pointed out that developmental counseling is virtually by definition devoted to the primary prevention of psychological dysfunction. Positive growth and development with its emphasis on personal *empowerment, competence-building,* and the creation of *support networks* offers the best insurance against many kinds of psychological dysfunctions. Moving along the paths of optimal development that were described in Chapter 4 helps to build the qualities of resilience or hardiness described earlier.

It would be foolhardy, however, in our deeply flawed and sadly imperfect world to believe that all human beings really enjoy reasonable opportunities to embark on the journey to optimal growth and development without the assistance of clearly focused and effective preventive interventions on their behalf.

Developmental counseling has two separate but interrelated facets. The first is the nurture and facilitation of optimal human development. The second is the removal or reduction of *barriers* to such development. The latter emphasis centers around the concept of *prevention*.

THE SCIENCE OF PREVENTION

For more than 20 years, human services professionals and researchers have grappled with both the practical and theoretical problems involved in designing and evaluating effective prevention programs in the mental health field (Albee, 1986; Kazdin, 1979).

Many of the recent theoretical formulations and research finding in the area of prevention center around the dual concepts of *vulnerability* and *resilience* (National Advisory Mental Health Council, NAMHC, 1996).

The goal of such a science is to prevent or at least ameliorate various kinds of psychological dysfunctions. Preventive efforts occur by definition *before* such dysfunctions are fully manifested, or reach disabling or disintegrative levels of severity. Generally this means levels of severity that lead to hospitalization or other institutionalization, or otherwise prevent the victim from living a reasonably independent and productive life.

Prevention research is focused primarily around the study of two kinds of factors that can be identified *prior* to the onset of major psychological problems. These are termed *risk factors* and *protective factors*.

Risk factors are variables associated with a high probability of onset, greater severity, and longer duration of major dysfunctions or mental health problems. Protective factors on the other hand refer to conditions that improve people's resistance to risk and related problems. Protective factors, thus are those that contribute to *resilience*. Identifying these two sets of factors helps counselors both to target high-risk groups or individuals, and to build on assets available to them.

Even though prevention science is very new as a field of inquiry it has already established several basic principles that are important to counselors and other professionals engaged in the practice of prevention (Coie et al., 1993). These include:

1. The relationship between risk factors and specific mental health problems is complex. Exposure to risk factors may occur in diverse ways and in numerous settings. They may exist in family, peer group, school, or larger community environments. An individual's overall risk may result from the *interaction* of personal dispositions

and environmental risk factors. In other words, overall risk is a function of *person-environment interaction.*

2. The effects of various risk factors may vary developmentally, that is with the age and life stage of the individual. Some risk factors seem to trigger problems only at specific points in the individual's development, while others seem to predict problems across the life-span. For example, close relationships with deviant peers, as in gang membership, relates to antisocial behavior primarily in adolescence and young adulthood. Poor parental bonding on the other hand is consistently related to problems in childhood, adolescence, and on into adulthood.

3. Exposure to many risk factors has cumulative effects, some of which tend to increase exponentially. The more factors present in the life of the individual the higher the probability and the greater the severity of problems. The combination of several risk factors can produce extremely high probabilities of psychological problems.

4. Different problems or disorders may be produced in different individuals by similar risk factors. The particular type of problem may vary depending on the age, sex, or genetic predisposition of the individual.

5. There is no single source of either resilience or vulnerability. Many interacting factors come into play. These include individual characteristics such as temperament, personality, intelligence, and physical health. The impact of both risk and protective factors is best understood by a careful study of the individual's developmental history.

PREVENTIVE FACTORS

Understanding how and why things go wrong in an individual's development is important, but equally important are the factors that help things to go right. Research suggests that human beings can survive major traumas both in childhood and adolescence. Resilience, the ability to survive, to overcome adversity, and to regain a degree of control is related to the ability to understand, explain, and comprehend what has happened (Elliott & Marmarosh, 1995).

An important finding is that personality patterns *can* change for the better even after years of exposure to multiple risk factors and consequent traumas. Even thoroughly established patterns of delinquency or dysfunctional behavior in adolescence can be altered in young adulthood when individuals are able to participate in stable and enriching relationships and enter satisfying and rewarding occupations (NAMHC, 1996).

Protective factors include supportive relationships, understanding of major influences and forces that impact one's life, a sense of control over at least some of those forces, and competence in dealing with practical problems in everyday life.

General Protective Factors in Children

1. At least average academic achievement
2. At least grade-level educational skills
3. Identification and development of special talents (musical, artistic, athletic, etc.)
4. A working family support system (may involve extended family or older siblings)
5. Good general health and physical development
6. Active involvement in school and community youth activities (clubs, teams, programs, organizations, etc.)
7. Positive peer acceptance (network of peer relationships with "healthy, pro-social friends")

General Risk Factors in Children

1. Family conflict, separation, divorce, or domestic violence
2. Inadequate parental monitoring
3. Poor parental bonding
4. History of child abuse or neglect
5. Neighborhood disorganization (random violence, danger, or victimization)
6. Chronic truancy
7. Extreme poverty (failure to access welfare or other social safety nets)
8. Parental mental illness, alcoholism, or drug abuse
9. Chronic untreated health problems or disabilities
10. Peer rejection, alienation, and isolation
11. Untreated learning disabilities
12. Attention deficits and hyperactivity

General Protective Factors with Adolescents

In addition to the protective factors listed for children, adolescent factors include:

1. Positive relationships with caring, responsible, and successful adults
2. Successful part-time or summer work experiences
3. Good interpersonal and social skills
4. Staying in and graduating from high school

5. Participation in school or community extracurricular activities
6. Involvement in positive peer relationships

Risk Factors in Adolescents

In addition to those mentioned for children, adolescent risk factors include:

1. Gang membership
2. Substance abuse
3. Delinquency, probation, or parole
4. Runaway, abandonment, or homelessness
5. Sexual promiscuity
6. Sexual victimization, rape, incest, or prostitution

The kinds of risk factors cited for children and adolescents should constitute a set of warning flags or distress signals to counselors and to the community about the need for special preventive programs or interventions. These may involve individual counseling, or in settings where considerable numbers of high-risk children and adolescents have been identified, it may mean referral to comprehensive ongoing preventive programs.

Many of the risk factors cited are the direct result of social and economic problems including poverty, racism, urban decay, crime, and other aspects of social disorganization. These will not be significantly ameliorated by counselors alone.

Research shows that many of the factors that lead to developmental problems are compounded by poverty (McCloyd, 1998). Similarly, many of these factors are exacerbated by the effects of social disorganization and decay in many community settings (Black & Krishnakumar, 1998). Often improving the lives and futures of children and adolescents involves actively working for social change in a given community (Ewart, 1991). For many counselors, prevention may mean active involvement in advocacy programs aimed at improving neighborhoods, controlling crime, increasing public awareness of social problems, and improving community services and resources (Wandersman & Nation, 1998).

PREVENTION PROGRAMS FOR ADULTS

Prevention programs aimed at adults have received considerably less attention than those targeted toward children and adolescents. Many adult

ORGANIZING FOR PREVENTION

Over the course of several months, a counselor doing intakes in a community family service agency notices that there have been more than two dozen referrals involving 11- to 14-year-old youngsters from the same part of the city. The incidents that precipitated the referrals varied widely. They included truancy, vandalism, shoplifting, and alcohol and drug abuse. A number appeared to be gang-related. Two involved possession of guns. The referrals were initiated by parents, schools, police, and the juvenile court.

The counselor decided to do a systems analysis that involved studying the characteristics of both the referred clients and the community environment. First, she plotted the addresses of the referred youngsters on a city map. More than three-fourths of the cases cluster within an eight-block radius.

Next the counselor studied the intake summaries. Fifteen of the cases involved single-parent families in which the custodial parent, usually the mother, worked full-time. All of the youngsters from the cluster attend the same middle school. Fifteen of the 19 precipitating incidents occurred after school or on weekends. The remaining incidents occurred in the school.

The counselor next contacted other professionals from the target area. These included the counselor from the middle school, a social worker from another agency, and a juvenile officer operating out of the local precinct. Information obtained from the school counselor indicated that all of the referred students were doing badly in school with failing grades, repeated absences, and disciplinary problems. The juvenile officer reported that several of the youngsters were involved in gang activity, and most were known to local police officers.

The social worker noted that the neighborhood is in the process of a major transition. The area had formerly been one of stable middle-class family dwellings surrounding a commercial area of small shops. Recent freeway construction has made the area more accessible to a large industrial area a few miles away.

As a result, a large shopping mall has opened at one end of the area, many of the small shops have closed, several apartment complexes have been constructed, and many of the larger houses have been converted into apartments. High rents and shortages of affordable housing have forced many families with low and moderate incomes into the area.

Very few social services, parks, or playgrounds are available in the area. The Middle School feeds into the most academically oriented and competitive high school in the city. The middle school curriculum was largely designed to equip students to enter the high school's college preparatory curriculum. Few remedial programs are available and many of the new transfer students have difficulty coping. Discipline problems are increasing rapidly, and many experienced teachers are requesting transfers.

The counselor collated and organized this information and presented the analysis to her agency director. They decided to request an interagency conference to examine the problems outlined in the analysis.

Such a conference was held. It included the counselors assigned to the referred children and their families, representatives from the schools, juvenile authorities, and several other social and recreational agencies. The local alderman, two local ministers, and the chairperson of the local business association were also invited to attend. After discussing the situation from a number of perspectives, the group made a set of recommendations to be sent to the school district, city government, and several civic groups. These included:

- Establishing parent support groups for single parents
- Establishing after school recreational programs at local playgrounds and gymnasiums
- Establishing peer helping and support groups in the school
- Increasing counseling services and remedial programs in the schools
- Establishing a neighborhood police-community liaison center
- Increasing police investigative activity to eliminate sources of illegal drugs and alcohol for youngsters
- Organizing neighborhood community improvement programs to combat urban blight

All of the agencies and groups represented agreed to continue to advocate for prevention programs.

---

prevention programs involve stress management and/or the development of good health habits and a healthy lifestyle.

In Chapter 5, we discussed stress factors as inevitable aspects of an individual's life space. Stress is defined very broadly as any threat or perceived threat to significant material or psychological resource or values (Hobfoll, 1989). Although, as we saw, stress is by no means always harmful, excessive, uncontrolled exposure to stress is implicated in a wide range of physical, psychological, and behavioral problems. Since some degree of stress is virtually inescapable and the psychological and practical cost of avoiding many sources of stress are prohibitive, the reasonable alternative is to help people learn to manage stress in their lives in ways that reduce the probability of physical or psychological damage. In some occupations and in some social roles, relatively high levels of chronic stress are virtually inescapable.

Coping with Stress

Human beings cope with psychological stress in a variety of ways. Two different general strategies for coping have been termed *problem-focused coping* and *emotion-focused coping* (R.S. Lazarus & Folkman, 1984).

Problem-focused coping consists of active efforts to manage or manipulate objective conditions that are sources of stress through problem solving. These kinds of strategies are sometimes called *engagement strategies* since the individual remains actively involved and engaged in efforts to master or control the situation (Long & Schutz, 1995).

Emotion-focused coping responses, on the other hand, represent attempts to reduce the level of emotional discomfort experienced in response to the stressful situation. They may include reappraising the stressful situation to downplay its significance, wishful thinking in hoping that it will go away, efforts to ignore the offending stimuli, avoiding contact with the situation as much as possible, or distracting oneself with other thoughts or activities. In extreme situations, it may involve the use of alcohol, sedatives, or other drugs to control emotional responses. These kinds of coping approaches are sometimes termed *disengagement strategies.* Some of these are obviously very expensive in terms of other values.

Research (Bowman & Stern, 1995; Long & Schutz, 1995) suggests that problem-focused approaches or engagement strategies are more effective than disengagement strategies in reducing discomfort or dissatisfaction when in fact the stress situations *is* amenable to some degree of control.

An important aspect of effective coping with stress is the ability to make accurate appraisals of both the stress situation and one's own reactions to it. The emotional response to a stress situation is often more a function of the individual's appraisal of it than of the actual situation itself. Thus, people's emotional responses to the same situation may vary widely.

Appraisals of threat or of the potential severity of stress situations are influenced by the individual's prior success in coping, resources such as material and social support, general health and stamina, optimism, sense of control over demands, and relevant life skills (Matheny, Aycock, Pugh, Curlette, & Canella, 1986).

STRESS MANAGEMENT PROGRAMS

A variety of stress management programs have been developed to help people anticipate, prepare for, and cope successfully with stress. All are intended to prevent or minimize exposure to damaging stress. Such programs have been used successfully with adolescents as well as adults (Compas, Malcarne, & Fondacaro, 1988; Kiselica, Baker, Thomas, & Reedy, 1994).

Stress management treatment programs have been used in a wide variety of settings including the workplace (Kagan, Kagan, & Watson, 1995), health care settings (Auerbach, 1989), and with victims of catastrophic events or abuse or assault. Such programs have been evaluated and meta-analyses support their effectiveness, (Matheny et al., 1986).

Stress training programs employ a variety of strategies and techniques to help people cope with or manage stress. These approaches are combined in various ways in specific treatment packages.

ANTICIPATORY COPING

Some stress management training programs prepare people to anticipate, appraise, and cope with stress situations that occur frequently in given settings or situations. As we noted in Chapter 3, stress is most easily managed when it is seen as *predictable* and *controllable*. Participants are taught to identify the conditions that precede or precipitate the onset of the stressful situation and to be ready to use specific coping strategies. This approach is sometimes called *behavioral rehearsal.*

Anticipatory coping can also involve assembling and organizing coping resources including social support and planning for their use in meeting anticipated stress. It may also involve seeking information about stressors to reduce fear of what is unknown and to improve one's responses to specific stressors.

Another aspect of anticipatory coping involves *stress monitoring.* This includes increased awareness of tension buildup and awareness of those situations, events and thoughts that typically accompany the onset of stress. It also involves helping the individual to become aware of tolerance limits beyond which withdrawal from the stressful situation is advisable.

Anticipatory coping is aimed at increasing knowledge about stress and stressors, organizing resources available to manage stress, self-awareness of stress reactions, rehearsal of specific coping strategies, and awareness of limits beyond which withdrawal from the situation is appropriate.

Programs that focus on anticipatory coping are aimed at helping the participant to experience the stress situation as understandable, predictable, and controllable.

EMOTION-FOCUSED COPING

When stress situations are relatively uncontrollable and stress levels are severe, a variety of emotion-focused approaches are appropriate to relieve discomfort and prevent physiological or psychological damage. These include:

1. *Relaxation Training.* Participants are taught to use progressive relaxation techniques to relieve stress symptoms and to allow them to rest or sleep better. Relaxation techniques are often used as part of anxiety-management training (Suinn & Deffenbacher, 1988). They are also used to desensitize participants to highly fearful or anxiety-arousing situations.

2. *Cognitive-Restructuring.* Participants are taught to avoid catastrophising and to reduce self-defeating or self-pitying ways of thinking about stress situations that simply increase tension levels or compound feelings of helplessness or hopelessness. Participants are encouraged to focus on past achievements and successes and to build feelings of self-esteem, self-efficacy, and optimism. Such thoughts or self-statements are associated with stress buffering and mood enhancement (Lightsey, 1994).

3. *Self-Disclosure and Catharsis.* One emotion-oriented coping strategy simply involves disclosing and talking out feelings and fears about the stressful situation and one's reactions to it. Such talking out reduces feelings of isolation and helps to put the situation into a more balanced perspective. The sharing of feelings may be with family members or close friends or with a professional counselor. This approach is an aspect of social support. Research (Matheny et al., 1986) indicated that this approach is a part of the treatment package in about a third of stress managements programs.

Many stress management treatment packages may combine several of the approaches described earlier.

PROBLEM-FOCUSED COPING

When stress situations are at all amenable to control, the most effective strategies are those that emphasize active problem solving. Research has demonstrated rather conclusively that problem-solving ability is related to the alleviation of psychological distress and the attainment of positive feeling states. Further research indicates that confidence in one's problem-solving ability acts as a buffer to strong emotional reactions to stress (Elliott, Sherwin, Harkins, & Marmarosh, 1995).

Unfortunately, less agreement and clarity exist around the question of how to help clients acquire effective problem-solving skills across the wide range of situations in which they are needed. Problem solving has been recognized as an essential part of counseling for some 30 years (D'Zurilla &

Goldfried, 1971). A wide variety of personal problem-solving models have been proposed and studied. Strangely enough knowledge of problem solving has remained a relatively minor part of most counselor's technical expertise (P.P. Heppner & Krauskopf, 1987).

One of the reasons that research on problem solving has had little impact on the practice of counseling is that most of the research has been done in the laboratory under conditions that are very different than those encountered in counseling or stress management situations. The kinds of problem situations encountered in these settings are considerably different from laboratory exercises.

One of the most significant realities inherent in the kinds of problems that confront clients and counselors is that all personal problems are *emotional* problems. That is all real and immediate personal problems have an emotional component. A personal problem is by definition an *obstacle* to the attainment of a goal, or the satisfaction of a basic need. As we saw, such an obstacle always triggers stress, and unrelieved or chronic stress in turn arouses negative emotions such as frustration, fear, and anger.

The first indication of the existence of a problem is usually *frustration*. It seems intuitive that when people feel frustration they would immediately engage in problem-solving behavior. This is not, unfortunately, the usual reaction. For many people, in many stressful situations, the reaction is explosive and emotional or even passive and avoidant rather than rational and systematic (P.P. Heppner, Cook, Wright, & Johnson, 1995).

One frequent reaction to frustration is aggression. People who are frustrated tend to strike out physically or verbally at some other person, thing, or organization. The most common error in coping with stress or frustration involves slipping into the person-blame stance.

In this way of reacting to stressful situations people begin to search for someone to blame, rather than for a way to overcome the obstacle or cause of the problem. The person-blame approach may actually result in a temporary reduction of emotional arousal. It seldom, however, eliminates the real obstacle.

One of the flaws in approaches that move directly into elaborate and rational problem-solving formulas with frustrated and stressed-out people is that they have often not either identified or accepted ownership of their problem. When frustrated people are in the person-blame stance, they very often attempt to place ownership of a problem on others. They may say things like "I am upset because they have a problem." The person who is upset, frustrated, or stressed out is the person who owns the problem.

The first steps in helping a client move into a problem-focused coping strategy is to help that person acknowledge, identify, and accept ownership of a personal problem.

PROBLEM-SOLVING STRATEGIES

A multitude of logical problem-solving strategies have been developed. All of these approaches help the problem solver to increase the number and range of possible alternative solutions and then to choose and implement the most effective and efficient one. For any of these rational, systematic approaches to work, the successful problem solvers must control their emotional arousal at a level that allows them to operate in deliberate, systematic, and logical ways. Often before this kind of cognitive functioning can occur, the counselor must help the client to engage in some of the emotion-focused approaches described earlier.

Almost all of the common problem-solving strategies deal with five basic aspects or phases of the problem-solving process. These are:

1. Sensing and locating the problem
2. Assessing and defining the problem
3. Finding, considering, and choosing among alternative solutions
4. Implementing one or more alternatives
5. Evaluating the results

Problems-solving training programs have been effective in helping children, adolescents, and adults to cope more effectively with stressful situations (Kazdin, Esveld-Dawson, French, & Unis, 1987; Matheny et al., 1986; Nezu & Perri, 1989).

LIFE SKILLS TRAINING

Implementing problem-solving strategies in stress situations often requires the exercise of basic social skills. Long-term interpersonal conflict in family or workplace is probably the most common and most destructive source of chronic stress. Stress management and other preventive and remedial programs are often built around training in various life skills. Indeed, comprehensive programs of life skills training have been developed and demonstrated as the core of preventive and developmental treatment programs (Gazda, 1984). Social skills programs may focus around teaching interpersonal communication skills, assertiveness, conflict resolution, and negotiation skills, and career-related interviewing and job-seeking skills. Training is often done in groups and in conjunction with individual or group counseling.

Such programs have been used successfully with adolescents (Kiselica, Baker, Thomas, & Reedy, 1994), in workplace settings (Kagan et al., 1995), in hospitals (Gazda, 1984), and in a wide variety of other applications (Hollin & Trower, 1986).

LEISURE AND RECREATION AS STRESS REDUCERS

Another disengagement strategy for managing stress is the constructive use of leisure and recreational opportunities. As we saw in Chapter 9, leisure activities represent important aspects of lifespan career development (Super, 1990). Research has shown that the choice of leisure activities represents an effort to satisfy a variety of psychological needs (Tinsley & Eldredge, 1995).

For many people, leisure time is the only time in which they can escape stresses built into work or other responsibilities. For many people, leisure activities represent opportunities to find intrinsic satisfaction in one's efforts, while work represents things done for extrinsic rewards of pay, status, or security (Tinsley, Hinson, Tinsley, & Holt, 1993). For many people, stress is an outgrowth of boredom, monotony, or lack of meaning in work.

One of the goals of preventive and developmental programs is to help people integrate work and leisure within a total lifestyle that is productive, growth-enhancing, and physically and psychologically *healthy.*

It is obvious that large numbers of men and women who think of themselves as successful and well-adjusted in a vocational sense also experience chronic stress and other vocationally related patterns that are destructive and even life threatening (Sauter et al., 1990). It is estimated that over a hundred million workers in the United States suffer from work-induced health problems, the majority of which are stress related (Levi, 1990). For many people, the development of healthy, satisfying leisure pursuits offers the most direct and practical way to restore a healthy balance in their lives and to alleviate the effects of occupational stress.

Work and leisure are psychologically related concepts that connect to the ways people construe and interpret themselves and the world (Blocher & Siegal, 1984). For some people, the dichotomy between work and leisure may have little psychological meaning. The highly competitive business executive, for example, may play tennis or handball with very similar intensity and for much the same set of motives with which he or she pursues a business deal. In both situations, work and leisure activities stem from the same psychological drives and leisure may provide little in the way of tension reduction.

As we saw in Chapter 9, however, for many people work and leisure interact to provide both consistency and variety within an individual's lifestyle and also to reduce stress and promote health.

ENHANCING RESILIENCE IN ADULTS

As noted in earlier chapters, resilience and hardiness are important attributes that mark and facilitate progress along a path to optimal development. The ingredients in these kinds of protective factors in adults are less obvious than they are in children or adolescents. By the same token, factors leading to vulnerability are also more subtle.

SOCIAL SUPPORT AS A PROTECTIVE FACTOR

In both children and adults, the single most significant protective factor is the presence of an effective social support system. Support systems for children generally consist of identified caregivers such as parents or extended family and expand in adolescence to include peers and sometimes teachers or other youth workers. Support systems for adults are considerably more complex. For adults, social support is not a simple matter of being part of a circle of acquaintances. Social support is a multidimensional concept and varies both in its nature and in the role that it plays in buffering stress and nurturing development (Brown, Brady, Lent, Wolfert, & Hall, 1987). For adults feeling the effects of job loss, for example, the most important supportive factors may be reassurance of personal worth, that is, responses that assure the individual that others perceive and acknowledge their competence and abilities (Mallinckrodt & Bennett, 1992). In other situations, practical assistance in coping such as in giving help after a natural disaster may have profound psychological effects in buffering stress (Thoits, 1986).

Similarly, not all close relationships are supportive in the sense of buffering stress or nurturing development. Strained marriages or other family relationships may well be more sources of stress than support. Circles of casual acquaintances or emotionally distant relatives may offer little or no support to the victim of a life-threatening illness, for example.

Social support is more a product of the way in which a relationship is perceived by the distressed individual than of the objective circumstances or formal definition of the relationship (Coyne & DeLongis, 1986).

A quality that does seem to run through all genuinely supportive relationships is *empathy*. People feel support when they perceive that others are able to understand their circumstances, feel their pain, and are moved to care and offer help.

PSYCHOLOGICAL RESOURCES AS PROTECTIVE FACTORS

One of the differences in the nature of protective factors in children and adults is in the relatively larger role played by basic personality characteristics in adults. Beliefs, values, and attitudes play a very large role in the development of resilience in adults.

One way of looking at personality factors that affect resilience is a model that conceptualizes general personality tendencies or predispositions under three major headings: *positive emotionality, negative emotionality,* and *constraint* (Tellegen, 1985).

Positive emotionality is linked to self-efficacy and to positive social relationships, while negative emotionality is linked to strong stress reactions, negative mood swings, and difficulties in interpersonal relationships. The third cluster of personality characteristics is labeled constraint and consists of emotional control and openness to new experience (Church, 1994). Some personality researchers believe that these personality factors have strong genetic bases and that about half of the variance in them is accounted for by heredity and half by environment (Lightsey, 1996). Since little can be done about the genetic factors, it is all the more important from a preventive standpoint to identify individuals with a predisposition to depression, social isolation, or other mood disorders early on and to begin preventive and developmental counseling.

As we reiterated earlier, the best preventive insurance involves *empowering* people, helping them to develop *competence* in terms of life skills and helping them to build a network of genuinely supportive social relationships.

WELLNESS PROGRAMS

Another part of preventive, developmental counseling approaches involves programs aimed at the protection and enhancement of general health. As we saw in Chapter 4, contemporary definitions of health are very broad and inclusive. One aspect of health psychology involves helping people to build lifestyles that will conserve and enhance total human functioning, that is health.

Wellness programs may focus on factors like smoking cessation, diet and exercise regimes, as well as stress management and emotional control.

Stress-related personality patterns may account for as much as 4% of the variance in the incidence of life-threatening illnesses (Lightsey, 1996). This translates into many thousands of preventable deaths each year. The relationships between chronic anger or other strong negative feelings and health are about as large as the relationship between diet and health. Thus, the link between health and stress and various related personality patterns is about as important as is the effects of smoking or cholesterol levels (Friedman, 1991). Research using meta-analyses to integrate research findings suggests that a general negative affective style marked by depression, anxiety, and hostility may be associated with the development of a broad range of diseases including coronary heart disease, asthma, headache, and arthritis (Taylor, 1990).

Personality factors have also been associated with longevity and "successful aging" (Schulz & Heckhausen, 1996). Successful aging involves continued engagement with the environment and the ability to control the most important aspects of that environment as long as possible. Again, the factors of empowerment, competence, and social involvement are reiterated as crucial factors in successful aging. Analyses of the famous Terman longitudinal studies of gifted individuals also suggests that early death is closely associated with maladaptive personality and lifestyle patterns (Freidman et al., 1995).

PREVENTIVE ROLES FOR
DEVELOPMENTAL COUNSELORS

In a very broad sense, almost all professional work with children or adolescents can be considered preventive. Progress along the path of optimal development is virtually by definition also primary prevention. When barriers to such development are evident, a number of special roles for counselors in working with at risk children or adolescents are appropriate. These include:

1. *Child Advocacy.* Counselors, because of their positioning in school and community, are often aware of deficits in human services

programs and of individuals or groups who fall through the cracks. They can help to increase the awareness of the general public as well as public policy makers about the need for services and the urgency of attention to social problems. Sometimes they need to advocate for individuals who are victims of abuse or neglect.

2. *Consultation.* Consultation with parents, teachers, or other caregivers and service providers is an important role. Counselors can identify and interpret the developmental needs and characteristics of children and adolescents to those who are in a position to provide direct help.

3. *Supportive Counseling.* Counselors can provide support for at-risk children and adolescents who are victims or potential victims of violence or abuse. Supportive counseling for children of separation, divorce, or abandonment is an important role for counselors. Probably the most common cause of stress in children is family conflict, separation, and divorce (Hetherington et al., 1998).

4. *Research and Evaluation.* Counselors can help to evaluate existing programs and identify unmet needs. An example of such a role may be to identify the population of at-risk children or adolescents in various categories within a community or school district and to determine whether they are being reached and helped by school or community services. The vignette on page 271 provides an example of such an effort.

5. *Teaching and Training.* Counselors can help to educate parents, train other workers or volunteers, and provide educational services directly to children and adolescents. They can operate or help in educational programs in areas such as tobacco, alcohol and drug education, prevention of AIDS and other sexually transmitted diseases, prevention of teenage pregnancy, and prevention of violence.

6. *Supporting School and Community Peer-Helping Programs.* Another major preventive role for developmental counselors involves the identification, training, and support of the wide variety of helpers and potential helpers who already reside in every community. Such helpers are found in a wide variety of settings including schools, churches, youth groups, hospices, recreational organizations, neighborhood councils, parent associations, and many others. These are the people who are quite literally the first line of prevention within the community. When these peer or lay helpers can learn to recognize, relate to, and/or refer vulnerable, at-risk individuals, they can greatly strengthen the fabric of a community. One of the interesting

findings regarding peer-helping programs is that they almost invariably benefit the helpers as much as the people being helped.

THE NEED FOR PREVENTION

Each night in America in the last decade of the twentieth century an estimated 100,000 children and adolescents were homeless. Some sleep in shelters, some try to survive on the mean streets of every inner city. Some 25% of children under 5 live in poverty. Thousands more are awakened each night by the sound of gun shots. Over 7.5 *million* children suffer from a diagnosable mental health condition.

For millions of children and adolescents the opportunity to grow and flourish, to move along the path of optimal development, and to participate in the good life is little more than an empty promise.

There is no more urgent role for developmental counselors than in joining in efforts to remove the barriers left by decades of ignorance and indifference that block the paths to development of these children.

CHAPTER 14

Ethical and Professional Issues

The primary significance of ultimate moral principles is in their application. . . . Moral failures are the result of careless, perverse judgments in concrete situations.

—John Dewey (1916)

N OT LONG ago this classified advertisement appeared in a small town newspaper:

> Wanted: Counselor and part-time janitor for local human services agency. Experience (in counseling) not required.

The concept of professionalism is not readily understood or easily defined. For many people, the term *professional* is a mark of status, a kind of lofty pedestal from which to look down on others less educated or privileged. However, for counselors, the concept of professionalism represents much more than a mere status symbol.

THE ESSENCE OF PROFESSIONALISM

Nothing is more central to the practice of counseling than trust. Counseling, by its very nature, involves a relationship built on mutual confidence, respect, trust, and consideration. Effective counseling involves the client in a process of self-exploration and self-disclosure. The client becomes more vulnerable as he or she is asked to risk more in terms of dropping facades and defenses and opening up to rigorous examination. Much of the art of interviewing is aimed at helping the client to proceed with this process with feelings of safety and comfort.

To a considerable degree, each counselor depends not only on clinical skills, but also on general expectations of trustworthiness, expertness, and integrity that the client brings to the counseling situation from experiences as a member of society. These hard-won expectations of trust, confidence, and faith in counseling and counselors are the product of many years of commitment, concern, and service provided by an entire profession.

The concept of *professionalism* is often used loosely by those who seek the status, power, and autonomy that the title professional tends to imply. Professionals do not define their identities based on the size of the fees they charge, the number of certificates or diplomas hanging on their walls, or whether they practice privately or work for an agency or institution. These superficial characteristics do not convey the essence of one's professional identity. The reality is that all professions rise out of and are maintained on the basis of public trust.

The public trust that defines and distinguishes any profession is fragile. However, it is easily the most precious asset possessed by any profession. It is trust, respect, and confidence that brings clients to the counselor in the first place. Without public acceptance, counselors would lose the autonomy and independence in judgment and action to do their jobs.

Public trust is not quickly or easily won. It accumulates slowly out of the shared experiences of people, but it can be quickly damaged. Public trust is based in great part on three expectations of the counseling profession and its individual members: competence, regulation, and public service.

The Expectation of Competence

Professionals are recognized, sought out, and given respect primarily because they are believed to have special, useful, and current knowledge and skill not available from other members of society. Professional competence is generally attested to by credentials such as advanced degrees, licenses, or certificates. It may also be affirmed by membership in professional associations.

When incompetent or unqualified people are allowed to enter, remain in, or pass themselves off as members of a profession, the public faith in that profession's competence will be diminished. For this reason, most professional groups attempt to perform some sort of gate-keeping function. This is done by accrediting preparation programs, offering recognition based on special examinations, or by lobbying for legislation to provide for licensure or certification.

The Expectation of Regulation

A second core expectation on which public trust is based is that professional conduct and practice will be regulated for the interest and protection of consumers. Usually, there is an expectation that the profession will regulate itself by disciplining or removing unethical or unqualified members. Similarly, there is an expectation that such regulation will be exercised by public agencies.

Self-regulation of professionals is usually accomplished by their associations. These organizations typically develop, disseminate, and attempt to enforce ethical codes and standards for professional practice. These codes and standards provide both the professionals and the public with a way to understand the duties, obligations, and responsibilities undertaken by these professionals. When these obligations and responsibilities are not met, the professional association can act to protect the public and its own reputation by disciplining or expelling the offending member.

Ethical codes and standards for practice are based on principles laid down by a profession to guide its members in their practice (American Psychological Association [APA], 1992). Many of the ethical and professional issues confronting counselors are complex. It is not easy to compile a simple set of rules or laws to be followed mechanically (APA, 1994). Most of the human services professions have tried to identify and clarify a set of basic general principles that can be applied in a wide range of professional relationships and situations (APA, 1987). The code presently used by the American Psychological Association is included in the Appendix.

The Expectations of Public Service

A third expectation is that members of a profession are genuinely motivated to serve the people with whom they work. This belief is perhaps the most fragile of the expectations. It is faith that the professional is committed to values that go beyond status needs, or monetary interests, and that professional practice will be guided by those values (Meara, Schmidt, & Day, 1996).

ETHICAL PROBLEMS IN COUNSELING

Ethical questions, because they are rooted in the public trust that defines any profession, are of central concern to all of its members. Whenever the trust and respect of the public are eroded by the unethical, unprofessional, or irresponsible behavior of one member of the profession, all members are harmed, and their ability to function in fully professional ways is diminished or impaired.

The profession of counseling is especially concerned with ethical problems. The effectiveness and future development of the counseling profession is directly related to its ability to nurture and deserve the trust of the public. Counseling is a relatively new or emerging profession with fewer years of professional history around which to establish trust and credibility than some more established groups.

Second, counseling deals with clients on a deeply personal and intimate level. Obtaining help in a counseling relationship requires a high level of self-disclosure and personal risk-taking that can only be expected when the client trusts the counselor's competence and integrity.

Finally, ethical concerns are especially significant for professional counseling because the profession is not clearly defined and easily identified by the public. As noted in Chapter 1, the title of counselor is widely used and easily misunderstood. A wide variety of professionals and nonprofessionals can and do utilize the term *counseling* to describe all or part of what they do. Bankers, stockbrokers, or real estate or insurance salespeople, for example, may call what they do *investment counseling*. Physicians, lawyers, ministers, and even architects or librarians may describe some aspects of their professional functions as counseling.

The public may be easily confused and sometimes misled by the generalized use of this term. Even in the area of psychological counseling, clear and widely observed standards for levels and types of training have not yet been fully defined or accepted. People practicing under the title of counselor and engaging in psychological counseling activities may have from a sub-baccalaureate level to a doctoral level of preparation.

Professional preparation may occur in a variety of settings. Counselor education programs may be housed in departments of psychology or educational psychology, in schools of education, or in departments of rehabilitation medicine, family studies, criminal justice, or health sciences. Practicing counselors may hold a variety of credentials and may differ in terms of specific competence and organizational affiliations.

The most widely sanctioned contemporary preparation pattern for professional counselors is at the level of a two-year master's degree program. Such a program typically includes basic graduate level work in psychology and other social and behavioral sciences, and has major components of supervised practice, personal growth experiences, and professional seminars.

Generally, when we speak of a professional counselor, we refer to people prepared in this way. Such patterns of professional training are not universal, however. The clients that any professional counselor encounters in his or her own practice may have had experience with people called counselors who were prepared at various levels and in different ways. Counselors often find it necessary to structure or explain their own ethical codes and commitments much more carefully and explicitly than do some other human services professionals.

ETHICAL PRINCIPLES IN COUNSELING

Several basic issues tend to dominate any discussion of professional ethics in counseling. These are issues that are encountered frequently and that are of major concern to both counselors and clients as they begin any counseling relationship (Pope & Vetter, 1992). The first and most familiar of these issues is *confidentiality*.

CONFIDENTIALITY

Most counseling situations require the client to disclose a great deal of significant and often intimate information about themselves. Clients are concerned with how that information will be treated by the counselor. Problems about confidentiality provide the most frequent ethical dilemmas for practicing counselors.

Questions of confidentiality are best discussed in terms of *levels* of confidentiality. Confidentiality involves a commitment to retain information that is always relative, rather than absolute. No ethical code, for example, requires a counselor to withhold information when such action would clearly endanger human life. For example, we would certainly not expect a counselor to withhold information that a client had just placed a bomb on an airliner. In such a case, the sanctity and value of human life clearly outweighs the importance of the promise to treat information in confidence.

We can look at three levels of confidentiality within a counseling situation. The first level of confidentiality concerns the professional handling of information. Every counselor has the obligation to treat all information arising from professional contacts in a professional way.

This includes information about clients, their friends and families, and information about relevant organizations. Such information acquired in a professional situation, no matter how harmless or trivial it may seem to the counselor, should never be used in a loose or irresponsible way. It should never be used in social conversations, to entertain or impress others, or to build the ego of the counselor. If the information is to be used in a serious professional context for teaching or staff development purposes, great care should be exercised to protect the identity of the people or organizations involved.

This obligation extends not only to information from counseling sessions, but also to any kind of personal information contained in files, cumulative records, records of telephone conversations, information from referral sources, and so on. All information about clients or client systems should be handled in ways that respect the privacy and worth of the people involved. The most frequent example of unethical breaches of confidentiality stem from loose, careless, or thoughtless handling of information.

Records, test scores, and other kinds of information should not be released to anyone without the client's explicit consent. This precludes furnishing information to people such as employers, insurance companies, or even colleges without the client's consent. Whenever there is doubt about the release of information, the best policy is not to release it.

One problem that arises more and more frequently concerns the handling of information about minor children. This problem is especially vexing when the parents are separated or divorced, and when legal custody of the child is disputed, shared, or simply unclear. Normally, formal records about minor children are made available to custodial parents with a qualified professional present to interpret the information or answer questions. When legal custody is not clear or when the parent requesting information does not have custody, information should not be released without consent of the custodial parent or the court.

Maintaining confidentiality is simply good professional practice and should be observed by all professionals whether they are physicians, lawyers, counselors, teachers, or others.

The ethical principle involved may be stated as follows:

> Information arising out of a counseling contact is the joint property of the counselor or counseling agency and the client or client system, and should not be used in any way that may be objectionable to either party.

When this simple principle is observed, the most frequent breaches of confidentiality can be avoided. We might note that this principle could, under some circumstances, preclude the counselor from releasing information even with the client's consent. An example might be a former client who consults a clearly unethical or unqualified practitioner or "quack." In such cases, the counselor might actually refuse to share information even at the client's request.

The second level of confidentiality relates to special kinds of information arising out of counseling processes. In many situations, it is highly desirable to share certain information with other professionals who are working with the same client or client system. The purpose of this sharing is clearly to enhance the welfare of the client. Such persons may include other counselors, teachers, social workers, physicians, or psychologists. In certain circumstances, this situation may also include parents or spouses.

Even though the purpose of sharing information in this way is to help the client, very complicated ethical problems may arise. Often, in order to make referrals or to secure desirable changes in the client's environment, some sharing of information seems necessary. For a variety of reasons, clients may be extremely reluctant to have the information shared in any way, even though in the counselor's judgment, it may be in the client's best interest. Conflicts arising from this kind of situation often confront the counselor with very difficult ethical dilemmas.

The best way to avoid this kind of ethical problem is to prevent it. Explain very clearly, in advance to the client how information will be handled regarding parents, spouses, or other professionals within the agency or community. When a clear policy exists, and is explained to the client before confidences are accepted, many ethical and professional problems can be avoided.

This level of confidentiality can be summed up with the following principle:

> Clients should be informed, in advance, of the counselor's policy in regard to sharing of information with relatives or other professionals when such sharing is judged to be in the client's best interest.

When the counselor structures his or her position regarding the sharing of information with others in the client's best interest, then many of the ensuing decisions are simply professional judgments rather than ethical dilemmas. Ethical breaches of confidentiality occur primarily where the counselor encourages the client to expect that information will be withheld under a given set of conditions and then proceeds to divulge it.

It is possible to base a counseling practice solely on the two levels of confidentiality described previously. In some circumstances, it may even be desirable to do so. Yet, when only these two levels of confidentiality are observed, clients will not bring some kinds of problems to the counselor.

A third level of confidentiality is one in which the counselor holds a communication in complete confidence, except in the case of clear and imminent danger to human life. At this level of confidentiality, the counselor would not divulge the communication without the client's consent, even if the counselor felt strongly that it was in the client's best interest to do so. The only grounds for breaking this kind of confidence involve some extraordinary circumstance involving danger to human life. The fact that it might be better for the client or for society if the information were divulged, is not in itself, an ethical reason for breaking a confidence accepted under such conditions.

The basis for accepting a communication at this level of confidentiality is that it is desirable for clients to have available a professionally trained person with whom they can share information in almost total confidence, rather than to have no such person in whom to trust. The counselor, in providing the client with a trustworthy and professional relationship, is discharging an important societal role. In this role, the counselor's *primary* function is not to protect society by some direct intervention, but rather to enhance society by providing a confidential and expert helping relationship to the client.

The significance of our earlier discussion of public trust seems clear here. In accepting and honoring confidential communications that are often of a troubling and disturbing nature, the counselor is discharging the responsibilities that go along with his or her status as a professional.

Client confidences should not be accepted lightly. The counselor should choose carefully and explain clearly the level of confidentiality at which he or she is willing to work in a particular setting or with a specific client population. Counselors should thoroughly discuss problems of confidentiality with their coworkers and administrators so that all of those with whom they work understand as completely as possible the nature of the ethical constraints and obligations within which they operate. The ethical principle involved here can be stated in this way:

> When a counselor encourages a client to believe that a communication will be held in full and complete confidence, the only ethical ground for breaking that confidence is in terms of danger to human life.

The counselor who is personally or professionally unable or unwilling to accept disturbing and shocking communications at the highest level of confidentiality should structure his or her relationships with clients in advance. The counselor will then have to accept the limitations that working at a lower level of confidentiality may impose on his or her usefulness in certain situations. Deciding at which of these levels of confidentiality to operate is a matter of professional judgment. Keeping a confidence once it has been accepted at a particular level is a matter of ethical integrity. The counselor who does not keep a confidence in an ethical manner will soon have no confidences to keep and will bring the profession into disrepute.

One note should be made at this point regarding confidentiality with minors. Normally, custodial parents have legal and moral rights to information about their minor children. Such rights are not to be taken lightly. On the other hand, often the nature of counseling relationships with children and adolescents encourages them to share information with counselors that they may be reluctant to share with parents. In situations that involve counseling with minors, it is important to discuss confidentiality explicitly with the client and if appropriate, with the parents.

Children and adolescents should be especially clear about the policies and practices of the counselor and the agency or institution in regard to privacy and confidentiality. Once a communication has been accepted from a child or adolescent with expectations of complete confidentiality, the promise made is certainly no less ethically binding than a similar commitment made to an adult.

LEGAL IMPLICATIONS OF CONFIDENTIALITY

A number of important legal principles affect the nature of professional-client communication. One of these is called *privileged communication.* The concept of privileged communication is based on the notion that some kinds of professional relationships are so important to the welfare of individuals, and ultimately to society, that they should not be intruded upon even by courts of law. In practice, privileged communication means that a professional cannot be compelled to testify against his or her client in a criminal proceeding regarding anything that was communicated within their professional relationship.

Privileged communication for professionals is generally given only to physician-patient, lawyer-client, and minister-parishioner relationships. In most states and under most circumstances, counselors are not accorded privileged status by the courts. In part, this is due to the point made earlier about the difficulty of defining precisely who is a counselor. Some states are beginning to accord privileged communication to psychologists under certain conditions.

Counselors do have certain legal rights as witnesses of which they should be aware. Normally, all formal records and files of a counselor, or counseling agency, are subject to subpoena and can be used as evidence in a legal proceeding. This includes the counselor's interview notes if they are part of the formal records. Counselors should be aware of this possible legal access when they enter interview notes into formal files or records.

If a counselor wishes to keep confidential case notes or memoranda about cases that are not subject to subpoena, such notes must be clearly addressed to themselves, used primarily for their own professional development, and kept in a secure place not accessible to others, including supervisors or clerical workers. Such personal memoranda may not be ordinarily subject to subpoena, but the counselor may be compelled to testify about them.

While testifying in any legal proceeding or making any statements to authorities, counselors should be aware that many kinds of client communications constitute hearsay evidence rather than factual knowledge, and are therefore inadmissable as evidence in a court of law. Typically, counselors are not required to report client's statements about legal responsibility or their accusations against others to authorities. In some situations, counselors could be guilty of slander or libel if they did report such statements.

Recent court decisions have placed some added responsibilities on counselors and other professionals. Some courts (Monahan, 1993) have held that counselors or therapists have a clear obligation to warn an intended victim in the event that threats against that person are made by a client in the course of treatment. Since such threats involve danger to human life, the counselor has no ethical obligation to treat them in confidence. The counselor instead may have a responsibility to warn the possible victim directly, or to notify appropriate authorities to insure that such warning is accomplished.

A third legal consideration in handling confidential information is that counselors and therapists are in some situations and in some states required by law to report cases of abuse or neglect of children or other vulnerable individuals such as the mentally retarded, mentally ill, or aged. When counselors are "mandated reporters," it is very important to make this fact known to all concerned in advance of any pledges of confidentiality.

Issues of Competence

An equally important ethical issue concerns the scope of professional competence. Ethical practice for any professional is more than a matter of good intentions. Since the work of the counselor is based on trust in his or her competence, that trust must be respected. Counselors have two primary ethical obligations in regard to professional competence. First, they have an obligation not to work beyond their own areas of competence and second, they are obligated not to misrepresent that area of professional competence to clients or prospective clients.

Because the term *counselor* is an ambiguous one, and counselors are prepared in a variety of settings and ways, the demarcation of boundaries of professional competence is a particularly difficult and important aspect of ethical practice for counselors. It is essential that professional counselors be clear and honest with themselves about the limits of their own expertise. Making distinctions about cases or issues that one is competent to work with is not easy.

If it is hard for professionals to make such distinctions clearly and neatly, it is unreasonable to suppose that clients or prospective clients will be able to do so. Clients may bring problems and concerns to counselors that are inappropriate for the counselor to deal with. In this event, it is the counselor's ethical obligation to make that determination, and to refer the client to a more appropriate resource. In some cases, if no other referral resource is available, or if the client is unwilling to accept referral, the counselor must ethically refuse to treat the client. One of the somber realities of professional life is that in some cases, inexpert treatment is worse than no treatment at all. Some attempts at counseling interventions can be harmful.

Because of the great variability in clients and in the counseling profession, it is difficult to prescribe rules of thumb by which to assess competence boundaries. A conservative, but defensible, approach to take is that a counselor is presumed to be competent to work with those kinds of cases, and practice those techniques, with which he or she has had successful *supervised* experience. Supervised experience may be acquired as part of preservice professional preparation programs in practicum and internship. The counselor who wishes to expand his or her areas of professional competence after entering practice should do so through obtaining supervision from a clearly qualified professional. Reading a book or attending a weekend workshop devoted to a particular topic does not qualify a counselor to begin unsupervised experience in a new area.

In making referrals for clients whom they view as inappropriate to work with, counselors have an obligation to help clients understand the reasons for the referral and the distinctive qualifications of the professionals to whom the referral is made. Considerable confusion often exists in the minds of clients about the qualifications and credentials of helping professionals. Referral to a psychiatrist or to a clinical psychologist may be frightening or upsetting to a client, or to the client's family. Making a successful referral may involve not only ethical integrity, but considerable professional skill.

In such situations, clients need to understand that psychiatrists are physicians practicing a medical specialty. As such, they are legally able to prescribe controlled drugs and to admit patients to hospitals. Psychologists are generally licensed or certified by the state, but in some states, the certification only regulates the use of the title *psychologist.* It may not signify competence in a specific area of professional practice. The American Board of Examiners in Professional Psychology does grant diplomate status upon examination to the various professional psychological specialties. Social workers are also licensed in some states and practice in a variety of settings providing professional help. The term *psychotherapist* is, in itself, not descriptive of any specific kind of professional qualification, and does not, by itself, denote the possession of any kind of professional credential.

When professionals are guilty of failure to practice at a reasonable level of competence, they may incur liability for damage due to malpractice. The general rule for defining malpractice is a failure to meet prevailing, professionally accepted standards for practice. Physicians and psychologists may be sued for malpractice and found liable for damages by the courts. Malpractice suits against counselors are rare because it is so difficult to determine standards of competence in a field as varied and loosely defined as counseling. Counselors are not, however, immune from malpractice suits and certainly they are ethically responsible for providing competent professional services.

One of the marks of any professional is the ability and motivation to evaluate the quality of his or her own professional services. Counselors have an obligation to their clients and to their profession to be accountable for the quality of professional services offered. Ethical counselors will establish formal and systematic methods for evaluating client satisfaction and client outcomes. They will keep careful and thorough case records, and will attempt to assess their own effectiveness with particular types of clients, cases, and treatment approaches. One such evaluation model was described in Chapter 8. Counselors will use this information and all available knowledge and resources to improve the quality of their own professional practice.

Conflicts of Interest

Another major ethical issue involves conflicts of interest. As professionals ethically obligated to act in the best interests of clients, counselors are committed to avoid situations in which there are conflicts between the best interests of the client and the self-interest, or other commitments, of the counselor. This means, among other things, that counselors do not engage in counseling with close friends, immediate family members, or those with whom they have employer-employee relationships. It also means that sexual relationships with clients are unethical. In some states, these relationships may also constitute a felony. To avoid even the appearance of unethical behavior, counselors should conduct counseling sessions in professional settings, during well-defined hours, and in places that are not unusually secluded or remote.

An area of ethical conduct that is of increasing concern is that of sexual harassment. Sexual harassment can be defined as any kind of unwanted or uninvited attention of a sexual nature forced on someone in a subordinate or otherwise vulnerable position. Ill-considered, crude, or distasteful remarks in a conversation between a counselor and client, or counselor and employee can be construed as sexual harassment. Such behavior is *illegal, unethical, unprofessional,* and is certain to bring both the counselor and the profession into disrepute.

Some kinds of counseling situations present particular difficulties for counselors in regard to conflicts of interest. Counselors in schools, colleges, correctional facilities, or other institutions may find that they are faced with dual roles and dual expectations in regard to their professional practice. Administrators may view them as arms of administration rather than as agents or advocates of students or inmates. Problems regarding sharing of information, the nature of advice given to clients, or even questions of client's rights within the institution may trigger controversy.

Generally, as we noted, these kinds of expectations should be discussed very thoroughly in advance of specific crisis situations. Clear and explicit understanding of the roles and responsibilities of counselors in regard both to clients and employing institutions are the best safeguards against being put into agonizing ethical dilemmas. As professionals, however, it is not possible for counselors to delegate their ethical responsibilities to others. Being ordered to do something that is unethical is not an excuse.

When professional counselors are unable to discharge their ethical obligations within a given setting after reasonable efforts to clarify and resolve differences, they may have no ethical alternative except to leave the setting.

Certain other kinds of counseling situations may also trigger conflict of interest problems. In some situations, clients are referred by or their treatment is paid for by an employer, an ex-spouse, a noncustodial parent, or other relative. In such situations, the person or company paying for treatment may feel entitled to receive information about counseling, or even to influence the course of treatment. The primary ethical obligation of the counselor is to the identified client. Before accepting this kind of referral, the counselor should clearly establish the ethical ground rules to all concerned. Paying for a program of professional treatment does not, by itself, confer *any* special privileges to the payer in regard to that treatment. Sometimes, bitterly contested divorce or custody battles may involve counselors in situations that are difficult to resolve. In such cases, it is often necessary to place ethical standards and the welfare of clients, ahead of being approved or liked by the contesting parties.

INFORMED CONSENT

One important ethical issue that is sometimes neglected is that of obtaining full and informed consent from clients prior to the beginning of counseling. Many clients are not sophisticated about the nature of counseling processes, or about the policies and practices of human services agencies.

It is important that the client be carefully and explicitly informed as fully as possible about the nature of counseling procedures, the handling of information and records, the fees charged, the nature of third-party payment procedures, the legal requirements regarding reporting of abuse or neglect, and any other pertinent information affecting the client. When research or training activities are involved, it is especially important that clients be informed in advance and that explicit informed consent be obtained (Pope & Vasquez, 1991).

USING ETHICAL CODES

Fortunately, the individual counselor is not alone in confronting all of the complex and confusing ethical dilemmas that may arise in professional practice. As we noted, ethical questions are the concern of all members of a profession and their professional associations. Ethical codes are established to help individual counselors to resolve problems ethically and fairly.

All of these codes involve principles that practitioners must attempt to apply in the very complex context of real-life situations. Going from abstract principles to practical applications is often not an easy task.

When confronted with a complex ethical dilemma, the first thing that any counselor should do is to consult with a fellow professional. Often sorting out the issues and principles involved with another informed and concerned counselor who is not caught up in the conflicting pressures of the situation can help resolve the dilemma. When the situation is very unclear, or when ethical guidelines seem confusing or contradictory, counselors can often consult with ethics committees of local, state, or national organizations to obtain more specialized and expert assistance.

Seeking assistance and consultation on ethical problems is not a one-way street. All professional counselors should be willing to provide assistance and consultation to colleagues.

Since ethical behavior is a concern of *all* professionals, responsibility is not solely limited to one's own behavior. When one counselor observes unethical behavior by another counselor, there is a clear obligation to intervene. Usually, the first step in such an intervention is to call the unethical nature of the behavior to the attention of the colleague in question. Often unethical behavior is inadvertent or the result of ignorance or simply thoughtlessness. When such situations are discussed between colleagues in a tactful and concerned way, the result is positive for both the individual and the profession.

When such an approach does not work, the counselor may have to take more formal action within the employing institution or within the appropriate professional organization. Ethical complaints are generally handled by professional associations in ways that provide for fair, impartial, and private hearings for all concerned. While professional associations do not have the force of law, they can use the collective weight and opinion of the profession to obtain compliance with ethical standards so long as a professional wishes to continue as a member of the association. In some very serious situations, unethical behavior may be called to the attention of licensing boards or other governmental agencies concerned with maintaining professional standards.

Upholding and enhancing the ethical standards of any profession rests primarily with its individual members. Ethical behavior primarily involves the courage and integrity to banish self-deceptions and self-serving realizations about one's ability to be all things to all people. The ethical counselor must have the courage to be consistent and effective within the limitations of his or her proven professional competence. The counselor must put his or her concern for the welfare of clients and respect for the profession ahead of needs to be admired, approved, or even liked by the host of others who at times may want to influence professional commitments and decisions. To the extent that a professional counselor is committed to and involved with this kind of professional role, sound ethical decisions and obligations will flow out of that commitment. To some extent, ethical considerations put boundaries around professional relationships. It is important that these boundaries do not result in relationships that clients perceive as cold, impersonal, or dehumanizing (Lazarus, 1994).

DERIVING ETHICAL PRINCIPLES AND VALUES

Most people in our society must face disturbing issues and questions as they confront and cope with the realities of a complex and deeply imperfect world. Usually, however, people confront those realities in the comfort and security of their own living rooms as they watch the 6:00 o'clock news or read the feature stories in a newspaper.

Counselors, unfortunately, do not have the luxury of distancing themselves from the ugly realities of daily life in this way. Almost daily counselors are likely to be confronted in direct and personal ways with human dilemmas that involve situations such as child abuse or neglect, abortion, rape, incest, domestic violence, or other potentially tragic and deeply emotionally charged issues.

Dealing with these kinds of issues ethically and rationally while maintaining one's personal commitment to some consistent and coherent set of values and principles is one of the most formidable challenges confronting any counselor.

Counselors like other well-integrated and morally responsible adults have personal value systems. They cannot and should not attempt to avoid the realities of a complex and often morally confused and confusing world by attempting to maintain some empty pretense of moral neutrality or ethical indifference. Indeed, much of what is discussed in counseling interviews is centered around moral issues in human relationships (Sugarman & Martin, 1995).

To communicate themselves as mature, caring, and committed adults, counselors must be able to articulate a deeply consistent and well-elaborated kind of moral and ethical sensitivity.

This does not mean that counselors exist to impose their own views on every client who comes into contact with them. It does mean that in most ethical or moral situations, they cannot and should not try to avoid exposing their own deeply held value commitments.

Such exposure of values also does not mean that in every situation the counselor acts as the watchdog or mouthpiece for the established society. Indeed, throughout the twentieth century, many of the great crises of conscience that have confronted men and women have stemmed from their conviction that to preserve their own moral integrity they must oppose and perhaps even disobey the dictates of government or organized society. Events like the Holocaust, the Civil Rights Movement, or the Vietnam War have made it abundantly clear that moral and ethical individuals can never delegate their deeply felt sense of right and wrong to either politicians or bureaucrats.

Counselors must communicate themselves as sensitive, committed, and consistent people who can be trusted with heartfelt confidences and deeply personal self-disclosures. Counselors must be *principled people* (Meara, Schmidt, & Day, 1996).

To be principled in the ethical and moral sense of being trustworthy and above behaving solely on the basis of expedience or self-interest, the counselor must first be a principled thinker. A principled thinker is one who is cognitively complex enough to recognize and sort out the many diverse and often conflicting issues and values at stake in a complicated human dilemma, yet be able to integrate these elements within a set of basic and general moral principles out of which a deeply personal and consistent resolution can be found.

Moral development, that is, the development of principled thinking, is a part of cognitive growth. For the counselor, it is a vital part of professional development.

BASIC ETHICAL FRAMEWORKS

One way in which people are able to reason in complex ethical situations and to make moral judgments is through the use of general moral frameworks or worldviews that provide consistent bases for making decisions about what is good and true and beautiful within themselves, their fellows, and within the social world.

These global frameworks are sometimes called "first order principles" because they are very basic and all encompassing. Even principled people of good will and conscience can and do disagree on many of their moral judgments in given situations. Some of this disagreement stems from the fact that they appeal to different sets of first-order principles or moral theories as they begin the moral judgment process.

We can identify several of the most commonly used moral reasoning frameworks or sets of first-order principles below:

THEISM

In the history of Western thought, theism has been a primary source of moral principles. Basically, theism as a framework for making moral judgments is based on the view that human beings should act to please God or to do whatever is the will of God. Obviously, there are many interpretations of what exactly constitutes the will of God. Usually, however, theistic frameworks are derived from theological principles based on religious teachings and interpretations of Scriptures or other divine revelations. Within such theological interpretations, a consistent and comprehensive basis for moral judgments can often be found.

MORAL RATIONALISM

A second global framework for making moral judgments is organized around the view that human beings are rational by nature and hence are able to engage in a logical process of moral reasoning. Sometimes the origin of this view is attributed to Aristotle who held that virtue and reason were closely related. Just as in the theistic model, however, there may be many disagreements about what kinds of moral judgments are reasonable and hence virtuous.

Within this kind of framework, much depends on the specific assumptions with which one begins the moral reasoning process. When these basic assumptions differ, equally rational or logical processes may lead to vastly different decisions.

MORAL IMPERATIVES

This model or approach to ethical and moral reasoning is based upon Kant's concept of categorical imperatives. It, too, is in a sense a rational model of moral decision making, but one that insists that the basic premises or assumptions from which we begin the process should be universal in scope and relevance. If we build our process of moral reasoning on a principle of what is good, that principle should be applicable to all people and all situations. For example, if we began with a basic principle of the importance of being truthful, we would logically have to believe that being truthful was good for all people in all situations. The point of this approach is that before people can genuinely base their moral judgments on logical processes, they must get down to a kind of bedrock of *universally* applicable first principles.

UTILITARIAN REASONING

A fourth general framework for making moral judgments deals with the consequences of those decisions. This view holds that the primary purpose of moral behavior is to secure the happiness and welfare of human beings. Acts are good, therefore, and judgments are moral when they maximize the happiness and well-being of people. This is a kind of moral framework that seeks the greatest good (happiness) for the greatest number of people for the greatest possible part of the time. This view asserts, in effect, that one should, in making a moral decision, consider primarily its effects upon the happiness of human beings who may be affected.

ETHICAL EGOISM

This framework is one that is unabashedly selfish or self-centered in its view. It asserts that people should behave in terms on their own long-term best interests. In other words, the best guide in making a moral judgment is whether or not its long-term consequences serve one's own interests and personal welfare. This view does distinguish between immediate expediency and long-term interest, so that it is quite possible to make pro-social or even philanthropic decisions on the grounds that strengthening the general social fabric and promoting the general welfare are really the best ways to serve one's own long-term interests.

MORAL INTUITIONISM

In this framework, the primary guides to moral decision making are viewed to be one's own immediate and personal *feelings* about a situation. The moral person is one who is deeply aware and sensitive, and who is willing to *act* upon strong feelings. Generally, this view holds that people's intuitions or deepseated feelings are in the direction of compassion, and concern for others.

Moral intuitionism generally assumes that people have both moral obligations and inherent tendencies to behave with compassion, fidelity, justice, and in other essentially pro-social and positive ways. In this view, when one is fully aware of personal feelings and impulses, decisions and behaviors will be moral.

THE SEARCH FOR SOCIAL JUSTICE

The final global moral framework that we will describe is based upon notions of social justice. This position holds that people should act justly and fairly toward their fellow human beings without regard for differences in power, status, or wealth, and without racial, sexual, age, or ethnic bias or discrimination. It holds that moral behavior should promote the cause of a just and fair world for all. This view is essentially egalitarian and puts great emphasis on human freedom.

We have briefly sketched some basic parameters of several fundamental ethical theories or frameworks within which basic moral principles may be derived It should be clear that differences in views of what is ethical may stem from differences in cultural backgrounds, religious beliefs, and even gender. Many of the considerations discussed in Chapters 10 and 11 addressed this point.

Not all moral principles are as global or sweeping in their scope as those derived from the kinds of frameworks or worldviews described.

SPECIFIC PRINCIPLES

We can also identify a number of more specific and concrete moral principles that can be used as guides to moral and ethical reasoning. These can be called second-order principles. They need not be derived directly from highly abstract and global views of the world or of mankind. Such principles or values include:

- Respect for human life
- Respect for truth
- Respect for privacy
- Respect for freedom and autonomy
- Respect for promises and commitments
- Concern for the weak, vulnerable, or helpless
- Concern for the growth and development of people
- Concern lest others be harmed

- Concern for human dignity and equality
- Concern for gratitude and reparation
- Concern for human freedom

These more focused principles reflect somewhat more specific and simple decencies. They are, in one sense, more easily made relevant and applicable to moral dilemmas arising out of social interaction than are some of the more profound and abstract principles derived directly out of sweeping philosophical or theological frameworks.

As we search for a set of either general or specific moral principles we may ask a number of questions, including:

1. How universal is this principle, or framework? Is it essentially timeless and part of the total human experience, or is it rooted in a set of beliefs or customs that are simply part of a contemporary scene, or is it the view of a specific subculture?
2. How applicable is this moral framework or principle to the kinds of dilemmas that I face as a professional counselor?
3. How consistent is this moral principle or framework as a guide across many situations and circumstances?
4. Does this ethical principle or framework provide a *practical* guide for moral reasoning, decision making, and behavior?
5. Is this moral principle or framework comprehensible and reasonable to any serious and intelligent person who tries to understand and apply it?
6. How will this particular framework or principle be perceived or understood by clients or colleagues with differing cultural backgrounds?

A MODEL FOR APPLYING ETHICAL PRINCIPLES

Complex moral and ethical dilemmas are never easy to resolve. Often we find ourselves torn and confused by all of the conflicting options, obligations and circumstances that are involved. One way to provide greater clarity is to impose a logical, step-by-step reasoning process to the problem. The following model lists five basic steps in thinking about a difficult ethical or moral dilemma.

1. Review the general ethical frameworks or first-order principles to which you feel committed as the fundamental basis for moral reasoning.

2. List the second-order principles that seem most relevant to the situation at hand.
3. Gather all relevant information about the specific situations and circumstances surrounding the dilemma. Review the relevant parts of professional codes of ethics.
4. List the major options within which you must choose in resolving the dilemma.
5. Compare these options in terms of the degree to which they reflect commitment to your first and second order principles and the ethical standards of the profession.

When counselors are able to develop a set of ethical and moral principles on which to base their professional relationships and to define their

---

AN ETHICAL DILEMMA

Jane was doing her counseling internship at a metropolitan senior high school. One of her first assignments was to visit a nearby middle school whose students next went into the high school. The middle school had no counselor, so Jane was to explain the high school's curriculum, counseling program, course options, and registration procedures to students in their English class.

After meeting three classes in the morning, Jane was eating her bag lunch in a vacant classroom when a girl from one of the classes came in. The eighth-grade girl, Marie, began by asking, "If I tell you something, will you promise not to tell anyone?" Without much consideration, Jane agreed.

Marie proceeded to explain that she was five months pregnant. That morning before school her parents confronted Marie about her condition. After an hour of name calling and near hysterics, Marie's father announced that he would take her that evening to a physician he knew who would perform an abortion.

Marie maintains that she does not want an abortion, and that her 17-year-old boyfriend, Gary, wants to marry her. After the confrontation with her parents, Marie called Gary and they planned to run away together that afternoon. Gary plans to steal a car and they will drive to Chicago where he has friends.

Jane now is faced with a major ethical dilemma. She has promised to keep a confidence. She realizes that the situation presents drastic consequences for Marie, her boyfriend, Gary, Marie's parents, and the school.

Try to put yourself in Jane's position, and using the five-step model for applying ethical principles (pp. 304–305), try to think through the situation and reach a decision about how you would resolve it.

obligations, they are able to deal with others in more consistent ways and are able to earn the trust of both clients and colleagues. In a sense, trust in any person arises partially out of belief that the trusted person will behave toward us in dependable, consistent, and predictable ways.

When we are able to clarify and articulate our ethical and moral commitments to ourselves, we can make consistent, principled decisions. When we are able to communicate and demonstrate our ethical and moral principles to others in quiet, yet clear ways, we can show our trustworthiness.

CHAPTER 15

The Professional Development of the Counselor

[A]ny careful analysis of the "higher" stages of ego, moral or social development indicates that an enlarged social perspective, acceptance of social convention and law, an effort to consider other's rights and to be fair . . . are at the heart of the individual's development.

—Ralph Mosher (1979)

WE VERY often hear that counseling is a developing profession. Although the roots of counseling go back into our history for nearly a century, that statement probably still has some validity. In another sense, counseling is a profession of developing *people*, that is, developmental counseling begins with the counselor's *own* development.

THE EMPATHY-HELPING CONNECTION

In Chapter 2, we described briefly the development of social role-taking ability. Empathy and the understanding and compassion that flows from it are not innate characteristics, or the genetic endowment of a fortunate few. Rather, the ability both to feel *with* and to feel *for* others is *developed* out of the social experiences and interactions that shape personality. For most of the history of psychology, personality theories and social psychological conceptualizations have tended to ignore or even to deny that human beings were genuinely capable of altruistic behavior, or that we as human beings can actually come to care for someone other than ourselves.

More recent research and views of caring behavior support the notion that as people develop the capacity to *empathize*, that is, both to mirror and to understand another's needs and feelings, the capacity for caring, compassion, and helping emerges (Batson, 1990). This phenomenon is sometimes called the empathy-helping connection and it is a crucial component of counseling and other helping relationships.

CONCEPTS OF EMPATHIC FUNCTIONING

Empathy is a concept that has long been considered central to the process of counseling. The early writing and research done by Carl Rogers more than 40 years ago have made empathy a key concept in understanding how and why counseling works.

The development of empathic responding has been of interest to many branches of psychology (Duan & Hill, 1996). Some personality theorists have contended that empathy is the essential element in all human interaction (Kohut, 1977).

Empathy is a concept that is as hard to define as it is rare to observe. Empathy has been defined as a process of coming to *know* and even to *feel* with another person. It is sometimes described as feeling as if one were in the other person's shoes (Gladstein, 1983), or transposing oneself into the thinking, feeling, and acting of another (Dymond, 1950). Many of the definitions given of empathy seem more poetic than operational.

The voluminous studies of empathy have tended to focus on three separate, but clearly interrelated, aspects of empathic functioning. The first of these, *sensitivity to people,* has been considered to be a fairly stable characteristic of individuals, and to be virtually a personality trait. There have been, however, successful programs to increase the level of interpersonal functioning of people through sensitivity training (Faith, Wong, & Carpenter, 1995). Indeed, such efforts are part of the curriculum in many counselor education programs.

SENSITIVITY TO PEOPLE

Sensitivity to people consists partly of the ability to *recognize* and *react* to cues from another person that convey the existence of strong emotional arousal or unique perceptions or interpretations of situations and events. It is the ability to sense that something unusual and significant is happening in the inner world of another human being at that moment. It also involves letting the other person know that such an inner state has been recognized and accepted as a legitimate part of the relationship.

Sensitivity to people seems to develop out of a number of factors or experiences in the life of an individual. Perhaps the most important of these involves a deep interest in other people. Sensitivity to people varies widely across people with different life interests or aspirations. Groups showing the highest levels of sensitivity tend to be those with interests in the arts including literature, drama, and other aesthetic endeavors. The study of empathy really began with the study of aesthetic appreciation (Duan & Hill, 1996).

A second important factor seems to involve family and cultural norms governing the expression and ways of attending to feelings in social situations. In some subcultures, norms for interpersonal behavior discourage or even punish both the *expression* of strong emotion, and even the *recognition* and *acceptance* of such expressions in others. In the early stages of group counseling, for example, members frequently express strong feelings as they re-experience anger, frustration, or fear. Sometimes the individual is in tears, sobbing audibly. In almost every group, some members will simply ignore the other member's expression of distress. This phenomenon has been called the "nothing-unusual-is-happening" syndrome and has the effect of distancing and insulating one person from others.

In counseling, the desired emphasis is exactly the opposite. The presumption is that something unusual (and significant) is always happening in the inner world of the client, and it is the counselor's job to sense, respond to, and follow the client's experiencing. The ability of the counselor to be sensitive to the client's inner life and to accept and relate to it is sometimes called *comfort with psychological intimacy.* It has been shown to be closely linked to the establishment of effective working alliances in counseling (Dunkle & Friedlander, 1996).

For some counselors, comfort with psychological intimacy may be a natural part of their personal and family experiences. For others, achieving such comfort with closeness may represent a major developmental task. Some research suggests that counselors who themselves perceive greater social support and acceptance from others, who have less self-directed hostility, and who are interested in and intellectually stimulated by others are more empathic and better able to establish effective helping relationships (Dunkle & Friedlander, 1996; Lafferty, Beutler, & Crago, 1989).

Affective Empathy

A second aspect of empathic functioning involves the ability to *resonate* to another person's emotional state or expression. As one person communicates strong emotion, the other person is actually able to feel the emotion being communicated. In this sense, an emotional arousal is *contagious;* that is, it is transmitted from one person to another. This phenomenon is well established and is apparent in everyday experiences. People sobbing at the tragic conclusion of a play or movie, a lump in the throat at a tribute to a fallen hero, or the collective mood of a group of mourners at a funeral all attest to the contagious character of strong emotion.

To resonate to the expression of strong emotion, however, one must first open oneself to the experience. Because feeling deeply can be disturbing and disquieting, many people choose to distance themselves physically or psychologically from emotionally charged encounters. Further, because empathic resonation often triggers the need to reach out to help another person, it always carries the risk of feeling helpless or inadequate in being unable to relieve another's pain. Finally, such encounters may carry the risk, or imagined risk, of losing control of one's own emotions and being seen as weak, immature, or unprofessional.

One of the most important developmental tasks for counselors-in-preparation is to learn to remain open to and sensitive to others' feelings, able to feel *with* them and *for* them, while managing one's own feelings at a level that permits a personalized but professional perspective. The task of managing psychological intimacy in a professional and therapeutic way involves continued growth in self-awareness as well as growth in emotional maturity and personal security.

Cognitive Empathy

The third aspect of empathic functioning can be called *cognitive empathy* (Gladstein, 1983). It is closely related to role taking in the cognitive developmental literature described in Chapter 2. Cognitive empathy is the ability to *understand* the perspective of another person in perceiving or construing a complex social or intellectual issue or situation. It involves understanding another person's experience, perceptions, and point of view. A number of studies of counseling process and outcome have shown the counselor's cognitive empathy to be related to positive client outcomes (Duan & Hill, 1996). For Carl Rogers, this kind of empathy was part of what he considered to be the necessary and sufficient conditions for positive outcomes in counseling and psychotherapy. Although such an extreme position has never been fully supported by research, few counselors would deny the importance of cognitive empathy in a counseling relationship.

Cognitive empathy is related to the counselor's level of cognitive complexity (Lutwak & Hennessy, 1982), ego development (Carlozzi, Gaa, & Liberman, 1983), and conceptual level, a measure of general cognitive development (Holloway & Wampold, 1986). Cognitive complexity has also been shown to be related to formulating and testing relevant hypotheses about clients (Spengler & Strohmer, 1994).

Whether viewed as *sensitivity, affective resonance,* or *intellectual understanding,* or as a composite of all of these, the capacity for empathy is an important characteristic of an effective counselor.

Effective counselor education programs should facilitate the development of empathic functioning in students. Indeed, the very process of supervision of counseling practicum and internship experiences has been conceptualized as one of nurturing this kind of development (Blocher, 1983; Loganbill, Hardy, & Delworth, 1982; Stoltenberg, McNeill, & Crethar, 1995).

COUNSELOR PREPARATION AS DEVELOPMENTAL EDUCATION

For many years, programs of "deliberate psychological education" (Sprinthall & Mosher, 1970) have been used as strategies for prevention of psychopathology and nurturing development. Many of these strategies reflected in what we now term *developmental education* were created out of pioneering research on counselor education and development. As we saw in Chapter 11, for many years psychologists have known that people's perceptions of each other were more a function of the *perceiver* than of the actual person being perceived or described. The study of these phenomena is called *developmental person perception* research. As we saw, this line of theory and research has established that an individual's perceptions of others tends to develop in the direction of greater complexity, a decreasing reliance on stereotypes, and greater ability to integrate discordant of inconsistent information about the behavior of others. This kind of development is required for the kind of counselor functioning discussed earlier (Spengler & Strohmer, 1994). It is crucial in all kinds of counseling situations, and is, as we saw in Chapter 11, the psychological infrastructure for successful multicultural counseling.

The primary function of counselor preparation is to nurture the psychological development of its students as they in turn to facilitate the development of clients.

Unfortunately, the psychological development of students either in a counselor preparation program or in other kinds of educational enterprises does not happen solely as a result of reading a book, attending a lecture or passing an examination. Some important kinds of learning that contribute to the growth of an effective counselor do begin at least with traditional learning experiences in reading, listening to, and discussing relevant issues, ideas, and findings.

The core of developmental experiences in any counselor preparation program tends to center in the supervised practicum and internship opportunities that offer *hands-on* experiences working directly with clients. These are the experiences that provide opportunities for the student to bring together all of the other relevant learning experiences, and to organize and integrate them into a new and uniquely personal way of thinking, feeling, and acting. Such an integration is exactly what constitutes a higher level of personal and professional development.

THE DYNAMICS OF COUNSELOR DEVELOPMENT

In Chapter 2, some of the essential elements in developmentally potent learning environments were briefly discussed in terms of their impact on children and adolescents. Some of these same dynamics are equally important to the professional development of counselors.

Also in Chapter 2, four key elements in a developmentally responsive learning environment were discussed. They were (1) challenge; (2) involvement; (3) structure; and (4) support. Each learner has an optimal level or band relative to each of these elements that will best nurture his or her growth.

The very nature of counselor preparation programs imposes high levels of challenge and involvement into the learning situation. As counselors-in-preparation begin the hands-on phases of their programs, that is practicum and internship experiences, they are faced with new and usually complex, abstract, ambiguous, and emotionally charged tasks and situations.

CHALLENGE AND INVOLVEMENT

The process of learning to be a counselor is virtually unique in that the learner is confronted with the challenge of growing, adapting, and re-shaping self while at the same time working with real clients for whose welfare the fledgling counselor has increasing levels of professional, ethical, and moral responsibility.

In terms of involvement, the counselor-in-preparation undertakes the simultaneous challenges of learning to *grow* and learning to *help* while knowing that his or her own professional future is at stake. It is small wonder that research shows that novice counselors experience considerable anxiety and threats to self-esteem and self-efficacy (Larson, 1998; Nutt-Williams & Hill, 1997; Williams, Judge, Hill, & Hoffman, 1997).

SUPPORT AND STRUCTURE

The novice counselor can cope with high levels of challenge and involvement and their consequent stress only by seeking *support* and building *structure* into the counselor education experience. Support can come from three sources: (1) positive relationships with supervisors, (2) positive relationships with fellow students, and (3) positive relationships with friends and family. All are important.

THE SUPERVISORY WORKING ALLIANCE

The concept of working alliance was discussed earlier in Chapter 8. The emotional bond and focus on mutual goals that characterize a working alliance in counseling is seen as a crucial ingredient in therapeutic effectiveness. Actually, the ingredients represented in the concept are central to any human developmental process. In counselor education, the concept of a Supervisory Working Alliance extends the idea to the relationship between a novice counselor, or counselor-in-preparation, and a more experienced supervisor, teacher, or mentor. Research (Patton & Kivlighan, 1997) suggests that the quality of the supervisory working alliance between novice and mentor is closely related to the quality of the working relationship between the novice counselor and his or her own clients. It is also related to the progress of the student in following through on and progressing in the mutual goals established between student and supervisor.

An effective supervisory working alliance provides the student with both support and structure. The emotional bond between the two helps to provide support while the delineation of mutually agreed upon and clearly defined goals helps to provide structure. As novice counselors progress, they frequently are able to reduce the level of supervisor-initiated structure needed and to function as more self-directed learners.

Such continuous renegotiation is part of a good supervisory working alliance. Research suggests that the core of good supervision as perceived by the student consists of support, empathy, and validation that fosters openness (Worthen & McNeill, 1996).

No matter how skillful or caring a supervisor may be much of the responsibility for cementing an effective supervisory alliance always remains with the student. Research shows that counselors in preparation are often reluctant to be open and confiding in the supervisory relationship (Ladany, Hill, Corbett, & Nutt, 1996). Just as we have concepts of *defensiveness* and *resistance* to explain why clients are sometimes unable to function effectively within a counseling relationship, so too counselors-in-preparation often have difficulty utilizing their supervisory relationships. In counseling as in other professional activities one's sense of self-efficacy must be tempered by accurate and objective estimates of actual effectiveness. Often the supervisor is an essential part of this process (M.J. Heppner, Multon, Gysbers, Ellis, & Zook, 1998).

Peer Relationships

Another important source of support and structure in the counselor education environment are peer relationships among students. As students develop a strong and caring network of relationships these not only provide immediate support and structure but they are also the beginning of what is optimally a career-long process of forming and utilizing collegial relationships to nurture life-long learning and development.

Without such relationships, a counselor's life can be lonely. As novice counselors review cases, they frequently have negative "self talk" or thoughts (Nutt-Williams & Hill, 1997). Sharing perceptions and problems with colleagues is often a way of moving from self-blame to positive problem solving.

Relationships with Friends and Family

Both counselor-preparation and counseling practice are stress-laden activities. The most crucial resource to cope with this stress is active engagement in a network of positive social and familial relationships. A counselor's own feelings of being part of a warm and supportive network of personal relationships is closely related to that counselor's ability to form effective working alliances with clients (Dunkle & Friedlander,

1996). This finding is not surprising in that as we noted in Chapter 5, one of the major aftereffects of unrelieved stress is a sharp decrease in sensitivity to people (S. Cohen, 1980).

COUNSELOR EDUCATION AS LIFE-LONG LEARNING

The process of preparing to be a counselor is optimally the first step in a life-long program of personal and professional growth. Counselor education *is* education, not just a program of indoctrination in the theory of the moment or a mechanical sequence of simple skill-building exercises. Education is what is left after you forget everything that you learned in school. Psychological theories come and go. Each has its moment and soon passes into obscurity. Research findings are continually superseded by other findings as science slowly but inexorably grinds ahead.

What are permanent and therefore do constitute a foundation for future growth are deeply engrained ways of *thinking, analyzing,* and *acting* in response to what we observe in our clients and what we become aware of in ourselves.

REFLECTIVITY: THE ACTION-REFLECTION CYCLE

The career-long challenge to counselors that begins in the preparation phase is how to convert experience into life-long learning and an ongoing pattern of personal and professional development. This is experiential learning. Actually, all real learning is experiential in the sense that it derives from direct experience. The term is often used to differentiate active, immediate, and personally relevant learning from the more formal, passive, and teacher-directed classroom experiences in traditional schooling. The latter are sometimes called "fact-and-memory" approaches to education.

The learning of facts is important, but the crucial tasks of organizing them into a coherent set of ideas, integrating them with past experiences, and then applying them to practical situations is sometimes neglected. The concept of experiential learning is intended to embrace a comprehensive process of understanding and relating to new knowledge, organizing and internalizing that knowledge, and then applying it to problematic situations.

One model of experiential learning is described next. It consists of a four-step process or *action-reflection cycle.*

1. *Tuning in to Immediate Experience.* The learner focuses intently on the immediate situation. In counseling this is or should be a normal procedure. It means, however, focusing on all aspects of a client's communication, verbal and nonverbal, while at the same time being as aware as possible of one's own reactions and responses.

2. *Reflecting on the Concrete Experience.* After the termination of the immediate learning situation (in our example, the counseling interview), *reflect* thoroughly and thoughtfully on what has been experienced. In the reflection process, the learner tries to tie together as many of the elements (including personal responses) recalled from the concrete experience as possible. In counseling, this is sometimes done by reviewing audio or videotapes, reviewing the case with a supervisor, or compiling and studying case notes and summaries. Reflection leads to *conceptualization.* As disparate elements of the concrete experience are recalled, they are organized into concepts, terms that capture the commonalities and essences that bring them together and give them meaning. The crucial concepts in turn are organized into themes that recur and together give the entire experience coherence and logical structure. Such themes make the experience *understandable as a whole.* Next questions of when, how often, and to what effect are considered. Finally tentative hypotheses are formulated. A mini-theory about the experience is formulated.

3. *Integrating and Internalizing.* As the concrete experience becomes coherent and understandable, the learner compares and contrasts it with prior learning experiences and ways of understanding self, others, and social interactions. The new experience may challenge some of the learner's presuppositions and assumptions about self, clients, and the counseling process while it supports and validates others. Integration and internalization involve the process of examining old learning in the light of new learning and in the process creating a clearer more consistent and more fully conscious way of construing self and the world.

4. *Acting on New Understanding.* For learning to be translated into development, it must be acted on. Reflection without action can lead to what is sometimes called "paralysis through analysis." Action based on newly modified ways of perceiving, construing, and relating can be thought of as *experiments.* No matter how logical and well-thought through our abstract ways of understanding are, they are best tested through action. In the case of counseling, such action may involve testing hypotheses about the client or about the

counseling process. Action may mean setting new goals for oneself or new ways of measuring progress in professional development. As action experiments are acted on, they become new experiential learning opportunities and are cycled through the same four-step process just described. The process can be utilized with a wide range of professional problems as well as counseling cases.

"REFLECTIVITY" AS A CAREER STYLE

This process of life-long learning and development or action-reflection cycle is also called *reflectivity*. It has been considered the crucial variable in long-term professional development in a variety of occupations and endeavors (Neufeldt, Karnon, & Nelson, 1996; Skovalt & Ronnestad, 1992). For such a process to have real potency, it must become part of a counselor's *career style,* that is it must permeate professional preparation and practice. Unfortunately many of the stresses and pressures that beset both counselor preparation and practice mitigate against the internalization of a genuinely reflective career style.

Many practicing counselors feel that they are too busy helping clients to afford the luxury of reflecting, integrating, and testing new learnings. The result is often a kind of professional "mindlessness" in which rather than gaining and growing from experience the professional merely repeats over and over months and years of developmentally and professionally sterile rituals and exercises.

STAYING COOL VERSUS BURNING OUT

The profession of counseling is an ever-interesting, ever-changing yet emotionally arduous and intellectually demanding way of making a living. Counselors are inevitably confronted by the turmoil and tragedy that besets the lives of their clients. They must, in some part at least, resonate to what are often deep-seated feelings of pain and despair. On bad days, it sometimes feels the counselor is swimming against an unending tide of human despair and misery.

At the same time that counselors resonate to the pain and perplexity that clients bring to them, counselors also often represent the last best hope the client has in the eventual triumph of reason and responsibility over helplessness and despair. The counselor is frequently the one who helps a client in crisis mobilize both inner and outer resources to bring them to bear on seemingly insurmountable problems. An often unanswered question is how does the counselor share the client's pain and yet preserve a sense of optimism and remain a fountain of psychological energy?

One of the factors that is frequently left out of the counselor-client equation, as theories of counseling are formulated and debated, is the essential fact that counselors too are *human*. Sometimes counselors feel compelled to assume a sort of professional facade or mask that covers and conceals many of the normal doubts and inevitable frailties that are experienced by all human beings. They may attempt to create a kind of myth of personal invulnerability in which denial takes the place of self-awareness and avoidance is substituted for active coping.

One of the strange paradoxes of the professional socialization of counselors is that they often have the greatest difficulty in acknowledging psychological pain in themselves and in seeking support and assistance from others (Deutch, 1985). The Greek myth of the wounded healer who could heal the wounds of everyone other than himself is often all too much of a reality.

Several major sources of stress confront most practicing counselors. We can classify these as organizational stressors, clinical stressors, and personal stressors.

ORGANIZATIONAL STRESS

Most counselors work within the framework of organizations. Unfortunately, organizations comprised of professional helpers are no more immune from confusion and conflict than are any others. Human services organizations are often beset with problems of inadequate staffing, excessive case loads and mountains of paperwork. The work loads of staff are often set with little regard for variability in problems and level of difficulty. The pressures on staff of brief therapy models and third-party payers often creates a climate more conducive to stress than reflectivity. The most important factor in managing this kind of stress is the existence of a positive collegial support network among professional staff.

CLINICAL STRESS

Research (Deutch, 1984) suggests that much of the clinical stress confronting counselors comes from dealing with especially difficult kinds of situations. Obviously, severely disturbed or depressed or potentially suicidal clients are sources of stress. Where it is ethically feasible, some of the stress on an individual counselor can be alleviated by utilizing case

conferences, staff development sessions, or collegial consultation to provide for mutual support and shared expertise.

Three other kinds of clinical situations are also reported as particularly
troubling and stress-producing. These are (1) client expressions of anger
and hostility to the counselor; (2) client apathy, indifference, and general
lack of motivation for counseling; and (3) premature termination.

All of these situations present real difficulties, yet to some extent when
they trigger strong emotional upset in the counselor it is likely that the
situation is compounded by the counselor's own unrealistic expectations
and irrational beliefs.

No matter how experienced or how skilled a counselor may be, no
counselor is able to save clients from themselves. In counseling, you can't
win them all. Counselors are not God and the only certain consequence
of trying to be God, or allowing others to cast one into a God-like role is
grief and disappointment for all concerned. No counselor can help every
conceivable client. The primary ingredient in every successful counseling
outcome is *within the client* in the form of a deep and sincere desire to use
the counseling situation to change, grow, and gain more control over his
or her own life.

Clients sometimes do feel and express hostility for a variety of reasons.
They often come to counseling at the insistence of others, or even under
threats of dire consequences. Counselors are often the target of frustration and aggression caused by many circumstances outside the counseling situation. No matter how sincere the counselor's desire to help may
be, simply wanting to help does not ward off the venting of anger, nor
does such venting reflect on the competence or character of the counselor.
A strong need to be liked and admired by everyone is likely to lead to disappointment and frustration for the practicing counselor.

A client's decision to terminate counseling is a personal choice. It is not
necessarily a rejection of the counselor, or a rejection of counseling, itself.
Not every counselor-client pair is perfectly matched for either success or
compatibility. Most counselors encounter clients who have failed in earlier attempts to obtain professional help. The success or failure of any single counseling case is not by itself an indication of the worth of either the
counselor or the profession.

Many of the sources of excessive clinical stress on counselors stem from
a set of untenable beliefs and assumptions, including:

1. My professional worth as a counselor stems from my ability to help
   everyone, every time, under *every* circumstance.

2. If my attempt to help is greeted with anger, ingratitude, and rejection, I must have done something wrong.
3. If I try hard enough and skillfully enough, I can make up for the client's apathy, indifference, and lack of motivation for counseling.
4. My success as a counselor in any single case is an indicator of my *personal* worth as a human being.
5. I should be able to totally submerge my own personal needs and motivations in the service of the noble cause of helping others.

PERSONAL STRESS

Counselors like everyone else are subject to stress in their personal lives. In Chapter 13, we discussed sources of personal stress and strategies for stress management. They apply to the counselors' personal lives as much as they apply to the clients. Maintaining a reasonable level of physical and emotional health is as much a part of being a competent and ethical professional as is continuing professional education, membership in professional organizations, or evaluating programs and procedures.

THE NATURE OF BURNOUT

The effects of prolonged stress and occupational dissatisfaction on the performance of professionals is a well-known and frequently studied phenomenon. It is particularly a problem in the human services professions where some degree of emotional involvement with clients and client problems is a constant factor.

Burnout is characterized by a progressive loss of energy, idealism, sense of purpose, and satisfaction from work. It is experienced as a kind of chronic physical and emotional exhaustion and gradually deepening feelings of apathy, indifference, and defeat in the performance of one's essential duties. Intellectually, the burned out professional often experiences a growing cynicism about the worth of counseling, and a deepening indifference to the plight of clients. The burned out counselor is sometimes described as "case hardened."

Burnout may lead to personal feelings of depression, loss of morale, and feelings of isolation and rejection. The burned out professional may withdraw from colleagues and show increasing disillusionment and resentment toward the employing agency and to its administration.

Burnout is a psychological process. It is a product of a long-term pattern of unhealthy person-environment interaction. Preventing or reducing burnout can best be approached by building positive social supports within the organization, giving support and recognition to the efforts of individuals, sharing and savoring successes, and treating failures as experiences to be learned from rather than occasions for blame and recrimination.

THE IMPAIRED COUNSELOR

One of the convenient but erroneous myths that surrounds the counseling profession is that counselors are not subject to substance abuse, depression, or other psychological problems. Research (Good, Thoreson, & Shaughnessy, 1995) suggests that around 10% of psychologists admit to having problems with alcohol or drugs, while nearly one-half report knowing a colleague with such a problem. Studies also indicate that counselors tend to be reluctant to confront or even to offer help to an impaired colleague (Vandenbos & Duthie, 1986).

THE POSITIVE SIDE OF COUNSELOR DEVELOPMENT

While there are undeniably hazards to positive growth and development within the counseling profession, burnout and disillusionment are by no means inevitable. One of the same studies that looked at counselor impairment (Good et al., 1995) also found that as a group counselors hold fairly positive views of their personal and professional satisfaction. They report moderate levels of work-related stress and experience minimal psychological distress. All of these variables—personal satisfaction, professional satisfaction, and freedom from psychological distress—were highly correlated. In other words, managing professional life and satisfaction is highly related to satisfaction with personal life and both are related to positive psychological functioning.

THE CAREER DEVELOPMENT OF THE COUNSELOR

Counseling as a profession is practiced in increasingly varied settings and situations. Although counseling began almost simultaneously in schools and settlement houses, recent years have seen a tremendous proliferation of settings and specialties in the profession. These new settings provide greater opportunities for the practice of counseling, but also provide real challenges to the individual counselor in career planning, continuing professional education, and identification of career paths and professional competencies. Some of these professional settings are described next.

COUNSELING IN ELEMENTARY AND SECONDARY SCHOOLS

The special emphasis on facilitating human development that distinguishes counseling from other helping professions stems from its long history in schools. Counseling owes much to the American tradition of comprehensive education for all. Today's counselors are widely employed in elementary schools, middle schools, and high schools. They have their own professional organizations, licensing credentials, and a long history of service in school organizations.

The history of counseling in school settings has been a stormy one. For many years, counselors have struggled to define and defend a truly unique and fully appreciated role for themselves in schools. The first stage of this endeavor involved the separation of counseling as a profession from the profession of teaching. While such a separation was necessary to allow for the constantly expanding nature of counselor expertise and education, it sometimes eroded the base of understanding and cooperation between teachers and counselors that is necessary for the development of effective and comprehensive personnel programs.

Similarly school counselors have struggled to avoid being swallowed by the expansion of school administration. In many settings, counselors have been saddled with minor administrative functions that have taken away from both their time and ability to work directly with students.

A career in school counseling demands both the ability to work cooperatively and constructively with teachers and administrators, and the sense of professional commitment and personal identity to avoid being swallowed up in a torrent of administrative trivia and quasi-professional expectations. School counselors frequently have specialized expertise in working with developmental and educational problems of specific age groups. High school counselors are often expert in college placement and availability of scholarships. Counselors at all levels consult with parents. School counselors work closely with school psychologists and social workers, and with a variety of community agencies.

The career ladders available to school counselors are somewhat limited unless they choose to enter school administration. Counselors may move into chairs of departments within schools, and may become directors of guidance or psychological services within systems. There are also professional positions in state or federal departments of education, and in private business organizations that supply guidance or testing materials to schools. Many of the higher level positions require the completion of a doctoral degree.

COUNSELING IN COLLEGES AND UNIVERSITIES

Large numbers of counselors are employed in college and university counseling centers and related offices. For many years, the profession of college personnel work pioneered in the development and operation of student services. Counselors presently operate not only in counseling centers, but in residence halls, study skills centers, student health services, centers for continuing education, programs for minority students, and special services for international students. Each of these settings requires special knowledge and expertise in addition to basic counseling skills. The increasingly diverse college student population requires multicultural competencies for counselors.

Career ladders for college counselors include promotion to directorships of centers or programs, movement into dean of students positions or vice presidents for student affairs. College counselors are frequently also involved in counselor education programs particularly in the supervision of practicum and internship activities.

COMMUNITY COUNSELING

Over the past 20 years, the greatest growth in and proliferation of counseling services has been in community agencies. Community mental health centers employ mental health counselors and counseling psychologists, clinical psychologists, and social workers, as well as paraprofessional staff. Programs are generally headed by psychiatrists.

The philosophy that drives most of the community mental health centers has been one of prevention of serious mental health problems through close cooperation with schools, family services, and other human services agencies. Staff in community mental health centers typically consult with community action groups, work closely with the criminal justice system and with welfare agencies.

The typical administrative structure utilizes a team approach that utilizes the special skills of several professionals. In most community mental health centers, the psychiatrist is the captain, coach, and general manager of the team.

In most urban centers, there are a variety of special programs and agencies that work with specific problems such as domestic violence, child abuse and neglect, substance abuse, homelessness, delinquency prevention, and a variety of other social problems. Counselors may be employed in any or all of these agencies. Some of these programs are run directly by local government, while some are private nonprofit organizations operating with combinations of private and public funding.

Career ladders involve promotion to program director positions or coordinating positions in local government.

HEALTH CARE COUNSELING

Counselors have been increasingly involved in the delivery of health services in hospitals and clinics. This development is part of the burgeoning of health care psychology. Health care psychology is built around several basic assumptions.

First, all types of illnesses are inherently stressful and therefore likely to involve strong emotional reactions. Such reactions are important factors in patients success in treatment and time of recovery.

Second, any human being responds to illness as a total organism, not merely in terms of sets of separate and discrete physical versus emotional reactions. In this sense, health care psychology is closely related to concepts shared by holistic and psychosomatic medicine.

Finally, most serious or lengthy illnesses impose a variety of special problems in daily living for patients and their families. Traditional medical services are often limited in their ability to deal with these problems.

Health care counseling services are delivered in a variety of ways. Counselors may help patients deal with anxiety about pending surgical or other procedures. They may work with patients in managing chronic pain or discomfort such as in migraine headaches, arthritis, or circulatory problems.

Counseling also helps patients and their families to manage long-term chronic diseases such as diabetes, allergies, hypertension, arthritis, and other conditions that require special regimens of diet, medication, exercise, or avoidance of toxic substances. Counseling and training may be especially important for children afflicted with such conditions.

Counselors frequently run support groups for terminally ill patients and/or their families. They may do geriatric counseling or work with bereaved families.

As we saw in Chapter 13, one of the most important and fastest growing areas of health care counseling is in the operation of wellness programs designed to prevent serious illness through the acquisition of positive health habits and lifestyles. Programs aimed at smoking cessation, weight management, exercise habits, and nutrition are rapidly growing applications. Many times such programs are operated by professionals who are cross-trained both as counselors and in fields such as nursing, or other paramedical specialities. Health care counselors are frequently employed in hospitals, health maintenance organizations, or in close collaboration with family practice physicians or pediatricians. They may also work in comprehensive medical centers or clinics and in health education programs. In the latter setting, they may provide counseling or educational programs to prevent the spread of communicable diseases such as AIDS or the spread of addictions.

REHABILITATION COUNSELING

A major setting in which counselors have worked for many years is the field of rehabilitation medicine. In these settings, counselors work closely with other medical personnel. Rehabilitation counselors may work with both physically and psychologically disabled patients.

Rehabilitation medicine and counseling is aimed at helping patients in restoring as much of their previous functioning as possible and with helping the patient to accept and manage life with the remaining impairment. Counseling may include extensive physical and psychological assessment and career counseling and placement.

Rehabilitation counselors have, in addition to their counseling skill, specialized expertise relating to the nature of various illnesses and disabilities, especially as these relate to functioning in work settings. Rehabilitation counselors usually have taken additional education programs devoted to this specialty.

Rehabilitation counselors may be employed in hospitals or medical centers, by state rehabilitation agencies, the Veterans Administration, or by insurance companies or private rehabilitation agencies. They are also frequently employed in alcohol or drug treatment programs and in correctional facilities.

Career ladders typically involve movement into managerial and supervisory roles within agencies or in state or federal government.

COUNSELORS IN PRIVATE PRACTICE

An increasing number of counselors operate in private practice, delivering services directly to the public. They also frequently provide services on a contract basis to schools, business organizations, or unions. These services may include staffing employee assistance programs, outplacement services, wellness programs, or family counseling services. Private practice counselors may run groups in assertiveness training, sensitivity training, or parent effectiveness training for a variety of organizations. The ability to provide services directly to the public frequently depends on the nature of state licensing or credentialling requirements.

In many ways, the counseling profession exists in a kind of limbo in regard to professional credentials. The great variation in types and levels of preparation often causes great consternation and confusion. Credentialling requirements vary widely from state to state. Some counselors may be licensed as psychologists, or even as social workers. Mental health counselors currently are seeking licensure in some states.

The great variations in professional settings and situations make career planning and continuing education particularly challenging. Many settings require special expertise well beyond that offered in most preservice preparation programs including even those at the doctoral level.

COUNSELOR COMPETENCIES

To function effectively in most settings and particularly to move up career ladders, counselors need a variety of skills and understandings. A few of these are listed here that apply across most counseling settings and specialties:

1. *Program Management Skills.* Most agencies expect senior level staff to be able to develop and operate budgets, maintain financial records, supervise clerical or paraprofessional staff, recruit and train volunteers, and develop and justify staffing patterns and workload requirements.

2. *Program Design and Evaluation Skills.* Most counseling agencies are responsible for the design and evaluation of treatment programs. This is sometimes done with the assistance of outside consultants. Designing such programs involves the identification, articulation, and communication of agency missions, goals, and priorities. Treatment approaches involve the interpretation and application of current research findings in terms of agency goals and capabilities. Evaluation components are generally based upon both qualitative and quantitative assessments and typically require an understanding of at least basic statistical concepts and procedures. Computer skills are generally required.

   The design, articulation, and evaluation of treatment programs are the major ingredients in "grantsmanship." Since most human services programs are operated on a "soft funding" basis, the struggle to attract resources is never-ending. Good writing and public speaking skills are also important.

3. *General Professional Leadership Skills.* As counselors move up career ladders, they typically assume greater and greater leadership responsibilities. Sometimes these responsibilities must be assumed very early in the counselor's career. In many human services settings, the arrival of a fully qualified, certified, and graduate degreed counselor on the scene evokes immediate expectations of both professional expertise and leadership.

Leadership skills involve establishing two-way communication with associates and colleagues, articulating ideas clearly, setting agendas for staff meetings, and managing them in efficient yet open ways. Professional leadership frequently involves helping to recruit, train, supervise, and evaluate paraprofessionals or volunteers as well as colleagues.

Leadership may also involve creating staff development programs and building staff morale to prevent burnout. In most professional organizations, effective leadership styles involve open communication, consensus formation, team building, and nurturing trust and confidence among colleagues. Highly authoritarian or "top down" leadership styles in professional organizations often lead to conflict, staff turnover, and burnout.

4. *Consultation and Training Skills.* Most senior level staff in human services agencies consult on an ongoing basis with schools, other human services agencies, community action groups, parent and teacher organizations, and other interested groups in the community. Many of these consulting relationships involve training or assisting with staff development for other agencies, operating public information programs, or simply establishing visibility and credibility in the community. While consulting relationships are sometimes similar to counseling situations, the consultant is always an "outsider" who comes in to *listen* and *offer* new possibilities without taking over either responsibility for, or ownership of the consultee's problems.

5. *Interprofessional Collaboration and Cooperation.* Most human services organizations and the larger systems of which they are a part involve mixed teams of professionals who represent different training and professional socialization experiences, as well as differing professional self-concepts. Carrying out a treatment plan in a medical setting might mean coordinating the efforts of psychiatrists, neurologists, physiatrists, or other medical specialists, as well as nurses,

social workers, psychologists, occupational or physical therapists, and paraprofessionals or volunteers. In a school setting, such plans might involve counselor, school nurse, school psychologist or social worker, several teachers, and a school principal or assistant principal.

Working with a problem family might additionally entail the co-operation of police, child protection agencies, welfare agencies, juvenile courts, and probation departments.

The problem of interprofessional and interagency cooperation and coordination is one of the most vexing and time-consuming activities in the whole human services field. Frequently counselors are designated as case managers responsible for coordination of services and managing case conferences. Such roles usually require the patience and tact to listen to and understand the points of view of other professionals, a willingness to share information where ethically possible, along with negotiation and mediation skills to help resolve disagreements or conflicts. In some situations, professionals feel that one set of staff is needed just to go to the meetings and another to do the counseling.

Similar skills are needed in working through interagency competition or conflict or in dealing with political and governmental organizations that allocate resources.

CONTINUING EDUCATION AND LIFE-LONG LEARNING

The list of competencies needed for successful career progress and development described appears to be formidable if not mind-boggling. Certainly, no counselor is going to leave a pre-service preparation program equipped with all of the skills and understanding just discussed. The curriculums of most counselor education programs are far too crowded and time is too short to permit even passing attention to most of these issues. The introduction to some of these challenges may be started in the full time internship experience that is the capstone of many programs. Career development for the professional counselor, however, means a commitment to lifelong learning and a career style centered around the processes of *reflectivity* discussed earlier. Fortunately there are several kinds of resources available to support this kind of development.

One process vital to the career development of all kinds of professions is called *mentoring*. Entry counselors need to seek out, heed, and utilize the know-how of more experienced colleagues. The greatest single resource of any beginning counselor is a relationship with a knowledgeable, caring, and supportive mentor.

A second basic resource is in-service professional development programs. These help colleagues share experiences and expertise and often bring in outside consultants or resource people to help with specific issues or problems.

A third source is continuing professional education. In one sense a professional counselor never graduates, but always seeks new knowledge, understanding, and skills. Continuing professional education opportunities are offered by universities and colleges, professional associations, and a wide variety of private and public organizations. In many metropolitan areas, advanced degree programs are offered in ways that allow professionals to continue in full-time employment while progressing in work toward the doctorate. The quality of such programs may vary rather widely.

Characteristics of "Master Counselors"

A qualitative study of the cognitive, emotional, and relational characteristics of a group of professionals nominated by their colleagues and associates as "master therapists" produced findings that are significant for those who aspire to excellence in the field (Jennings & Skovalt, 1999). The study involved intensive interviews with 10 such designated experts.

The researchers reported a number of characteristics shared by these outstanding practitioners, including:

1. They are *voracious learners.* Continuous professional development was one of the hallmarks of the group. When speaking about learning, many used terms such as "hunger or thirst" for knowledge and new understanding.
2. They draw upon *accumulated experience* in a thoughtful and systematic way. They draw upon rich life and professional experiences. These seem to have increased these counselors depth and competence as human beings and as professionals.
3. These master counselors value cognitive complexity and are fascinated by the ambiguity and mystery of the human condition. They seek out and try to unravel inconsistencies and contradictions in their clients and in life.
4. These master clinicians appear to be emotionally open, self-aware, and reflective and nondefensive. They seek feedback from clients

and associates. They report learning much from clients over the course of professional practice.

5. These counselors appear mentally healthy and mature. They attend to their own physical and emotional well-being. They are not self-centered or grandiose and seem to have struck a healthy balance between confidence and humility.

6. These counselors possess strong relationship skills and tend to see the relationship and working alliance as the core of their practice.

In short these Master Counselors appear to be mature, healthy individuals who have focused upon both personal and professional development.

It seems clear that the most important resource is in the counselor, himself or herself. An unflagging intellectual curiosity, a deep interest in people, a voracious appetite for professional reading along with the internalization of reflective patterns of experiencing are what most facilitates the development of the developmental counselor.

Action and
Reflection Issues

CHAPTER 1
THE NATURE OF DEVELOPMENTAL
COUNSELING: AN OVERVIEW

SYNOPSIS

The history of counseling in the United States beginning with the Guidance Movement in the early twentieth century is traced. It explains some of the historical events that contributed to the rise of professional counseling. Developmental emphases that had shaped the field are also traced.

The basic philosophical and psychological concepts that distinguish developmental counseling from other approaches are delineated. The eclectic-integrative approach to counseling theory is discussed. The ecological view of human behavior as arising from interaction with the environment is similarly introduced.

CHAPTER OUTLINE

A Brief History of Developmental Counseling
Basic Principles of Developmental Counseling and Therapy
- Philosophical Concerns and Commitments
- Concepts and Constructs in Developmental Counseling
- Concepts of Development
Distinguishing Characteristics of Developmental Counseling

QUESTIONS TO CONSIDER

1. How has the history of professional counseling helped to shape its present status?
2. Why has the developmental influence been so pervasive?

3. How do concerns for human freedom and autonomy help to define developmental counseling?

4. How does an ecological view affect the ways in which developmental counselors work with clients?

5. How does an ecological approach differ from an intrapsychic approach?

6. Why is a systematic eclectic-integrative approach important?

7. How is the developmental approach different from the adjustment focus?

RECOMMENDED READINGS

Benjamin, L.T., Jr. (Ed.). (1992). *American Psychologist, Special Issue: The History of American Psychology, 47.*

Freedheim, D.K. (Ed.). (1993). *History of psychotherapy: A century of change.* Washington, DC: American Psychological Association.

Whiteley, J.M. (1984). A historical perspective on the development of counseling psychology as a profession. In S.D. Brown & R.W. Lent (Eds.), *Handbook of counseling psychology* (pp. 3–55). New York: Wiley.

Willi, J. (1998). *Ecological psychotherapy: Improving interactive effectiveness.* Mansfield, OH: Hogrefe and Huber.

RELEVANT JOURNALS

American Psychologist
The Counseling Psychologist
The Journal of Counseling Psychology
The Journal of Counseling and Development

CHAPTER 2
THEORETICAL APPROACHES TO
HUMAN DEVELOPMENT

SYNOPSIS

Two major streams of theory about human development are discussed. The first stems from psychoanalytic theory and as modified by Neo-Freudian theorists is called the psychosocial approach. The second line of theory is called the cognitive developmental approach and was pioneered by Jean Piaget.

These theories are described and the implications of developmental theory for learning and learning environments are discussed.

QUESTIONS TO CONSIDER

1. Have you experienced discontinuity in your life? When? Where? How did it feel?
2. Have you seen people you know experience developmental crises? How did they cope?
3. How do the needs to exert control, make meaning of life, and build relationships affect you and those you know?
4. How can you assess the degree of person-environment fit in an individual's life?
5. What are the best and worst learning environments that you have experienced? How did they affect you?

RECOMMENDED READINGS

Dent-Read, C., & Jukow-Goldring, P. (Eds.). (1997). *Evolving explanations of development: Ecological approaches to organism-environment systems.* Washington, DC: American Psychological Association.

Glantz, M.D., Johnson, J., & Huffman, L. (Eds.). (1999). *Resilience and development: Positive life adaptations.* New York: Plenum Press.

Haggerty, R.J., Sherrod, L.R., Garmezy, N., & Rutter, M. (Eds.). (1996). *Stress, risk and resilience in children and adolescents: Processes, mechanisms and interventions.* New York: Cambridge University Press.

Hetherington, E.M. (Ed.). (1998). *American Psychologist: Special Issue: Applications of Developmental Science, 53.*

RELEVANT JOURNALS

The Journal of Personality and Social Psychology
Child Development
Journal of Applied Developmental Psychology

CHAPTER 3
THE CYCLE OF LIFE-SPAN DEVELOPMENT

SYNOPSIS

Life stages that define life-span development are discussed. The characteristic developmental tasks and needed coping behaviors at each life stage are described. Problems associated with each stage are discussed and concerns for counseling approaches are discussed.

CHAPTER OUTLINE

The Organization Stage (Birth–15 years)
- Infancy (Birth–3 years)
- Early childhood (3–6 years)
- Later childhood (6–12 years)
- Early adolescence (12–15 years)

The Exploration Stage (Ages 16–30)
- Later adolescence (16–23 years)
- Young adulthood (24–30 years)

The Realization Stage (39–45)
The Stabilization Stage (45–60+)
The Examination Stage (60+–Death)
Using a Life-Span Framework in Counseling

QUESTIONS TO CONSIDER

1. As you look back on your own life history, can you recognize key developmental tasks that helped you to grow?
2. Who were the key helpers who assisted you with such tasks? How did they help?

3. How do people at mid-life and beyond cope with changes in their life?

4. What are some key coping behaviors that you are using right now?

5. What are the roles in your life right now that provide the greatest challenges and satisfactions?

6. What are some of the key ingredients in successful aging? How have members of your family handled retirement and aging?

RECOMMENDED READINGS

Billig, N. (1992). *Growing older and wiser: Coping with expectations, challenges and change in the later years.* New York: Lexington.

Klein, W.C., & Bloom, M. (1997). *Successful aging: Strategies for healthy living.* New York: Plenum Press.

Lachman, M.E., & James, J.B. (Eds.). (1997). *Multiple paths to mid-life development.* Chicago: University of Chicago Press.

Takanishi, R. (Ed.). (1993). *American Psychologist, Special Issue: Adolescence, 48.*

Young, G.D. (1996). *Adult development, therapy and culture: A postmodern synthesis.* New York: Plenum Press.

RELEVANT JOURNALS

Journal of Early Adolescence
Human Development
Journal of College Student Development
Journal of Youth and Adolescence
Journal of Applied Gerontology
Journal of Psychology and Aging
International Journal of Aging and Human Development
Journal of Adolescence
Developmental Psychology

CHAPTER 4
CONCEPTS OF OPTIMAL DEVELOPMENT

SYNOPSIS

A wide range of views about the nature of optimal development or human effectiveness are introduced. These range from extensive, highly idealized models to simple common sense definitions of effective human functioning. Research on people's own concepts of quality of life is reviewed.

The Loevinger model of ego development is described. The counseling implications of ego development and related concepts are discussed. The relationship between health and human effectiveness is described.

CHAPTER OUTLINE

The Nature of Human Effectiveness
The Bag of Virtues Approach
- Maslow's Hierarchy and Self-Actualization
- Jahoda's Concept of Normal Behavior
- Shoben's Version of Normal Behavior
- Goleman's Concept of Emotional Intelligence
- Heath's Concept of Human Excellence

Roger's Concept of Directions of Development
Clients Own Values and Aspirations
Cognitive Developmental Schemas
Loevinger's Stages of Ego Development
Cognitive Development in Children and Adolescents
Health and Human Effectiveness

QUESTIONS TO CONSIDER

1. How do the virtues described by Maslow, Goleman, and so on compare to those you have observed in the people you most admire and respect?

2. How does the increasing emphasis on interpersonal or social skills as part of optimal development fit with what is needed for success today?

3. How do the things that people report valuing in their own lives compare with the "bag of virtues" approach? Which should we give greatest priority to in developmental counseling?

4. How do you define your goals as a developmental counselor?

5. How can you combine the various developmental and diagnostic factors to form a clear, comprehensive, and coherent impression of your client?

RECOMMENDED READINGS

Csikszentmihalyi, M., Rathunde, K., & Whalen, S. (1993). *Talented teenagers: The roots of success and failure.* New York: Cambridge University Press.

Gardner, H. (1993). *Frames of mind*. New York: Basic.

Goleman, D. (1998). *Working with emotional intelligence*. New York: Bantam.

Goodhart, C.D., & Lansing, M.H. (1997). *Treating people with chronic disease: A psychological guide*. Washington, DC: American Psychological Association.

Spencer, L.M., Jr., & Spencer, S.M. (1993). *Competence at work: Models for superior performance*. New York: Wiley.

Sternberg, R.J., & Wagner, R.K. (1986). *Practical intelligence: Nature and origin of competence in the everyday world*. Cambridge: Cambridge University Press.

Westenberg, P.M., Blasi, A., & Cohn, L.C. (Eds.). (1998). *Personality development: Theoretical, empirical and clinical investigation of Loevinger's conception of ego development*. Mahwah, NJ: Erlbaum.

RELEVANT JOURNALS

Exceptional Child
Journal of American Orthopsychiatry
Health Psychology
Youth and Society

CHAPTER 5
DEVELOPMENTAL DIAGNOSIS

SYNOPSIS

Implications of an ecological and developmental approach for understanding human behavior and counseling clients are discussed. Three basic concepts for understanding clients are described. These are: life stages, lifestyles, and life space. The importance of social roles in structuring behavior is discussed and the concept of stress is explained. A five-level model of diagnosis is described. The levels include panic, apathy, striving, coping, and mastery. Their implication for counseling are described.

CHAPTER OUTLINE

The Question of Diagnosis
Understanding Development Rather Than Deficits
- Life Stage Elements
- Life Style Concepts for Understanding Clients
- Life Space Contexts
- Stress and Life Space
- Stress Factors
- Health and Personal Resources
- Support and Life Space

Levels of Immediate Functioning
- Panic
- Apathy
- Striving
- Coping
- Mastery

Counseling and Levels of Effectiveness

QUESTIONS TO CONSIDER

1. What are some of the normative influences that have helped to shape your development so far?
2. How have you experienced developmental crises?
3. What are your principal coping styles?
4. What are the principal sources of stress in your life now?
5. Have you ever tried to help someone in a panic state? How did you experience the situation?
6. How would you approach a client in an apathetic state?

RECOMMENDED READINGS

Friedman, S.L., & Wachs, T.D. (Eds.). (1999). *Measuring environments across the life-span: Emerging methods and concepts.* Washington, DC: American Psychological Association.

Lazarus, R.S. (1999). *Stress and emotion: A new synthesis.* New York: Springer.

Wapner, S. (Ed.). (1995). Relations between environmental psychology and allied fields. *Environment and Behavior: Special Issue, 27.*

RELEVANT JOURNALS

Environmental and Behavior
Journal of Research in Personality
Personality and Individual Differences

CHAPTER 6
COUNSELING THEORIES AS SOURCES OF GAIN

SYNOPSIS

The role of theory in counseling is introduced. So-called "counseling theories" are treated as "sources of gain" that are useful as ways of conceptualizing counseling processes that can be combined and integrated in a variety of ways. A number of these models are described and the usefulness of each is discussed. The unique contributions of each is summarized.

CHAPTER OUTLINE

Defining the Term Theory
Counseling Models as Sources of Gain
The Relationship Model
- Phenomenology
- Rogerian Concepts
- Relationship Conditions
- Research on Counseling Relationships
Cognitive Models
Behavioral and Cognitive-Behavioral Models
- Operant Conditioning
- Behavior Modification
- Implications of the Operant Model
- Objections to the Operant Model
- The Classical Conditioning Model
- The Social Learning Model
- Applications of Social Learning
- Cognitive Behavioral Approaches
The Social Influence Model
Summarizing Sources of Gain

QUESTIONS TO CONSIDER

1. What is the difference between scientific theories and what we usually consider counseling theories?
2. Why do we still have so many competing theories after all these years?
3. Are the behavioral and client-centered approaches totally incompatible? Why?
4. What can you learn and use from each of the approaches?

RECOMMENDED READINGS

Bergin, A.E., & Garfield, L. (Eds.). (1994). *Handbook of psychotherapy and behavior change.* New York: Wiley.

Brown, S.D., & Lent, R.W. (Eds.). (1992). *Handbook of counseling psychology* (2nd ed.). New York: Wiley.

Okun, B.F. (1990). *Seeking connections in psychotherapy.* San Francisco: Jossey-Bass.

Richards, P.S., & Bergin, A.E. (1997). *A spiritual strategy for counseling and psychotherapy.* Washington, DC: American Psychological Association.

RELEVANT JOURNALS

Behavior Modification
Psychotherapy
Behavior Therapy
Journal of Humanistic Psychology
Journal of Cognitive Therapy and Research

CHAPTER 7
ECLECTIC-INTEGRATIVE THERAPIES

SYNOPSIS

The concept of eclectic-integrative approaches to counseling and psychotherapy is defined. Several eclectic/integrative therapeutic frameworks are described. These include Lazarus' multimodal therapy, Beutler's systematic-eclectic therapy, Prochaska and DiClemente's transtheoretical approach, Wachtel's cyclical psychodynamics, and Garfield's eclectic-integrative approach. Ways of drawing on these to develop a personal approach are discussed.

CHAPTER OUTLINE

The Need for Eclectic-Integrative Approaches
Eclectic-Integrative Frameworks
- Lazarus' Multimodal Therapy
- Beutler's Systematic Eclectic Therapy
- The Transtheoretical Approach
- Wachtel's Cyclical Psychodynamics
Common Factors Approaches
- Garfield's Eclectic-Integrative Therapy
- Jerome Frank's Common Factors Approach
- Utilizing Eclectic-Integrative Therapies

1. What does it mean to you to be an eclectic-integrative counselor?
2. How will differences in client characteristics determine what approaches you will choose?
3. How will your own professional style and personal characteristics influence your choice of approaches?
4. What are the most important common factors that you see in all effective counseling?

RECOMMENDED READINGS

Lazarus, A.A. (1997). *Brief comprehensive psychotherapy: The multimodal way.* New York: Springer.
Prochaska, J.O., DiClemente, C.C., & Norcross, J.C. (1994). *Changing for good.* New York: Morrow.

RELEVANT JOURNALS

International Journal of Eclectic Psychotherapy
Journal of Psychotherapy Integration

CHAPTER 8
APPLYING AN ECLECTIC-INTEGRATIVE APPROACH

SYNOPSIS

An eclectic-integrative model for developmental counseling is described. It includes sources of gain drawn from relationship conditions, the therapeutic alliance, insight and cognitive approaches, and learning and behavior changes.

A sample eclectic-integrative counseling model based on accomplishing a sequence of counseling tasks is described. A practical developmental counseling case illustrates the approach.

CHAPTER OUTLINE

Sources of Gain in Developmental Counseling
- Relationship Conditions and the Working Alliance
- Insight and Cognitive Restructuring
- Learning and Behavior Change

Process Models
Basic Therapeutic Tasks
Building on Common Elements
Fundamental Ingredients of Effective Counseling
A Case Example: The Case of Lynne
Evaluating Counseling Outcomes

QUESTIONS TO CONSIDER

1. How would you have approached Lynne if she were your client?
2. How will you go about building your own personal theory or process model?
3. How well do the series of tasks described in the chapter define what you want to do? Are there additional ones that you see?
4. How will you evaluate success in counseling cases?

RECOMMENDED READINGS

Hubble, M.A., Duncan, B.L., & Miller, S.D. (Eds.). (1999). *The heart and soul of change: What works in therapy.* Washington, DC: American Psychological Association.

Safran, J.D., & Muran, J.C. (Eds.). (1998). *The therapeutic alliance in brief psychotherapy.* Washington, DC: American Psychological Association.

RELEVANT JOURNALS

Psychotherapy
Psychotherapy: Theory, Research and Practice

CHAPTER 9
CAREER COUNSELING

SYNOPSIS

Career counseling and its importance are discussed. The concept of career development is introduced and its role in developmental counseling is described. A chronological framework for career development is described. Cognitive developmental approaches are also outlined. Models of person-environment interaction and the Holland model is described in detail. The interrelated concepts of work and leisure are discussed. Career counseling and the use of tests is analyzed. The effectiveness of career counseling is critiqued. The process of career counseling is described.

CHAPTER OUTLINE

The Need for Career Counseling
The Concept of Career
The Meaning of Career Development
Chronological Aspects of Career Development
Cognitive Approaches to Career Development
Developmental Self-Concepts
Personal-Environmental Fit (or Flow)
Work and Leisure
Career Counseling and the Use of Tests
The Effectiveness of Career Counseling
Life Stage Considerations in Career Counseling
Counseling Processes in Career Counseling

QUESTIONS TO CONSIDER

1. How did *you* decide on counseling as a career choice?
2. How does a career differ from a series of jobs?
3. What have been the most important influences on you career development?
4. How will you know when clients simply need information versus needing self-exploration?
5. What are your most important concerns in using tests and inventories in counseling?

RECOMMENDED READINGS

Barling, J., & Kelloway, E.K. (Eds.). (1999). *Young workers: Varieties of experience.* Washington, DC: American Psychological Association.

Kapes, J.T., Mastie, M.M., & Whitfield, E.A. (Eds.). (1997). *A counselor's guide to career assessment instruments.* Baltimore: National Career Development Association.

Peterson, N.G., Mumford, M.D., Borman, W.C., Jeanneret, P.R., & Flishman, E.A. (Eds.). (1999). *An occupational information system for the 21st Century: The development of O net.* Washington, DC: American Psychological Association.

RELEVANT JOURNALS

Journal of Vocational Behavior
Journal of Occupational Health Psychology
Career Development Quarterly

Journal of Career Development
Journal of Career Assessment
Measurement and Evaluation in Counseling and Development
Journal of Applied Psychology

CHAPTER 10
GENDER ISSUES IN DEVELOPMENTAL COUNSELING

SYNOPSIS

Research on gender differences and the different developmental problems confronting men and women are discussed. Issues of gender are discussed in terms of counseling approaches. Feminist therapy and the reluctance of men to engage in counseling is examined. Gender role conflict in men is discussed. Principles for counseling women developed by professional groups are presented. Cautions in counseling men are noted.

CHAPTER OUTLINE

Gender Differences
- Male Vulnerability
- Cognitive and Intellectual Differences
- Social Behavior
- Social Relationships
- Differences in Moral Reasoning
- The Meaning of *les Differences*

Gender and Psychological Well-being
Gender and Life-Span Development
- Women's Career Development
- Men's Career Development

Gender Role Conflict in Men
Gender and the Counseling Process
- Feminist Therapy
- Principles for Counseling Women
- Counseling Men

QUESTIONS TO CONSIDER

1. How do you see the most important differences between men and women?

2. How did your own family and social life affect your perceptions of gender roles?

3. Have you witnessed gender discrimination? How? When? Where?

4. How is your view of gender roles similar and different from your parents' views?

5. Have you experienced gender role conflict as a man?

6. Have you experienced gender discrimination as a woman in your own life?

RECOMMENDED READINGS

Cook, E.P. (1993). *Women, relationships and power: Implications for counseling.* Washington, DC: American Counseling Association.

Hales, D. (1999). *Just like a woman: How gender science is redefining what make us female.* New York: Bantam.

Hart, D.A. (1992). *Becoming men: The development of aspirations, values and adaptational styles.* New York: Plenum Press.

Levant, R.F., & Pollack, W.S. (Eds.). (1995). *A new psychology of men.* New York: Basic.

Miller, J.B., & Stiver, I.P. (1998). *The healing connection: How women form relationships in therapy and in life.* Boston: Beacon Press.

Philpot, C.L., Brooks, G.R., Lusterman, D.D., & Nult, R.L. (1997). *Bridging separate gender worlds.* Washington, DC: American Psychological Association.

Swann, W.B., Langlois, J.H., & Gilbert, L.A. (1999). *Sexism and stereotypes in modern society: The gender science of Janet Taylor Spence.* Washington, DC: American Psychological Association.

RELEVANT JOURNALS

Psychology of Women Quarterly
Sex Roles

CHAPTER 11
COUNSELING IN A MULTICULTURAL WORLD

SYNOPSIS

The nature of cultural differences and their effects in distancing people is introduced. Developmental person perception is discussed as the basis for stereotyping and perseverating social psychological distances. The realities of a multicultural world are described as is the "new diversity." The mythology of race is discussed. The process of acculturation is described. The psychological bases for cross-cultural counseling are presented.

CHAPTER OUTLINE

Culture and Social Psychological Distance
Developmental Person Perception
The Concept of Culture
- The Reality of a Multicultural World
- The New Diversity

Race and Ethnicity
- Culture and Ethnicity

Building Social Psychological Bridges
- States of Acculturation
- Approaches to Cross-Cultural Competence

Keys to Cross-Cultural Competence

QUESTIONS TO CONSIDER

1. How have your family and personal experiences equipped you to function in a multicultural world?
2. How has bigotry or prejudice touched your life?
3. Where are you in terms of acculturation to your own ethnic group?
4. How do you plan to increase your level of cross-cultural competence?
5. How can you begin to transcend your cultural limitations and break out of your cultural cocoon?

SYNOPSIS

Lee, Y., McCauley, C., & Draguns, J. (Eds.). (1998). *Personality and person perception across cultures.* Mahwah, NJ: Erlbaum.

McFadden, J. (Ed.). (1999). *Transcultural counseling* (2nd ed.). Washington, DC: American Counseling Association.

Pedersen, P.B., Draguns, J.G., Lonner, W.J., & Trimble, J.E. (Eds.). (1996). *Counseling across cultures* (4th ed.). Thousand Oaks, CA: Sage.

RELEVANT JOURNALS

Journal of Black Psychology
Journal of Multicultural Counseling and Development
Journal of Cross Cultural Psychology

CHAPTER 12
WORKING WITH FAMILIES

Synopsis

Ways in which families function are described. Changes in family organization are discussed. The role of cohesiveness and adaptability are described, as are primary themes and issues in family functioning. The varied patterns of family life, the problems of single parent families and of teen-age parents are discussed. The systems approach to understanding family interaction is introduced and four models of family counseling are discussed.

Chapter Outline

How Families Function
- Crucial Factors in Family Functioning
- Themes in Family Functioning
- Family Functions and Optimal Development

Children in Nontraditional Households
- Family Composition
- Parental Distress
- Individual Characteristics
- Development of Children in Nontraditional Households
- Children Having Children
  - Effects on Children of Teenage Parents
- Men, Women, and Child Care
  - Children's Day Care
- Understanding Family Interaction
- General Systems Theory and Cybernetics
  - Cybernetics
  - Feedback
  - Family Systems Theory
- Models of Family Counseling
  - The Family Communications Approach
  - Structural Family Therapy
  - Family Networking
  - Family Consultation and Training

QUESTIONS TO CONSIDER

1. How can counselors help nontraditional families provide nurturing environments for children?
2. Which of the themes in family functioning were most problematic in your family history? How were they handled?
3. How can counselors help families that are isolated from the mainstreams of community life?
4. What are the most important principles of child rearing that parents should understand?

RECOMMENDED READINGS

Boss, P.G., Doherty, W.J., LaRossa, R., Schumn, W.R., & Sternmetz, S.K. (Eds.). (1993). *Sourcebook of family theories and methods.* New York: Plenum Press.

Brown, P.M., & Shalett, J.S. (Eds.). (1998). *Cross-Cultural practice with couples and families.* Binghampton, NY: Haworth Press.

Goldenberg, I., & Goldenberg, H. (1991). *Family therapy: An overview* (3rd ed.). Pacific Grove, CA: Brooks/Cole.

Johnston, F.R., & Rosely, V. (1997). *In the name of the child: A developmental approach to understanding and helping children of conflicted and violent divorce.* New York: Free Press.

Kerr, M.E., & Bowen, M. (1988). *Family evaluation: An approach based on Bowen theory.* New York: Norton.

Odell, M., & Campbell, C.E. (1998). *The practical practice of marriage and family therapy: Things my training supervisor never told me.* Binghampton, NY: Haworth Press.

RELEVANT JOURNALS

Journal of Marriage and Family Therapy
Journal of Marriage and the Family
American Journal of Family Therapy

CHAPTER 13
COUNSELING AS PREVENTION

SYNOPSIS

The need for preventive services is discussed. Risk factors and protective factors for children and adolescents are described. The effects of stress and the role of psychological support are discussed. The effects of leisure and recreation in coping with stress are described. Psychological resources in coping with stress are described. Wellness programs are introduced. Prevention roles for counselors are enumerated.

CHAPTER OUTLINE

The Science of Prevention
- Preventive Factors
- General Protective Factors in Children
- General Risk Factors in Children
- General Protective Factors with Adolescents
- Risk Factors in Adolescents

Prevention Programs for Adults
Coping with Stress
Stress Management Programs
Anticipatory Coping
Emotion-Focused Coping
Problem-Focused Coping
Problem-Solving Strategies
Life Skills Training
Leisure and Recreation as Stress Reducers
Enhancing Resilience in Adults
- Social Support as a Protective Factor
- Psychological Resources as Protective Factors

Wellness Programs
Preventive Roles for Developmental Counselors
The Need for Prevention

QUESTIONS TO CONSIDER

1. How does the ability to understand, explain, and comprehend what is happening help to prevent catastrophic reactions?
2. How do I decide whether to use emotion-focused or problem-focused approaches with a stressed out client?
3. How can counselors help clients develop and mobilize social support?
4. How can counselors help to empower clients?
5. How can counselors help to advocate for better programs of prevention?

RECOMMENDED READINGS

Becker, R., Rankin, E., & Rickel, A.A. (1998). *High-risk sexual behavior: Interventions with vulnerable populations.* New York: Plenum Press.

Bryant, K.J., Windle, M., & West, S.G. (1997). *The science of prevention: Methodological advances from alcohol and substance abuse research.* Washington, DC: American psychological Association.

Daugherty, R.P., & Leukefeld, C. (1998). *Reducing the risks for substance abuse: A lifespan approach.* New York: Plenum Press.

D'Zurilla, T.J., & Nezu, A.M. (1999). *Problem-solving therapy: A social competence approach to clinical intervention* (2nd ed.). New York: Springer.

McClam, T., & Woodside, M. (1994). *Problem-solving in the helping professions.* Pacific Grove, CA: Brooks/Cole.

Pierce, G.R., Lakey, B., Sarason, I.G., & Sarason, B.R. (1997). *Sourcebook of social support and personality.* New York: Plenum Press.

Rickel, A.U., & Becker, E. (1997). *Keeping children from harm's way: How national policy affects psychological development.* Washington, DC: American Psychological Association.

Weybrew, B.B. (1992). *The ABC's of stress: A submarine psychologist's perspective.* New York: Praeger.

Wilson, D.K., Rodrequlz, J.R., & Taylor, W.C. (Eds.). (1997). *Health-promoting and health compromising behaviors among minority adolescents.* Washington, DC: American Psychological Association.

RELEVANT JOURNALS

Applied and Preventive Psychology
Development and Psychopathology

CHAPTER 14
ETHICAL AND PROFESSIONAL ISSUES

SYNOPSIS

Bases of professionalism as rooted in public trust are introduced. The bases for public trust in terms of competence, self-regulation, and commitment to public service are discussed. The nature of ethical problems in counseling and ethical principles are discussed. Confidentiality, issues of competence, and conflicts of interest are discussed. The roles of ethical codes and professional associations are discussed. Basic frameworks for deriving ethical principles and values are described.

CHAPTER OUTLINE

The Essence of Professionalism
- The Expectations for Competence
- The Expectation of Regulation
- The Expectation of Public Service

Ethical Problems of Counseling

Ethical Principles in Counseling
- Levels of Confidentiality
- Legal Implications of Confidentiality
- Issues of Competence
- Conflicts of Interest

Using Ethical Codes

Driving Ethical Principles and Values

Basic Ethical Frameworks

Specific Principles

A Model for Applying Ethical Principles

QUESTIONS TO CONSIDER

1. What does it mean to me to be a professional?
2. How will I handle confidentiality in my counseling cases?
3. How will I know the limits of my professional competence?
4. How will I handle ethical breaches by my colleagues or in my agency?
5. What are my most important first order principles?
6. What are my most important specific ethical principles?

RECOMMENDED READINGS

Anderson, R.M., Needels, T.L., & Hall, H.V. (1998). *Avoiding ethical misconduct in psychology specialty areas.* Springfield, IL: Thomas.

Bersoff, D.N. (1995). *Ethical conflicts in psychology.* Washington, DC: American Psychological Association.

Canter, M.B., Bennett, B.E., Jones, S.E., & Nagy, T.K. (1994). *Ethics for psychologists: A commentary on the APA Ethics Code.* Washington, DC: American Psychological Association.

Pope, K.S., & Vasquez, M.J.T. (1991). *Ethics in psychotherapy and counseling: A practical guide for psychologists.* San Francisco: Jossey-Bass.

Small, R.F., & Barnhill, L.R. (Eds.). (1998). *Practicing in the new mental health marketplace: Ethical, legal and moral issues.* Washington, DC: American Psychological Association.

RELEVANT JOURNALS

Professional Psychology: Research and Practice
Journal of Theoretical and Philosophical Psychology
Ethics and Behavior

CHAPTER 15
THE PROFESSIONAL DEVELOPMENT
OF THE COUNSELOR

SYNOPSIS

Chapter 15 deals with the basic professional and personal development of the counselor. The concept of empathy is elaborated. The role and limitations of counselor education programs are described. The dynamics of counselor development are discussed. The importance of peer and family supports is stressed. Professional development as life-long learning is discussed. Burnout and its prevention are discussed. The career opportunities open to counselors are described. Characteristics of "Master Counselors" are described.

CHAPTER OUTLINE

The Empathy-Helping Connection
- Sensitivity to People
- Affective Empathy
- Cognitive Empathy

Counselor Preparations as Developmental Education
The Dynamics of Counselor Development
- The Supervisory Working Alliance
- Peer Relationships
- Relationships with Friends and Family

Counselor Education as Life-Long Learning
- Reflectivity: The Action-Reflection Cycle
- Reflectivity as a Career Style

Staying Cool versus Burning Out
- Organizational Stress
- Clinical Stress
- Personal Stress
- The Nature of Burnout
- The Impaired Counselor
- The Positive Side of Counselor Development

The Career Development of the Counselor
- Counseling in Elementary and Secondary Schools
- Counseling in Colleges and Universities
- Community Counseling
- Health Care Counseling
- Rehabilitation Counseling
- Counseling in Private Practice

Counselor Competencies

Continuing Education and Life-Long Learning

Characteristics of Master Counselors

QUESTIONS TO CONSIDER

1. How have my personal experiences affected my capacity for empathic responding?
2. How are my experiences in counselor preparation contributing to my development?
3. Am I started on an action-reflection pattern of professional growth?
4. How will I deal with potential burnout in my career?
5. What are my career directions in counseling?
6. What gaps are there in my professional preparation? How can I address them?

RECOMMENDED READINGS

Breggin, P.R. (1998). *The heart of being helpful: Empathy and the creation of a healing presence.* New York: Springer.

Rest, J.R., & Narvaez, D.F. (Eds.). (1994). *Moral development in the professions: Psychology and applied ethics.* Hillsdale, NJ: Erlbaum.

RELEVANT JOURNALS

Professional Psychology: Research and Practice
The School Counselor
Rehabilitation Counseling Bulletin
Elementary School Guidance and Counseling
Journal of Mental Health Counseling
The Journal of Community Psychology

Appendix

Ethical Principles of Psychologists and Code of Conduct

CONTENTS

Introduction

The American Psychological Association's (APA's) Ethical Principles of Psychologists and Code of Conduct (hereinafter referred to as the Ethics Code) consists of an Introduction, a Preamble, six General Principles (A–F), and specific Ethical Standards. The Introduction discusses the intent, organization, procedural considerations, and scope of application of the Ethics Code. The Preamble and General Principles are *aspirational* goals to guide psychologists toward the highest ideals of psychology. Although the Preamble and General Principles are not themselves enforceable rules, they should be considered by psychologists in arriving at an ethical course of action and may be considered by ethics bodies in interpreting the Ethical Standards. The Ethical Standards set forth *enforceable* rules for conduct as psychologists. Most of the Ethical Standards are written broadly, in order to apply to psychologists in varied roles, although the application of an Ethical Standard may vary depending on the context. The Ethical Standards are not exhaustive. The fact that a given conduct is not specifically addressed by the Ethics Code does not mean that it is necessarily either ethical or unethical.

Reprinted from *American Psychologist*, Vol. 47, pp. 1597–1611. Copyright 1992 by the American Psychological Association.

This version of the APA Ethics Code was adopted by the American Psychological Association's Council of Representatives during its meeting, August 13 and 16, 1992, and its effective beginning December 1, 1992. Inquiries concerning the substance or interpretation of the APA Ethics Code should be addressed to the Director, Office of Ethics, American Psychological Association, 750 First Street, NE, Washington, DC 20002-4242.

This Code will be used to Adjudicate complaints brought concerning alleged conduct occurring on or after the effective date. Complaints regarding conduct occurring prior to the effective date will be adjudicated on the basis of the version of the Code that was in effect at the time the conduct occurred, except that no provisions repealed in June 1989, will be enforced even if an earlier version contains the provision. The Ethics Code will undergo continuing review and study for future revisions; comments on the Code may be sent to the above address.

The APA has previously published its Ethical Standards as follows:

American Psychological Association. (1953). *Ethical standards of psychologists.* Washington, DC: Author.
American Psychological Association. (1958). Standards of ethical behavior for psychologists. *American Psychologist, 13,* 268–271.
American Psychological Association. (1963). Ethical standards of psychologists. *American Psychologist, 18,* 56–60.
American Psychological Association. (1968). Ethical standards of psychologists. *American Psychologist, 23,* 357–361.
American Psychological Association. (1977, March). Ethical standards of psychologists. *APA Monitor,* pp. 22–23.
American Psychological Association. (1979). *Ethical standards of psychologists.* Washington, DC: Author.
American Psychological Association. (1981). Ethical principles of psychologists. *American Psychologist, 36,* 633–638.
American Psychological Association. (1990). Ethical principles of psychologists (Amended June 2, 1989). *American Psychologist, 4,* 390–395.

Request copies of the APA's Ethical Principles of Psychologists and Code of Conduct from the APA Order Department, 750 First Street, NE, Washington, DC 20002-4242, or phone (202) 336-5510.

Membership in the APA commits members to adhere to the APA Ethics Code and to the rules and procedures used to implement it. Psychologists and students, whether or not they are APA members, should be aware that the Ethics Code may be applied to them by state psychology boards, courts, or other public bodies.

This Ethics Code applies only to psychologists' work-related activities, that is, activities that are part of the psychologists' scientific and professional functions or that are psychological in nature. It includes the clinical or counseling practice of psychology, research, teaching, supervision of trainees, development of assessment instruments, conducting assessments, educational counseling, organizational consulting, social intervention, administration, and other activities as well. These work-related activities can be distinguished from the purely private conduct of a psychologist, which ordinarily is not within the purview of the Ethics Code.

The Ethics Code is intended to provide standards of professional conduct that can be applied by the APA and by other bodies that choose to adopt them. Whether or not a psychologist has violated the Ethics Code does not by itself determine whether he or she is legally liable in a court action, whether a contract is enforceable, or whether other legal consequences occur. These results are based on legal rather than ethical rules. However, compliance with or violation of the Ethics Code may be admissible as evidence in some legal proceedings, depending on the circumstances.

In the process of making decisions regarding their professional behavior, psychologists must consider this Ethics Code, in addition to applicable laws and psychology board regulations. If the Ethics Code establishes a higher standard of conduct than is required by law, psychologists must meet the higher ethical standard. If the Ethics Code standard appears to conflict with the requirements of law, then psychologists make known their commitment to the Ethics Code and take steps to resolve the conflict in a responsible manner. If neither law nor the Ethics Code resolves an issue, psychologists should consider other professional materials[1] and the dictates of their own conscience, as well as seek consultation with others within the field when this is practical.

The procedures for filing, investigating, and resolving complaints of unethical conduct are described in the current Rules and Procedures of the APA

---

[1]Professional materials that are most helpful in this regard are guidelines and standards that have been adopted or endorsed by professional psychological organizations. Such guidelines and standards, whether adopted by the American Psychological Association (APA) or its Divisions, are not enforceable as such by this Ethics Code, but are of educative value to psychologists, courts, and professional bodies. Such materials include, but are not limited to, the APA's *General Guidelines for Providers of Psychological Services* (1987), *Specialty Guidelines for the Delivery of Services by Clinical Psychologists, Counseling Psychologists, Industrial/Organizational Psychologists, and School of Psychologists* (1981), *Guidelines for Computer Based Tests and Interpretations* (1987), *Standards for Educational and Psychological Testing* (1985), *Ethical Principles in the Conduct of Research With Human Participants* (1982), *Guidelines for Ethical Conduct in the Care and Use of Animals* (1986), *Guidelines for Providers of Psychological Services to Ethnic, Linguistic, and Culturally Diverse Populations* (1990), and *Publication Manual of the American Psychological Association* (3rd ed., 1983). Materials not adopted by APA as a whole include the APA Division 41 (Forensic Psychology)/American Psychology–Law Society's *Specialty Guidelines for Forensic Psychologists* (1991).

Ethics Committee. The actions that APA may take for violations of the Ethics Code include actions such as reprimand, censure, termination of APA membership, and referral of the matter to other bodies. Complainants who seek remedies such as monetary damages in alleging ethical violations by a psychologist must resort to private negotiation, administrative bodies, or the courts. Actions that violate the Ethics Code may lead to the imposition of sanctions on a psychologist by bodies other than APA, including state psychological associations, other professional groups, psychology boards, other state or federal agencies, and payors for health services. In addition to actions for violation of the Ethics Code, the APA Bylaws provide that APA may take action against a member after his or her conviction of a felony, expulsion or suspension from an affiliated state psychological association, or suspension or loss of licensure.

Preamble

Psychologists work to develop a valid and reliable body of scientific knowledge based on research. They may apply that knowledge to human behavior in a variety of contexts. In doing so, they perform many roles, such as researcher, educator, diagnostician, therapist, supervisor, consultant, administrator, social interventionist, and expert witness. Their goal is to broaden knowledge of behavior and, where appropriate, to apply it pragmatically to improve the condition of both the individual and society. Psychologists respect the central importance of freedom of inquiry and expression in research, teaching, and publication. They also strive to help the public in developing informed judgments and choices concerning human behavior. This Ethics Code provides a common set of values upon which psychologists build their professional and scientific work.

This Code is intended to provide both the general principles and the decision rules to cover most situations encountered by psychologists. It has as its primary goal the welfare and protection of the individuals and groups with whom psychologists work. It is the individual responsibility of each psychologist to aspire to the highest possible standards of conduct. Psychologists respect and protect human and civil rights, and do not knowingly participate in or condone unfair discriminatory practices.

The development of a dynamic set of ethical standards for a psychologist's work-related conduct requires a personal commitment to a lifelong effort to act ethically; to encourage ethical behavior by students, supervisees, employees, and colleagues, as appropriate; and to consult with others, as needed, concerning ethical problems. Each psychologist supplements, but does not violate, the Ethics Code's values and rules on the basis of guidance drawn from personal values, culture, and experience.

General Principles

Principle A: Competence

Psychologists strive to maintain high standards of competence in their work. They recognize the boundaries of their particular competencies and the limitations of their expertise. They provide only those services and use only those techniques for which they are qualified by education, training, or experience. Psychologists are cognizant of the fact that the competencies required in serving, teaching, and/or studying groups of people vary with the distinctive characteristics of those groups. In those areas in which recognized professional standards do not yet exist, psychologists exercise careful judgment and take appropriate precautions to protect the welfare of those with whom they work. They maintain knowledge of relevant scientific and professional information related to the services they render, and they recognize the need for ongoing education. Psychologists make appropriate use of scientific, professional, technical, and administrative resources.

Principle B: Integrity

Psychologists seek to promote integrity in the science, teaching, and practice of psychology. In these activities psychologists are honest, fair, and respectful of others. In describing or reporting their qualifications, services, products, fees, research, or teaching, they do not make statements that are false, misleading, or deceptive. Psychologists strive to be aware of their own belief systems, values, needs, and limitations and the effect of these on their work. To the extent feasible, they attempt to clarify for relevant parties the roles they are performing and to function appropriately in accordance with those roles. Psychologists avoid improper and potentially harmful dual relationships.

Principle C: Professional and Scientific Responsibility

Psychologists uphold professional standards of conduct, clarify their professional roles and obligations, accept appropriate responsibility for their behavior, and adapt their methods to the needs of different populations. Psychologists consult with, refer to, or cooperate with other professionals and institutions to the extent needed to serve the best interests of their patients, clients, or other recipients of their services. Psychologists' moral standards and conduct are personal matters to the same degree as is true for any other person, except as psychologists' conduct may compromise their professional responsibilities or reduce the public's trust in psychology and psychologists. Psychologists are concerned about the ethical compliance of their colleagues' scientific and professional conduct. When appropriate, they consult with colleagues in order to prevent or avoid unethical conduct.

Principle D: Respect for People's Rights and Dignity

Psychologists accord appropriate respect to the fundamental rights, dignity, and worth of all people. They respect the rights of individuals to privacy, confidentiality, self-determination, and autonomy, mindful that legal and other obligations may lead to inconsistency and conflict with the exercise of these rights. Psychologists are aware of cultural, individual, and role differences, including those due to age, gender, race, ethnicity, national origin, religion, sexual orientation, disability, language, and socioeconomic status. Psychologists try to eliminate the effect on their work of biases based on those factors, and they do not knowingly participate in or condone unfair discriminatory practices.

Principle E: Concern for Others' Welfare

Psychologists seek to contribute to the welfare of those with whom they interact professionally. In their professional actions, psychologists weigh the welfare and rights of their patients or clients, students, supervisees, human research participants, and other affected persons, and the welfare of animal subjects of research. When conflicts occur among psychologists' obligations or concerns, they attempt to resolve these conflicts and to perform their roles in a responsible fashion that avoids or minimizes harm. Psychologists are sensitive to real and ascribed differences in power between themselves and others, and they do not exploit or mislead other people during or after professional relationships.

Principle F: Social Responsibility

Psychologists are aware of their professional and scientific responsibilities to the community and the society in which they work and live. They apply and make public their knowledge of psychology in order to contribute to human welfare. Psychologists are concerned about and work to mitigate the causes of human suffering. When undertaking research, they strive to advance human welfare and the science of psychology. Psychologists try to avoid misuse of their work. Psychologists comply with the law and encourage the development of law and social policy that serve the interests of their patients and clients and the public. They are encouraged to contribute a portion of their professional time for little or no personal advantage.

Ethical Standards

1. General Standards

These General Standards are potentially applicable to the professional and scientific activities of all psychologists.

1.01 Applicability of the Ethics Code

The activity of a psychologist subject to the Ethics Code may be reviewed under these Ethical Standards only if the activity is part of his or her work-related functions or the activity is psychological in nature. Personal activities having no connection to or effect on psychological roles are not subject to the Ethics Code.

1.02 Relationship of Ethics and Law

If psychologists' ethical responsibilities conflict with law, psychologists make known their commitment to the Ethics Code and take steps to resolve the conflict in a responsible manner.

1.03 Professional and Scientific Relationship

Psychologists provide diagnostic, therapeutic, teaching, research, supervisory, consultative, or other psychological services only in the context of a defined professional or scientific relationship or role. (See also Standards 2.01, Evaluation, Diagnosis, and Interventions in Professional Context, and 7.02, Forensic Assessments.)

1.04 Boundaries of Competence

(a) Psychologists provide services, teach, and conduct research only within the boundaries of their competence, based on their education, training, supervised experience, or appropriate professional experience.

(b) Psychologists provide services, teach, or conduct research in new areas or involving new techniques only after first undertaking appropriate study, training, supervision, and/or consultation from persons who are competent in those areas or techniques.

(c) In those emerging areas in which generally recognized standards for preparatory training do not yet exist, psychologists nevertheless take reasonable steps to ensure the competence of their work and to protect patients, clients, students, research participants, and others from harm.

1.05 Maintaining Expertise

Psychologists who engage in assessment, therapy, teaching, research, organizational consulting, or other professional activities maintain a reasonable level of awareness of current scientific and professional information in their fields of activity, and undertake ongoing efforts to maintain competence in the skills they use.

1.06 Basis for Scientific and Professional Judgments

Psychologists rely on scientifically and professionally derived knowledge when making scientific or professional judgments or when engaging in scholarly or professional endeavors.

1.07 Describing the Nature and Results of Psychological Services

(a) When psychologists provide assessment, evaluation, treatment, counseling, supervision, teaching, consultation, research, or other psychological services to an individual, a group, or an organization, they provide, using language that is reasonably understandable to the recipient of those services, appropriate information beforehand about the nature of such services and appropriate information later about results and consultations. (See also Standard 2.09, Explaining Assessment Results.)

(b) If psychologists will be precluded by law or by organizational roles from providing such information to particular individuals or groups, they so inform those individuals or groups at the outset of the service.

1.08 Human Differences

Where differences of age, gender, race, ethnicity, national origin, religion, sexual orientation, disability, language, or socioeconomic status significantly affect psychologists' work concerning particular individuals or groups, psychologists obtain the training, experience, consultation, or supervision necessary to ensure the competence of their services, or they make appropriate referrals.

1.09 Respecting Others

In their work-related activities, psychologists respect the rights of others to hold values, attitudes, and opinions that differ from their own.

1.10 Nondiscrimination

In their work-related activities, psychologists do not engage in unfair discrimination based on age, gender, race, ethnicity, national origin, religion, sexual orientation, disability, socioeconomic status, or any basis proscribed by law.

1.11 Sexual Harassment

(a) Psychologists do not engage in sexual harassment. Sexual harassment is sexual solicitation, physical advances, or verbal or nonverbal conduct that is sexual in nature, that occurs in connection with the psychologist's activities or roles as a psychologist, and that either: (1) is unwelcome, is offensive, or creates a hostile workplace environment, and the psychologist knows or is told this; or (2) is sufficiently severe or intense to be abusive to a reasonable person in the context. Sexual harassment can consist of a single intense or severe act or of multiple persistent or pervasive acts.

(b) Psychologists accord sexual-harassment complaints and respondents dignity and respect. Psychologists do not participate in denying a person academic admittance or advancement, employment, tenure, or promotion, based solely upon their having made, or their being the subject of, sexual-harassment charges. This does not preclude taking action based upon the outcome of such proceedings or consideration of other appropriate information.

1.12 Other Harassment

Psychologists do not knowingly engage in behavior that is harassing or demeaning to persons with whom they interact in their work based on factors such as those persons' age, gender, race, ethnicity, national origin, religion, sexual orientation, disability, language, or socioeconomic status.

1.13 Personal Problems and Conflicts

(a) Psychologists recognize that their personal problems and conflicts may interfere with their effectiveness. Accordingly, they refrain from undertaking an activity when they know or should know that their personal problems are likely to lead to harm to a patient, client, colleague, student, research participant, or other person to whom they may owe a professional or scientific obligation.

(b) In addition, psychologists have an obligation to be alert to signs of, and to obtain assistance for, their personal problems at an early stage, in order to prevent significantly impaired performance.

(c) When psychologists become aware of personal problems that may interfere with their performing work-related duties adequately, they take appropriate measures, such as obtaining professional consultation or assistance, and determine whether they should limit, suspend, or terminate their work-related duties.

1.14 Avoiding Harm

Psychologists take reasonable steps to avoid harming their patients or clients, research participants, students, and others with whom they work, and to minimize harm where it is foreseeable and unavoidable.

1.15 Misuse of Psychologists' Influence

Because psychologists' scientific and professional judgments and actions may affect the lives of others, they are alert to and guard against personal, financial, social, organizational, or political factors that might lead to misuse of their influence.

1.16 Misuse of Psychologists' Work

(a) Psychologists do not participate in activities in which it appears likely that their skills or data will be misused by others, unless corrective mechanisms are available. (See also Standard 7.04, Truthfulness and Candor.)

(b) If psychologists learn of misuse or misrepresentation of their work, they take reasonable steps to correct or minimize the misuse or misrepresentation.

1.17 Multiple Relationships

(a) In many communities and situations, it may not be feasible or reasonable for psychologists to avoid social or other nonprofessional contacts with persons such as patients, clients, students, supervisees, or research participants. Psychologists must always be sensitive to the potential harmful effects of other contacts on their work and on those persons with whom they deal. A psychologist refrains from entering into or promising another personal, scientific, professional, financial, or other relationship with such persons if it appears likely that such a relationship reasonably might impair the psychologist's objectivity or otherwise interfere with the psychologist's effectively performing his or her function as a psychologist, or might harm or exploit the other party.

(b) Likewise, whenever feasible, a psychologist refrains from taking on professional or scientific obligations when preexisting relationships would create a risk of such harm.

(c) If a psychologist finds that, due to unforeseen factors, a potentially harmful multiple relationship has arisen, the psychologist attempts to resolve it with due regard for the best interests of the affected person and maximal compliance with the Ethics Code.

1.18 Barter (With Patients or Clients)

Psychologists ordinarily refrain from accepting goods, services, or other nonmonetary remuneration from patients or clients in return for psychological services because such arrangements create inherent potential for conflicts, exploitation, and distortion of the professional relationship. A psychologist may participate in bartering only if (1) it is not clinically contraindicated, and (2) the relationship is not exploitative. (See also Standards 1.17, Multiple Relationships, and 1.25, Fees and Financial Arrangements.)

1.19 Exploitative Relationships

(a) Psychologists do not exploit persons over whom they have supervisory, evaluative, or other authority such as students, supervisees, employees, research participants, and clients or patients. (See also Standards 4.05–4.07 regarding sexual involvement with clients or patients.)

(b) Psychologists do not engage in sexual relationships with students or supervisees in training over whom the psychologist has evaluative or direct authority, because such relationships are so likely to impair judgment or be exploitative.

1.20 Consultations and Referrals

(a) Psychologists arrange for appropriate consultations and referrals based principally on the best interests of their patients or clients, with appropriate consent, and subject to other relevant considerations, including applicable law and contractual obligations. (See also Standards 5.01, Discussing the Limits of Confidentiality, and 5.06, Consultations.)

(b) When indicated and professionally appropriate, psychologists cooperate with other professionals in order to serve their patients or clients effectively and appropriately.

(c) Psychologists' referral practices are consistent with law.

1.21 Third-Party Requests for Services

(a) When a psychologist agrees to provide services to a person or entity at the request of a third party, the psychologist clarifies to the extent feasible, at the outset of the service, the nature of the relationship with each party. This clarification includes the role of the psychologist (such as therapist, organizational consultant, diagnostician, or expert witness), the probable uses of the services provided or the information obtained, and the fact that there may be limits to confidentiality.

(b) If there is a foreseeable risk of the psychologist's being called upon to perform conflicting roles because of the involvement of a third party, the psychologist clarifies the nature and direction of his or her responsibilities, keeps all parties appropriately informed as matters develop, and resolves the situation in accordance with this Ethics Code.

1.22 Delegation to and Supervision of Subordinates

(a) Psychologists delegate to their employees, supervisees, and research assistants only those responsibilities that such persons can reasonably be expected to perform competently, on the basis of their education, training, or experience, either independently or with the level of supervision being provided.

(b) Psychologists provide proper training and supervision to their employees or supervisees and take reasonable steps to see that such persons perform services responsibly, competently, and ethically.

(c) If institutional policies, procedures, or practices prevent fulfillment of this obligation, psychologists attempt to modify their role or to correct the situation to the extent feasible.

1.23 Documentation of Professional and Scientific Work

(a) Psychologists appropriately document their professional and scientific work in order to facilitate provision of services later by them or by other professionals, to ensure accountability, and to meet other requirements of institutions or the law.

(b) When psychologists have reason to believe that records of their professional services will be used in legal proceedings involving recipients of or participants in their work, they have a responsibility to create and maintain documentation in the kind of detail and quality that would be consistent with reasonable scrutiny in an adjudicative forum. (See also Standard 7.01, Professionalism, under Forensic Activities.)

1.24 Records and Data

Psychologists create, maintain, disseminate, store, retain, and dispose of records and data relating to their research, practice, and other work in accordance with law and in a manner that permits compliance with the requirements of this Ethics Code. (See also Standard 5.04, Maintenance of Records.)

1.25 Fees and Financial Arrangements

(a) As early as is feasible in a professional or scientific relationship, the psychologist and the patient, client, or other appropriate recipient of psychological services reach an agreement specifying the compensation and the billing arrangements.

(b) Psychologists do not exploit recipients of services or payors with respect to fees.

(c) Psychologists' fee practices are consistent with law.

(d) Psychologists do not misrepresent their fees.

(e) If limitations to services can be anticipated because of limitations in financing, this is discussed with the patient, client, or other appropriate recipient of services as early as is feasible. (See also Standard 4.08, Interruption of Services.)

(f) If the patient, client, or other recipient of services does not pay for services as agreed, and if the psychologist wishes to use collection agencies or legal measures to collect the fees, the psychologist first informs the person that such measures will be taken and provides that person an opportunity to make prompt payment. (See also Standard 5.11, Withholding Records for Nonpayment.)

1.26 Accuracy in Reports to Payors and Funding Sources

In their reports to payors for services or sources of research funding, psychologists accurately state the nature of the research or service provided, the fees or charges, and where applicable, the identity of the provider, the findings, and the diagnosis. (See also Standard 5.05, Disclosures.)

1.27 Referrals and Fees

When a psychologist pays, receives payment from, or divides fees with another professional other than in an employer–employee relationship, the payment to each is based on the services (clinical, consultative, administrative, or other) provided and is not based on the referral itself.

2. Evaluative, Assessment, or Intervention

2.01 Evaluation, Diagnosis, and Interventions in Professional Context

(a) Psychologists perform evaluations, diagnosis services, or interventions only within the context of a defined professional relationship. (See also Standard 1.03, Professional and Scientific Relationship.)

(b) Psychologists' assessments, recommendations, reports, and psychological diagnostic or evaluative statements are based on information and techniques (including personal interviews of the individual when appropriate) sufficient to provide appropriate substantiation for their findings. (See also Standard 7.02, Forensic Assessments.)

2.02 Competence and Appropriate Use of Assessments and Interventions

(a) Psychologists who develop, administer, score, interpret, or use psychological assessment techniques, interviews, tests, or instruments do so in a manner and for purposes that are appropriate in light of the research on or evidence of the usefulness and proper application of the techniques.

(b) Psychologists refrain from misuse of assessment techniques, interventions, results, and interpretations and take reasonable steps to prevent others from misusing the information these techniques provide. This includes refraining from releasing raw test results or raw data to persons, other than to patients or clients as appropriate, who are not qualified to use such information. (See also Standards 1.02, Relationship of Ethics and Law, and 1.04, Boundaries of Competence.)

2.03 Test Construction

Psychologists who develop and conduct research with tests and other assessment techniques use specific procedures and current professional knowledge for test design, standardization, validation, reduction or elimination of bias, and recommendations for use.

2.04 Use of Assessment in General and With Special Populations

(a) Psychologists who perform interventions or administer, score, interpret, or use assessment techniques are familiar with the reliability, validation, and related standardization or outcome studies of, and proper applications and uses of, the techniques they use.

(b) Psychologists recognize limits to the certainty with which diagnoses, judgments, or predictions can be made about individuals.

(c) Psychologists attempt to identify situations in which particular interventions or assessment techniques or norms may not be applicable or may require adjustment in administration or interpretation because of factors such as individuals' gender, age, race, ethnicity, national origin, religion, sexual orientation, disability, language, or socioeconomic status.

2.05 Interpreting Assessment Results

When interpreting assessment results, including automated interpretations, psychologists take into account the various test factors and characteristics of the person being assessed that might affect psychologists' judgments or reduce the accuracy of their interpretations. They indicate any significant reservations they have about the accuracy or limitations of their interpretations.

2.06 Unqualified Persons

Psychologists do not promote the use of psychological assessment techniques by unqualified persons. (See also Standard 1.22, Delegation to and Supervision of Subordinates.)

2.07 Obsolete Tests and Outdated Test Results

(a) Psychologists do not base their assessment or intervention decisions or recommendations on data or test results that are outdated for the current purpose.

(b) Similarly, psychologists do not base such decisions or recommendations on tests and measures that are obsolete and not useful for the current purpose.

2.08 Test Scoring and Interpretation Services

(a) Psychologists who offer assessment or scoring procedures to other professionals accurately describe the purpose, norms, validity, reliability, and applications of the procedures and any special qualifications applicable to their use.

(b) Psychologists select scoring and interpretation services (including automated services) on the basis of evidence of the validity of the program and procedures as well as on other appropriate considerations.

(c) Psychologists retain appropriate responsibility for the appropriate application, interpretation, and use of assessment instruments, whether they score and interpret such tests themselves or use automated or other services.

2.09 Explaining Assessment Results

Unless the nature of the relationship is clearly explained to the person being assessed in advance and precludes provision of an explanation of results (such as in some organizational consulting, preemployment or security screenings, and forensic evaluations), psychologists ensure that an explanation of the results is provided using language that is reasonably understandable to the person assessed or to another legally authorized person on behalf of the client. Regardless of whether the scoring and interpretation are done by the psychologist, by assistants, or by automated or other outside services, psychologists take reasonable steps to ensure that appropriate explanations of results are given.

2.10 Maintaining Test Security

Psychologists make reasonable efforts to maintain the integrity and security of tests and other assessment techniques consistent with law, contractual obligations, and in a manner that permits compliance with the requirements of this Ethics Code. (See also Standard 1.02, Relationship of Ethics and Law.)

3. Advertising and Other Public Statements

3.01 Definition of Public Statements

Psychologists comply with this Ethics Code in public statements relating to their professional services, products, or publications or to the field of psychology. Public statements include but are not limited to paid or unpaid advertising, brochures, printed matter, directory listings, personal resumes or curricula vitae, interviews or comments for use in media, statements in legal proceedings, lectures and public oral presentations, and published materials.

3.02 Statements by Others

(a) Psychologists who engage others to create or place public statements that promote their professional practice, products, or activities retain professional responsibility for such statements.

(b) In addition, psychologists make reasonable efforts to prevent others whom they do not control (such as employers, publishers, sponsors, organizational clients, and representatives of the print or broadcast media) from making deceptive statements concerning psychologists' practice or professional or scientific activities.

(c) If psychologists learn of deceptive statements about their work made by others, psychologists make reasonable efforts to correct such statements.

(d) Psychologists do not compensate employees of press, radio, television, or other communication media in return for publicity in a news item.

(e) A paid advertisement relating to the psychologist's activities must be identified as such, unless it is already apparent from the context.

3.03 Avoidance of False or Deceptive Statements

(a) Psychologists do not make public statements that are false, deceptive, misleading, or fraudulent, either because of what they state, convey, or suggest or because of what they omit, concerning their research, practice, or other work activities or those of persons or organizations with which they are affiliated. As examples (and not in limitation) of this standard, psychologists do not make false or deceptive statements concerning (1) their training, experience, or competence; (2) their academic degrees; (3) their credentials; (4) their institutional or association affiliations; (5) their services; (6) the scientific or clinical basis for, or results or degree of success of, their services; (7) their fees; or (8) their publications or research findings. (See also Standards 6.15, Deception in Research, and 6.18, Providing Participants With Information About the Study.)

(b) Psychologists claim as credentials for their psychological work, only degrees that (1) were earned from a regionally accredited educational institution or (2) were the basis for psychology licensure by the state in which they practice.

3.04 Media Presentations

When psychologists provide advice or comment by means of public lectures, demonstrations, radio or television programs, prerecorded tapes, printed articles, mailed material, or other media, they take reasonable precautions to ensure that (1) the statements are based on appropriate psychological literature and practice, (2) the statements are otherwise consistent with this Ethics Code, and (3) the recipients of the information are not encouraged to infer that a relationship has been established with them personally.

3.05 Testimonials

Psychologists do not solicit testimonials from current psychotherapy clients or patients or other persons who because of their particular circumstances are vulnerable to undue influence.

3.06 In-Person Solicitation

Psychologists do not engage, directly or through agents, in uninvited in-person solicitation of business from actual or potential psychotherapy patients or clients or other persons who because of their particular circumstances are vulnerable to undue influence. However, this does not preclude attempting to implement appropriate collateral contacts with significant others for the purpose of benefiting an already engaged therapy patient.

4. *Therapy*

4.01 Structuring the Relationship

(a) Psychologists discuss with clients or patients as early as is feasible in the therapeutic relationship appropriate issues, such as the nature and anticipated course of therapy, fees, and confidentiality. (See also Standards 1.25, Fees and Financial Arrangements, and 5.01, Discussing the Limits of Confidentiality.)

(b) When the psychologist's work with clients or patients will be supervised, the above discussion includes that fact, and the name of the supervisor, when the supervisor has legal responsibility for the case.

(c) When the therapist is a student intern, the client or patient is informed of that fact.

(d) Psychologists make reasonable efforts to answer patients' questions and to avoid apparent misunderstandings about therapy. Whenever possible, psychologists provide oral and/or written information, using language that is reasonably understandable to the patient or client.

4.02 Informed Consent to Therapy

(a) Psychologists obtain appropriate informed consent to therapy or related procedures, using language that is reasonably understanding to participants. The content of informed consent will vary depending on many circumstances; however, informed consent generally implies that the person (1) has the capacity to consent, (2) has been informed of significant information concerning the procedure, (3) has freely and without undue influence expressed consent, and (4) consent has been appropriately documented.

(b) When persons are legally incapable of giving informed consent, psychologists obtain informed permission from a legally authorized person, if such substitute consent is permitted by law.

(c) In addition, psychologists (1) inform those persons who are legally incapable of giving informed consent about the proposed interventions in a manner commensurate with the persons' psychological capacities, (2) seek their assent to those interventions, and (3) consider such persons' preferences and best interests.

4.03 Couple and Family Relationships

(a) When a psychologist agrees to provide services to several persons who have a relationship (such as husband and wife or parents and children), the psychologist attempts to clarify at the outset (1) which of the individuals are patients or clients and (2) the relationship the psychologist will have with each person. This clarification includes the role of the psychologist and the probable uses of the services provided or the information obtained. (See also Standard 5.01, Discussing the Limits of Confidentiality.)

(b) As soon as it becomes apparent that the psychologist may be called on to perform potentially conflicting roles (such as marital counselor to husband and wife, and then witness for one party in a divorce proceeding), the psychologist attempts to clarify and adjust, or withdraw from, roles appropriately. (See also Standard 7.03, Clarification of Role, under Forensic Activities.)

4.04 Providing Mental Health Services to Those Served by Others

In deciding whether to offer or provide services to those already receiving mental health services elsewhere, psychologists carefully consider the treatment issues and the potential patient's or client's welfare. The psychologist discusses these issues with the patient or client, or another legally authorized person on behalf of the client, in order to minimize the risk of confusion and conflict, consults with the other service providers when appropriate, and proceeds with caution and sensitivity to the therapeutic issues.

4.05 Sexual Intimacies With Current Patients or Clients

Psychologists do not engage in sexual intimacies with current patients or clients.

4.06 Therapy With Former Sexual Partners

Psychologists do not accept as therapy patients or clients persons with whom they have engaged in sexual intimacies.

4.07 Sexual Intimacies With Former Therapy Patients

(a) Psychologists do not engage in sexual intimacies with a former therapy patient or client for at least two years after cessation or termination of professional services.

(b) Because sexual intimacies with a former therapy patient or client are so frequently harmful to the patient or client, and because such intimacies undermine public confidence in the psychology profession and thereby deter the public's use of needed services, psychologists do not engage in sexual intimacies with former therapy patients and clients even after a two-year interval except in the most unusual circumstances. The psychologist who engages in such activity after the two years following cessation or termination of treatment bears the burden of demonstrating that there has been no exploitation, in light of all relevant factors, including (1) the amount of time that has passed since therapy terminated, (2) the nature and duration of the therapy, (3) the circumstances of termination, (4) the patient's or client's personal history, (5) the patient's or client's current mental status, (6) the likelihood of adverse impact on the patient or client and others, and (7) any statements or actions made by the therapist during the course of therapy suggesting or inviting the possibility of a posttermination sexual or romantic relationship with the patient or client. (See also Standard 1.17, Multiple Relationships.)

4.08 Interruption of Services

(a) Psychologists make reasonable efforts to plan for facilitating care in the event that psychological services are interrupted by factors such as the psychologist's illness, death, unavailability, or relocation or by the client's relocation or financial limitations. (See also Standard 5.09, Preserving Records and Data.)

(b) When entering into employment or contractual relationships, psychologists provide for orderly and appropriate resolution of responsibility for patient or client care in the event that the employment or contractual relationship ends, with paramount consideration given to the welfare of the patient or client.

4.09 Terminating the Professional Relationship

(a) Psychologists do not abandon patients or clients. (See also Standard 1.25e, under Fees and Financial Arrangements.)

(b) Psychologists terminate a professional relationship when it becomes reasonably clear that the patient or client no longer needs the service, is not benefiting, or is being harmed by continued service.

(c) Prior to termination for whatever reason, except where precluded by the patient's or client's conduct, the psychologist discusses the patient's or client's views and needs, provides appropriate pretermination counseling, suggests alternative service providers as appropriate, and takes other reasonable steps to facilitate transfer of responsibility to another provider if the patient or client needs one immediately.

5. *Privacy and Confidentiality*

These Standards are potentially applicable to the professional and scientific activities of all psychologists.

5.01 Discussing the Limits of Confidentiality

(a) Psychologists discuss with persons and organizations with whom they establish a scientific, or professional relationship (including, to the extent feasible, minors and their legal representatives) (1) the relevant limitations on confidentiality, including limitations where applicable in group, marital, and family therapy or in organizational consulting, and (2) the foreseeable uses of the information generated through their services.

(b) Unless it is not feasible or is contraindicated, the discussion of confidentiality occurs at the outset of the relationship and thereafter as new circumstances may warrant.

(c) Permission for electronic recording of interviews is secured from clients and patients.

5.02 Maintaining Confidentiality

Psychologists have a primary obligation and take reasonable precautions to respect the confidentiality rights of those with whom they work or consult, recognizing that confidentiality may be established by law, institutional rules, or professional or scientific relationships. (See also Standard 6.26, Professional Reviewers.)

5.03 Minimizing Intrusions on Privacy

(a) In order to minimize intrusions on privacy, psychologists include in written and oral reports, consultations, and the like, only information germane to the purpose for which the communication is made.

(b) Psychologists discuss confidential information obtained in clinical or consulting relationships, or evaluative data concerning patients, individual or organizational clients, students, research participants, supervisees, and employees, only for appropriate scientific or professional purposes and only with persons clearly concerned with such matters.

5.04 Maintenance of Records

Psychologists maintain appropriate confidentiality in creating, storing, accessing, transferring, and disposing of records under their control, whether these are written, automated, or in any other medium. Psychologists maintain and dispose of records in accordance with law and in a manner that permits compliance with the requirements of this Ethics Code.

5.05 Disclosures

(a) Psychologists disclose confidential information without the consent of the individual only as mandated by law, or where permitted by law for a valid purpose, such as (1) to provide needed professional services to the patient or the individual or organizational client, (2) to obtain appropriate professional consultations, (3) to protect the patient or client or others from harm, or (4) to obtain payment for services, in which instance disclosure is limited to the minimum that is necessary to achieve the purpose.

(b) Psychologists also may disclose confidential information with the appropriate consent of the patient or the individual or organizational client (or of another legally authorized person on behalf of the patient or client), unless prohibited by law.

5.06 Consultations

When consulting with colleagues, (1) psychologists do not share confidential information that reasonably could lead to the identification of a patient, client, research participant, or other person or organization with whom they have a confidential relationship unless they have obtained the prior consent of the person or organization or the disclosure cannot be avoided, and (2) they share information only to the extent necessary to achieve the purposes of the consultation. (See also Standard 5.02, Maintaining Confidentiality.)

5.07 Confidential Information in Databases

(a) If confidential information concerning recipients of psychological services is to be entered into databases or systems of records available to persons whose access has not been consented to by the recipient, then psychologists use coding or other techniques to avoid the inclusion of personal identifiers.

(b) If a research protocol approved by an institutional review board or similar body requires the inclusion of personal identifiers, such identifiers are deleted before the information is made accessible to persons other than those of whom the subject was advised.

(c) If such deletion is not feasible, then before psychologists transfer such data to others or review such data collected by others, they take reasonable steps to determine that appropriate consent of personally identifiable individuals has been obtained.

5.08 Use of Confidential Information for Didactic or Other Purposes

(a) Psychologists do not disclose in their writings, lectures, or other public media, confidential, personally identifiable information concerning their patients, individual or organizational clients, students, research participants, or other recipients of their services that they obtained during the course of their work, unless the person or organization has consented in writing or unless there is other ethical or legal authorization for doing so.

(b) Ordinarily, in such scientific and professional presentations, psychologists disguise confidential information concerning such persons or organizations so that they are not individually identifiable to others and so that discussions do not cause harm to subjects who might identify themselves.

5.09 Preserving Records and Data

A psychologist makes plans in advance so that confidentiality of records and data is protected in the event of the psychologist's death, incapacity, or withdrawal from the position or practice.

5.10 Ownership of Records and Data

Recognizing that ownership of records and data is governed by legal principles, psychologists take reasonable and lawful steps so that records and data remain available to the extent needed to serve the best interests of patients, individual or organizational clients, research participants, or appropriate others.

5.11 Withholding Records for Nonpayment

Psychologists may not withhold records under their control that are requested and imminently needed for a patient's or client's treatment solely because payment has not been received, except as otherwise provided by law.

6. _Teaching, Training Supervision, Research, and Publishing_

6.01 Design of Education and Training Programs

Psychologists who are responsible for education and training programs seek to ensure that the programs are competently designed, provide the proper experiences, and meet the requirements for licensure, certification, or other goals for which claims are made by the program.

6.02 Descriptions of Education and Training Programs

(a) Psychologists responsible for education and training programs seek to ensure that there is a current and accurate description of the program content, training goals and objectives, and requirements that must be met for satisfactory completion of the program. This information must be made readily available to all interested parties.

(b) Psychologists seek to ensure that statements concerning their course outlines are accurate and not misleading, particularly regarding the subject matter to be covered, bases for evaluating progress, and the nature of course experiences. (See also Standard 3.03, Avoidance of False or Deceptive Statements.)

(c) To the degree to which they exercise control, psychologists responsible for announcements, catalogs, brochures, or advertisements describing workshops, seminars, or other non-degree-granting educational programs ensure that they accurately describe the audience for which the program is intended, the educational objectives, the presenters, and the fees involved.

6.03 Accuracy and Objectivity in Teaching

(a) When engaged in teaching or training, psychologists present psychological information accurately and with a reasonable degree of objectivity.

(b) When engaged in teaching or training, psychologists recognize the power they hold over students or supervisees and therefore make reasonable efforts to avoid engaging in conduct that is personally demeaning to students or supervisees. (See also Standards 1.09, Respecting Others, and 1.12, Other Harassment.)

6.04 Limitation on Teaching

Psychologists do not teach the use of techniques or procedures that require specialized training, licensure, or expertise, including but not limited to hypnosis, biofeedback, and projective techniques, to individuals who lack the prerequisite training, legal scope of practice, or expertise.

6.05 Assessing Student and Supervisee Performance

(a) In academic and supervisory relationships, psychologists establish an appropriate process for providing feedback to students and supervisees.

(b) Psychologists evaluate students and supervisees on the basis of their actual performance on relevant and established program requirements.

6.06 Planning Research

(a) Psychologists design, conduct, and report research in accordance with recognized standards of scientific competence and ethical research.

(b) Psychologists plan their research so as to minimize the possibility that results will be misleading.

(c) In planning research, psychologists consider its ethical acceptability under the Ethics Code. If an ethical issue is unclear, psychologists seek to resolve the issue through consultation with institutional review boards, animal care and use committees, peer consultations, or other proper mechanisms.

(d) Psychologists take responsible steps to implement appropriate protections for the rights and welfare of human participants, other persons affected by the research, and the welfare of animal subjects.

6.07 Responsibility

(a) Psychologists conduct research competently and with due concern for the dignity and welfare of the participants.

(b) Psychologists are responsible for the ethical conduct of research conducted by them or by others under their supervision or control.

(c) Researchers and assistants are permitted to perform only those tasks for which they are appropriately trained and prepared.

(d) As part of the process of development and implementation of research projects, psychologists consult those with expertise concerning any special population under investigation or most likely to be affected.

6.08 Compliance With Law and Standards

Psychologists plan and conduct research in a manner consistent with federal and state law and regulations, as well as professional standards governing the conduct of research, and particularly those standards governing research with human participants and animal subjects.

6.09 Institutional Approval

Psychologists obtain from host institutions or organizations appropriate approval prior to conducting research, and they provide accurate information about their research proposals. They conduct the research in accordance with the approved research protocol.

6.10 Research Responsibilities

Prior to conducting research (except research involving only anonymous surveys, naturalistic observations, or similar research), psychologists enter into an agreement with participants that clarifies the nature of the research and the responsibilities of each party.

6.11 Informed Consent to Research

(a) Psychologists use language that is reasonably understandable to research participants in obtaining their appropriate informed consent (except as provided in Standard 6.12, Dispensing With Informed Consent). Such informed consent is appropriately documented.

(b) Using language that is reasonably understandable to participants, psychologists inform participants of the nature of the research; they inform participants that they are free to participate or to decline to participate or to withdraw from the research; they explain the foreseeable consequences of declining or withdrawing; they inform participants of significant factors that may be expected to influence their willingness to participate (such as risks, discomfort, adverse effects, or limitations on confidentiality, except as provided in Standard 6.15, Deception in Research); and they explain other aspects about which the prospective participants inquire.

(c) When psychologists conduct research with individuals such as students or subordinates, psychologists take special care to protect the prospective participants from adverse consequences of declining or withdrawing from participation.

(d) When research participation is a course requirement or opportunity for extra credit, the prospective participant is given the choice of equitable alternative activities.

(e) For persons who are legally incapable of giving informed consent, psychologists nevertheless (1) provide an appropriate explanation, (2) obtain the participant's assent, and (3) obtain appropriate permission from a legally authorized person, if such substitute consent is permitted by law.

6.12 *Dispensing With Informed Consent*

Before determining that planned research (such as research involving only anonymous questionnaires, naturalistic observations, or certain kinds of archival research) does not require the informed consent of research participants, psychologists consider applicable regulations and institutional review board requirements, and they consult with colleagues as appropriate.

6.13 *Informed Consent in Research Filming or Recording*

Psychologists obtain informed consent from research participants prior to filming or recording them in any form, unless the research involves simply naturalistic observations in public places and it is not anticipated that the recording will be used in a manner that could cause personal identification or harm.

6.14 *Offering Inducement for Research Participants*

(a) In offering professional services as an inducement to obtain research participants, psychologists make clear the nature of the services, as well as the risks, obligations, and limitations. (See also Standard 1.18 Barter [With Patients or Clients].)

(b) Psychologists do not offer excessive or inappropriate financial or other inducements to obtain research participants, particularly when it might tend to coerce participation.

6.15 *Deception in Research*

(a) Psychologists do not conduct a study involving deception unless they have determined that the use of deceptive techniques is justified by the study's prospective scientific, educational, or applied value and that equally effective alternative procedures that do not use deception are not feasible.

(b) Psychologists never deceive research participants about significant aspects that would affect their willingness to participate, such as physical risks, discomfort, or unpleasant emotional experiences.

(c) Any other deception that is an integral feature of the design and conduct of an experiment must be explained to participants as early as is feasible, preferably at the conclusion of their participation, but no later than at the conclusion of the research. (See also Standard 6.18, Providing Participants With Information About the Study.)

6.16 Sharing and Utilizing Data

Psychologists inform research participants of their anticipated sharing or further use of personally identifiable research data and of the possibility of unanticipated future uses.

6.17 Minimizing Invasiveness

In conducting research, psychologists interfere with the participants or milieu from which data are collected only in a manner that is warranted by an appropriate research design and that is consistent with psychologists' roles as scientific investigators.

6.18 Providing Participants With Information About the Study

(a) Psychologists provide a prompt opportunity for participants to obtain appropriate information about the nature, results, and conclusions of the research, and psychologists attempt to correct any misconceptions that participants may have.

(b) If scientific or humane values justify delaying or withholding this information, psychologists take reasonable measures to reduce the risk of harm.

6.19 Honoring Commitments

Psychologists take reasonable measures to honor all commitments they have made to research participants.

6.20 Care and Use of Animals in Research

(a) Psychologists who conduct research involving animals treat them humanely.

(b) Psychologists acquire, care for, use, and dispose of animals in compliance with current federal, state, and local laws and regulations, and with professional standards.

(c) Psychologists trained in research methods and experienced in the care of laboratory animals supervise all procedures involving animals and are responsible for ensuring appropriate consideration of their comfort, health, and humane treatment.

(d) Psychologists ensure that all individuals using animals under their supervision have received instruction in research methods and in the care, maintenance, and handling of the species being used, to the extent appropriate to their role.

(e) Responsibilities and activities of individuals assisting in a research project are consistent with their respective competencies.

(f) Psychologists make reasonable efforts to minimize the discomfort, infection, illness, and pain of animal subjects.

(g) A procedure subjecting animals to pain, stress, or privation is used only when an alternative procedure is unavailable and the goal is justified by its prospective scientific, educational, or applied value.

(h) Surgical procedures are performed under appropriate anesthesia; techniques to avoid infection and minimize pain are followed during and after surgery.

(i) When it is appropriate that the animal's life be terminated, it is done rapidly, with an effort to minimize pain, and in accordance with accepted procedures.

6.21 Reporting of Results

(a) Psychologists do not fabricate data or falsify results in their publications.

(b) If psychologists discover significant errors in their published data, they take reasonable steps to correct such errors in a correction, retraction, erratum, or other appropriate publication means.

6.22 Plagiarism

Psychologists do not present substantial portions or elements of another's work or data as their own, even if the other work or data source is cited occasionally.

6.23 Publication Credit

(a) Psychologists take responsibility and credit, including authorship credit, only for work they have actually performed or to which they have contributed.

(b) Principal authorship and other publication credits accurately reflect the relative scientific or professional contributions of the individuals involved, regardless of their relative status. Mere possession of an institutional position, such as Department Chair, does not justify authorship credit. Minor contributions to the research or to the writing for publications are appropriately acknowledged, such as in footnotes or in an introductory statement.

(c) A student is usually listed as principal author on any multiple-authored article that is substantially based on the student's dissertation or thesis.

6.24 Duplicate Publication of Data

Psychologists do not publish, as original data, data that have been previously published. This does not preclude republishing data when they are accompanied by proper acknowledgment.

6.25 Sharing Data

After research results are published, psychologists do not withhold the data on which their conclusions are based from other competent professionals who seek to verify the substantive claims through reanalysis and who intend to use such data only for that purpose, provided that the confidentiality of the participants can be protected and unless legal rights concerning proprietary data preclude their release.

6.26 Professional Reviewers

Psychologists who review material submitted for publication, grant, or other research proposal review respect the confidentiality of and the proprietary rights in such information of those who submitted it.

7. Forensic Activities

7.01 Professionalism

Psychologists who perform forensic functions, such as assessments, interviews, consultations, reports, or expert testimony, must comply with all other provisions of this Ethics Code to the extent that they apply to such activities. In addition, psychologists base their forensic work on appropriate knowledge of and competence in the areas underlying such work, including specialized knowledge concerning special populations. (See also Standards 1.06, Basis for Scientific and Professional Judgments; 1.08, Human Differences; 1.15, Misuse of Psychologists' Influence; and 1.23, Documentation of Professional and Scientific Work.)

7.02 Forensic Assessments

(a) Psychologists' forensic assessments, recommendations, and reports are based on information and techniques (including personal interviews of the individual, when appropriate) sufficient to provide appropriate substantiation for their findings. (See also Standards 1.03, Professional and Scientific Relationship; 1.23, Documentation of Professional and Scientific Work; 2.01, Evaluation, Diagnosis, and Interventions in Professional Context; and 2.05, Interpreting Assessment Results.)

(b) Except as noted in (c), below, psychologists provide written or oral forensic reports or testimony of the psychological characteristics of an individual only after they have conducted an examination of the individual adequate to support their statements or conclusions.

(c) When, despite reasonable efforts, such an examination is not feasible, psychologists clarify the impact of their limited information on the reliability and validity of their reports and testimony, and they appropriately limit the nature and extent of their conclusions or recommendations.

7.03 Clarification of Role

In most circumstances, psychologists avoid performing multiple and potentially conflicting roles in forensic matters. When psychologists may be called on to serve in more than one role in a legal proceeding—for example, as consultant or expert for one party or for the court and as a fact witness—they clarify role expectations and the extent of confidentiality in advance to the extent feasible, and thereafter as changes occur, in order to avoid compromising their professional judgment and objectivity and in order to avoid misleading others regarding their role.

7.04 Truthfulness and Candor

(a) In forensic testimony and reports, psychologists testify truthfully, honestly, and candidly and, consistent with applicable legal procedures, describe fairly the bases for their testimony and conclusions.

(b) Whenever necessary to avoid misleading, psychologists acknowledge the limits of their data or conclusions.

7.05 Prior Relationships

A prior professional relationship with a party does not preclude psychologists from testifying as fact witnesses or from testifying to their services to the extent permitted by applicable law. Psychologists appropriately take into account ways in which the prior relationship might affect their professional objectivity or opinions and disclose the potential conflict to the relevant parties.

7.06 Compliance With Law and Rules

In performing forensic roles, psychologists are reasonably familiar with the rules governing their roles. Psychologists are aware of the occasionally competing demands placed upon them by these principles and the requirements of the court system, and attempt to resolve these conflicts by making known their commitment to this Ethics Code and taking steps to resolve the conflict in a responsible manner. (See also Standard 1.02, Relationship of Ethics and Law.)

8. *Resolving Ethical Issues*

8.01 *Familiarity With Ethics Code*

Psychologists have an obligation to be familiar with this Ethics Code, other applicable ethics codes, and their application to psychologists' work. Lack of awareness or misunderstanding of an ethical standard is not itself a defense to a charge of unethical conduct.

8.02 *Confronting Ethical Issues*

When a psychologist is uncertain whether a particular situation or course of action would violate this Ethics Code, the psychologist ordinarily consults with other psychologists knowledgeable about ethical issues, with state or national psychology ethics committees, or with other appropriate authorities in order to choose a proper response.

8.03 *Conflicts Between Ethics and Organizational Demands*

If the demands of an organization with which psychologists are affiliated conflict with this Ethics Code, psychologists clarify the nature of the conflict, make known their commitment to the Ethics Code, and to the extent feasible, seek to resolve the conflict in a way that permits the fullest adherence to the Ethics Code.

8.04 *Informal Resolution of Ethical Violations*

When psychologists believe that there may have been an ethical violation by another psychologist, they attempt to resolve the issue by bringing it to the attention of that individual if an informal resolution appears appropriate and the intervention does not violate any confidentiality rights that may be involved.

8.05 *Reporting Ethical Violations*

If an apparent ethical violation is not appropriate for informal resolution under Standard 8.04 or is not resolved properly in that fashion, psychologists take further action appropriate to the situation, unless such action conflicts with confidentiality rights in ways that cannot be resolved. Such action might include referral to state or national committees on professional ethics or to state licensing boards.

8.06 Cooperating With Ethics Committees

Psychologists cooperate in ethics investigations, proceedings, and resulting requirements of the APA or any affiliated state psychological association to which they belong. In doing so, they make reasonable efforts to resolve any issues as to confidentiality. Failure to cooperate is itself an ethics violation.

8.07 Improper Complaints

Psychologists do not file or encourage the filing of ethics complaints that are frivolous and are intended to harm the respondent rather than to protect the public.

References

Ainsworth, M., & Bowlby, J. (1991). An ethnological approach to personality development. *American Psychologist, 46*, 353–341.

Albee, G.H. (1986). Toward a just society: Lessons from observations on the primary prevention of pathology. *American Psychologist, 41*, 891–898.

Albee, G.H. (1999). Prevention not treatment. *Counselling Psychology Quarterly, 12*, 133–146.

Altmaier, E.M., & Johnson, B. (1992). Health related applications of counseling psychology: Toward health promotion and disease prevention across the life span. In S. Brown & R. Lent (Eds.), *Handbook of counseling psychology* (pp. 315–348). New York: Wiley.

American Psychological Association. (1987). *Casebook on ethical principles of psychologists*. Washington, DC: Author.

American Psychological Association. (1992). Ethical principles of psychologists and code of conduct. *American Psychologist, 47*, 1597–1611.

Andrews, F.M., & Withey, S.B. (1976). *Social indicators of well-being: Americans perceptions of life quality*. New York: Plenum Press.

Archer, J. (1996). Sex differences in social behavior: Are the social role and evolutionary explanations compatible? *American Psychologist, 51*, 909–917.

Atkinson, D.R., Thompson, C.E., & Grant, S.K. (1993). A three dimensional model for counseling racial/ethnic minorities. *Counseling Psychologist, 21*, 257–277.

Auerbach, S.M. (1989). Stress management and coping research in the health care setting: An overview and methodological commentary. *Journal of Consulting and Clinical Psychology, 57*, 388–395.

Bandura, A. (1977). Self efficacy: Toward a unifying theory of behavioral change. *Psychological Review, 84*, 191–215.

Bandura, A. (1982). Self-efficacy mechanism in human agency. *American Psychologist, 37*, 122–147.

Batson, C.D. (1990). How social an animal? *American Psychologist, 45*(3), 336–346.

Baumeister, R.F., & Leary, M.R. (1995). The need to belong: Desire for interpersonal attachments as a fundamental human motivation. *Psychological Bulletin, 117*, 497–529.

Bechtel, R. (1977). *Enclosing behavior*. Stroudsberg, PA: Dowden, Hutchinson and Ross.

Beck, A.T. (1976). *Cognitive therapy and emotional disorders*. New York: International Universities Press.

Beck, A.T. (1991). Cognitive therapy: A 30 year perspective. *American Psychologist, 46,* 368–375.

Becvar, D.S., & Becvar, R.J. (1993). *Family therapy: A systematic integration* (2nd ed.). New York: Allyn & Bacon.

Behrens, J.T. (1997). Does the White Racial Identity Attitude Scale measure racial identity? *Journal of Counseling Psychology, 44,* 3–12.

Betancourt, H., & Lopez, S.R. (1993). The study of culture ethnicity and race in American psychology. *American Psychologist, 38,* 629–637.

Beutler, L., & Consoli, A.J. (1992). Systematic eclectic psychotherapy. In J. Norcross & M. Goldfried (Eds.), *Handbook of psychotherapy integration* (pp. 264–299). New York: Basic Books.

Black, M.M., & Krishnakumar, A. (1998). Children in low-income, urban settings: Interventions to promote mental health and well-being. *American Psychologist, 53,* 635–646.

Blocher, D.H. (1983). Toward a cognitive developmental approach to counseling supervision. *Counseling Psychologist, 11*(1), 27–34.

Blocher, D.H. (1987). *The professional counselor.* New York: Macmillan.

Blocher, D.H. (1988). On the uses and misuses of the term theory. *Journal of Counseling and Development, 66,* 67–68.

Blocher, D.H., & Siegal, R. (1981). Toward a cognitive developmental theory of work and leisure. *Counseling Psychologist, 9,* 33–44.

Blustein, D.L. (1992). Toward the reinvigoration of the vocational realm of counseling psychology. *Counseling Psychologist, 20,* 712–723.

Bodden, J. (1970). Cognitive complexity as a factor in appropriate vocational choice. *Journal of Counseling Psychology, 17,* 364–368.

Borders, L.D., & Drury, S.M. (1992). Comprehensive school counseling programs: A review for policy makers and practitioners. *Journal of Counseling and Development, 70,* 487–498.

Bordin, E.S. (1979). The generalizability of the psychoanalytic concept of the working alliance. *Psychotherapy: Theory, Research and Practice, 16,* 252–260.

Bordin, E.S. (1994). Theory and research on the therapeutic working alliance. In A.O. Horvath & L.S. Greenberg (Eds.), *The working alliance: Theory, research and practice* (pp. 13–37). New York: Wiley.

Borgen, F.H. (1992). Expanding scientific paradigms in counseling psychology. In S.D. Brown & R.W. Lent (Eds.), *Handbook of counseling psychology* (pp. 111–139). New York: Wiley.

Borow, H. (1959). Modern perspectives in personnel research. In *National Society for the Study of Education Yearbook* (Vol. 58, pp. 210–231). Washington, DC: National Society for the Study of Education.

Borow, H. (1964). Milestones: A chronology of notable events in the history of vocational guidance. In H. Borow (Ed.), *Man in the world of work* (pp. 45–66). Boston: Houghton Mifflin.

Bowman, G.D., & Stern, M. (1995). Adjustment to occupational stress: The relationship of perceived control to effectiveness of coping strategies. *Journal of Counseling Psychology, 42,* 294–303.

Brammer, L.M., Abrego, P.J., & Shostrum, E. (1993). *Therapeutic counseling and psychotherapy* (6th ed.). Inglewood Cliffs, NJ: Prentice Hall.

Brewer, J. (1932). *Education as guidance*. New York: Macmillan.

Brim, O., & Kagan, J. (Eds.). (1980). Introduction. *Constancy and change in human development*. Cambridge, MA: Harvard University Press.

Bronfenbrenner, A. (1979). *The ecology of human development*. Cambridge, MA: Harvard University Press.

Brown, S.D., Brady, R., Lent, R.W., Wolfert, J., & Hall, S. (1987). Perceived support among college students: Three studies of the psychometric characteristics and counseling uses of the Social Support Inventory. *Journal of Counseling Psychology, 34*, 337–354.

Brown, S.D., Regan, N.E., & McPartland, E.B. (1996). Why are so many people happy and what do we do for those who aren't ? A reaction to Lightsey. *Counseling Psychologist 24*, 751–756.

Bruch, M.A., Berko, E.H., & Haase, R.F. (1998). Shyness, masculine ideology, physical attractiveness and emotional inexpressiveness: Testing a mediational model of men's interpersonal competence. *Journal of Counseling Psychology, 45*, 84–97.

Buehler, C. (1933). *Der menschliche Lebenslauf als psychologisches Problem*. Leipzig, Germany: Hirzel.

Buss, D.M. (1995). Psychological sex differences: Origins through sexual selection. *American Psychologist, 50*, 164–168.

Cahan, E.D. (1984). The genetic psychologies of James Mark Baldwin and Jean Piaget. *Developmental Psychology, 20*, 128–135.

Canter, M.B., Bennett, B.E., Jones, S.E., & Nagy, F.F. (1994). *Ethics for psychologists*. Washington, DC: American Psychological Association.

Capurso, R., & Blocher, D.H. (1985). The effects of sex-role consistent and inconsistent information on the social perceptions of complex, non-complex, androgynous and sex-typed women. *Journal of Vocational Behavior, 26*, 79–91.

Carkhuff, R. (1966). Counseling research, theory and practice. *Journal of Counseling Psychology, 13*, 450–467.

Carkhuff, R. (1969). *Helping and human relations* (Vol. 2). New York: Holt, Rinehart and Winston.

Carlozzi, A.F., Gaa, J.P., & Liberman, D.B. (1983). Empathy and ego development. *Journal of Counseling Psychology, 30*, 113–116.

Carver, C.S., & Schier, M.F. (1990). Origins and function of positive and negative affect: A control-process review. *Psychological Review, 97*, 19–35.

Catanzaro, S.J., Horaney, F., & Creasey, G. (1995). Hassles, coping and depressive symptoms in an elderly community sample: The role of mood regulation and expectancies. *Journal of Counseling Psychology, 42*, 259–265.

Church, T.A. (1994). Relating the Tellegen and five factor models of personality structure. *Journal of Personality and Social Psychology, 67*, 898–909.

Cicchetti, D., & Toth, S.L. (1998). The development of depression in children and adolescents. *American Psychologist, 53*, 221–241.

Cohen, C.R., Chartrand, J.M., & Jowdy, D.P. (1995). Relationships between career indecision subtypes and ego identity development. *Journal of Counseling Psychology, 42*, 440–447.

Cohen, S. (1980). After effects of stress on human performance and social behavior: A review of research and theory. *Psychological Bulletin, 88*(1), 82–108.

Coie, J.D., Watt, N.F., West, S.G., Hawkins, J.D., Asarnow, J.R., Markman, H.J., Ramey, S.L., Shure, M.B., & Long, B. (1993). The science of prevention. *American Psychologist, 48*, 1013–1022.

Coleman, H., Wampold, B.E., & Casali, S.L. (1995). Ethnic minorities ratings of ethnically similar and European American counselors: A meta-analysis. *Journal of Counseling Psychology, 42*, 55–64.

Coley, R.L., & Chase-Lansdale, P.L. (1998). Adolescent pregnancy and parenthood: Recent evidence and future direction. *American Psychologist, 53*, 152–166.

Committee on Definition. (1956). Division 17 of the American Psychological Association: Counseling psychology as a specialty. *American Psychologist, 11*, 282–285.

Compas, B.E., Malcarne, V.L., & Fondacaro, K.M. (1988). Coping with stressful events in older children and young adolescents. *Journal of Consulting and Clinical Psychology, 56*, 405–411.

Conyne, R. (1988). The counseling ecologist: Helping people and environments. In R. Hays & R. Aubrey (Eds.), *New directions for counseling and development* (pp. 304–324). Denver: Love.

Cooper, R.S., Rotomi, C.N., & Ward, R. (1999). The puzzle of hypertension in African-Americans. *Scientific American, 280*(2), 56–63.

Corey, G., Corey, M.S., & Callanan, P. (1993). *Issues and ethics in the helping professions*. Pacific Grove, CA: Brooks/Cole.

Corrigan, J.D., Dell, D.M., Lewis, K.N., & Schmidt, L.D. (1980). Counseling as a social influence process. *Journal of Counseling Psychology, 27*, 395–441.

Corsini, R. (1995). Introduction. In R. Corsini & D. Wedding (Eds.), *Current psychotherapies* (pp. 1–13). Itasca, IL: Peacock.

Cournoyer, R.J., & Mahalik, J. (1995). Cross-sectional study of gender role conflict: Examining college-aged and middle-aged men. *Journal of Counseling Psychology, 42*, 11–19.

Coyne, J.C., & DeLongis, A. (1986). Going beyond social support: The role of social relationships in adaptation. *Journal of Consulting and Clinical Psychology, 54*, 454–460.

Csikszentmihalyi, M. (1990). *Flow: The psychology of optimal experience*. New York: Harper & Row.

Culbertson, F.M. (1997). Depression and Gender: An international review. *American Psychologist, 52*, 25–31.

D'Andrea, M. (1988). The counselor as pacer: A model for revitalization of the counseling profession. In R. Hayes & R. Aubrey (Eds.), *New directions for counseling and human development* (pp. 22–44). Denver: Love.

Danish, S.J. (1981). Life span development and intervention: A necessary link. *Counseling Psychologist, 9*, 40–44.

Davis, K.L. (1996). Division 17 Presidential Address: Defining questions, charting possibilities. *Counseling Psychologist, 24*, 144–160.

Deffenbacher, J.L. (1992). Counseling for anxiety management. In S.D. Brown & R.W. Lent (Eds.), *Handbook of counseling psychology*. New York: Wiley.

DeHeer, N.D., Wampold, B.E., & Freund, R.D. (1992). Do sex-typed and androgynous subjects prefer counselors on the basis of gender of effectiveness? They prefer the best. *Journal of Counseling Psychology, 39*, 175–184.

Denmark, F.I. (1994). Engendering psychology. *American Psychologist, 49,* 329–334.

Deutch, C.J. (1984). Self-reporting sources of stress among psychotherapists. *Professional Psychology: Research and Practice, 15*(6), 833–845.

Deutch, C.J. (1985). A survey of therapists personal problems and treatment. *Professional Psychology: Research and Practice, 16,* 305–316.

Dewey, J. (1916). *Education and democracy.* New York: Macmillan.

Diener, E. (1984). Subjective well-being. *Psychological Bulletin, 95,* 542–575.

Dobson, K. (Ed.). (1988). *Handbook of cognitive behavioral therapies* (pp. ix–xi). New York: Guilford Press.

Dollard, J., & Miller, N. (1950). *Personality and psychotherapy.* New York: McGraw-Hill.

Duan, C., & Hill, C.E. (1996). The current status of empathy research. *Journal of Counseling Psychology, 43*(3), 261–274.

Duckett, J. (1992). Psychology and prejudice: A historical analysis and integrative framework. *American Psychologist, 47,* 1182–1193.

Dunkle, J.H., & Friedlander, M.L. (1996). Contributions of therapist experience and personal characteristics to the working alliance. *Journal of Counseling Psychology, 43*(4), 456–460.

Dymond, R.F. (1950). Personality and empathy. *Journal of Consulting and Clinical Psychology, 14,* 343–350.

D'Zurilla, T., & Goldfried, M.N. (1971). Problem solving and behavior modification. *Journal of Abnormal Psychology, 78,* 107–126.

Eagly, A.H. (1995). The science and politics of comparing women and men. *American Psychologist, 50,* 145–158.

Eccles, J.S., Midgley, C., Wigfield, A., Buchanan, C.M., Reuman, D., Flanagan, C., & MacIver, D. (1993). Development during adolescence: The impact of stage-environment fit on young adolescents' experiences in school and in families. *American Psychologist, 48,* 90–101.

Elliott, T.R., & Marmarosh, C. (1995). Social-cognitive processes in behavioral health: Implications for counseling. *Counseling Psychologist, 23,* 666–681.

Elliott, T.R., Shapiro, D., Firth-Cozens, J., Stiles, W., Hardy, G., Llewelyn, S., & Margison, F. (1994). Comprehensive process analysis of insight events in cognitive-behavioral and psychodynamic-interpersonal psychotherapies. *Journal of Counseling Psychology, 41,* 449–463.

Elliott, T.R., Sherwin, E., Harkins, S.W., & Marmarosh, C. (1995). Self-appraised problem-solving and psychological distress. *Journal of Counseling Psychology, 42,* 105–115.

Emery, R.E., & Laumann-Billings, L. (1998). An overview of the nature causes and consequences of abusive family relationships: Toward differentiating maltreatment and violence. *American Psychologist, 53,* 121–135.

Emmelkamp, P.M.G. (1994). Behavior therapy with adults. In A.E. Bergin & S.L. Garfield (Eds.), *Handbook of psychotherapy and behavior change* (4th ed., pp. 379–427). New York: Wiley.

Enright, R., & Lapsely, O. (1980). Social role-taking: A review of the constructs, measurement and measurement procedures. *Review of Educational Research, 50,* 647–674.

Ericsson, K., & Charness, N. (1994). Expert performance. *American Psychologist, 49,* 725–747.

Erikson, E. (1950). *Childhood and society.* New York: Norton.

Erikson, E. (1963). *Childhood and society* (2nd ed.). New York: Norton.

Eskapa, R. (1992). Multimodal therapy. In W. Dryden (Ed.), *Integrative and eclectic therapy: A handbook.* Philadelphia: Open University Press.

Evans, D.R., Pellizzari, J.R., Culbert, B.J., & Metzen, M.E. (1993). Personality, marital and occupational factors associated with quality of life. *Journal of Clinical Psychology, 49,* 477–485.

Ewart, C.K. (1991). Social action theory for a public health psychology. *American Psychologist, 46,* 931–946.

Faith, M.S., Wong, F.Y., & Carpenter, K.M. (1995). Group sensitivity training: Update, meta-analysis and recommendations. *The Journal of Counseling Psychology, 42*(3), 259–265.

Farmer, H.S., Wardrop, J.L., Anderson, M.Z., & Risinger, R. (1995). Women's career choices: Focus on science, math and technology careers. *Journal of Counseling Psychology, 42,* 155–170.

Fassinger, R.E., & Richie, B.S. (1994). Being the best: Preliminary results from a national study of the achievement of prominent black and white women. *Journal of Counseling Psychology, 41,* 191–204.

Fassinger, R.E., & Schlossberg, N. (1992). Understanding the adult years: Perspectives and implications. In S.D. Brown & R.W. Lent (Eds.), *Handbook of counseling psychology* (2nd ed., pp. 217–250). New York: Wiley.

Feingold, A. (1988). Cognitive gender differences are disappearing. *American Psychologist, 43,* 96–102.

Fiske, S.F. (1993). Controlling other people: The impact of power on stereotyping. *American Psychologist, 48,* 621–628.

Fitzgerald, L.F., & Nutt, R. (1986). The Division 17 Principles concerning the counseling psychotherapy of women: Rationale and implementation. *Counseling Psychologist, 14,* 180–216.

Flanagan, J.C. (1978). A research approach to improving our quality of life. *American Psychologist, 33,* 138–147.

Folkman, S., & Lazarus, R.S. (1986). Coping processes and depressive symptoms. *Journal of Abnormal Psychology, 95,* 107–113.

Forsyth, D.R., & Leary, M.R. (1997). Achieving the goals of the scientist-practitioner model: The seven interfaces of social and counseling psychology. *Counseling Psychologist, 25,* 180–200.

Fowers, B.J., & Richardson, F.C. (1996). Why is multi-culturalism good? *American Psychologist, 51,* 609–621.

Frank, J.D. (1961). *Persuasion and healing.* Baltimore: Johns Hopkins University Press.

Frank, J.D. (1971). Therapeutic factors in psychotherapy. *American Journal of Psychotherapy, 25,* 350–361.

Frank, J.D. (1982). Therapeutic components shared by all therapies. In J.H. Harvey & M.M. Parks (Eds.), *Psychotherapy research and behavior change: The master lecture series* (Vol. 1, pp. 73–122). Washington, DC: American Psychological Association.

Friedman, H.S. (1991). *The self-healing personality.* New York: Henry Holt.

Friedman, H.S., Tucker, J., Schwartz, J.E., Tomlinson-Keasey, C., Martin, L.R., Wingard, D.L., & Criqui, M.H. (1995). Psychosocial and behavioral predictors of longevity. *American Psychologist, 50,* 69–78.

Fromm, E. (1941). *Escape from freedom.* New York: Farrar and Rinehart.

Garfield, S.L. (1995). *Psychotherapy: An eclectic-integrative approach* (2nd ed.). New York: Wiley.

Garfield, S.L., & Bergin, A.E. (1994). Introduction and historical overview. In A.E. Bergin & S.L. Garfield (Eds.), *Handbook of psychotherapy and behavior change* (pp. 3–18). New York: Wiley.

Garfield, S.L., & Kurtz, R. (1977). A study of eclectic views. *Journal of Consulting and Clinical Psychology, 45,* 78–83.

Garmezy, N. (1974). The study of children at risk for severe psychopathology. In E.J. Anthony & C. Koupernik (Eds.), *The child and his family: Children at psychiatric risk* (Vol. 3, pp. 77–97). New York: Wiley.

Garmezy, N. (1994). Reflections and commentary on risk, resilience and development. In R.J. Haggerty, L.R. Sherrod, & M. Rutter (Eds.), *Stress, risk and resilience in children and adolescents: Processes and mechanisms* (pp. 1–18). Cambridge, England: Cambridge University Press.

Gati, I., Houminer, D., & Aviram, T. (1998). Career compromises framings and their implications. *Journal of Counseling Psychology, 45,* 505–514.

Gati, I., Osipow, S.H., & Givon, M. (1995). Gender differences in career decision-making: The content and structure of preferences. *Journal of Counseling Psychology, 42,* 204–216.

Gazda, G.M. (1984). Multiple impact training: A life skills approach. In D. Larson (Ed.), *Teaching psychological skills.* Monterey, CA: Brooks/Cole.

Gelso, C.J., & Carter, J.A. (1994). Components of the psychotherapy relationship: Their interaction and unfolding during treatment. *Journal of Counseling Psychology, 41,* 296–306.

Gelso, C.J., & Fassinger, R.E. (1992). Personality development and counseling psychology: Depth, ambivalence and actualization. *Journal of Counseling Psychology, 39,* 275–298.

Gibson, J., & Brown, S.D. (1992). Counseling adults for life transition. In S.D. Brown & R.W. Lent (Eds.), *Handbook of counseling psychology* (2nd ed., pp. 285–314). New York: Wiley.

Gilligan, C. (1982). *In a different voice: Psychological theory and women's development.* Cambridge, MA: Harvard University Press.

Gladstein, G. (1983). Understanding empathy: Integrating counseling, developmental, and social psychology perspectives. *Journal of Counseling Psychology, 30*(4), 467–482.

Goldfried, M.R. (1980). Toward the delineation of therapeutic change principles. *American Psychologist, 35,* 991–999.

Goldin, C. (1990). *Understanding the gender gap: An economic history of American women.* New York: Oxford University Press.

Goleman, D. (1998). *Working with emotional intelligence.* New York: Bantam Books.

Good, G.E., Thoreson, R.W., & Shaughnessy, P. (1995). Substance abuse, confrontation of impaired colleagues and psychological functioning among counseling psychologists. *Counseling Psychologist, 23*(4), 703–721.

Gossett, T.F. (1963). *Race: The history of an idea in American.* Dallas, TX: Southern Methodist University Press.

Gould, R. (1978). *Transformations: Growth and change in adult life.* New York: Simon & Schuster.

Greenberg, L.S., Elliot, R.K., & Lietaer, G. (1994). Research on experiential therapies. In A.E. Bergin & S.L. Garfied (Eds.), *Handbook of psychotherapy and behavior change* (4th ed., pp. 509–539). New York: Wiley.

Hackett, G. (1995). Self-efficacy in career choices and development. In A. Bandura (Ed.), *Self-efficacy in adaptation of youth in changing societies* (pp. 232–258). Cambridge, England: Cambridge University Press.

Hackett, G. (1997). Promise and problems in theory and research on women's career development. *Journal of Counseling Psychology, 44,* 184–188.

Hall, C.C.I. (1997). Cultural malpractice: The growing obsolescence of psychology with the changing U.S. population. *American Psychologist, 52,* 642–651.

Halleck, S.L. (1963). The impact of professional dishonesty on behavior of disturbed adolescents. *Social Work, 8,* 48–56.

Halpern, D.F. (1997). Sex differences in intelligence: Implications for education. *American Psychologist, 52,* 1091–1102.

Hamrin, S., & Erickson, C. (1939). *Guidance in the secondary school.* New York: Appleton-Century-Crofts.

Hare-Mustin, R.T. (1983). An appraisal of the relationship between women and psychotherapy: 80 years after the case of Dora. *American Psychologist, 38,* 593–601.

Hare-Mustin, R.T., & Marecek, J. (1988). The meaning of difference. *American Psychologist, 43,* 455–464.

Hartmann, H. (1939). *Ego psychology and the problem of adaptation.* New York: International Universities Press.

Hartup, W. (1989). Social relationships and their developmental significance. *American Psychologist, 44,* 120–126.

Harvey, O.J., Hunt, D.E., & Schroder, H.M. (1961). *Conceptual systems and personality organization.* New York: Wiley.

Havighurst, R. (1953). *Human development and education.* London: Longmans, Green.

Havighurst, R. (1972). *Developmental tasks and education* (3rd ed.). New York: David McKay.

Heath, D.H. (1994). *Schools of hope.* San Francisco: Jossey-Bass.

Helms, J.E. (1997). Implications of Behrens (1997) for the validity of the White Racial Identity Attitude Scale. *Journal of Counseling Psychology, 44,* 13–16.

Heppner, M.J., Multon, K.D., Gysbers, N.C., Ellis, C.A., & Zook, C.E. (1998). The relationship of trainee self-efficacy to the process and outcome of career counseling. *Journal of Counseling Psychology, 45,* 393–402.

Heppner, P.P., & Claiborn, C.D. (1989). Social influence research in counseling: A review and critique. *Journal of Counseling Psychology, 36,* 365–387.

Heppner, P.P., Cook, S.W., Wright, D.M., & Johnson, C.W., Jr. (1995). Progress in resolving problems: A problem-focused style of coping. *Journal of Counseling Psychology, 42*, 279–293.

Heppner, P.P., & Krauskopf, C.J. (1987). An information-processing approach to personal problem solving. *Counseling Psychologist, 15*, 371–447.

Hermans, J.M., & Kempen, H.J.G. (1998). Moving cultures: The perilous problems of cultural dichotomies in a globalizing society. *American Psychologist, 53*, 1111–1120.

Hersch, C. (1968). The discontent explosion in mental health. *American Psychologist, 23*, 497–506.

Hetherington, E.M., Bridges, M., & Insabella, R. (1998). What matters? What does not? Five perspectives on the association between marital transitions and children's adjustment. *American Psychologist, 53*, 167–184.

Hill, C.E. (1994). What is the therapeutic relationship? A reply to Sexton and Whiston. *Counseling Psychologist, 22*, 90–97.

Ho, D.Y.F. (1995). Internalized culture, culturocentrism and transcendence. *Counseling Psychologist, 23*, 4–24.

Hobbs, N. (1962). Sources of gain in psychotherapy. *American Psychologist, 17*, 741–747.

Hobfoll, S. (1989). Conservation of resources: A new attempt at conceptualizing stress. *American Psychologist, 44*, 513–524.

Holland, J.L. (1992). *Making vocational choices: A theory of vocational personalities and work environments* (2nd ed.). Odessa, FL: Psychological Assessment Resources.

Holland, J.L. (1996). Exploring careers with a typology. *American Psychologist, 51*, 397–406.

Holland, J.L., Magoon, R.M., & Spokane, A.R. (1981). Counseling psychology: Career interventions, research and theory. *Annual Review of Psychology, 32*, 279–305.

Hollin, C.R., & Trower, P. (1986). Social skills training: A retrospective analysis and summary of applications. In C.R. Hollin & P. Trower (Eds.), *Handbook of social skills training* (Vol. 1, pp. 1–10). Oxford, England: Pergamon Press.

Hollingsworth, L. (1927). Leta Stetter Hollingsworth: Literature of opinion and the study of individual differences. In G.A. Kimble, M. Wertheimer, & C. White (Eds.). [Quoted in Shields, S.A. (1991)] *Portraits of pioneers in psychology.* Washington, DC: American Psychological Association.

Hollon, S.D., & Beck, A.T. (1994). Cognitive and cognitive-behavioral therapies. In A.E. Bergin & S.L. Garfield (Eds.), *Handbook of psychotherapy and behavior change* (4th ed., pp. 428–466). New York: Wiley.

Holloway, E.L., & Wampold, B.E. (1986). Relation between conceptual level and counseling related tasks: A met-analysis. *Journal of Counseling Psychology, 33*(3), 310–319.

Holt, R.R. (1967). *Loevinger's measure of ego development: Reliability and national norms for short male and female forms.* Unpublished manuscript, New York University.

Horney, K. (1950). *Neurosis and human growth.* New York: Norton.

Humphries, K. (1996). Clinical psychologists as psychotherapists. *American Psychologist, 51*, 190–197.

Hunt, J.M. (1961). *Intelligence and experience.* New York: Ronald Press.

Hurst, J. (1989). Division 17 presidential address. *Counseling Psychologist, 17,* 157–162.

Hyde, J.S., & Plant, E.A. (1995). Magnitude of psychological gender differences. *American Psychologist, 50,* 159–161.

Iscoe, I. (1974). Community psychology and the competent community. *American Psychologist, 29,* 611–613.

Jacklyn, C.N. (1989). Female and male: Issues of gender. *American Psychologist, 44,* 127–133.

Jahoda, M. (1958). *Current concepts of positive mental health.* New York: Basic Books.

Jennings, L., & Skovalt, T.M. (1999). The cognitive, emotional and relational characteristics of master therapists. *Journal of Counseling Psychology, 46,* 3–11.

Jessor, R. (1993). Successful adolescent development among youth in high risk settings. *American Psychologist, 48,* 117–126.

Johnson, S.D. (1987). Knowing that versus knowing how: Toward achieving expertise through multi-cultural training for counseling. *Counseling Psychologist, 15,* 320–331.

Jung, C. (1933). *Modern man in search of a soul.* New York: Harcourt Brace.

Kaczmarek, P.G., & Riva, M.T. (1996). Facilitating adolescent development: Training considerations for counseling psychologists. *Counseling Psychologist, 24,* 400–432.

Kagan, N., Armsworth, M.W., Altmaier, E.M., Dowd, E.T., Hansen, J.C., Milk, D.H., Schlossberg, N., Sprinthall, N.A., Tanney, M.F., & Vasquez, M.J.T. (1988). Professional practice of counseling psychology in various settings. *Counseling Psychologist, 16,* 347–365.

Kagan, N., Kagan-Klein, H., & Watson, M.G. (1995). Stress reduction in the workplace: The effectiveness of psychoeducational programs. *Journal of Counseling Psychology, 42,* 71–78.

Karasu, T.B. (1986). The specificity vs. non-specificity dilemma: Toward identifying therapeutic change agents. *American Journal of Psychiatry, 143,* 687–695.

Kazdin, A.E. (1979). Advances in child behavior theory. *American Psychologist, 34,* 981–987.

Kazdin, A.E. (1993). Adolescent mental health: Prevention and treatment programs. *American Psychologist, 48,* 127–141.

Kazdin, A.E. (1994). Psychotherapy for children and adolescents. In A.E. Bergin & S.L. Garfield (Eds.), *Handbook of psychotherapy and behavior change* (4th ed., pp. 543–594). New York: Wiley.

Kazdin, A.E., Esveld-Dawson, S., French, N.H., & Unis, A.S. (1987). Problem-solving skills training and relationship therapy in the treatment of antisocial child behavior. *Journal of Consulting and Clinical Psychology, 55,* 76–85.

Kegan, N. (1980). Making meaning: The constructive-developmental approach to persons and practice. *The Personnel and Guidance Journal, 58,* 373–380.

Kelly, J.G. (1955). *A theory of personality: The psychology of personal constructs.* New York: Norton.

Kelly, J.G. (1963). *A theory of personality: The psychology of personal constructs.* New York: Norton.

Kelly, J.G. (1966). Ecological constraints on mental health services. *American Psychologist, 21,* 535–539.

Kelly, T. (1916). *Educational guidance.* New York: Teachers College.

Kerr, M.E., & Bowen, M. (1988). *Family evaluation.* New York: Norton.

Kingsburg, N., & Scanzoni, J. (1993). Structural-functionalism. In P.G. Boss, W.J. Doherty, R. LaRossa, W.R. Schumm, & S.K. Steinmetz (Eds.), *Sourcebook of family theories and methods* (pp. 195–217). New York: Plenum Press.

Kipnis, D. (1997). Ghosts, taxonomies and social psychology. *American Psychologist, 52,* 205–211.

Kiselica, M.S., Baker, S.B., Thomas, R.N., & Reedy, S. (1994). Effects of stress inoculation training on anxiety, stress and academic performance among adolescents. *Journal of Counseling Psychology, 41,* 335–342.

Klein, M. (1932). *The psychoanalysis of children.* London: Hogarth Press.

Kobasa, S.C. (1979). Stressful life events, personality and health: An inquiry into hardiness. *Journal of Personality and Social Psychology, 37,* 1–11.

Kohlberg, L. (1969). *Stages in the development of moral thought and action.* New York: Holt, Rinehart and Winston.

Kohlberg, L. (1984). *The psychology of moral development: The nature and validity of moral stages.* San Francisco: Harper & Row.

Kohut, H. (1977). *The restoration of the self.* New York: International Universities Press.

Koreleski, S.F., & Larson, L.M. (1997). A partial test of the transtheoretical model with adult survivors of childhood sexual abuse. *Journal of Counseling Psychology, 41,* 302–315.

Koss, M.P., & Schiang, J. (1994). Research on brief psychotherapy. In A.E. Bergin & S.L. Garfield (Eds.), *Handbook of psychotherapy and behavior change* (4th ed., pp. 664–700). New York: Wiley.

Krumboltz, J.D. (1996). A social learning theory of career-decision-making. In M.L. Savickas & W.B. Walsh (Eds.), *Handbook of career counseling theory and practice* (pp. 55–80). Palo Alto, CA: Davies-Black.

Krumboltz, J.D. (1998). Serendipity is not serendipitous. *Journal of Counseling Psychology, 45,* 390–392.

Lachman, M.E., & James, J.B. (1997). Charting the course of mid-life development: An overview. In M.E. Lachman & J.B. James (Eds.), *Multiple paths of mid-life development* (pp. 1–17). Chicago: University of Chicago Press.

Ladany, N., Hill, C.E., Corbett, M., & Nutt, E. (1996). Nature, extent and importance of what psychotherapy trainees do not disclose to their supervisors. *Journal of Counseling Psychology, 43*(1), 10–14.

Lafferty, P., Beutler, L., & Crago, M. (1989). Differences between more and less effective psychotherapists: A study of select therapist variables. *Journal of Consulting and Clinical Psychology, 57*(1), 71–80.

Lambert, M.J., & Bergin, A.E. (1994). The effectiveness of psychotherapy. In A.E. Bergin & S.L. Garfield (Eds.), *Handbook of psychotherapy and behavior change* (4th ed., pp. 143–189). New York: Wiley.

Lambert, M.J., & Hill, C.E. (1994). Assessing psychotherapy outcomes and processes. In A.E. Bergin & S.L. Garfield (Eds.), *Handbook of psychotherapy and behavior change* (4th ed., pp. 19–71). New York: Wiley.

Lambert, M.J., Shapiro, D.A., & Bergin, A.E. (1986). The effectiveness of psychotherapy. In S.L. Garfield & A.E. Bergin (Eds.), *Handbook of psychotherapy and behavior change* (4th ed., pp. 157–212). New York: Wiley.

Larson, L. (1998). The social cognitive model of counselor training. *Counseling Psychologist, 26*, 219–273.

Lazarus, A.A. (1976). *Multimodal behavior therapy.* New York: Springer.

Lazarus, A.A. (1994). How certain boundaries and ethics diminish therapeutic effectiveness. *Ethics and Behavior, 4*(3), 255–261.

Lazarus, A.A. (1995). Multimodal therapy. In R. Corsini & D. Wedding (Eds.), *Current Psychotherapies* (5th ed., pp. 322–355). Itasca, IL: Peacock.

Lazarus, R.A. (1966). *Psychological stress and the coping process.* New York: McGraw-Hill.

Lazarus, R.S., & Folkman, S. (1984). *Stress, appraisal and coping.* New York: Springer.

Leaf, P.J., & Bruce, W.L. (1987). Gender differences on the use of mental health related services. *Journal of Health and Social Behavior, 28*, 171–183.

Lehman, S. (1971). Community and community psychology. *American Psychologist, 26*, 544–560.

Lemle, R., & Miskind, M.E. (1989). Alcohol and masculinity. *Journal of Substance Abuse Treatment, 6*, 213–222.

Lent, R.W., Brown, S.D., & Larkin, K.C. (1986). Self-efficacy in the prediction of academic performance and perceived career options. *Journal of Counseling Psychology, 33*, 265–269.

Lent, R.W., Brown, S.D., & Larkin, K.C. (1987). Comparison of three theoretically derived variables in predicting career and academic behavior: Self-efficacy, interest congruence and consequence thinking. *Journal of Counseling Psychology, 34*, 293–298.

Levi, L. (1990). Occupational stress: Spice of life or kiss of death. *American Psychologist, 45*, 1142–1145.

Levinson, D. (with Danow, C., Klein, E., Levinson, M., & McKee, B.). (1978). *The seasons of a man's life.* New York: Ballantine Books.

Levinson, D. (1986). A conception of adult development. *American Psychologist, 41*, 3–13.

Lewin, K. (n.d.). *The practical theorist: The life and work of Kurt Lewin.* [Quoted in Marrow, A.J. (1969)] New York: Basic Books.

Lightsey, O.R. (1994). "Thinking positive" as a stress buffer: The role of positive automatic cognitions in depression and happiness. *Journal of Counseling Psychology, 41*, 325–334.

Lightsey, O.R. (1996). What leads to wellness? The role of psychological resources in well-being. *Counseling Psychologist, 24*, 589–735.

Link, A.S., & Catton, W.B. (1963). *American epoch: A history of the United States since the 1980s* (Vol. 1). New York: Knopf.

Linton, R. (1943). *The science of man in world crisis.* New York: Columbia University Press.

Loevinger, J. (1976). *Ego development.* San Francisco: Jossey-Bass.

Loganbill, C., Hardy, E., & Delworth, U. (1982). Supervision: A conceptual model. *Counseling Psychologist, 10*(1), 3–42.

London, P. (1986). *The modes and morals of psychotherapy.* New York: Holt, Rinehart and Winston.

London, P. (1988). Metamorphosis in psychotherapy: Slouching toward integration. *Journal Integrative and Eclectic Therapy, 7,* 3–12.

Long, B.C., & Schutz, R.W. (1995). Temporal stability and replicability of a workplace stress and coping model for managerial women: A multiwave panel study. *Journal of Counseling Psychology, 42,* 266–278.

Lopez, F.G. (1992). Family dynamics and late adolescent identity development. In S.D. Brown & R.W. Lent (Eds.), *Handbook of counseling psychology* (2nd ed., pp. 251–284). New York: Wiley.

Lopez, F.G. (1995). Contemporary attachment theory: An introduction with implications for counseling psychology. *Counseling Psychologist, 23,* 395–415.

Lowenthal, M.F., Thurnher, M., & Chiriboga, D. (1975). *Four stages of life.* San Francisco: Jossey-Bass.

Lutwak, N., & Hennessy, J. (1982). Conceptual systems functioning as a mediating factor in the development of counseling skills. *Journal of Counseling Psychology, 29,* 265–260.

Lykken, D., & Tellegen, A. (1996). Happiness is a stochastic phenomenon. *Psychological Science, 7,* 186–189.

Maccoby, E.E. (1990). Gender and relationships: A developmental account. *American Psychologist, 45,* 513–520.

Maccoby, E.E., & Jacklyn, C.N. (1974). *The psychology of sex differences.* Palo Alto, CA: Stanford University Press.

Mahalik, J.R. (1990). Systematic eclectic models. *Counseling Psychologist, 18,* 655–679.

Mahoney, M., & Lyddon, W.J. (1988). Recent developments in cognitive approaches to counseling and psychotherapy. *Counseling Psychologist, 16,* 190–234.

Mallinckrodt, B., & Bennett, J. (1992). Social support and impact of job loss in dislocated blue-collar workers. *Journal of Counseling Psychology, 39,* 482–489.

Marcia, J.E. (1980). Identity in adolescence. In J. Adelson (Ed.), *Handbook of adolescent psychology* (pp. 159–187). New York: Wiley.

Maslow, A. (1968). *Toward a psychology of being* (2nd ed.). Princeton, NJ: Van Nostrand.

Maslow, A. (1970). *Motivation and personality* (2nd ed.). New York: Harper & Row.

Masten, A.S., & Coatsworth, J.D. (1998). The development of competence in favorable and unfavorable environments: Lessons from research on successful children. *American Psychologist, 53,* 205–220.

Masterpasqua, F. (1989). A competence paradigm for psychological practice. *American Psychologist, 44,* 1366–1371.

Matheny, K.B. (1988). Stress management. In R. Hayes & R. Aubrey (Eds.), *New directions for counseling and development* (pp. 418–445). Denver, CO: Love.

Matheny, K.B., Aycock, D.W., Pugh, J.L., Curlette, W.L., & Silva Canella, K.A. (1986). Stress coping: A qualitative and quantitative syntheses with implications for treatment. *Counseling Psychologist, 14,* 499–549.

McCloyd, V.C. (1998). Socioeconomic disadvantage and child development. *American Psychologist, 53*, 185–204.

McCreary, D.R., Newcomb, M.D., & Sadava, S.W. (1999). The male role, alcohol use, and alcohol problems: A structural modeling examination in adult women and men. *Journal of Counseling Psychology, 46*, 109–124.

Meara, N.M., Schmidt, L.D., & Day, J.D. (1996). Principles and virtues: A foundation for ethical decisions, policies and character. *Counseling Psychologist, 24*, 4–77.

Miller, C. (1961). *Foundations of guidance.* New York: Harper & Row.

Mischel, W. (1984). Convergences and challenges in the search for consistency. *American Psychologist, 39*, 351–364.

Monahan, J. (1993). Limiting therapist exposure to *Tarasoff* liability. *American Psychologist, 48*(3), 242–250.

Moore, M.A., & Neimeyer, G.J. (1992). Using occupational information to increase vocational differentiation. *Journal of Career Development, 19*, 3–12.

Mosher, R. (1979). Introduction. In R Mosher (Ed.), *Adolescent's development and education.* Berkeley, CA: McCutchan.

Murphy, G. (1973). Work and the productive personality. In H. Borow (Ed.), *Career guidance for a new age* (pp. 151–176). Boston: Houghton Mufflin.

Muuss, R.E. (1968). *Theories of adolescence.* New York: Random House.

Myers, D.G., & Diener, E. (1995). Who is happy? *Psychological Science, 6*, 10–19.

Myers, R.A., & Cairo, P.C. (1992). Counseling and career adjustment. In S.D. Brown & R.W. Lent (Eds.), *Handbook of counseling psychology* (2nd ed., pp. 549–580). New York: Wiley.

National Advisory Mental Health Council. (1996). Basic behavioral science research for mental health: Vulnerability and resilience. *American Psychologist, 51*, 22–28.

National Institute for Occupational Safety and Health. (1988). *Prevention of occupationally-generated illnesses: A proposed synoptic national strategy to reduce neurotoxic disorders in the U.S. workplace.* In proposed national strategies for the prevention of leading work-related diseases and injuries. (Pt. 2, NTIS No. P 1389–130348, pp. 31–50). Washington, DC: Author.

Neimeyer, G.J. (1988). Cognitive integration and differentiation in vocational behavior. *Counseling Psychologist, 16*, 440–475.

Neimeyer, G.J., Metzler, A.E., & Bowman, R. (1988). Effects of sex, career orientation and occupational type on vocational integration differentiation and conflict. *Journal of Counseling Psychology, 35*, 139–143.

Nelson, M.L. (1993). A current perspective on gender differences: Implications for research in counseling. *Journal of Counseling Psychology, 40*, 200–209.

Neufeldt, S., Karno, M., & Nelson, M. (1996). A qualitative study of expert's conceptualization of supervisee reflectivity. *Journal of Counseling Psychology, 43*(1), 3–9.

Neugarten, B. (1979). Time, age and the life cycle. *American Journal of Psychiatry, 36*, 887–898.

Newcomb, M.D. (1996). Adolescence: Pathologizing a normal process. *Counseling Psychologist, 24*, 482–490.

Nezu, A.M., & Perri, M.G. (1989). Social problem-solving therapy for unpolar depression: An initial dismantling investigation. *Journal of Consulting and Clinical Psychology, 57*, 408–413.

Nichols, M.P., & Schwartz, R.C. (1998). *Family therapy: Concepts and methods* (4th ed.). Boston: Allyn & Bacon.

Norcross, J.C., & Arkowitz, H. (1992). The evolution and current status of psychotherapy integration. In W. Dryden (Ed.), *Integrative and eclectic therapy: A handbook* (pp. 1–40). Philadelphia: Open University Press.

Norcross, J.C., & Newman, C.F. (1992). Psychotherapy integration: Setting the context. In J. Norcross & M.R. Goldfried (Eds.), *Handbook of psychotherapy integration* (pp. 3–45). New York: Basic Books.

Norcross, J.C., Prochaska, J.O., & Farber, J.A. (1993). Psychologists conducting psychotherapy: New findings and historical comparisons on the psychotherapy division membership. *Psychotherapy, 30*, 692–697.

Nutt-Williams, E., & Hill, C.E. (1997). The relationship between self-talk and therapy process variables for novice therapists. *Journal of Counseling Psychology, 43*(2), 170–177.

Nutt-Williams, E., Soeprapto, K.L., Tourodji, P., Hess, S., & Hill, C.E. (1998). Perceptions of serendipity: Career paths of prominent academic women in counseling psychology. *Journal of Counseling Psychology, 45*, 370–389.

O'Brien, K.M., & Fassinger, R.E. (1993). A casual model of the career orientation and career choice of adolescent women. *Journal of Counseling Psychology, 40*, 456–469.

Okun, B.F. (1984). *Working with adults: Individual family and career development.* Monterey, CA: Brooks/Cole.

Okun, B.F. (1990). *Seeking connections in psychotherapy.* San Francisco: Jossey-Bass.

Oliver, L.W., & Spokane, A.R. (1988). Career intervention outcome: What contributes to client gain? *Journal of Counseling Psychology, 35*, 447–462.

Olson, D.H. (1970). Marital and family therapy: Integrative review and critique. *Journal of Marriage and the Family, 32*, 501–538.

O'Neil, J.M. (1981). Patterns of gender role conflict and strain: Sexism and fear of femininity in men's lives. *Personnel and Guidance Journal, 10*, 203–210.

Orlinsky, D.E., Grawe, K., & Parks, B.K. (1994). Process and outcome in psychotherapy. In A.E. Bergin & S.L. Garfield (Eds.), *Handbook of psychotherapy and behavior change* (4th ed., pp. 270–376). New York: Wiley.

Parker, R.A., & Aldwin, C.M. (1997). Do aspects of gender identity change from early to middle adulthood? Disentangling age, cohort and period effects. In M.E. Lachman & J.B. James (Eds.). *Multiple paths of mid-life development* (pp 67–107). Chicago: University of Chicago Press.

Parr, J., & Neimeyer, G.J. (1994). Effects of gender construct type, occupational information and career relevance on vocational differentiation. *Journal of Counseling Psychology, 42*, 27–33.

Parsons, F. (1909). *Choosing a vocation.* Boston: Houghton Mufflin.

Patton, M.J., & Kivlighan, D.M., Jr. (1997). Relevance of the supervisory alliance to the counseling alliance and to treatment adherence in counseling training. *Journal of Counseling Psychology, 44*(1), 108–114.

Pederson, P. (1991). Multiculturalism as a generic approach to counseling. *Journal of Counseling and Development, 70,* 6–12.

Perry, W.D., Jr. (1970). *Intellectual and ethical development in the college years.* New York: Holt, Rinehart and Winston.

Pervin, L.A. (1968). Performance and satisfaction as a function of individual-environment fit. *Psychological Bulletin, 69,* 56–68.

Phares, V. (1992). Where's Poppa? The relative lack of attention to the role of father in child and adolescent psychopathology. *American Psychologist, 47,* 656–664.

Phares, V., & Compas, B.E. (1992). The role of fathers in child and adolescent psychopathology: Make room for daddy. *Psychological Bulletin, 111,* 387–412.

Phillips, S.D. (1982). The development of career choices: The relationship between patterns of commitment and career outcomes in adulthood. *Journal of Vocational Behavior, 20,* 141–152.

Phillips, S.D. (1992). Career counseling: Choice and implementation. In S.D. Brown & R.W. Lent (Eds.), *Handbook of counseling psychology* (2nd ed., pp. 513–548). New York: Wiley.

Phinney, J.S. (1996). When we talk about American ethnic groups what do we mean? *American Psychologist, 51,* 918–927.

Piaget, J. (1929). *The child's conception of the world.* New York: Harcourt Brace.

Pope, K.S., & Vasquez, M. (1991). *Ethics in psychotherapy and counseling.* San Francisco: Jossey-Bass.

Pope, K.S., & Vetter, V.A. (1992). Ethical dilemmas encountered by members of the American Psychological Association. *American Psychologist, 47*(3), 397–411.

Pope-Davis, D.B., Vandiver, B.J., & Stone, G.L. (1999). White identity attitude development: A psychometric examination of two instruments. *Journal of Counseling Psychology, 46,* 70–79.

Powers, S.I., Hauser, S.T., & Kilner, L.A. (1989). Adolescent mental health. *American Psychologist, 44*(2), 200–208.

Poznanski, J.J., & McLennan, J. (1995). Conceptualizing and measuring counselors' theoretical orientation. *Journal of Counseling Psychology, 42,* 411–422.

Prochaska, J.O., & DiClemente, C.C. (1984). *The transtheoretical approach: Crossing the traditional boundaries of therapy.* Homewood, IL: Dow Jones-Irwin.

Prochaska, J.O., DiClemente, C.C., & Norcross, J.C. (1992). In search of how people change. *American Psychologist, 47,* 1102–1114.

Prugh, D.J. (1973). Criteria for psychosocial functioning of children in Joint Commission on Mental Health for Children (Eds.). *The mental health of children* (pp. 363–373). New York: Harper & Row.

Ramey, C.T., & Ramey, S. (1998). Early intervention and early experience. *American Psychologist, 53,* 109–120.

Rapoza, R.S., & Blocher, D.H. (1976). The Cinderella effect: Planning avoidance in girls. *Counseling and Values, 28,* 12–18.

Rest, J.R., & Narvaez, D.F. (Eds.). (1994). *Moral development in the professions: Psychology and applied ethics.* Hillsdale, NJ: Erlbaum.

Reynolds, S., & Gilbert, P. (1991). Psychological impact of unemployment: Interactive effects of vulnerability and protective factors on depression. *Journal of Counseling Psychology, 38,* 76–84.

Richardson, M.S. (1993). Work in people's lives: A location for counseling psychologists. *Journal of Counseling Psychology, 40,* 425–433.

Richie, B.S., Fassinger, R.E., Linn, S.G., Johnson, J., Prosser, J., & Robinson, S. (1997). Persistence, connection and passion: A qualitative study of the career development of highly achieving African American black and white women. *Journal of Counseling Psychology, 44,* 133–148.

Ridley, C.R., Mendoza, D.W., Kanitz, B.E., Angermeier, L., & Zank, R. (1994). Cultural sensitivity in multi-cultural counseling: A perceptual schema model. *Journal of Counseling Psychology, 41,* 125–136.

Roberts, J.M., & Fitzgerald, L.F. (1992). Overcoming the masculine mystique: Preferences for alternative forms of assistance among men who avoid counseling. *Journal of Counseling Psychology, 39,* 240–246.

Rodgers, R.F. (1984). Theories of adult development: Research status and counseling implications. In S.D. Brown & R.W. Lent (Eds.), *Handbook of counseling psychology* (pp. 479–519). New York: Wiley.

Rogers, C.R. (1951). *Client centered therapy.* Boston: Houghton Mifflin.

Rogers, C.R. (1957). The necessary and sufficient conditions of therapeutic and personality change. *Journal of Consulting Psychology, 21,* 95–103.

Rogers, C.R. (1961). *On becoming a person.* Boston: Houghton Mifflin.

Rogers, C.R. (1962). The interpersonal relationships: The core of guidance. In R. Mosher, R. Carle, & C. Kehas (Eds.), *Guidance an examination* (pp. 50–65). Boston: Harcourt Brace.

Rogers, C.R. (1964). Toward a modern approach to valuing in the mature person. *Abnormal and Social Psychology, 68,* 160–167.

Rubenstein, A.K., & Zager, K. (1995). Training in adolescent treatment: Where is the psychology? *Psychotherapy, 32,* 2–6.

Ryff, C.D. (1989). Happiness is everything, or is it? Explorations on the meaning of psychological well-being. *Journal of Personality and Social Psychology, 57,* 1069–1087.

Satir, V. (1988). *The new peoplemaking.* Mountain View, CA: Science and Behavior Books.

Satterfield, W.A., Buelow, S.A., Lyddon, W.J., & Johnson, J.F. (1995). Client stages of change and expectations about counseling. *Journal of Counseling Psychology, 42,* 476–478.

Sauter, S.L., Murphy, L.R., Hurrell, J.J., Jr. (1990). Prevention of work-related psychological disorders. *American Psychologist, 45,* 1146–1158.

Scarr, S. (1993). Genes, experience and development. In D. Magnusson (Ed.), *Longitudinal research on individual development* (pp. 26–50). London: Cambridge University Press.

Scarr, S. (1998). American child care today. *American Psychologist, 53,* 95–108.

Schlossberg, N.K. (1981). A model for analyzing human adaptation to transition. *Counseling Psychologist, 9,* 2–18.

Schlossberg, N.K. (1989). *Overwhelmed: Coping with life's ups and downs.* Lexington, MA: Lexington Books.

Schneider, B. (1987). E=F (P,B): The road to a radical approach to person-environment fit. *Journal of Vocational Behavior, 26* 306–343.

Schulz, R., & Heckhausen, J. (1996). A life span model of successful aging. *American Psychologist, 51,* 702–714.

Seeman, J. (1989). Toward a model of positive health. *American Psychologist, 44,* 1099–1109.

Segall, M.H., Lonner, W.J., & Berry, J.W. (1998). Cross-cultural psychology as a scholarly discipline: On the flowering of culture in behavioral research. *American Psychologist, 53,* 1101–1110.

Sexton, T.L., & Whiston, S.C. (1994). The status of the counseling relationship: An empirical review, theoretical implications and research directions. *Counseling Psychologist, 22,* 6–78.

Shaffer, L.F., & Shoben, E.J. (1956). *The psychology of adjustment.* Boston: Houghton Mifflin.

Shoben, E.J. (1957). Toward a concept of the normal personality. *American Psychologist, 12,* 183–190.

Shoben, E.J. (1962). Guidance: Remedial function or social reconstruction. In R. Mosher, R. Carle, & C. Kehas (Eds.), *Guidance: An examination* (pp. 110–126). New York: Harcourt Brace.

Siegler, R.S., & Crowley, K. (1991). The microgenetic method: A direct means for studying cognitive development. *American Psychologist, 46,* 606–620.

Skovalt, T.M., & Ronnestad, M.H. (1992). *The evolving professional self: Stages and themes in therapist and counselor development.* Chichester, England: Wiley.

Smith, K.J., Subich, L.M., & Kalodner, C. (1995). The transtheoretical model's stages and processes of change and their relation to premature termination. *Journal of Counseling Psychology, 42,* 34–39.

Solberg, V.S., Good, G.E., Fischer, A.R., Brown, S.D., & Nord, D. (1995). Career decision-making and career search activities: Relative effects of career search self-efficacy and human agency. *Journal of Counseling Psychology, 42,* 448–458.

Spengler, P.M., & Strohmer, D. (1994). Clinical judgmental biases. The moderating roles of counselor cognitive complexity and counselor client preferences. *Journal of Counseling Psychology, 41*(1), 8–17.

Spengler, P.M., Strohmer, D., Dixon, D., & Shivy, V. (1995). A scientist-practitioner model of psychological assessment: Implications for training practice and research. *Counseling Psychologist, 23,* 506–534.

Sprinthall, N., & Mosher, R. (1970). Psychological education in secondary schools: A program to promote individual and human development. *American Psychologist, 25,* 911–924.

Stern, M., & Newland, L.M. (1994). Working with children: Providing a framework for the roles of counseling psychologists. *Counseling Psychologist, 22,* 402–425.

Stewart, A.J., & Ostrove, J.M. (1998). Women's personality in middle-age: Gender, history and mid-course correction. *American Psychology, 53,* 1185–1194.

Stoltenberg, C.D., McNeill, B., & Crethar, H. (1995). Persuasion and development in counselor supervision. *Counseling Psychologist, 23*(4), 633–648.

Strong, S.R., & Claiborn, C. (1982). *Change through interaction: Social psychological processes of counseling and psychotherapy.* New York: Pergamon Press.

Strong, S.R. (1997). Enhancing the social-counseling interface. *Counseling Psychologist, 25,* 274–279.

Strong, S.R., Welsh, J.A., Corcoran, J.L., & Hoyt, W.T. (1992). Social psychology and counseling psychology: The history, products and promise of an interface. *Journal of Counseling Psychology, 39,* 139–157.

Sue, S. (1998). In search of cultural competence in psychotherapy and counseling. *American Psychologist, 53,* 440–448.

Sugarman, J., & Martin, J. (1995). The moral dimension: A conceptualization and empirical demonstration of the moral nature of psychotherapeutic conversations. *Counseling Psychologist, 23*(2), 324–347.

Suinn, R.M. (1979). Behavior pathology. In M. Meur (Ed.), *Foundations of contemporary psychology* (pp. 651–679). New York: Oxford University Press.

Suinn, R.M., & Deffenbacher, J.L. (1988). Anxiety management training. *Counseling Psychologist, 16,* 31–49.

Sullivan, H.S. (1953). *The interpersonal theory of psychiatry.* New York: Norton.

Super, D.E. (1957). *The psychology of careers.* New York: Harper & Row.

Super, D.E. (1980). A lifespan, life space approach to career development. *Journal of Vocational Behavior, 16,* 282–298.

Super, D.E. (1985). Coming of age in Middletown: Careers in the making. *American Psychologist, 40,* 405–414.

Super, D.E. (1990). A life-span, life space approach to career development. In D. Brown, L. Brooks, & Associates (Eds.), *Career choice and development* (2nd ed., pp. 197–261). San Francisco: Jossey-Bass.

Swenson, C.H. (1980). Ego development and a general model for counseling and psychotherapy. *Personal and Guidance Journal, 58,* 382–388.

Takanishi, R. (1993). The opportunities of adolescence: Research interventions, and policy. *American Psychologist, 48,* 85–87.

Taylor, S.E. (1990). Health psychology: The science and the field. *American Psychologist, 45,* 40–50.

Tellegen, A. (1985). Structures of mood and personality and their relevance in assessing anxiety with an emphasis on self-report. In A.H. Tuma & J.D. Maser (Eds.), *Anxiety and anxiety disorders* (pp. 681–706). Hillsdale, NJ: Erlbaum.

Terry, D.J. (1994). Determinants of coping: The role of stable and situational factors. *Journal of Personality and Social Psychology, 66,* 895–910.

Thoits, P.A. (1986). Social support as coping assistance. *Journal of Consulting and Clinical Psychology, 54,* 416–423.

Thomas, L. (1984). Human responsibility: In Cooper-Hewitt Museum. *The phenomenon of change* (pp. 6–8). New York: Rizzoli.

Tinsley, H.E.A., & Eldredge, B. (1995). Psychological benefits of leisure participation: A taxonomy of leisure activities based on their need-gratifying properties. *Journal of Counseling Psychology, 42,* 123–132.

Tinsley, H.E.A., Hinson, J.A., Tinsley, D., & Holt, M.S. (1993). Attributes of leisure and work experiences. *Journal of Counseling Psychology, 40,* 447–455.

Traxler, A. (1945). *Techniques of Guidance.* New York: Harper & Row.

Truax, C.B. (1966). Reinforcement and non-reinforcement in Rogerian counseling. *Journal of Abnormal Psychology, 71,* 1–9.

Tyler, L. (1958). Theoretical principles underlying the counseling process. *Journal of Counseling Psychology, 5,* 3–10.

Tyler, L. (1964). The methods and processes of appraisal and counseling. In A. Thompson & D. Super (Eds.), *The professional preparation of counseling psychologist* (pp. 76–89). New York: Columbia University, Teachers College.

Tyler, L. (1983). *Thinking creatively: A new approach to psychology and individual lives.* San Francisco: Jossey-Bass.

Vaillant, G. (1977). *Adaptation to life.* Boston: Little, Brown.

Vandenbos, G.R., & Duthie, R.F. (1986). Confronting and supporting colleagues in distress. In R. Kilburg, P. Nathan, & R. Thoreson (Eds.), *Professionals in distress: Issues, syndromes and solutions in psychology* (pp. 211–231). Washington, DC: American Psychological Association.

Van Slyck, M., Stern, M., & Zak-Place, J. (1996). Promoting optimal adolescent development through conflict resolution education, training and practice: An innovative approach for counseling psychologists. *Counseling Psychologist, 24,* 433–461.

Wachtel, P.L. (1987). *Action and insight.* New York: Guilford Press.

Wachtel, P.L. (1997). *Psychoanalysis, behavior therapy and the relational world.* Washington, DC: American Psychological Association.

Wagner, W.G. (1996). Facilitating optimal development in adolescence. *Counseling Psychologist, 24,* 360–399.

Wampold, B.E., Mondin, G.W., & Hyun-nie-ahn. (1999). Preference for people and tasks. *Journal of Counseling Psychology, 46,* 35–41.

Wandersman, A., & Nation, M. (1998). Urban neighborhoods and mental health: Psychological contributions to understanding toxicity, resilience and interventions. *American Psychologist, 3,* 647–656.

Wang, L., Heppner, P.P., & Berry, T.R. (1997). Role of gender-related personality traits, problem-solving appraisal, and perceived social support in developing a mediational model of psychological adjustment. *Journal of Counseling Psychology, 44,* 245–255.

Wapner, S. (1987). A holistic, developmental, systems-oriented environmental psychology: Some beginnings. In D. Stokols & I. Altman (Eds.), *Handbook of environmental psychology* (pp. 1433–1465). New York: Wiley.

Watkins, C.E., Lopez, F.G., Campbell, V.L., & Hinmell, C.D. (1986). Contemporary counseling psychology: Results of a national survey. *Journal of Counseling Psychology, 33,* 301–309.

Whiston, S.C., Sexton, T.L., & Lasoff, D. (1998). Career-intervention outcome: A replication and extension of Oliver and Spolane (1998). *Journal of Counseling Psychology, 45,* 150–165.

White, R.W. (1959). Motivation reconsidered: The concept of competence. *Psychological Review, 66,* 297–333.

Williams E.N., Judge, A., Hill, C.E., & Hoffman, M.A. (1997). Experiences of novice therapists in pre-practicum: Trainees, clients and supervisors' perceptions of therapist's personal reactions and management strategies. *Journal of Counseling Psychologist, 44*(4), 390–399.

Williamson, E.G. (1939). *How to counsel students.* New York: McGraw-Hill.

Williamson, E.G. (1950). A concept of counseling. *Occupations, 29,* 182–189.

Williamson, E.G. (1958). Value orientation in counseling. *Personnel and Guidance Journal, 36,* 520–528.

Winer, J.L., Cesari, J., Haase, R.F., & Bodden, J.L. (1979). Cognitive complexity and career maturity among college students. *Journal of Vocational Behavior, 15,* 186–192.

Wolfe, B.E., & Goldfried, M.R. (1988). Research on psychotherapy integration: Recommendations and conclusions from an NIMIT workshop. *Journal of Consulting and Clinical Psychology, 56,* 448–451.

World Health Organization. (1964). *Basic documents* (15th ed.). Geneva, Switzerland: Author.

Worthen, B., & McNeill, B. (1996). A phenomenological investigation of "good" supervision events. *Journal of Counseling Psychology, 43*(1), 25–34.

Wrenn, C.G. (1962). *The counselor in a changing world.* Boston: Houghton Mifflin.

Wrenn, C.G. (1965). The culturally encapsulated counselor. In R. Mosher, R. Carle, & C. Kehas (Eds.), *Guidance: An examination* (pp. 214–224). New York: Harcourt-Brace and World.

Yee, A.H., Fauchild, H.H., Weizmann, F., & Wyatt, G.E. (1993). Addressing psychology's problems with race. *American Psychologist, 48,* 1132–1140.

Zeig, J.K. (1985). Introduction. In J.K. Zeig (Ed.), *The evolution of psychotherapy* (p. xxi). New York: Brunner/Mazel.

Zuckerman, M. (1990). Some dubious premises in research and theory on racial differences: Scientific, social and ethical issues. *American Psychologist, 45,* 1297–1303.

Author Index

Subject Index